BIG PICTURE REALITIES

BIG PICTURE REALITIES

Canada and Mexico at the Crossroads

Daniel Drache, editor

Wilfrid Laurier University Press

WLU

We acknowledge the financial support of the Government of Canada through the Book Publishing Industry Development Program for our publishing activities.

Library and Archives Canada Cataloguing in Publication

Big picture realities : Canada and Mexico at the crossroads / Daniel Drache, editor.

Includes bibliographical references and index.
ISBN 978-1-55458-045-3

1. Canada—Foreign relations—Mexico. 2. Mexico—Foreign relations—Canada. I. Drache, Daniel, 1941–

FC640.B53 2008   327.71072   C2008-902714-0

© 2008 Wilfrid Laurier University Press
Waterloo, Ontario, Canada
www.wlupress.wlu.ca

Cover images by Duncan Walker/iStockphoto. Cover design by Blakeley Words+Pictures. Text design by Kathe Gray Design.

(∞)

This book is printed on Ancient Forest Friendly paper (100% post-consumer recycled).

Printed in Canada

CONTENTS

Part 4 North American Security Perimeter: The Mega Agenda

Part 5 Open Regionalism and the National Interest: New Dynamics of Divergence

Part 6 Asian Turbo-Capitalism and the Brazilian Miracle: Winners and Losers?

Part 7 Building the Canada-Mexico Relationship: Thinking Outside the Box

Acknowledgements

"Canada–Mexico Big Picture Realities" was the subject of a major conference organized by the Robarts Centre for Canadian Studies at York University in November 2005. It was a unique event because it brought together a group of Mexican and Canadian experts to work on the big picture realities that are defining inter-state relations in North America. It is infrequent that Canada and Mexico have such an opportunity to explore the ways in which social and economic agendas are being rethought following the introduction of the *North American Free Trade Agreement*. This collection includes the papers—albeit all significantly reworked—from this conference. By also publishing it in Spanish, I am hoping to reach out to a larger audience and significantly strengthen Canadian-Mexican relations.

Numerous individuals and organizations supported this project throughout its development. Ambassador Carlos Pujalte, consulate general in Toronto, played a critical role in finding resources both for the initial meeting and for the publication of this book. We owe him a special debt of thanks. The Robarts Centre for Canadian Studies played a singular role in hosting the conference, which was remarkable for the high level of participation and widespread interest from the academic and policy-making community. In particular, we owe a special debt to Laura Taman, who flawlessly organized this complex event. Her sharp editorial eye and pencil has improved the subsequent manuscript. Professor Seth Feldman, director of the Robarts Centre for Canadian Studies, has been very helpful in supporting this initiative, and I would like to offer him special thanks as well.

Professor Duncan Wood of the Instituto Tecnológico Autónomo de México (ITAM) generously offered to help with the preparation of this volume and facilitated the publication with Porrua edición. He provided badly needed resources and oversaw the translation. To Daniela Rivera, our translator, we owe the most thanks of all for doing excellent work faced under numerous time constraints while overseeing the preparation of the manuscript in Mexico. She has done an excellent job of discharging her responsibilities and has played a critical role in the final preparation of the manuscript. Professor Rena Carces, an accomplished Costa Rican historian, checked the translation, and I am much indebted to her for her detailed work. Thanks to Jaigris Hodson, a research assistant at the Robarts Centre for Canadian Studies, for her terrific assistance in the final stages of preparation of the manuscript, in preparing the index, and for her most careful proofing. The task of editing has been made much easier by the cooperation and enthusiasm of all of the contributors. They also have been a pleasure to work with. We owe a special thanks for Daniel Schwanen, CIGI, as well as David Dewitt, associate vice president, research, York University, for timely financial support. Muchas gracias.

Daniel Drache

Big Picture Realities in a Post-NAFTA Era

Daniel Drache

North America Transformed

The attentive reader will discover that the primary concept behind this collection refers to the dramatic sea changes in the political-economic order of North America. Ideally, every government wants to manage these big picture realities rather than be managed by them. Public authority has to be focused in order not to be blind-sided. At present, leading, pace-setting institutions such as the labour market, education, and health systems are being required to change and adapt to the new power dynamics triggered by the deep-seeded reorganization of the system of production, wealth creation, new citizenship practices, and public expectations (Hollingsworth and Boyer 1997). In a way that no expert has predicted, these forceful expressions of national interest and domestic priorities have reappeared as the new and authoritative agenda-setting priorities for all three signatories of the North American Free Trade Agreement (NAFTA).[1]

Canada and Mexico are highly differentiated societies that need to come to terms with the cumulative and contradictory effects of these micro and macro changes. If, in the 1990s, the contour of North America was organized around a grand commercial project driven by neo-liberal deregulation and deep market access, in this new century, security and immigration have overtaken the once seemingly unstoppable dynamic of NAFTA as the driver of the North American community (Randall and Konrad 1992). Many, if not all, of these changes are breathtaking in their consequences.

At one time, Canada boasted of having the world's longest undefended border. Today, the great northern and southern borders are militarized and securitized to an unprecedented degree. In 2006, President George W. Bush authorized the stationing of more than two thousand troops to guard the US side of the border along the forty-ninth parallel. On the southern border, twenty thousand US troops have been put on duty on the US side of the Rio Grande. The centrepiece of the Bush administration has been to create a North American security perimeter with a singular focus on protecting US sovereignty. Border security is the high-maintenance public policy that cuts across the length and breadth of US government departments (Susskind 2007). Responsibility for North American continental security lies with the super-sized US Department of Homeland Security with its budget of more than one hundred and fifty billion dollars annually and its vast and intrusive reach across the length and breadth of the US government. Support for the US security-first border has transformed the institutional dynamics of the continent, arguably forever (Haglund 2003). Its vast program for the inspection of every passenger vehicle, truck, ship, and plane that enters the United States has no precedent. US authority must monitor, verify, and screen the vast transmovement of people between Canada, the United States, and Mexico.

With over three hundred and fifty million annual cross-border visits between the NAFTA partners, the task is daunting, if not next to impossible, to carry out with one hundred percent effectiveness (Canada 2007). According to the US government's Accountability Office, many of the problems undermining US security efforts have developed at home. Budget cuts have led to the serious under-staffing of US border agents and poor training for border officials (Blumenthal 2007). As of November 2007, more than seventy-five thousand names were included on the US no-fly list (Hall 2007). Yet, there have been so many errors made that in 2006 more than fifteen thousand people appealed to the Department of Homeland Security to have their names cleared. The backlog of complaints is growing faster than names can be removed (Hall 2007).

Stepping Up to the Plate

Canadian governments have not been idle or passive spectators to the world of homeland security. They were quick off the mark to legislate a made-in-Canada security policy after 9/11. Canada's security-first border has been transformed beyond recognition over the last seven years. Both Liberal and Conservative governments have spent more than ten billion dollars upgrading, enhancing, and securitizing Canada's intelligence and security capacity. The activity on securing the border has been intense and unprecedented (Canada 2006). Customs officials have been given new responsibilities and, for the first time in Canadian history, are armed. Passengers arriving by air, sea, and rail are required to show a valid passport. Yet, by far the greatest change has come for Canadians and Americans who cross the border.

As of January 2008, in a dramatic reversal of policy, the old practice of "flashing and dashing" documents to customs agents will be replaced. Every Canadian and American will have to show his or her passport at the border (Drache 2007). With over three hundred million border crossings annually, wait times will lengthen unless the number of border guards is increased dramatically. Existing staffing levels are inadequate to meet the new rules of transborder screening since wait times are already aggravatingly long and unpredictable between Windsor and Detroit. By contrast, one of the busiest pre-clearance operations is at Pearson International Airport. Daily, more than ten thousand passengers embark to the United States, and, with twenty or more US customs officials on duty for peak periods, wait times are minimal. However, the highly efficient processing of a high-volume passenger airport is the exception in the world of border co-management.[2] Under the new rules coming into effect in 2008, the decision whether to inspect the documents of all passengers or just the drivers' will be left to the discretion of US officials. At Canadian land border crossings, wait times will vary enormously, depending on the time of day, the ad hoc practice of custom's inspectors, and the volume of traffic. Travellers should count on several hours to cross, but the times will vary enormously particularly at peak periods and holidays.

Canadian governments have tightened many other related border management practices. The issuance of Canadian passports has been overhauled, and new administrative procedures have been implemented, including background security checks. Stephen Harper's Conservative government is spending millions of dollars to provide cities with security alert systems, even in urban areas that are far from the border and are not primary immigration destinations. Canada's east and west coast harbours have seen their security upgraded as the government has spent hundreds of millions of dollars installing new surveillance equipment. These are the more visible signs of the new security age.

Goods and services continue to move across the continent largely unimpeded beyond the anticipated delays at border crossings. Empirical studies reveal that 95 percent of all shipments cross without any inspection from US border services (Drache 2007). Just-in-time systems of production have not been disrupted in the auto, steel, and electronic industries except when the Canadian-US border was shut down tight in the days following 9/11. In an economic analysis of security affecting wait times, one of the most authoritative studies found that trucks had to wait up to one-and-a-half hours at the border. This delay has had a significant financial impact, resulting in Canadian truckers paying close to CDN $500 million in extra costs for US security measures. Most of the burden comes from US measures imposed by homeland security (Chase 2007). American authorities are proposing new inspections for food and drug products. In effect, Canadian shippers are being charged for the new US security measures—a unique form of downloading. Only 14 percent of these border fees stem from Canadian government initiatives. Nonetheless, Canadian exporters continue to lobby for shorter wait times at the border and have learned the value of the skilled intervention of customs' brokers and other service industries that ensure that administrative glitches are kept to the minimum. Exporters do not like the new security rules that add costs to their lean margins, but they are learning to adapt to them.

Leading Canadian business organizations continue to lobby Ottawa for exemptions, but none appear to be forthcoming (Clarkson 2003). Contrary to the NAFTA provisions, the Bush administration has imposed new taxes at the border requiring Canadian exporters to pay for the increased surveillance and the cost of a "thicker border" (Chase 2007a). Intense lobbying by Canadian chief executives has not resulted in rule changes since US officials have turned a deaf ear to Canadian corporate complaints. Canadian business is largely on its own. In the last five years, no leading American chief executive officer has publicly challenged the new rules of border security. Patriotic compliance is the norm, not public criticism.

At the political level, Canadian authorities regularly co-operate and liaise with their counterparts in homeland security on a daily basis. This new-found security focus extends to the top of the political hierarchy. There is a permanent liaison committee between the prime minister's office and its US counterparts. Former prime minister Jean Chrètien established a cabinet committee on security to coordinate the security file across the face of government. Paul Martin, his successor, gave the security file greater visibility with the appointment of Anne McLellan, a senior minister with responsibility for public safety and security.

Under Harper, security concerns continue to be a major priority of the government. Canada's public safety minister is a senior member of Cabinet responsible for all aspects of implementation of security as a cross-cutting issue. Stockwell Day, the present minister, regularly interacts with his US counterpart, Michael Chertoff, the serving secretary of homeland security. Nothing comparable exists in Mexico, although Mexican officials would like to move up the security chain and occupy a status similar to Canada's. Finally, in this long list of initiatives, Canada and the United States have signed a number of agreements in the security area. The most important is the 2005 Security and Prosperity Partnership, which is a framework for deepening the trilateral relationship that explicitly links prosperity to the goals and objectives of the Bush administration's commitment to security first.[3] So far, it has acquired no policy legs, and the one-day annual meeting for the heads of state is largely a photo opportunity for the leaders (Freeman and Curry 2007).

The Security Backlash

Despite the massive investment in the security-first border, the idea of a North American security perimeter has not found much favour in Canadian public opinion. When Canadians are asked to rank their most important concerns, health rises to the top of the list followed by the environment ("State of Public Opionion" 2007).[4] Compared to Americans, Canadians view homeland security and terrorism as low-priority items. The Pew Research Centre for the People and the Press reports that the war on terrorism and immigration remain the major preoccupations of the majority of Americans surveyed, followed by economic concerns and health care worries (Pew Research Centre 2007).

It is not all that surprising that Canadians display a persistent ambivalence to the North American security perimeter for three principle reasons. First, Canadians are apprehensive that the Bush war on terror and its doctrine of unilateral regime changes undermine Canada's commitment to international law and its strong belief in multilateralism (Welsh 2004). Within Canada's multilateral security culture, support for human rights-based international law has made Canadians deeply skeptical of being drawn into the US security orbit any more than necessary. Public opinion has operated as an effective brake on Harper's ideological decision to be a Bush loyalist. The recent US Supreme Court rulings against military show trials of enemy combatants in Guantanamo and unauthorized spying on US citizens has hardened Canadian public opinion's opposition to the US homeland security doctrine. Canadians are skeptics about the idea of a "fortress North America." The public opinion divide between the two countries has grown larger as the political situation in Iraq continues to deteriorate (Goldsmith 2007).

Second, the homeland security doctrine has a rival in Canada's commitment to the broad policy goal of human security. Canadians have a very positive view of governmental institutions and look to the government for leadership and protection of the social bond (Clarkson 2003). Still, the Harper government has had to deal with the fallout from the Maher Arar case, the Canadian citizen of Syrian origin who was kidnapped in 2002 by US authorities on a return flight to Canada and returned to Syria where he was tortured. The previous liberal government and Harper tried to contain the political consequences of this outrageous violation of human rights by US authorities but were forced to set up a commission of inquiry headed by Supreme Court of Canada justice Dennis O'Connor (Canada 2007; Leeder 2007). Among other things, the commission has focused on the complicity of the Royal Canadian Mounted Police (RCMP) in handing Arar over to the US authorities based on the faulty, misleading information they supplied to the Central Intelligence Agency. After much hesitation, the government bowed to public opinion and apologized to Arar and his family. They were compensated with a CDN $10 million settlement, the largest of its kind in Canadian history. In December 2006, the head of the RCMP, Guiliano Zaccardelli, resigned for lying to the House of Commons committee investigating the role of the RCMP in the Arar rendition. He was the first commissioner in over one hundred years to be forced to leave his post as head of Canada's world famous police force. Another inquiry is underway for three other Canadian Muslims who were extradited and tortured in similar, though quite different, circumstances (Bell 2007).

Torture of Maher Arar, a Canadian Citizen: US Rendition

Canadians are angered by the fallout from the Arar inquiry since it highlights the unfairness of US anti-terrorist laws. Recently, the Arar story acquired new legs when US intelligence forces leaked a story in October 2007 to the Canadian press that one of their unnamed informants alleged that Arar attended an Afghan training camp when he travelled to that country (Leeder 2007). The continuing news campaign against Arar highlights the role of US intelligence services in attempting to divert public attention away from the US practice of "legalized" torture (Susskind 2007). Arar has been given no explanation as to why he remains a security threat. It is the view of experts that there is no reason to consider him a threat (Leeder 2007). So far, Arar remains on the US no-fly list, and secretary of state Condoleezza Rice has refused to issue any official apology.

Equally important, in 2006, the Supreme Court of Canada struck down the government's use of security certificates to hold individuals virtually without limit and to hold secret trials at which the accused are not able to see the evidence against them and are not represented by a lawyer ("Canadian Security Certificates" 2007). This legislation, loosely modelled on US practice, has further reinforced the Canadian view that anti-terrorists laws are intrusive. Here too, Canadian and American public opinion diverge sharply. An international Queen's University survey, published in November 2006, found that only 15 percent of Americans found the anti-terrorist laws to be highly intrusive. By comparison, 57 percent of Canadians believed that these laws invaded their privacy (Deveau 2006).

Risk Assessment: Why Top Experts Disagree

Finally, the third critical issue polarizing Canadian public opinion is that there is no shared understanding of how to benchmark risk assessment. For Canadian and US authorities to co-operate, they must have shared methodologies, definitions, operations, goals, and objectives. Wesley Wark, one of Canada's top security experts and a contributor to this volume, demonstrates that Canada and the United States cannot construct a North American defence perimeter without fundamental agreement on the basic issue of risk assessment (see Wark's chapter in this volume). Canada, Mexico, and the United States have parallel, competing, and often contradictory practices. Constitutionally in the three jurisdictions, the rights of the accused are subject to very different legal regimes. For many, this is a healthy state of affairs and operates as a brake on easily exporting the US security doctrine to the rest of the continent. From a national sovereignty perspective, the existence of rival and competing notions of risk assessment create leverage for Canada and Mexico to confront the US "security is first" doctrine (Byers 2005).

The fact that the US Supreme Court, the country's highest legal authority struck down key components of Bush's security package has had major repercussions on Canadians' thinking about continental security. It has reconfirmed the view of many Canadians that Canada should avoid having closer security ties with a doctrine that is regarded, in key aspects, as unconstitutional by American judges (Centre for Constitutional Rights 2007). The Bush security doctrine has, in the last several years, faced some stunning policy reversals. The US Supreme Court ruled against Bush's special military tribunals at Guantanamo Bay where detainees were tried without proper legal counsel and due process. The spectre of show trials, where the outcome is known in advance of the trial, has triggered deep disquiet among many Americans who remember the show trials in Eastern Europe and other countries after the Second World War. The illegal use of wiretaps on Americans has also registered with Canadians. The Department of Homeland Security and the Office of the Independent Counsel appear to have so much power and so little accountability that the US security doctrine appears to be out of control (Susskind 2007; Woodward 2006). For Harper, the Conservative leader of Canada's minority government, and Felipe Calderón Hinojosa, Mexico's current president, the bitterly contested debate over Bush's imperial presidency poses a huge dilemma. It is very difficult to publicly tie their administrations too closely to a security doctrine that has gone seriously off the rails. Both leaders have only so much political capital to expend on defending a doctrine that is unpopular and a lightening rod for anti-Americanism.

Further, these events regarding the constitutionality of Bush's homeland security doctrine have special immediacy for Canadians because one of the last Western citizens still incarcerated at Guantanamo Bay is Omar Khadr, a Canadian who has been held there since 2002 (Leeder 2007). He was captured as a fifteen year old by US troops in Afghanistan during the US operations against the Taliban. Unlike Egyptian, Australian, Saudi Arabian, and British nationals who were held in Guantanamo but have since been repatriated by their countries for trial, the Canadian government has done nothing to protect Khadr, who was a minor when seized (Bowker and Kaye 2007). All of the opposition political parties have demanded that Ottawa have Khadr returned to Canada for a fair trial. Yet, so far, the Harper government has opposed any intervention of this kind with US authorities. Britain, France, and Germany, close US allies, have all called for Guantanamo's closing, but not Canada. While many Canadians have misgivings about the Khadr family and its links to Osama Bin Laden, the consensus is that Omar Khadr deserves a fair trial where his rights as an accused are respected. It disturbs Canadians profoundly that the Harper government has done so little to protect one of its own citizens.

The US Courts Strike Back

While the intelligence communities in both Canada and Mexico co-operate with their American counterparts on an ad hoc basis, there is no appetite to institutionalize this co-operation. Indeed, Canadians and Mexicans have deep reservations about the legality of much of the US security doctrine for the very reasons identified earlier by Wark. For instance, the US prosecution of Muslim groups charged under the new legislation for allegedly financing terrorist organizations in the Middle East have ended in mistrials or not-guilty verdicts. In October 2007, in a flagship financing case, US prosecutors failed to convince a jury to convict any of the leaders from five charities or even to reach a verdict on any of the one hundred and ninety-seven counts. This decision is a stunning setback for the government (Eaton 2007). Legal experts have questioned the government tactic of freezing the assets of charities by using secret evidence that is unavailable to the charities and denying them the opportunity to cross-examine. According to David Cole, professor of constitutional law at Georgetown University, the government is really pushing beyond where the law allows them to go (Eaton 2007).

Bush has gone far beyond his predecessors in promoting an expansive theory of presidential authority. The Bush–Cheney administration has used signing statements to challenge more congressional laws than all of the previous administrations—a practice that began with Ronald Reagan, who evoked his right to defy congressional authority. The highly intrusive role of the Office of Legal Counsel has been at the forefront of the Bush presidency's expansion of powers. More than two hundred and thirty-two laws have asserted Bush's right to override Congress when their interpretation of the Constitution conflicts with Bush's (Goldsmith 2007). The American public is increasingly seized by this abuse of executive privilege in the White House, which has permitted the detention of suspects without trial, allowed for the eavesdropping of conversations of US citizens without judicial warrant, disregarded the Geneva Convention on torture, which former attorney general Alberto Gonzales called "quaint," sanctioned water-boarding as a legitimate form of interrogation, and denied fundamental legal rights to detainees in Guantanamo Bay.

In the public's mind, the Bush administration's highly skilled campaign of disinformation, followed by the media's revelation about their controversial terrorist surveillance program, have created much highly visible, bipartisan unease. Bush's plunge in popularity during his second mandate to a low of almost 30 percent is in part driven by these revelations and by the debate over the American use of torture. Polarizing political personalities such as former Attorney General Gonzales, Vice President Dick Cheney, former Secretary of Defence Donald Rumsfeld as well as Bush's refusal to explain clearly to the American public the absence of weapons of mass destruction in Iraq have cast a cloud over the US surveillance program and other key dimensions of homeland security (Greenberg 2007).

In October 2007 in Paris, human rights groups filed a fifth war crimes complaint against Rumsfeld who is held responsible, by Bob Woodward in his bestseller *State of Denial*, for much of the design and policy implementation of Bush's six-year war on terror.[5] Groups such as the International Federation of Free Human Rights, the US Centre for Constitutional Rights, the European Centre for Constitutional and Human Rights, and the French League of Human Rights filed the complaint with Paris prosecutors before the Court of First Instance, charging the former secretary of defence with ordering and authorizing torture. French courts have an obligation under the convention against torture to prosecute individuals present on French territory for acts of torture.[6] While this international coalition is unlikely to succeed for the time being, questions about the principle of impunity in the name of politics are not likely to go away, as Henry Kissinger ruefully discovered. International human rights law has evolved, and it has acquired new legitimacy with the establishment in 2002 of the International Criminal Court, which is mandated to bring to trial those who commit crimes of genocide, war crimes, and crimes against humanity (Goldsmith 2007).

Those on North America's political right and many in the security and intelligence community want to ratchet up the rhetoric and increase surveillance behind and at the border. They want tougher laws, a thick border, and a vigilant intelligence community working closely with US authorities. They are advocates of Washington's "security is first" doctrine and do not see a conflict when security needs to trump privacy rights, national regulatory standards, national sovereignty, and other fundamental public policy concerns. However, experience demonstrates that security regulation and control, and the screening of millions of licit cross-border visitors are most effective when border control practices are domestically organized and implemented. Experience also teaches that parallel policies between the NAFTA partners are preferable to a single coordinated policy from Washington since neither Canada nor Mexico has any standing or effective input into Washington's public policy-making process. Bluntly put, Canada and Mexico are on separate policy trajectories, and tight policy coordination is not in the cards.

The 2006 US Secure Fence Act and the Lou Dobbs Effect

For Mexico, border security has been a permanent reality defining much of Mexican political life for decades before 9/11 changed the security face of North America (Serrano 2007). The big picture reality for Mexico is symbolized by the two thousand-mile-long, twenty-foot-high wall that Congress has authorized to be built with the 2006 *Secure Fence Act* in order to prevent Mexican illegal immigration.[7] Each year, American border authorities remove close to one million Mexicans from the United States, but these draconian measures have not stemmed the tide of poor Mexicans trekking northward for a better life (Drache 2007).

It is estimated that three hundred thousand to five hundred thousand Mexicans enter the United States illegally, but no one really knows the exact number. Mexican economists and sociologists see the vast exodus of poor *campesinos* as a tragic "NAFTA effect." American competitiveness has been an ecological human disaster for Mexico's poor farmers. American farmers are unequalled in their productivity and have captured an even larger share of the Mexican market for corn to make tortillas, a staple of the Mexican diet. The very success of NAFTA has driven more than two million Mexican peasants off their land (see Rosalba Icaza Garza's chapter in this volume). A never-ending army of displaced persons treks north to be hired as cheap labour for the service, construction, and commercial industries of the American southwest and beyond (Gambrill 2006).

With the collapse of the US housing and construction industry, the number of undocumented immigrants has decreased, and, according to recent reports, the amount of money sent to Mexico by Mexicans working in the United States has tapered off. The year-to-year growth has flattened (Confessore 2007). Arizona has recently passed a law to sanction employers who hire illegal workers. If caught, an employer can lose his/her licence to operate and be shut down. This regulation may further discourage employers from hiring on the grey market, but it is too early to know whether the law will be effective. It faces opposition from employer's organizations and human rights groups. In 1971, then California governor Ronald Reagan enacted a law to sanction employers, but it was abandoned as being ineffective and too costly politically (Calavita 1982).

The new law could have a chilling affect on employers as well as on immigrants. In the past, when faced with organized hostility from sections of the American public, such as the anti-Irish antagonism at the end of the nineteenth century or the enmity against Mexican labourers in the 1920s, the fear factor gave them a strong incentive to stay put. Certainly, the conditions for cheap labour have slackened recently, but the reasons why hundreds of thousands of Mexicans annually immigrate have not changed in the least. Sue Ann Goodman, the executive director of Humane Borders, suggests that illegal immigrants are crossing at more remote stretches of desert rather than avoiding the border (Holstege 2007). The increased pressure at the border is forcing migrants to take more risks. In the same article, police report that two hundred and two undocumented immigrants died in Arizona deserts between 1 October 2006 and 31 April 2007. The Tucson-based organization Humane Borders puts the number of dead at two hundred and forty-six immigrants, up from one hundred and ninety-nine deaths the previous year. Along the entire border, the US border patrol reports that four hundred people died while entering the United States from Mexico in 2007, a decrease from the four hundred and ninety-four deaths in 2005, which was the worst year on record. More than half the deaths occurred in Arizona, the busiest entry point for illegal migration into the United States (Associated Press 2007).

To understand the powerful presence of the US border in American life, it is sobering to watch the Lou Dobbs show on CNN. Dobbs is a popular host with one of the largest audiences on the network. Most Mexicans do not know who Lou Dobbs is, but he has ignited a growing anti-Mexican sentiment in the United States that has killed any further interest in the US Congress for deepening and broadening NAFTA. Dobbs and the US Right believe that US sovereignty is being compromised by NAFTA and that illegal immigration is a threat to the American polity's self-image as a nation of hard-working Americans. Mexicans are seen as illegal "spongers" who drain tax dollars but do not pay taxes. Yet when the *Wall Street Journal* surveyed economists on whether illegal immigration proved to be a gain or loss to the US economy, forty-four out of forty-six of them said there was a net benefit (Annett 2006).

Despite a blizzard of counter arguments and mass demonstrations at the grassroots level in support of immigration reform, this stereotype has incited a vitriol of racism that has inflamed the conservative blogosphere at the grassroots level.[8] Dobbs has become a lightening rod, leading a nightly crusade against Mexicans and illegal immigration. His venting against illegal Mexican workers, who are likened to an "army of invaders ... threatening the health of many Americans," has demonized NAFTA in the public mind. When New York governor Eliot Spitzer proposed to allow illegal immigrants to apply for driver's licences, Dobb's program was bombarded with angry e-mails from around the country. One such message read: "We will derail the illegal gravy train from within." Guests and interviewees are typically opposed to any legislative change that would make it easier for illegal immigrants to become legal residents in the United States (Confessore 2007; Archibold 2007).

The Fallout from Bush's 2007 Immigration Bill

The failure of the US Congress to pass Bush's immigration reform bill in June 2007 represents part of the "new normality" on Capitol Hill, which will likely last until Bush's successor is chosen. The Bush immigration bill included fines, removals, work permits, and an extremely complex process that would allow some Mexicans working in the United States without papers to eventually become citizens. Guest workers would have to return home for twelve months every two years. There was no provision for any kind of amnesty. The bill's promise of legalization was so restrictive that only a tiny percentage of families would have qualified. There was nothing in the Senate version that would give Mexican immigrants permanent, family-based status—too many provisions were anti-family and anti-worker. At its core, the bill provided for a temporary employment system but not for full legalization for the millions of undocumented Mexicans. Many immigrant groups as well as civil rights advocates believed that Bush's compromise, which penalized hundreds of thousands of Mexicans and would have led to increased enforcement and raids, deserved its fate when the compromise bill failed to pass (Rutenberg and Hulse 2007). Immigration has become so polarized in the United States that it now dominates the 2007 presidential primaries along with gay rights and abortion. Few Americans see NAFTA as representing the beginning of a new American-Mexican partnership.

Equally disturbing is the view held by a significant number of American senators that they are not obliged to enforce key NAFTA provisions with respect to Mexico. Under NAFTA, Mexican truckers were guaranteed access to US highways, but the Republican senator of Nebraska, Chuck Hagel, told an American audience on Lou Dobbs's program on 12 September 2007 that Mexican trucks were unsafe, its drivers a security risk, and that he did not care if the US Senate broke the law by ignoring its legal obligations under NAFTA. What matters to him, he declared, are jobs for millions of Americans and protecting US national interests. Evidently, the US Senate and Congress do not regard the southern border with Mexico as a nineteenth-century anachronism. They understand fully the importance of borders as a strategic instrument of US foreign policy. The United States continues to play hardball with Mexico, and, so far, Mexico, like Canada, has had to bite its tongue publicly on this and other trade disputes. Mexico does not have much leverage because leverage is a matter of political will, not entitlement (Vega et al. 2005). So even if Mexico is entitled under the legal rules of NAFTA, it does not have the leverage to deal with congressional disregard of international obligations. Politically speaking, is there anyone who will champion a revitalized North American community? Are there any supporters in the inner circle of power? Who is waiting in the wings to lead the charge?

The Canada-Mexico-US Strategic Partnership

In his recently published book *Memoirs 1939–1993*, Brian Mulroney, Canada's former prime minister and champion of the 1984 Canada-US free trade agreement, recounts how little enthusiasm there was in the higher echelons of Ronald Reagan's administration for the dramatic step of signing the Canadian-US free trade agreement—the big idea of Canadian conservatives at that time—which would open the road to NAFTA five years later. Up to the very end of the two years of difficult negotiations, Mulroney believed that the Canada-US free trade agreement would fail. In his account, he says that no one in Washington really cared. North American integration had no champion in the inner circles of the George H.W. Bush administration, and US negotiators operated in political silos (Mulroney 2007).

In the United States, Reagan had to ask the Senate Finance Committee for a green light before beginning negotiations. The vote was tied twelve to twelve. Under the committee's rules, this gave the Reagan administration the right to proceed. As late as 2 October 1984, in the final hours before the legal deadline to conclude the agreement, Mulroney told his cabinet that without a number of small concessions on the binding dispute resolution mechanism he had instructed Canada's chief negotiator, Simon Reisman, to walk away from the deal. Mulroney muses that it was easier for the United States to reach an agreement with its Cold War enemy, the Soviet Union, on limiting the number of strategic missiles than to negotiate free trade with its Canada (Mulroney 2007). Puzzled by his own government's lack of traction, he argues that no one in the Reagan administration seemed to care very much if negotiations succeeded. It was a huge risk for Mulroney's newly minted government to propose free trade with Canada's powerful neighbour, and the Conservatives were pummelled daily in Parliament by the opposition party. None of the high drama registered on Reagan's radar screen. Most curiously, Reagan's inner circle did not regard Canada as a strategic partner—a status that Britain enjoyed. The evidence, thus, contradicts the idea that Canada has a special relationship forged by geography, social values, and language. The first giant step toward North American free trade was largely a non-event, which hardly registered in the inner circles of the White House and Congress (Mulroney 2007).

Mulroney's autobiography should be read skeptically since he would like the reader to believe that the only reason a free trade debacle was avoided was due to his considerable diplomatic skills and wire-pulling with Bush, Sr., and his carefully cultivated personal relationship with Reagan. Scholars and the public must interrogate the absence of a strong geopolitical imperative at work. Scholars remind us that the negotiations and final agreement were in fact driven by the more powerful logic of self-interest and opportunism on both sides. Is it a big picture story? The historical record does not support such a grand assumption.

On the other hand, the NAFTA deal with Mexico involved a ferocious fight in the US Senate and Congress, led in part by billionaire Ross Perot, an enormously talented and savvy right-wing populist who warned against the loss of hundreds of thousands of US jobs to the *maquiladora* industries south of the border. He was wrong about this most publicized claim, but he was right about NAFTA depressing US working-class salaries for those who did not lose their jobs to outsourcing. Fast-forward to 2007, when the same arguments are still much in evidence. Economists and experts have failed to document, to anyone's satisfaction, the number of jobs lost or gained because of, or despite, belonging to the exclusive NAFTA club (see the divergent views of Daniel Drache and Gustavo Vega-Cànovas in this volume).

Canadians continue to be obsessed with how things work in government and how much policy autonomy they have with the United States. In their 2007 book, *Unexpected War, Canada in Kandahar,* Janice Gross Stein and Eugene Lang take to task the senior officials who were feeding politicians their best policy counsel about Canada's combat role in Afghanistan (Stein and Lang 2007). Like Mulroney, who was obsessed with the Americans, officials in the prime minister's office convinced themselves that if Canada turned down the Bush administration on Afghanistan "catastrophic" consequences would ensue.

None of this doom-laden mindset proved to be correct. The Americans hardly remembered that Canada had not sent troops to Iraq and had turned down participation in Bush's ballistic missile defence program. As Lang writes, "we grossly overstate our importance in Washington. They really don't care that much about us. But the advice our politicians get is that they care deeply. It's self-absorbed. It's not a realistic view of Canada's role in the world and our relationship with the US" (quoted in Wente 2007).

The Geo-Political Lessons Learned

The lesson learned is that the North American community ideal is a very fragile construction. Neither Canada nor Mexico has significant leverage in the corridors of power in Washington. Both countries remain neighbours rather than partners in the US public policy world. It is often lamented by policy elites in both countries that they never receive the "face time" that they merit. It is surely a bitter pill for the Mexican political class to swallow that Mexico's influence with Washington in key policy areas is markedly less today than it was when Vicente Fox became president in 2000. It is also sobering to note that Brazil has overtaken Mexico as the most influential geopolitical country in Latin America.

In this volume, Ed Dosman emphasizes that Mexico made the wrong choice with NAFTA. By focusing so exclusively on gaining access to the US market, Mexico's commercial and foreign policy is dangerously unbalanced with respect to the rest of Latin American and the European Union. No one could have predicted that Mexican industry would be mauled by China's rise to pre-eminence in the global economy. In addition, Mexicans can only be ambivalent at best about exporting hundreds of thousands of skilled and unskilled citizens to seek employment opportunities abroad. The out-migration of Mexicans has to be regarded as a human stain on Mexico's present and future. Many scholars, such as Dani Rodrick, have underlined the fact that Mexico's growth rate post-NAFTA is actually lower in 2006 than before the Mexican political class signed on to the NAFTA train (Rodrik, Birdsall, and Subramanian 2006). While it is unlikely that Mexico can easily sever its structural relationship of enormous complexity and inequality, it can be nuanced, downsized, and redirected. It is only a matter of time before Mexico rediscovers a need for a very different kind of developmental trajectory.

The planned exodus of social and human capital comes at a huge cost to Mexico's self-esteem and a more robust economic performance. There is now an emerging consensus that Mexico's annual growth rate of a paltry 3 percent of its gross domestic product (GDP) needs to be doubled or tripled if it expects to support a vigorous attack on poverty eradication and give the 40 percent of the population now living at or below the poverty line new life opportunities (Drache and Froese 2005). Despite more access to US markets than any other southern economy, Mexico's performance can only be described as substandard.

It has yet to address its many difficult, urgent domestic priorities. Belonging to NAFTA has become a crutch for a badly performing economy, not a solution to moving forward. The singular focus on the American market with NAFTA has created significant structural rigidities, and, with Mexico's benefits from NAFTA winding down, the pressures to address domestic problems can only increase for Calderón.

The three NAFTA partners are facing very different futures from their relations with the global South and the seismic changes unleashed by China and India. Mexico has lost hundreds of thousands of jobs to China as production has shifted out of the *maquilidoras* to cheap assembly zones in China (see Victor López Villafañe's chapter in this volume). With the Canadian dollar at a record thirty-year high at US $1.05, Ontario manufacturing has been clobbered, losing over 300,000 manufacturing jobs in the last two years. Strategically, China has the full attention of Washington and has replaced Canada as the United States's largest trading partner. This shift also will have immediate effects for both NAFTA partners (Arthurs 2000). In the United States, new evidence links the negative impact of global free trade to the policy-induced inequality experienced by a large proportion of the population whose jobs cannot be moved off-shore. Many economists estimate that US wages have persistently fallen throughout the NAFTA decade, depressed by highly competitive and fragmented union-free labour market practices (Bivens 2007). The transformation of North America and the new public policy space that has been opened up will have many significant effects. It is modifying and altering the power dynamics that have been implicit in the grand neo-liberal commercial vision of North America. North America is very much a continent in flux, and the post-Bush North America will look very different in the coming years.

Shrinking Governments: Competing National Agendas

North American state-market relations are more anchored than ever in the competing and conflicting big picture realities of each of the NAFTA partners. Quite independently, the Bush and Harper administrations have been busy shrinking their government tax base by cutting tax rates for wealthy individuals and corporations. Paul Krugman and many others have documented the Bush administration's corporate largesse as being the top 1 percent of American income earners. The top 2 percent of Americans own 18 percent of US wealth. This concentration of wealth is unprecedented and had created more millionaires and billionaires than at any other time. According to *Forbes,* thirty-nine US billionaires represent 4.5 percent of the US GDP (Wolf 2007). In 2007, the Harper government reduced the goods and services tax, one of the government's largest sources of revenue, and corporate income tax is scheduled to fall from 21 percent to 15 percent by 2010 and will be the lowest in the G-7 (Chase 2007b). What is

significant is that in taking these dramatic initiatives, both governments have
sent a clear message that the governance capacity of future administrations will
be much reduced. They will have fewer resources to invest in new broad-based
social programs such as childcare, a strengthened public commitment to medicare, and innovative measures to address global warming. These constraints are
not across the board, however, and areas such as defence and security expenditures will be largely exempt.

Strikingly, the Calderón presidency has passed a very modest tax reform
bill to hike taxes to pay for badly needed social reforms in health and education.
It is unclear to many observers whether the funds will find their way to these
critically important areas of public life. Taxation revenue is at all times critical
for promoting social solidarity and investing in human capital, although tax
reform is constantly a wedge issue for politicians and voters.

Compared to a decade ago, North America is entering a period of uncer-
tainty and volatility. In the United States, the growing backlash against the Bush
administration is likely to result in many more Democrats in the Senate and
Congress. The theory of a massive electoral change in US voting patterns with
Democrats and Republicans crossing party lines will be tested in the next period.
Yet, intuitively, the United States is heading toward a major course correction.
It has become isolated from its allies and from global public opinion, and this
fact is worrisome to the US political class. The next president, regardless of
party affiliation, will have to mend fences. New policy directions are needed.
A harbinger of things to come is that Rudolph Giuliani and John McCain, the
Republican front-runners, have distanced themselves from key elements of
Bush's foreign policy, including torture, water-boarding, rendition, and the war
in Iraq. This is by no means repudiation, but the nuance is vital in the run up
to the presidential race.

In Canada, although Harper's minority government was incapable of re-
versing its popularity decline in public opinion polls between 2006 and 2007, it
effectively overtook the much-weakened Liberal party led by Stéphane Dion in
the autumn of 2007. Significantly though, the Harper government has no seats
in the metropolitan centres of Toronto, Montreal, Winnipeg, and Vancouver,
where 60 percent of Canadians reside. Canadian public opinion remains dis-
trustful of the neo-conservative administration, and the minority government
operates as a brake on Harper's exercise of power. While the Liberals have been
disorganized and disoriented under Dion's leadership, they, along with the Bloc
Québécois and New Democratic Party, represent the values and aspirations of
two-thirds of Canadian voters.

In Mexico, the bitter presidential election in 2006 has left a legacy of suspi-
cion and partisanship. One of the unintended consequences of the fear of the
Chávez effect, named for Venezuela's controversial, left-wing president Hugo
Chávez, was to give Calderón his victory over Andrés Manuel López Obrador.

The twin issues of immigration and development now drive Mexico's electoral cycle. Mexico's precipitous decline in terms of American politics requires the political class to be more innovative and strategic. The fact that Cristina Fernández de Kirchner was elected the first woman president of Argentina in late October 2007 underscores for many Mexicans that Latin America is again on the move and that social reform is on the agenda. She is a dynamic advocate of democratic reform, and Argentina has an economy that has made a remarkable recovery since her husband, former president Nestor Kirchner, rejected the conditions imposed by the International Monetary Fund (IMF) to renegotiate its catastrophic debt in 2003. By explicitly citing the "inadmissible privileges" that the IMF-sponsored structural adjustment programs had imposed on the private sector, he reopened privatized utility contracts (Farmelo and Cibils 2003). Reforms such as these cast neo-liberal economic strategies in a very different light. Simplistic templates that have empowered private actors at the expense of the majority have lost much of their allure in the public mind throughout Latin America. Observant Mexicans can see how out of step Mexico is with Latin America's rapidly changing world.

What can be said with certainty is that the political electoral cycle in all three countries is responding to a new constellation of forces after a decade of commercial-driven integration. North America has become ungovernable as a coherent entity without a workable consensus about goals and outcomes. This hypothesis can be tested against the fast-moving set of domestic pressures and competing forces between the NAFTA partners. With so much pressure from below and above, where does this leave the Canada-Mexico relationship?

The Canada-Mexico Partnership

Economically, Canada and Mexico are very modest trading partners. Over the past ten-year period, Canadian exports to Mexico grew from .42 percent to .78 percent, hardly a blistering pace. Mexican exports to Canada are equally modest, hovering around the 2 percent mark. What is undeniable is that, however disappointing the Canada-Mexico bilateral economic relationship is, on the larger screen the two countries register on each other's diplomatic radar with an unprecedented degree of importance. Hundreds of thousands of Canadian tourists vacation in Mexico. More significantly, forty thousand Mexican students come to Canada to study. Canadian and Mexican non-governmental organizations regularly meet to discuss the "Canada-Mexico relationship," and Canadian business organizations such as the Council of Chief Executives frequently coordinate public policy interventions with their Mexican counterparts (Drache 2007).

Still, the Harper government has shifted policy priorities and made building Canada's relationship with Brazil its number one foreign policy objective in

Latin American. There have been missed opportunities, particularly in response to human rights violations in Latin America as well as to the environment. The high point in the Canada-Mexico relationship occurred at the United Nations in 2003 when both countries worked closely together to bridge the divisions between the Bush administration's unilateral action to invade Iraq and the UN system of multilateralism. Typically perhaps, this singular occasion for Canada and Mexico to co-operate closely came and went without the establishment of any further basis for diplomatic co-operation. Many observers, such as Andrew Cooper who has contributed to this volume, believe that the Canada-Mexico strategic connection has not matured sufficiently to affect a deeper and overdue shift from a relationship of convenience to one of perceived commitment.

If there is a final lesson to be learned, it is that despite the billions of dollars in trade and energy flow, our instinctive North American community is only partially anchored in security and commerce. The need for the tri-management of North American public policy did not begin with the signing of NAFTA in 1994 (Cameron and Tomlin 2000). Citizenship rights, state regulation, and security co-operation lie outside its complex mandate. In these critical areas, interstate co-operation is essential and unavoidable. It is also a curious omission of the narrow focus on economic integration that the strategic institution of the border and the government agencies responsible for setting the key policy goals for the cross-border management of the continent has been all but ignored.

Canada and Mexico are two very different societies attempting to come to terms with the cumulative and contradictory effects of these micro and macro changes. Public opinion research and new studies on social values call for a strengthening of popular sovereignty, not its dilution (Adams 2005). In the latest of a series of public opinion polls commissioned by Decima, one of Canada's largest polling firms, 70 percent of Canadians said that they want government to do more to limit foreign takeovers. Even among conservative respondents, 66 percent called on the government to be proactive. Significantly, 71 percent regarded a laissez-faire approach to the free movement of capital a bad thing (Deveau 2007).

The North American idea has been part of the policy arsenal of Washington, Mexico City, and Ottawa ever since Frederick Jackson Turner wrote his celebrated American frontier thesis at the turn of the twentieth century (Drache 2004). System and structure link Canada and Mexico irreversibly to the North American economy, but there are other policy competitors to the security and commerce view of North America. The most powerful and evocative is to envision North America through the lens of diversity and multiculturalism. Some years ago, the great Mexican author and poet, Octavio Paz correctly characterized the North American experience as a labyrinth of solitudes. He was referring to the experience of the Mexican migrant living in the barrios of Los Angeles (Paz 1985). While, for some, the labyrinth may be negative, it speaks, in fact, to the multi-level complexity of North America as a prototypical diverse social space encompassing the linguistic and cultural diversity of three distinct societies. The three countries have a need to address what they share in common— from human security, to development, to human rights, to the environment. North American diversity is our common destiny, and we should accept the need to be "friends at a distance." Thoreau's gentle words represent the best way for national communities to co-exist and thrive.

The Structure of This Book

The book is organized into seven sections. Daniel Drache explores the big picture reality of the asymmetrical benefits of a decade of North American integration. He challenges the idea that there will be a normalization of US realities with either of the NAFTA partners in a post-Bush world. Both Mexico and Canada have to come to terms with the fact that the competitive edge they believed would automatically result from intense continental integration has fallen well short of expectations. In Canada, more job losses are on the way with the Canadian dollar at parity with the US greenback. Mexico's productivity has lagged badly, and its GDP growth is the most disappointing in Latin America. In fact, Mexico experienced higher growth rates prior to signing NAFTA than it has in the past decade. With so much divergence between the three economies in view, the role of national authority in economic strategizing cannot be minimized. In the post-Bush world, US Congress is re-centring on US strategic needs and priorities. Mexico and Canada are being forced down the same policy path. Drache concludes that the NAFTA era is over and that deepening the North American partnership is not in the cards for the foreseeable future.

Gustavo Vega-Cànovas analyzes a second big picture reality that has changed the economic and political landscape of North America, namely the convergence of economic and security relations within the United States. He is optimistic that NAFTA has provided a platform to liberalize further the trade investment between the three NAFTA partners. Significantly, he points to the fact that Mexican state authorities have become aware of the potential benefits that exports can bring to their own states. Mexico has been the recipient of more than US $40 billion dollars of foreign direct investment since the early 1990s. He notes that job growth in Mexico under NAFTA has grown to over one million in jobs related directly or indirectly to export activity.

Significantly, Mexican workers have not seen a real increase in wages in over a decade. The dramatic drop in the workforce engaged in agriculture has been the single most important change in Mexican domestic policy. The percentage of workers involved in Mexican agriculture has dropped from 28 percent to 17 percent, and hundreds of thousands of Mexicans have left the country to seek work illegally in the United States. Mexico's economy must grow at a level of 6–7 percent to prevent the further exodus of Mexicans to the United States. Vega-Cànovas makes a powerful case that Mexico must address the 40 percent of its population that lives in poverty. His chapter is particularly important in detailing Mexico's challenges for the next decade; removing external barriers; developing smart border migration agreements with the United States; and addressing mutual security concerns on the northern and southern border. With strong leadership, North America can accommodate the new political realities of the continent.

In Alex Neve's chapter on rights at the borders, he explains that the new defining reality for North America is the need to come to terms with immigration flows, human rights, and political refugees in the Canada-Mexico relationship. While, for many, the border is only a commercial gate, Neve makes the compelling case that borders are a line in the sand for human rights and that human rights violations have been on the increase over the past decade. The number of Mexicans seeking asylum has grown markedly since 9/11, and immigration into Canada has become more difficult. During border crossings, migrants face many dangers including extortion, rape, threats, and other violence from *coyotes* and private militia groups.

The Security and Prosperity Partnership, which was adopted in March 2005 and strengthened in March 2006, only spoke of legitimate migration but was silent on the movement of people, human rights, and migration. Neve's chapter is particularly important because it reminds us that there are other parallel regional initiatives going on, such as the Puebla process, which address the precarious situation of regional migrants. It includes eight other countries from the region and offers an alternative to a narrowly defined security-related focus on refugees. One of the new realities facing North America is the need for extended human rights co-operation and the need for better protections and stronger laws to protect the basic human rights of migrants. It is one of the areas in which Canada and Mexico could co-operate more closely.

Ana Covarrubias has written a far-reaching analysis on the role of human rights in Mexican foreign policy. Mexico's foreign policy, like that of many other countries, has supported the principle of non-intervention while, at the same time, promoting the protection of human rights. It is only belatedly that the Mexican government has recognized that human rights are a legitimate foreign policy issue. Covabrrubias notes that under Carlos Salinas' presidential term, the government did not prioritize human rights issues and was more focused on aggressive commercial diplomacy. Under Vicente Fox's foreign minister, Jorge Castañeda, human rights were given a key place in Mexico's foreign policy. Castañeda was particularly interested in using human rights instruments to achieve a new political culture. This has never been easy for Mexico as its own human rights record has been subject to much criticism, particularly with respect to the treatment of illegal immigrants as well as earlier human rights violations against its own citizens. Still there has been considerable progress made with respect to the protection of human rights in Mexico, and the rights of immigrants and others remains a top priority for the new government.

The Bush revolution in foreign policy has had a major impact on Canada and Mexico. Stephen Clarkson details the complex nature of Canada's response to what he calls the "Bush foreign policy counter-revolution." The central dilemma is that the US war on terrorism has driven a wedge between the Canadian and American political class, while, at the same time, it has accelerated co-operation between Canadian and American military personnel. Jean Chrétien's refusal to send Canadian forces to Iraq represented an iconic moment for Canadian foreign policy. After much dithering, Chrétien correctly read the mind of the Canadian electorate and refused Washington's request for Canadian forces without a UN resolution in support of the Iraq invasion. It is important to recall that Canada was in good company since France, Germany, and Mexico as well as many other countries opposed Bush's unilateral declaration of war. It is also significant that Canada and Mexico worked closely together at the United Nations in an attempt to find a "third way."

While many experts warned that there would be serious consequences for Canada's refusal to support the United States in Iraq, there were none. In fact, many inside the Department of External Affairs and the Department of Defence have seriously underestimated Canada's scope for autonomous action on the Iraq war as well as on other policy issues. Clarkson's chapter underscores the depth of the conflict in the relationship between the two capitals and suggests that the strain on diplomatic relations with Washington represents a new level of maturity in which allies can and will differ.

Jorge Chabat's chapter serves as a useful counterpoint to Clarkson's. Chabat provides a detailed account of the Bush foreign policy revolution with its clear preference for unilateral action and its willingness to use pre-emptive military force to produce "needed regime change in rogue states." Chabat describes US foreign policy under Bush as democratic imperialism in which Washington believes that it has the right to change existing regimes when it is in its interest to do so. The rejection of UN multilateralism has left the United States looking neither strong nor benign in the eyes of world opinion. The undermining of international law and the abuse of prisoners in Iraq has radically changed public perception of US foreign policy. For Mexico, there have been many direct consequences of the 11 September attacks. Washington now regards Mexican border security as a very large problem and is contemplating erecting a North American security perimeter. Chabat's chapter contains an excellent overview of Mexico-US relations post-9/11. Among other things, it explains the increase in tensions between the Bush administration and its disdain for international organizations, such as the United Nations, and Mexico's strong support for an international system of multilateralism. Chabat, like Clarkson, concludes that Mexico has a large margin for manoeuvring in foreign policy despite the high level of interdependence between the two countries.

The single most important issue changing the political landscape of North America is US homeland security. The biggest picture reality in the post-9/11 world is the doctrine of the US security imperative. Wesley Wark analyzes Canadian border security policy since 9/11, and Jordi Díez shines fresh light on Mexico's place in the North American security perimeter. It is important to note that both Canada and Mexico have stepped up to the plate and dramatically overhauled their cross-border infrastructure, policing, intelligence, and passport issuance. If, in the past, trade was the tie that linked the three countries together, in the new century security trumps all other aspects of domestic policy. Simply put, security is first, but these three words are interpreted very differently by Canada and Mexico. The core reason for this difference, Wark suggests, is that there is no commonly shared definition of what constitutes a security risk. Without an agreed upon definition, it is unlikely that Canada and Mexico can meet the US demand to work in close partnership on security. In retrospect, it can be seen that it was naive on the part of many trade experts to think that there could ever be a single common policy on border security. Canadian policy lumped together a wide range of threats from terrorism to national disasters, organized crime, and health pandemics. In this "all hazards" approach, Canada did not prioritize terrorism.

In his chapter, Díez concurs that the North American security partnership is flawed in fundamental ways because it does not take into account the diversity of the national security documents of the "three amigo" partners. Díez's chapter is very important for assimilating the primary message that while there has been some institutionalization of security co-operation, Mexico's nationalist public opinion is against any formal engagement with the United States that would pose a threat to the country's sovereignty. Significantly, the need for underlining the importance of Mexico's sovereignty did not prevent the Fox government from co-operating with Washington on a bilateral level. Yet here too, Mexico's level of participation has been politicized by the refusal of the US Congress to establish a new migratory system for the ten to twenty million Mexican's without legal status. Díez is quite right to underline the fact that NAFTA and close economic integration was the agenda of the 1990s. Economic development, drug trafficking, personal security, and immigration define the new priorities of Mexican citizens. As US immigration policy has become barefacedly unilateral, Mexico's relationship with Washington has become more conflictual and complex. It is likely that the idea of North America will evolve on the bilateral axis with little prospect for trilateral security structures.

One of the most difficult areas for North American relations has to do with Canada and Mexico's oil and gas reserves. The NAFTA neighbours supply the United States with almost 30 percent of its energy needs. For more than three decades, the big idea of negotiating a continental energy partnership has captured the interest and attention of all US administrations and much of the North American oil and gas industry. Isidro Morales' chapter provides an authoritative account of the pros and cons standing in the way of a full-blown North American strategic partnership. Ontario, Quebec, and BC Hydro are all publicly owned state enterprises in the electrical sector. In Mexico, PEMEX (Petroleos Mexicanos) and the CFE (Comisión Federal de Electricidad) are vital state monopolies that play a critical role in keeping Mexico's energy prices below international levels.

Significantly, PEMEX is excluded from the NAFTA purview, and this important exception has angered US oil interests. Despite their efforts, neither Ernesto Zedillo, the former president in 1999, nor Fox were successful in passing major reforms to privatize the CFE or PEMEX. Readers would do well to absorb the analysis contained in Morales' chapter on the growing divergence between the future of Mexico's energy production and US security concerns. Despite predictions that homeland security would lead to a slam-dunk deal and the creation of a North American energy market, this pro-business, big vision reality is very far down on the horizon. There is no likelihood that Mexico's Congress will pass the needed constitutional reforms to privatize the energy sector. By way of conclusion, Morales proposes some interesting ideas with respect to the reform of Mexico's energy industry.

In her chapter, Rosalba Icaza Garza addresses the future of what she calls "neo-liberal regionalism," a policy framework composed of NAFTA and an economic partnership between the European Union and Mexico. Few would argue with the fact that the region of North America was transformed in the 1990s through the reorganization of production and changes in migratory and capital flows. The government of Carlos Salinas, 1988–1994, was a key promoter of the open regionalism that would transform Mexican national markets into fully integrated regional economies closely integrated with US supply management chains.

In theory, open regionalism was designed to strengthen domestic production capacity and to become successful export platforms for the auto, steel, textile, and agricultural industries. When NAFTA was signed, there were more than one million Mexicans employed in the *maquiladoras*. A decade later, the China factor has challenged Mexico's access to the US market. Mexico has lost more than 300,000 jobs in these export-processing zones. Equally disappointing is the fact that economic growth in Mexico was actually lower in 2005 than it was the decade earlier when NAFTA was signed. Civil society groups and social movements have grown disillusioned with neo-liberal regionalism and have sought a "reform of the reforms."

Many economists have also supported the view that narrowly based market policies have failed to generate more and better jobs, to reduce the number of migrants to the United States, and to develop a modern agricultural sector. The latter point is particularly crucial because, in the past decade, rural Mexico has lost close to 1.5 million jobs due to the flow of cheap subsidized farm products from the United States. Hundreds of thousands of displaced agricultural workers have joined the mass movement of illegal migrants to the United States. Mexico is very far from its goal of poverty eradication, let alone being able to reduce the number of Mexicans (nearly 40 percent) who live below the poverty line. For Mexico, the agreement with the European Union is an important counterweight to NAFTA, but, so far, Mexico has only enjoyed modest success in strengthening its relationship with Europe.

The emergence of China in the global economy has had dramatic effects on Mexico's place in North America. Conventional wisdom has suggested that NAFTA would secure Mexico's place in the North American economy and that its privileged relationship with the United States would transform Mexico's industries into world-class competitors. The expectation was that hundreds of thousands of jobs would be created and millions of Mexicans living in poverty would escape a life of drudgery and marginalization. Victor López Villafañe's chapter is an extremely important corrective and exploration of why Mexico, and, by implication, Canada, can no longer rely on NAFTA as its anchor point in an increasingly turbulent global economy. Critics in the past have pointed out that the asymmetrical benefits from NAFTA with respect to job loss and the destruction of the Mexican agricultural sector would be offset by the growth in Mexico's auto and textiles industries and exports to the United States. The picture has become increasingly complicated because China, which is emblematic of the global South, is "stealing" Mexican jobs and industrial capacity as US producers shift production out of Mexico to China. For some theorists, Mexico has taken a wrong turn by putting all of its eggs in the NAFTA basket. While this may be true, Mexico has to move forward and rethink its developmental strategy, faced not only with China as a dynamo but also with Brazil and India. López Villafañe's chapter is essential reading for anyone who wants to develop a detailed understanding of the new challenges facing Mexico as it attempts to reorient itself to compelling changes in the world order.

Edgar Dosman's chapter provides an important set of metrics with which to contextualize the profound domestic and global challenges faced by Mexico and Brazil. By far, the largest Latin American countries in population and economies, they have followed divergent trajectories and strategies. Dosman sets out to explain why Mexico is trapped in low growth cycles while Brazil's industrial strategy has made it one of the "super powers" of the global South. Brazil is one of the success stories of the decade with its powerful industrial competitiveness in the air craft, petrochemicals, agriculture, and auto industries. Dosman demonstrates in a close analysis of Brazil's export strategy that it has developed a balanced approach with more than 20 percent of exports going to the United States, 20 percent or better going to the European Union, and another 25 percent going to its partners in the Mercado Común del Sur (Mercosur). It has also developed important trade links with China. Dosman notes that, along with China, Brazil has one of the lowest brain drains among developed countries.

After years of relative stagnation, Brazil has achieved a very stable macro-economic environment. As we have already discussed, Mexico's strategy has been almost exclusively centred on the US market with none of the diversity and balancing that is evident in Brazil's regional-global strategy. Dosman makes the very important point that Mexico has abandoned its self-image as a bridging power in the Western hemisphere, while Brazil has pursued the bridging role for itself globally and in Latin America. Indeed, it has become the leader of the global South in Latin America at the expense of Mexico's influence and authority. President Luiz Inâcio Lula da Silva campaigned and was elected in Brazil in 2002 with a broad neo-liberal critique of the Washington consensus goals and objectives. In Mexico, Calderón, the narrowly victorious National Action Party candidate in 2006, has chosen to deepen Mexico's dependence on NAFTA rather than anything else. In conclusion, Dosman is pessimistic about the possibility for a rapprochement between the two Latin American giants.

Andrew Cooper examines the future of Canada-Mexico relations in a particularly challenging chapter. Many Mexicans and Canadians are of the view that the two like-minded countries can find ways to balance their relationship with the United States by strengthening their ties to each other. The reality is that the Canada-Mexico relationship remains modest and is in need of deepening and strengthening. Many experts have believed that NAFTA would automatically lead to raising Canada and Mexico's profiles with each other, but so far this is only a pious wish. Cooper is quite insightful when he argues that self-interested convenience does not always create a more fundamental set of understandings such as could lead the way to a significant political commitment on the part of Ottawa or Mexico City. Certainly, there have been plenty of missed opportunities as Cooper recounts. Both the 2001 Quebec Summit and the G-20 finance ministers meeting in 2003 in Cancun could have been the catalysts for setting in motion a significant realignment between the two countries. Cooper's idea of a value-based foreign policy combined with a strong commitment to multilateralism and international human rights provides an alternative framework for the Mexican and Canadian political class. Cooper is particularly skeptical that a smart borders policy and further militarization of the border will translate into a coincidence of interests. For many congressmen and senators, the southern border is broken, and Mexican illegal immigration now poses a major threat to US security. Although Cooper speaks of the need to balance "the powerful one," Canada and Mexico are subject to very different sets of competing pressures.

If anything, the Canada-Mexico relationship suffers from understatement and not infrequent neglect at the level of geopolitical intersection. Cooper is quite right to draw our attention to the absence of any big bang in design. Much more could be done by way of a course correction. In conclusion, Cooper is skeptical that in the short term there will be a different mental map with a trajectory that would transform a relationship of convenience into one of commitment. Clearly, Latin America is on the move, and the China factor cannot be underestimated as Canada and Mexico enter a long transition period of uncertainty and re-examination.

In his chapter, Duncan Wood presents a realistic, but positive, view of the future of Canada-Mexico relations. Many contributors have pointed out that the vast distance of geography separating Canada and Mexico has also supported a number of competing political and economic divisions. With lucidity, Wood presents an overview of the difficulties facing North American integration. Key among these is the fact that significant trilateral progress has stalled due to the inability to overcome the disparities in levels of economic development between the three countries.

At the present time, the Mexican economy is trapped between China's rise to prominence as a global power and its own failure to stem the massive and officially sanctioned illegal immigration flow to the United States. It is important to examine in detail the Fox government's record on immigration and its ill fit with the newly minted security-driven focus on homeland security and tight, secure borders. Wood very effectively analyzes the growing conflict between the national interests of each of the NAFTA partners and the growing anti-Bush nationalism that is much in evidence in Mexico and Canada. Wood underscores how important it is in the public's mind that Bush and the United States are increasingly seen as representatives of global capitalism and globalization. The intensity of the current wave of "anti-yanquismo" in Mexico is a phenomenon that was not present in the early years of the Fox and Bush administrations. Periodic outbursts of anti-Mexican xenophobia have sharply constrained the Mexican political class. On the other hand, the Canadian government and the business community are currently ambiguous about deepening the Canada-Mexico partnership. Still, Canada and Mexico have reached a level of cultural and societal understanding that offers much to build on should the elites in each country decide to get on each other's radar screens. Wood explores education, health, security, infrastructure, and energy as areas of future high-level co-operation.

In the final chapter, Carlos H. Waisman examines the dynamics between the state and society in Mexico and its process of democratization in the past two decades. Throughout Latin America, there is now a vigorous, well-organized, and articulate civil society, although the exact nature of civic engagement remains imprecise and highly fluid. Alexis de Tocqueville is one of the fundamental thinkers with respect to citizen group activities and the core ideas behind interest, promotion, and engagement that is voluntary and self-organizing. These dense networks of secondary associations increasingly contribute to social collaboration that is autonomous from the state and bound by a legal order and set of common regulatory assumptions. In an information age, there is nothing surprising about the newly empowered citizen/civil society actor acquiring a voice and presence throughout Latin American society. Waisman explores the increasing contention between a growing individualism and a renewed interest in equality rather than liberty. At one time, it was thought that the "art of association would improve at the same speed as equal conditions spread" (Waisman, page 269 in this volume). In fact, the United Nations Development Programme's studies on the development of inequality suggest the reverse to be true. Inequality has grown as civil society has become stronger and more autonomous from the state in many countries. Waisman's chapter provides an analytically powerful way to examine the growing importance of civil society to the deepening of democracy.

In this chapter, he examines the growing social and economic dualism in most Latin American societies where democracy has been corrupted by authoritarianism, residualism, clientalism, and state corporatism. Waisman explores the way in which economic liberalization has intensified these dualisms in Mexico as well as in other countries. He suggests that there are three analytical dimensions: density, autonomy, and self-regulation. He goes on to develop theoretical propositions about the uneven nature of Latin American democratic culture that results when density, autonomy, and self-regulation are low. The question becomes: is Mexico overcoming the legacy of poorly institutionalized rules and evolving toward a high-quality democracy. He particularly highlights the fact that social polarization has increased since the beginning of NAFTA, which, in turn, undermines the dynamics of democratization. Mexico faces a challenging future if it is to reduce inequality and expand the material side of citizenship. This is a fundamentally political choice and not one that is structurally determined. For Waisman, Mexico's future depends upon mastering the dualism of inequality and clientalism.

NOTES

1 Specific details about the new phase of North American integration are drawn from the 2007 edition of my book *La Ilusión Continental: Seguridad fronteriza y la búsqueda de una identidad Norteamericana* (Mexico City: Siglo XXI). North American Free Trade Agreement between the Government of Canada, the Government of Mexico and the Government of the United States, 17 December 1992, Can. T.S. 1994 No. 2, 32 I.L.M. 289.

2 Personal discussions of the author with US border authorities, October 2007.

3 Security and Prosperity Partnership, 23 March 2005, http://www.spp.gov.

4 In the Strategic Counsel poll, the actual breakdown is as follows: 18 percent identified healthcare as their top concern; 26 percent identified the environment; 6 percent identified foreign policy and political leadership; 6 percent terrorism; 6 percent economic issues; 4 percent unemployment; 3 percent taxes; 3 percent education; and 3 percent crime.

5 Two previous complaints were filed in Germany, another one was filed in Spain, and one in Argentina.

6   See French League of Human Rights, http://www.fidh.org, accessed 26 October
    2007.

7   *The Secure Fence Act of 2006*, http://www.whitehouse.gov/news/releases/2006/10/
    20061026-1.html.

8   See the Federation for American Immigration Reform's accuracy in the report-
    ing analysis of Lou Dobbs's advocacy journalism, http://www.fair.org/index.
    php?page=2867. Dobbs makes no effort to provide a balanced, factual, or nuanced
    view, which is not unusual at CNN.

REFERENCES

Adams, Michael. 2005. *American Backlash: The Untold Story of Social Change in
    the United States.* Toronto: Viking Canada.

Annett, Tim. 2006. "Illegal Immigrants and the Economy." *Wall Street Journal,*
    13 April.

Archibold, Randal C. 2007. "Debate Raging, Mexico Adds Consulates in U.S."
    New York Times, 23 May.

Arthurs, Harry. 2000. "The Hollowing Out of Canada?" In Jane Jenson and Boa
    de Sousa Santos, eds., *Globalizing Institutions.* London: Ashgate.

Associated Press. 2007. "Border Crossings Fall for Second Consecutive Year."
    New York Times, 8 November.

Bell, Stuart. 2007. "Terror. Report Blames CSIS." *National Post,* 30 October.

Bivens, Josh. 2007. "Globalization, American Wages and Inequality." *EPI Working
    Paper,* http://www.epi.org.

Blumenthal, Ralph. 2007. "Some Texans Say Border Fence Will Sever Routine."
    New York Times, 20 June.

Bowker, David, and David Kaye. 2007. "Guantanamo by Numbers." *New York
    Times,* 10 November.

Byers, Michael. 2005. *War Law: Understanding International Law and Armed
    Conflict.* New York: Grove Press.

Calavita, Kitty. 1982. "California's 'Employer Sanctions': The Case of the Disappearing
    Law." Research Report Series No. 39, Center for U.S-Mexican Studies,
    University of California, San Diego.

Cameron, Maxwell, and Brian Tomlin. 2000. *The Making of NAFTA: How the
    Deal Was Done.* Ithaca, NY: Cornell University Press.

Canada. 2005. *Borderline Insecure: An Interim Report of the Senate Committee
    on National Security and Defence.* Ottawa.

———. 2007. *Reports of the Auditor General,* http://www.gnb.ca/OAG-BVG/
    Reports-e.asp.

Canadian Government. 2007. Commission of Inquiry into the Actions of
    Canadian Officials in Relation to Maher Arar. http://epe.lac-bac
    .gc.ca/100/206/301/pco-bcp/commissions/maher_arar/index.html.

"Canadian Security Certificates and Secret Evidence." 2007. CBC News World, http://www.cbc.ca/news/background/cdnsecurity/securitycertificates_ secretevidence.html.

Centre for Constitutional Rights. 2007. *Illegal Detentions and Guantanamo and Government Abuse of Power,* http://www.ccrjustice.org/issues.

Chase, Stephen. 2007a. "Anti-Terror Costs Take Toll on Transporters." *Globe and Mail,* 22 November.

_____. 2007b. "Ottawa Doles Out $60 Billion in Tax Relief." *Globe and Mail,* 31 October.

Clarkson, Stephen. 2003. *Uncle Sam and Us.* Toronto: University of Toronto Press.

Confessore, Nicholas. 2007. "Lou Dobbs Crusade against Spitzer's Driver's License Plan for Illegal Immigrants." *New York Times,* 17 October.

Deveau, Scott. 2006. "Anti-Terrorism Laws Intrusive, Canadians Say." *Globe and Mail,* 14 November.

Drache, Daniel. 2004. *Borders Matter: Homeland Security and the Search for North America.* Halifax: Fernwood.

_____. 2007. *La Ilusión Continental: Seguridad fronteriza y la búsqueda de una identidad Norteamericana.* Mexico City: Siglo XXI.

Drache, Daniel, and Marc Froese. 2005. *The Great Poverty Debate,* http://www .robarts.yorku.ca.

Eaton, Leslie. 2007. "US Prosecution of Muslim Group Ends in Mistrial." *New York Times,* 23 October.

Farmelo, Martha, and Alan Cibils. 2003. "Argentina's President's First 100 Days Break from Thirty Years of Business-As-Usual," http://americas.irc-online .org/articles/2003/0309kirchner.html.

Freeman, Alan, and Bill Curry. 2007. "Border among Key Issues at Summit's Opening." *Globe and Mail,* 21 August.

Gambrill, Monica, ed. 2006. *Diez años del* TLCAN *en México.* Mexico City: CISAN.

Goldsmith, Jack. 2007. *The Terror Presidency Law and Judgement inside the Bush Administration.* New York: Norton.

Greenberg, Karen J. 2007. *The Torture Debate in America.* New York: Cambridge University Press.

Haglund, David G. 2003. "North American Cooperation in an Era of Homeland Security." *Orbis* 47: 4.

Hall, Mimi. 2007. "15,000 Want Off Terror Watch List Tsa Struggles to Handle Backlog." *USA Today,* 7 November.

Hollingsworth, J. Rogers, and Robert Boyer, eds. 1997. *Contemporary Capitalism: The Embeddedness of Institutions.* Cambridge: Cambridge University Press.

Holstege, Sean. 2007. "Chertoff Will Highlight Progress along Border." *Arizona Republic,* 6 November.

International Federation for Human Rights. 2007. "Complaint Filed against Former Defense Secretary for Torture, Abuse at Guantanomo and Abu Grahib," http://www.fidh.org.

Jang, Brent. 2007. "Air Security: Demand Angers Canadians." *Globe and Mail,* 11 October.

Jervis, Robert. 2004. "Understanding the Bush Doctrine." In G. John Ikenberry, ed., *American Foreign Theoretical Essay.* New York: Pearson-Longman.

Kershaw, Sarah. 2007. "U.S. Rule Limits Emergency Care for Immigrants." *New York Times,* 22 September.

Leeder, Jessica. 2007. "Arar Fallout Shows Anti-Terror Laws Unjust, Activists Say." *Globe and Mail,* 22 October.

Marotte, Bertrand. 2007. "Producers Slam U.S. Tests for Canadian Meat, Poultry." *Globe and Mail,* 5 November.

McKinley Jr., James. 2007. "In Mexico, Bush Seeks to Bolster Uneasy Alliance." *New York Times,* 13 March.

Mulroney, Brian. 2007. *Memoirs 1939–1993.* Toronto: Random House.

Paz, Octavio. 1985. *Labyrinth of Solitude.* New York: Grove Press.

Pew Research Centre for the People and the Press. 2007. *Survey Reports,* http://people-press.org/reports.

Randall, Stephen, and Herman Konrad, eds. 1992. *North America without Borders.* Calgary: University of Calgary Press.

Rutenberg, Jim, and Carl Hulse. 2007. "President's Push on Immigration Tests G.O.P. Base." *New York Times,* 3 June.

Serrano, Monica. 2007. "Integration and Security in North America." *International Journal* (summer): 611–32.

"The State of Public Opinion in Canada: The Greening of Canada, Strategic Counsel." 2007. *Globe and Mail,* 17 January, http://www.thestrategiccounsel.com/our_news/polls/2007-01-17%20GMCTV%20Jan%2011-14%20f.pdf.

Stein, Janice Gross, and Eugene Lang. 2007. *Unexpected War: Canada in Kandahar.* Toronto: Viking.

Susskind, Ron. 2007. *The One Percent Doctrine: Deep inside America's Pursuit of Its Enemies since 1911.* New York: Simon and Schuster.

Thompson, John Herd, and Stephan J. Randall. 2002. *Canada and the United States: Ambivalent Allies.* Kingston and Montreal: McGill-Queen's University Press.

Vega, Alba, et al., eds. 2005. *A Diiez anos del* TLCAN. Mexico City: Colegio de Mexico, programma Interinstitucional de Estudios sobre La Region de America del Norte.

Welsh, Jennifer. 2004. *At Home in the World: Canada's Global Vision for the Twenty-first Century.* Toronto: Harper Collins.

Wente, Margaret. 2007. "The Twisted Road to Kandahar." *Globe and Mail*, 20 October.
Wolf, Martin. 2007. "Why Plutocracy Endangers Emerging Market Economies." *Financial Times,* 7 November.
Woodward, Bob. 2006. *State of Denial Bush at War, Part III.* New York: Simon and Schuster.

1

NAFTA: A CLOSED CHAPTER OR A FRESH START?

Bon Anniversaire NAFTA:
The Elusive and Asymmetrical Benefits of
a Decade of North American Integration

Daniel Drache

Next Steps: Challenges Ahead

Almost fifteen years after the signing of the North American Free Trade Agreement (NAFTA) there is no urgent need to proceed to the next stage in integration.[1] Increasing trade facilitation, improving the system of trade dispute panels, and reducing the transaction costs of a security-first border remain a set of generalized concerns for all three governments. Further integration projects have met with powerful opposition from the US Congress. The Central American Free Trade Agreement received congressional consent by the barest majority after months of White House arm-twisting and vote-buying (Alden and Yeager 2005). The Bush administration is preoccupied with homeland security, and, as the quagmire in Iraq costs more American lives and consumes billions of tax dollars, there are few incentives for Washington to gear up for a battle with the Republican Congress to broaden and deepen North American integration. Public opinion in Mexico and Canada has expressed little enthusiasm for a big next step. There are a lot of doubts and reservations about a second round of North American integration discussions (Drache 2004).

Strikingly, many Canadian businesses do not see deepening NAFTA as the preferred initiative to resolve the many strategic challenges that will reshape their operations over the next five years. High costs and a rising Canadian dollar are forcing Canadian manufacturers to look inward to respond to rapidly changing supply and demand chains (Drache 2004). In an October 2005 survey of Canadian manufacturers and exporters, improved North American market access did not even make the top ten list of strategic challenges for the roughly 1,000 firms surveyed (Canadian Manufacturers and Exporters 2005). Without a strong consensus, the public in both countries would need a huge amount of convincing and arm-twisting in order to deepen NAFTA and constrain Canadian and Mexican sovereignty in new ways.

For Canada and Mexico, given these uncertainties, what is the next move in a post-NAFTA world—more integration; integration through trade only; or building closer ties through a new framework for economic cooperation? Will a NAFTA-plus agenda alleviate the disparities in economic development between the NAFTA countries? Does Mexico need a different economic strategy? Have most of the NAFTA effects already been captured? If this scenario is the case, a major re-evaluation of NAFTA is needed before any new round of integration is undertaken.

New Competitive Pressures: Market Access Cannot Be Guaranteed

It is not significantly clear what more secure "access" would entail in a highly protectionist environment. With tariffs already at historic lows, the NAFTA countries have little more to gain for consumers or for industries in terms of efficiency gains. Nor is it a simple case to identify those Canadian and Mexican industries that would benefit at the present time from further integration. Canadian and Mexican export industries are faced with changing consumer demands, widespread technological change, competition from China, and generally higher production costs. These companies need to become more agile and diversified and less dependent on traditional markets. Diversification and gaining access to developing markets in the global South will require a rethinking of trade fundamentals (Krugman 1995). Canada's premier business organizations such as the Conference Board of Canada and the C.D. Howe Institute could not be further apart in their thinking. The Conference Board of Canada is championing investment in new technology and high productivity growth as the top priority for Canada's private sector. The C.D. Howe Institute seems locked into yesterday's strategy of calling for more North American economic integration but offers few fresh ideas to medium-sized Canadian firms battered by a CDN $.90 dollar. The Mexican Council on North American Business is also stuck in a rut and is not ready to confront the new competitive pressures facing Mexican industry (Council on Foreign Relations 2005). Right-of-centre business groups are banking on an environment of trade determinism at the very time when Washington consensus goals are unravelling (Naim 2000).

On the political front, NAFTA, which was once a mid-range priority for the Clinton administration, has been downgraded as a strategic goal for US policy makers in the Bush administration. Certainly, NAFTA has promised to build a new trilateral relationship in North America, but, after a decade of existence, bilateral tensions have risen sharply with respect to immigration, softwood lumber, US unilateralism, homeland security, and US trade politics. Mexican illegal immigration and the debate over amnesty have replaced NAFTA as the North American question *par excellence*. Equally significant is the fact that the dispute resolution mechanism has been badly damaged by US arrogance and that country's refusal to comply with its NAFTA obligations on softwood lumber. Gordon Ritchie (2005), one of the agreement's architects and main supporters, has argued that US non-compliance has irreparably damaged NAFTA's legal regime for Canada and Mexico. In 2006, Washington offered Canada only limited access to the US market in defiance of the keystone principle of NAFTA—free trade. According to the deal, US forestry interests will retain US $500 million dollars in illegally imposed duties. There is no level playing field in sight, and the legal asymmetries continue to spin out of control.

Regional Markets, Trade Bilateralism, and Growing Policy Diversity

Canada and Mexico increasingly find themselves at a distance from Washington's strategy for the future of North America and a new global vision. In Canada, recent polls show that highly contentious trade issues have soured the prospect of establishing a stronger trilateral relationship. Even along the bilateral Canada-US axis, relations have been rocky since Ottawa's refusal to send Canadian soldiers to fight in the US war in Iraq. The decline in the North American partnership has been both qualitative and quantitative. Why?

The argument in a nutshell is that highly adverse structural adjustments will require that Canada and Mexico begin to look for other options, given that access to the US market is largely a *fait accompli* for many industries and that there is no likely prospect of any new major gains. Any new moves to negotiate a NAFTA-plus agreement are a second-best option when faced with a US Congress that is in a protectionist phase. Mexico has large decisions to make as it wrestles against the limits of neo-liberalism—its major policy framework of the last decade. Mexico needs to rethink immigration policy. Exporting a half a million jobless, rural workers to the United States is not a policy that can be sustained.

In a post-NAFTA era, Canada and Mexico face many more policy challenges. As security continues to trump the narrow focus of NAFTA, Canada and Mexico will have to look for a new policy platform that reflects their divergent national priorities. First, in an era of regional bilateralism, the election of Stephen Harper's Conservative government in Canada has made the process of developing the Canada-Mexico relationship a lot more problematic and challenging. South of the Rio Grande, Mexican foreign policy is likely to shift toward a more values-based approach, while Canada is looking to be an active partner of Washington inside the beltway (see Ana Covarrubias's chapter in this volume, page 87).

Second, whatever the future may hold, two constants are going to shape Canada's relations with Mexico. First, it is unrealistic to talk about the "normalization" of US relations with either of its NAFTA partners. There is no going back to a status quo. Second, despite significant economic disparities, Canada and Mexico will have to be ready to co-operate in ways they have never before entertained. The burden of this chapter is to explain that the future of North America will be organized around regional bilateralism as the next stage of the integration process. Canada and Mexico can either face their dependence on the United States without one another, or they can look across the continent to build a partnership with a focused and strategic sense of purpose.

Adding Up the Numbers: The Big Picture Overview

Since NAFTA came into effect, Canada and Mexico have become more export oriented. They have also felt the full effect of trade adversity from new competitive circumstances. Trade adversity occurred because Canada and Mexico were unprepared for the larger structural changes arising from growing competition with their most important trading partner. Paradoxically, despite becoming more export oriented between 2000 and 2004, Canada and Mexico's share of world trade actually shrunk (see Figure 1). Since 2000, belonging to a free trade zone has been no guarantee that the NAFTA partners would not be buffeted by the gale-like forces of international competition. The United States has seen its commanding position in the world economy dramatically decline by three percentage points; Germany has made impressive gains despite its unemployment crisis; and Mexico has been a loser in the global export winner-take-all stakes along with Canada. Belonging to NAFTA has not prepared either country for

FIGURE 1 Share of World Exports in Selected Countries

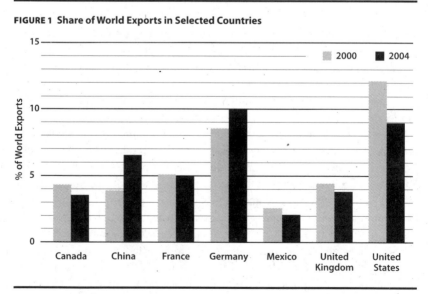

SOURCE: WORLD TRADE ORGANIZATION 2005.

the new competitiveness of China and India—countries that are powering their way into global markets. In addition, NAFTA's share of world exports in goods and services has dropped precipitously. In 1993, it accounted for 23 percent of total global exports. Yet by 2003, NAFTA's share of world exports had declined to 19 percent, while Europe's remained steady at 23 percent.

Concentration on a single market is no guarantee that NAFTA is providing Canada and Mexico with the competitive edge for the new challenges they are facing. In the next phase of continental integration, the link between a strong export performance and job creation is definitively uncoupled in the most export-oriented sectors such as auto and information technology. Productivity has increased dramatically, but employment is flat or declining, and more job cuts are on their way. The global commodity boom has created new employment growth in Canadian mining but not in the forest industries. For Mexico, export success has not triggered persistently high growth in the gross domestic product (GDP) either. Since 1994, per capita income growth has barely kept pace with Mexico's rapidly growing labour force. In 1995, per capita income plummeted by 9.11 percent. It recovered but was hardly a sparkler at 3.28 percent in 1999. Since 2000, per capita income has barely grown at all, minus 1.49 percent in 2001, minus 0.64 percent in 2002, and minus 0.01 percent in 2003. The paradox is that export wealth is not trickling down despite the fact that Mexico has become heavily dependent on exports in its role as the engine of the economy (Middlebrooke and Zepada 2003). For Canada, which is a developed economy, the NAFTA model of development has been largely job negative. Access to the giant American market has not noticeably slowed down the dramatic decline in manufacturing jobs in the economy (see Figure 2). The empirical data should set alarm bells ringing. Exports can have many effects for regions and sectors, but, in an efficiency-driven world, the single-minded pursuit of exports cannot be relied on for primary job creation. Globalization is requiring firms to shed jobs yet increase productivity with fewer workers on the factory floor (Peters 2005).

Concentration in a single market has proven to be a double-edge sword. Neither Canada nor Mexico has yet to assimilate the full implications of their decline globally. Over-reliance on NAFTA has led to a loss of industry-level flexibility on the one hand and to the growth of energy exports on the other hand, which has locked Canada and Mexico into the US-dominated energy market framework with little ability to capture upstream and downstream benefits for their own development goals. A recent Statistics Canada study reveals that NAFTA's biggest success has been to reinforce Canada's traditional competitive advantage in energy and natural resource industries. The same truth applies to Mexico as it has become more locked into the US energy and parts manufacturing market. Resource exports are not labour intensive, and oil and gas exports have given both countries a massive windfall from soaring energy prices. Yet the energy sector is not a model for the rest of the economy.

FIGURE 2 Canadian Share of Jobs in Manufacturing

SOURCE: CROSS 2005.

Canada and Mexico: The Weakest Link

Even if the North American trade in goods relative to GDP output has grown markedly for both countries, Canada-Mexico economic relations can only be described as feather weight. Between 1995 and 2004, Canada's exports to Mexico amounted to roughly .5 percent of Canada's total trade, rising to a very modest .8 percent by 2004. This number does not simply capture the way the two economies are "lost in translation" but also demonstrates a real absence of incentives to transform Canada-Mexico relations into a dynamic collaboration. There are few linkages between the two economies, and a decade of free trade has done little to lay the basis for any next steps or closer commercial collaboration.

For Mexico, the economic relationship has been small and limited to the export of cars and car parts to Canadian auto assemblers. This kind of arranged trade cannot properly be called a "NAFTA effect" since these exports are part of the negotiated 1965 Auto Pact (Canada 2007). The Detroit-based auto makers' share of the North American market is seriously under siege by Japanese imports. Even the once invincible Auto Pact is facing an increasingly uncertain future. Canada's top exports to Mexico are concentrated in agricultural products with some light manufacturing and auto related exports (see Figures 3 and 4).

Canada's branch plant subsidiaries are focused exclusively on the Canadian market, and US corporations rely on their Mexican-based subsidiaries to produce and assemble goods for the Mexican market. It is no surprise that the NAFTA linkages between Canada and Mexico are small, largely underdeveloped, and important to only a handful of industries. Many experts have argued that

NAFTA is really a hub-and-spoke free trade agreement, based on two bilateral trade deals with the United States. There is a lot of truth to the idea that the third bilateral agreement never really took off. Mexico's exports to Canada have risen by what can only be described accurately as a snail's pace (see Figures 4 and 5).

What Is a NAFTA Effect? What Is a Production Process Effect?

The single largest obstacle to a highly dynamic Canada-Mexico relationship is that there has been very little unbundling of production chains across North America other than in the automobile and energy sectors. Many experts wrongly believe that greater legal access has been determinant in creating more competitive industries. In fact, changes in the production process provide a more realistic basis for understanding the structural changes that many North American industrial clusters are currently experiencing. For instance, deep discounting by the auto industry's "big three" in Canada and the United States has not turned around the sagging sales figures for General Motors or Ford, and Chrysler has only recently recovered from a long slump. Detroit did not sufficiently reinvest the profits from surging sport utility vehicle sales for most of the past decade into new production processes and cheaper and more efficient cars. Asian and European-based manufacturers used to account for about 10 percent of the market, but now Honda is beating Ford and Chrysler in monthly sales, and General Motor's share has dropped by 40 percent compared

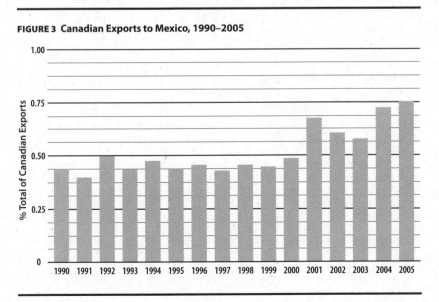

FIGURE 3 Canadian Exports to Mexico, 1990–2005

SOURCE: INDUSTRY CANADA 2006.

to little more than a decade ago. The Detroit-based assemblers' share of the North American market has fallen below the historic 50 percent mark, and many experts are of the view that it is impossible for the big three to return to dominance. The North American auto assembly is headed toward downsizing and the closure of assembly plants on an unprecedented scale. Both countries need a proactive industrial strategy in the auto assembly sector to manage these sweeping structural changes.

Second, Mexico and Canada have not developed a strategy to address the limitations of the hub-and-spoke arrangement that has kept their export growth confined to a narrow range of opportunities. Asymmetric growth between the NAFTA partners has accelerated over the decade, not diminished. More than ever before, Canada and Mexico have become energy and raw material export-ers to the US heartland as well as a vast market for American consumer and capital goods. Mexico is a primary exporter of immigrant labour to the US service and agricultural economy. This is without question the most troubling aspect of North American free trade. It was designed to modernize Mexico's

---

FIGURE 4 Canada's Top Ten Exports to Mexico, 1995–2004

Annual Value of Exports (Millions CDN $)

	1995	1996	1997	1998	1999	2000	2001	2002	2003	2004
Oil seeds, oleaginous fruits, industrial or medicinal plants, straw, and fodder	181	195	218	280	169	229	253	189	250	439
Meat and edible meat offal	5	4	8	12	58	163	272	245	172	400
Motor vehicles, trailers, bicycles, motorcycles, and other similar vehicles	207	235	238	226	356	463	568	410	319	338
Nuclear reactors, boilers, machinery, and mechanical applicances	263	191	147	177	216	201	406	304	300	282
Cereals	112	148	168	195	189	202	257	209	195	191
Electrical or electronic machinery and equipment	26	95	81	132	115	136	109	93	94	124
Aluminum and articles thereof	0.1	0.2	0.3	7	22	70	55	142	101	124
Rail transportation (including tramways and traffic signalling equipment)	04	0.3	0.6	11	25	39	65	119	6	123
Paper, paperboard, and articles made from these materials	8	3	12	11	35	48	69	76	86	88
Iron and steel	25	16	15	22	14	22	29	72	87	80

SOURCE: INDUSTRY CANADA, http://strategis.ic.gc.ca/sc_mrkti/tdst/engdoc/tr_homep.html.

economy and provide abundant work and employment for Mexican citizens. So far though, NAFTA has perpetuated most of Mexico's developmental weaknesses at the same time that Mexico's exports to the United States have soared in traditional areas such as auto parts, textiles, and agricultural products. There is nothing in the cards that suggests that either country will be able to change the division of labour without a focused and dedicated industrial strategy.

Under the NAFTA rules, both Canada and Mexico are seriously disadvantaged in a third way. Both countries have seen their export share of the world market decline as they have become more concentrated in the US mega-market. On the world stage, both countries have faced major structural adjustments from potential rivals in China, India, Brazil, and Eastern Europe. Mexico and Canada are living precipitously on the edge, benefiting from rising energy prices but facing enormous pressure on their labour-intensive processes in manufacturing.

Many experts are of the view that foreign direct investment is on an "investment binge," but it is not clear what kind of effect this will have on Canadian and

FIGURE 5 Canada's Top Ten Imports from Mexico, 1995–2004

Annual Value of Exports (Millions CDN $)

	1995	1996	1997	1998	1999	2000	2001	2002	2003	2004
Electrical or electronic machinery and equipment	1211	1452	1882	2369	2922	3583	3170	3418	3095	4199
Motor vehicles, trailers, bicycles, motorcycles, and other similar vehicles	1977	2022	2157	2009	2396	3508	3644	3685	3382	2993
Nuclear reactors, boilers, machinery, and mechanical applicances	802	1029	1035	1160	1731	2084	2140	2028	1896	2096
Furniture and stuffed furnishings; lamps and illuminated signs; prefabricated buildings	245	245	317	359	457	495	538	742	755	761
Optical, medical, photographic, scientific, and technical instrumentation	65	91	136	186	214	217	251	340	393	555
Mineral fuels, mineral oils, bituminous substances, and mineral waxes	111	193	267	206	267	397	431	275	418	363
Edible vegetables and certain roots and tubers	98	109	113	127	108	122	151	203	240	253
Woven clothing and articles of apparel	19	29	52	71	93	117	182	192	191	221
Miscellaneous articles of base metal	32	36	26	39	81	106	99	132	137	158
Articles of iron or steel	34	55	75	87	107	153	158	161	138	156

SOURCE: INDUSTRY CANADA, http://strategis.ic.gc.ca/sc_mrkti/tdst/engdoc/tr_homep.html.

Mexican industrial and service exports. Since 2000, Mexico has seen its share of global investment decline, losing out to China as the preferred place for multinational corporations' venture capital and new industrial enterprises. China is controlling the big game globally, and Mexico has found itself on the outside of the latest investment boom. On the service side of the economy, Canada and Mexico need to look to their own capital markets for start-ups and new equity financing. So far, there is little incentive for the NAFTA partners to bite the bullet and develop high performance financial services. It is not off the mark to state that Mexico and Canada have been coasting on their access to the American market and have had little incentive to rethink where they want to be at the end of the next decade. Neither country is lean, hungry, or ground-breaking in the area of financial service innovation. Since NAFTA came into effect, Mexico's major banks are now under foreign ownership. Canadian and Mexican public law have made these takeovers, which have been encouraged by public authorities, relatively easy to effect.

The major analytical point is that complex market and non-market forces no longer respond to the simple supply and demand signals of free trade in North America—if they ever did. Sorting out the real life cause-and-effect relationships in highly open economies has proven to be hazardous. The most authoritative study performed by Industry Canada demonstrated that the low Canadian dollar, rather than new market access, was responsible for Canada's export boom to the United States between 1995 and 2000.[2] Over 85 percent in the growth of Canadian exports was due to the unbeatably competitive CDN $ .62 dollar.

It is far more significant that any untapped access to US non-resource markets is unlikely to grow until Canada develops a clutch of homegrown multinational corporations who can power themselves into the US market. Canada would be better able to increase its access to world and North American markets by doubling its investment in research and development (R & D) from less than 1 percent of GDP to 2 percent or better in the next decade. Canadian companies have to turn their attention away from traditional markets and put their effort into responding to changes in the production process, developing new products, investing in the workforce, and improving education and training. Other than promising tax relief to Canadian exporters, the Canadian government has failed to take the lead and provide a strategic vision. Cutting taxes is no guarantee that firms will reinvest their profits in innovative equipment, new processes, and badly needed job skills and training. Despite record profits from the recent export boom, due to the super-competitive Canadian dollar, Canadian manufacturers did not use the high rate of return to become more competitive. The relationship between higher productivity growth and lower taxes is not well understood, and without proper institutional arrangements cutting taxes is always a high-risk activity that often backfires.

Human Capital, R & D, and Innovation

The challenge that globalization represents for Canada is how to acquire the policy tools and institutions that will enable it to adapt to the rapidly changing economic landscape (Rodrick 2001). The key to Canada's future lies in research and innovation, and Canada lags far behind the United States, Japan, and Germany in R & D and in investment in higher learning. The macro-economic benefits of globalization have been equally mixed. To move up the competition value-added ladder in a free trade agreement, Ottawa has to invest more in social capital and skills training. According to the Organisation for Economic Co-operation and Development, Canada spends 30 percent less on post-secondary education than the United States. In fact, spending on human capital and education declined in the 1990s, which is the exact opposite of what one would expect given that skill training is so important for efficiency purposes (Boltvinik 2003) (see Figure 6).

For Mexico, NAFTA was not a stand-alone policy. It was to have an equally impressive social reform dimension, but, over the last decade, spending on social capital and investment in post-secondary education has failed to materialize (United Nations 2005). Mexican governments forgot the other part of the NAFTA package and have not made social reform a priority. So while Mexican intra-firm exports have soared in some key sectors such as automobile and light electronics assembly, the larger picture remains skewed by the negative

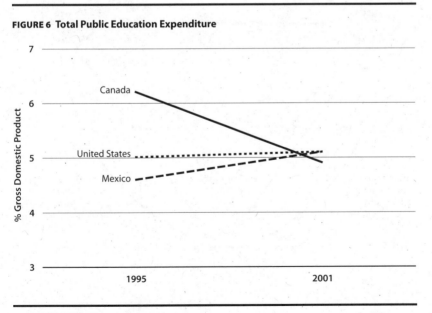

FIGURE 6 Total Public Education Expenditure

SOURCE: OED FACTBOOK 2005.

distributional effects of income and wealth polarization. NAFTA has provided Mexico with full duty-free access to the US market—market access that no other country shares. Mexico should have been a showcase for other developing countries. Yet, in per capita terms, Mexico's economy has grown since 1992 at barely over 1 percent—a fraction of its growth rate during the decades prior to NAFTA (Lustig 2001). In 2004, Mexico's economy grew at a snail's pace, averaging a rate of growth of 3 percent, which is not sufficient to stay ahead of the burgeoning number of people entering the labour market annually. It is small wonder that immigration is one of Mexico's leading exports. Access to US markets has not made up for the domestic factors that hold back Mexico's economic growth or for the lack of a strongly articulated development strategy. The asymmetrical commercial effects are pronounced (see Figure 7).

Reliance on NAFTA has not been a silver bullet for Mexico. Like many others in the global South, those individuals working in the most vulnerable and exposed industries such as textiles, agriculture, and primary resource extraction

FIGURE 7 The Asymmetrical NAFTA Triangular Trade

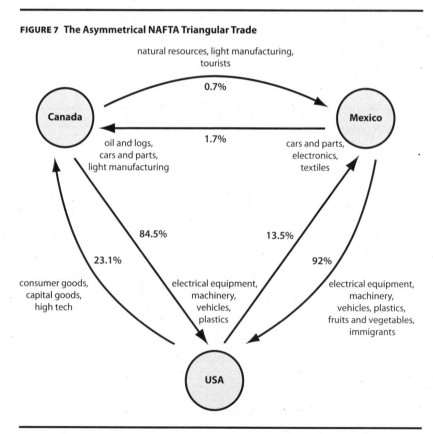

SOURCES: INDUSTRY CANADA, US TREASURY DEPARTMENT, WTO.
NOTE: Percentages indicate the percentage share of the exporting country's total exports for 2004.

and processing have seen their wages decline. In Mexico's *maquiladoras* sectors, the drive for international competitiveness has been the incentive for many industries to shed labour rather than to create employment. Since 2000, it is estimated that over 300,000 jobs have been lost. Employment growth remains negative, and many labour-intensive jobs have shifted to China and Guatemala. Manufacturing employment has grown persistently but not enough to absorb the massive influx of displaced agricultural workers into the cities. The predictions that NAFTA could double as a trade and development strategy were wrong and have left a legacy of policy failure.

The trickle-down theory, which suggests that free trade would lift the poorest out of poverty and become the great economic equalizer for the middle class, has not delivered on its basic promise. Mexico's structural problems preceded NAFTA, but the implementation of the export-led model of development is associated with the worsening of income distribution in Mexico as Boltvinik (2003), among others, has demonstrated. Regions in the north and centre of the country are better off than those in the south, which are disconnected from NAFTA-related production chains. Polarization between Mexico's regions is much worse today than a decade ago. Since 1994, Mexico has lost 1.3 million jobs in the agricultural sector and millions of new jobs in other sectors.

For Canada, NAFTA has also failed to generate hundreds of thousands of jobs in the export side of the economy. Instead, the auto, resource, and manufacturing sectors have taken incentives to downsize their workforce and produce more with fewer people. The drive to be competitive has had major negative consequences on blue collar employment. In a recent article in the *Canadian Economic Observer,* Cross documents how deep the decline in Canadian manufacturing employment has been over the NAFTA bookended decade. Manufacturing jobs peaked in 1980 at 19 percent and bottomed out in 1993 at 14 percent. Since then, manufacturing jobs have come back as the economy rebounded but are once again at an all-time low. Even the auto and the information and communication technology sectors have seen their growth stalled (Cross 2005).

It is disturbing that many of the high tech jobs in computer design that were created in the 1990s collapsed in the following decade. The boom-bust cycle in high-level jobs is a mirror image of manufacturing and resources. More generally, volatility in the labour market, which is dependent on the demand for goods and services in the United States, leads to instability for new entrants and older workers in particular. Export industries are the losers in the employment stakes (see Figure 8). The winners include those industries involved with the public sector, hospitals, education, real estate, and retail, all of which experienced better than average growth between 2000 and 2004 (Jackson 2005). The shedding of Canadian manufacturing jobs continues its downward trend, and, while not as dramatic as in the United States, the strongest source of job creation is on the domestic side of the economy.

FIGURE 8 Canadian Share of Jobs in Manufacturing

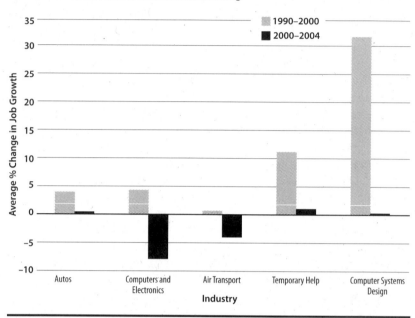

SOURCE: CROSS 2005.

Arthur Donner (2005) has examined job creation in the two countries and found that the majority of new jobs in Canada are in the construction, services, and public sectors. Employment in the United States is strong in the part-time sector and in the service industry but not in the public sector. The message here is unambiguous: exports cannot be relied on as a net creator of jobs. Aside from the commodity boom in mining, white-collar domestic job growth is almost twice that of blue-collar occupations. As Canada becomes more of an information economy, job creation is tied more directly to domestic conditions. A strong export performance requires a large and focused role for the public authority, a lot of fortuity from rising commodity prices, and a competitive currency. Even in situations when the effects if NAFTA are advantageous to Canadian industry, these results are largely washed out by other macro factors. Mexico is in the same situation. Export growth is strong, but GDP growth is disapprovingly weak. It peaked in 1997 at 6.8 percent annually, but, since 2000, Mexico's domestic growth has hovered around the 2 percent mark, when the economy needs to be growing at between 6 and 8 percent annually. Mexico faces the seemingly impossible challenge of obtaining a rate of growth equal to that of Argentina and Chile, which are both now in double-digit figures.

NAFTA Effects: Some Qualitative Measures—Growing Divergence, Institutional Constraints, and Neo-Liberal Competitiveness

NAFTA regulatory divergence is now a fact of life in North America. The markets have not been able to impose a single template on the way Mexican, Canadian, and American authorities govern the market. There is no agreement on its benefits let alone on its costs. Although Canadian and Mexican exports have surged year after year, market share and changes in the composition of trade for both countries are much more revealing of the actual benefits. On this fundamental point, NAFTA has not dramatically transformed Canada or Mexico's comparative advantage in high value-added sectors. Their traditional strengths in resources, agriculture, and, for Mexico, labour-intensive industries are not much different than they were a decade ago. A second discovery is that there is no scientific way to forecast NAFTA effects and outcomes (see Figure 9). From a political and legal perspective, the final text of NAFTA did not contain a definition of a subsidy or an arms-length procedure to resolve this issue. With such a gaping legal omission, it is not clear how NAFTA's legitimacy can be restored.

NAFTA's principle weakness from a public policy perspective is that it lacks concrete provisions regarding human rights or environmental protection. NAFTA's emphasis—to borrow Michael Trebilcock's (2003) critical distinction— has been on negative integration. Negative integration sets out the rules of what countries cannot do and is largely responsible for the "less state, less tax" policy harmonization process that has led to spending cuts everywhere. By contrast, positive integration would spell out the supranational regulatory rules and domestic policy standards that the United States, Mexico, and Canada must adopt. Without positive integration, there is no trinational framework that protects social standards and strengthens social inclusion. Each country will continue to decide for itself. In the absence of an institutional escalator, there is no built-in momentum that will propel all three countries to spend more on social North America, invest in human capital, and provide incentives to increase health and labour standards.

As far as public policy is concerned, economic divergence has undermined many of NAFTA's principal assumptions. North American integration is market driven, but the role of national authority cannot be minimized. What Canada and Mexico have learned painfully is that North American governance is a very imprecise term. Transnational authority is not the result of common policies and a grand political bargain that has limited the authority of the US Congress. Nor has there ever been a single North American economy but, rather, many competing regional ones. Most are nationally centred, and the massive growth in the transborder traffic of people, goods, and services has strengthened the

FIGURE 9 How Good Were the Experts' Predictions about NAFTA's Effects and Benefits?

Challenge	Prediction	Outcome
Challenges to government regulation	Significant policy harmonization with respect to taxes, social policy, and macro-economic coordination. A new Canada–US relationship envisaged with a level playing field.	Dramatic reduction in federal spending driven by zero inflation and zero deficit targeting. Federal spending as a percentage of GDP drops to 1950s levels. By 2005, Canadian social spending is more than 4 percent of GDP compared to the United States in per capita terms.
Future of Auto Pact	Neutral.	Global overcapacity more important. Canada maintains share of new investment and production. Canadian Auto Workers proves an astute bargainer at the table. Global overcapacity forces job and wage concessions in 2005.
Investor protection	Significant increase in investor rights.	Many new conflicts created by NAFTA provisions in a range of sectors with respect to national treatment. Most of the conflicts are in agriculture and cultural sectors.
Capital mobility	Increases.	Underestimated capital volatility and reverse flows. Canada's share of new investment flows is no greater than in previous years. Foreign direct investment is not driven by NAFTA text but by US shareholder capital and multinational corporation strategies. NAFTA effect dwarfed by US dot.com craze.
Mexico's economic inequality	Expected to decrease as free trade accelerates the modernization of the economy.	Dramatic fall in incomes and rise in unemployment. Mexican small business does not modernize, while worker productivity is up 36 percent since NAFTA was signed. Wages fall 29 percent between 1993 and 1997, and welfare gains are meagre for the mass of Mexican wage earners.
Cost of regulation	Sharp decrease.	Little evidence of major reduction in regulatory costs. Canadian business complains about increase in user fees.
Wages	Significant income gains for well-positioned workers in export industries.	In Canada, wage polarization is deeper than anticipated. Evidence is mixed. In the United States, the growth of wage inequality is explained by the growth of the union-free workplace. Exchange rates for Canada and Mexico are the key variable.

Labour restrictive practices	Diffusion of US norms and more competitive labour markets post-NAFTA.	Collapse of US labour movement has fewer knock-on effects and predates NAFTA. Canadian labour has not gone down US road of a union-free workplace. Roughly 35 percent of Canadian workers are covered by collective bargaining, compared to 15 percent in the United States.
Unemployment	With a stronger performance and stronger economy, unemployment levels expected to fall.	Underestimated the magnitude of the job loss for many sectors, but much job loss is not NAFTA driven. Eighty percent of the private sector jobs regained by 2000 when Canada outperforms US economy in the job Olympics.
Union bargaining power	Increased competitiveness will lead to a decrease in collective bargaining for Canadian unions.	Some significant decrease in collective bargaining arrangements in Canada, but high levels of unemployment reduce the effectiveness of Canadian labour.
Government decision making	Constrained.	Impossible to attribute to NAFTA. Too many other competing agendas. Divergence across a broad range of policy areas is pronounced.
Exports	Sharp increase.	The record is mixed. Trade asymmetries increase. Canada and Mexico's comparative advantages are not transformed, but traditional competences become the drivers of their export-oriented economies.

SOURCE: DRACHE 2007.

regional dimension of North America economically. Governance—meaning the policies and institutions that would co-ordinate and manage the trilateral relationship—is largely carried out by interdepartmental contacts in the three governments and at the highest level of government. Governance is not carried out through NAFTA, which has neither the institutional capacity nor the political clout to give the North American idea effective policy legs. At the centre, this elaborate system of interstate contacts encompasses the US Department of Homeland Security and its Canadian and Mexican counterparts in military, intelligence, transportation, immigration, and justice. The second pillar of North American integration is the management of the northern and southern border. Borders are fixed by law and geography but are changed by governments through circumstance and need.

Every border has four dimensions. it is a security moat, a regulatory wall, a commercial gate, and a line in the sand for citizenship purposes (Drache 2004). While NAFTA is the big player economically, it controls only 10 percent of the policy agenda and, since 9/11, has lost its place in the pecking order. In any event, discerning Canadians want to increase their sovereignty not compromise it any further. Parallel policies, rather than common ones, have always been at

centre stage in North America in the exercise of power and international co-
operation. This basic policy truth is more relevant than ever in an age of security
and integration.

Conclusion: Acquiring Willpower

Thus, when Canadian and Mexican macro-strategies and US policies go their
separate ways, will Mexico and Canada acquire the willpower and conceptual
tools to become effective conflict managers of North American integration?
Henry Kissinger (1973) was prescient when he wrote that "foreign policy is domestic policy," and if this is true for the United States it doubly applies to Canada
and Mexico—countries in which social diversity and multiculturalism define
the national identity. Both of them need to nurture and protect their strategic
interests (Welsh 2004).

If Ottawa expects to be a more effective actor globally, it needs to connect
with the Canadian public in ways that it has not chosen to do. Today, what
Joseph Nye (2004) has called "the soft power of public opinion" is more critical than ever to Canadian and Mexican foreign policy goals and practices. If
these NAFTA "twins" expect to chart their own course in the age of the smart
citizen and critical, informed counter-publics, public opinion has to be kept on
side, consulted, and mobilized.[3] Ottawa and Mexico cannot change the path
of the Bush revolution in foreign policy, but they will need to build leverage
and acquire voice on missile defence, peacekeeping, human rights, agricultural
subsidies at the World Trade Organization, and global governance in the post-
Bush era (Ibbitson 2005).

Increasingly, foreign policy will have to reflect the social values of Canadian
and Mexican society rather than, as in the past, the special interests of business
elites. In a prescient article in the *Globe and Mail,* Gordon Pitts (2005) argued
that the Canadian Council of Chief Executives has declined in influence in
Ottawa partly due to its support for outdated and economically deterministic
policies.[4] At present, Ottawa and Mexico City are caught somewhere between
denial and taking responsibility for setting new priorities for their relationship
and the future of North America. They are still reacting to every change coming
out of Washington. Managing conflict will require a lot of focus and smarts from
civil society. The new Harper government must accept that Canadian foreign
policy and continental free trade have to constantly change, adapt, and innovate
in this very charged global policy environment. Mexico's newly elected president
will have to grapple with the fallout from the NAFTA decade as a top priority.

Immigration and development require rethinking from the ground up.
NAFTA's distributional effects have skewed its macro-benefits in favour of the
United States. Negative distributional effects have seriously compromised the
competitive advantage that a handful of Mexican and Canadian industries have

derived from an era of North American free trade. With respect to the critical issues of enhanced citizenship rights, poverty eradication, and a return of public authority after the triumph of market fundamentalism, there is no room for ambiguity. Deepening the North American partnership remains a far-off reality short of strategic, economic, or intellectual substance.

NOTES

Thanks to Greg Smith for preparing the tables and for general assistance.

1   North American Free Trade Agreement between the Government of Canada, the Government of Mexico and the Government of the United States, 17 December 1992, Can. T.S. 1994 No. 2, 32 I.L.M. 289.
2   As a driver of Canadian exports, the competitive dollar rescued Canadian industry from the economic doldrums (Poloz 2004).
3   See Daniel Drache, *Defiant Publics: The Unprecedented Reach of the Global Citizen* (London: Polity Press, 2008).
4   Gordon Pitts (2005, B10) writes: "[D]espite this ability to command press coverage, there are questions about whether Ottawa pays much attention these days ... [The] glory days are over ... As a policy advocate ... Mr. d'Aquino has fallen into predictable habits, sounding the same drumbeat on every issue and rarely reaching out beyond his top-executive constituency."

REFERENCES

Alden, Edward, and Holly Yeager. 2005. "CAFTA Victory Revives Bush's Ambitions for US Trade Deals." *Financial Times,* 29 July, 9.

Boltvinik, Julio. 2003. "Welfare, Inequality, and Poverty in Mexico, 1970–2000." In Kevin J. Middlebrooke and Eduardo Zepada, eds., *Confronting Development: Assessing Mexico's Economic and Social Policy.* Stanford: Stanford University Press.

Canadian Government. 2007. "Key Economic Events: 1965—Canada–United States Auto Pact." http://canadianeconomy.gc.ca/english/economy/1965canada_US_auto_pact.html.

Canadian Manufacturers and Exporters. 2005. *CME 2005–2006 Management Issues Survey: Winning Strategies for the Future,* http://www.cme-mec.ca/national/media.asp?id=588.

Council on Foreign Relations. 2005. *Building a North American Community.* Independent Task Force Report No. 53. New York: Council on Foreign Relations.

Cross, P. 2005. "Recent Changes in the Labour Market." *Canadian Economic Observer* 18(3): 1–10.

Donner, Arthur. 2005. *Economic Review,* August.

Drache, Daniel. 2004. *Borders Matter: Homeland Security and the Search for North America*. Halifax: Fernwood.

Ibbitson, John. 2005. "Trading with the 'Schoolyard Bully.'" *Globe and Mail*, 20 August, A8

Jackson, Andrew. 2005. "Commentary." *The Economy*, March 2005.

Kissinger, Henry. 1973. *A World Restored*. Gloucester, MA: P. Smith.

Krugman, Paul. 1995. "Cycles of Conventional Wisdom on Economic Development." *International Affairs* 71(4): 717–32.

Lustig, Nora, ed. 2001. *Shielding the Poor: Social Protection in the Developing World*. Washington, DC: Brookings Institution Press.

Middlebrooke, Kevin J., and Eduardo Zepada, eds. 2003. *Confronting Development: Assessing Mexico's Economic and Social Policy*. Stanford: Stanford University Press.

Naim, Moises. 2000. "Washington Consensus or Washington Confusion?" *Foreign Policy* (Spring): 74–85.

Nye, S. Joseph. 2004. *Power in the Global Information Age from Realism to Globalization*. New York: Routledge.

Office of the United States Trade Representative. 2007. "Central America–United States Free Trade Agreement (CAFTA)." http://www.ustr.gov/Trade_Agreements/Regional/Section_Index.html.

Peters, Jeremy. 2005. "Shock and Resignation on GM Shop Floors Set to Close." *New York Times*, 22 November.

Pitts, Gordon. 2005. "Tom's Club: Only Chief Executives Need Apply." *Globe and Mail*, 4 July, B10.

Poloz, Stephen S. 2004. "Who Is Most Vulnerable to the Rising Dollar?" *Weekly Commentary*, Export Development Canada, 1 December. http://www.edc.ca/english/docs/ereports/commentary/publications_6710.htm.

Ritchie, Gordon. 2005. "Who's Afraid of NAFTA's Bite?" *Globe and Mail*, 15 February, A21.

Rodrik, Dani. 2001. "Four Simple Principles for Democratic Governance of Globalization." Paper prepared for the Friedrich Ebert Foundation. http://kgshome.harvard.edu/~drodrik/shortpieces.html.

Trebilcock, Michael. 2003. "Trade Liberalization, Regulatory Diversity and Political Sovereignty." Faculty of Law, University of Toronto, November.

United Nations. 2005. *United Nations Millennium Report*. New York: United Nations, http://un.org/docs/summit2005/MDGBook.pdf.

Welsh, Jennifer. 2004. *At Home in the World: Canada's Global Vision for the Twenty-first Century*. Toronto: HarperCollins.

2

Towards a North American Economic and Security Space

Gustavo Vega-Cànovas

Introduction

Mexico has reached a critical juncture in its economic and security relations with the United States. As a result of the North American Free Trade Agreement (NAFTA), the two countries saw their trade and investment relations undergo exponential growth.[1] In 2000, trade flows reached US $263 billion, making Mexico the second most important US trading partner and ranking it among the most important recipients of US foreign direct investment. NAFTA also made important contributions to Mexico's financial recovery and economic growth after the infamous financial crisis of the second half of the 1990s.

In light of this commercial and investment success, it is not surprising that within the two countries, and especially within Mexico, many people were calling by early 2001 for new measures to reduce border congestion and transaction costs. Along with President Vicente Fox, some observers advocated permanent open borders and the creation of a North American community (Pastor 2001). This attitude, however, changed with the attacks of 11 September 2001. US authorities imposed security measures along both of its north and south borders. Since the early post-attack weeks, the US Customs Service has beefed up staffing along the southern border, tripling the number of agents. The amount of cross-border retail shopping and tourism has plunged. Discussions about a migration agreement were placed on the back burner. These new policies, together with increased competition from China and other countries that have signed free trade agreements with the United States, have provoked a gradual deterioration of Mexican imports in the US market.

As a result, the NAFTA countries have negotiated new agreements on "smart borders," the aim of which is to secure the borders while keeping them open to legitimate commerce. The Security and Prosperity Partnership of North America seeks to address policies that stand in the way of more beneficial trade and investment flows, such as cumbersome rules of origin, complex anti-dumping procedures, burdensome regulatory requirements, and other restrictive measures.[2]

This chapter evaluates the role of NAFTA since its inception in 1994 in the achievement of economic development in Mexico. It is argued that trade liberalization in general, and NAFTA in particular, has helped Mexico to become a successful exporter of manufacturing products and an attractive location for foreign direct investment, which, in turn, made important contributions to Mexico's financial recovery and economic growth in the 1980s and 1990s and helped to maintain economic stability in the first six years of the twenty-first century. The chapter will explore not only Mexico's economic performance since trade liberalization and NAFTA went into effect but will also consider the domestic and global environment that Mexico confronted in the mid-1980s and final half of the 1990s. NAFTA's limitations will also be discussed. Despite its commercial and investment success, NAFTA has not meant that everyone in North America has prospered.

Mexicans, in particular, were devastated by the peso crisis of 1994–95, and many Mexicans have seen no increase in their real wages in over a decade. To make matter worse, political elites in Mexico have been unable to agree on important reforms that are desperately needed in order to address the structural problems in the Mexican economy. Canadians have, on average, done much better, but Canadian prosperity in the 1990s lagged behind the "new economy" boom that swept the United States. This situation did change, however, once the dot.com bubble burst and especially following 9/11 and the advent of the Iraq war. Trade agreements, however, cannot be held responsible for all of the financial and structural shortcomings that slow down (or even reverse) economic progress. Within a narrow commercial sphere, NAFTA has succeeded beyond the expectations of its advocates.

The chapter also addresses the policy opportunities and dilemmas faced by Mexico in its relations with the United States as a result of the 11 September attacks. The events of 9/11 have forced Mexico to look for a closer economic and security relationship with the United States in order to ensure that closure of the Mexico-US border does not occur again, as it did after 9/11. This closer relationship, which so far covers only border matters, should be expanded to include a new commercial policy to eliminate the external trade barriers that are still present in the region as well as a program for Mexican migrant workers and the legalization of immigrant workers already living in the United States. Both of these steps are necessary in the overall economic integration of North America. Some recommendations are made regarding the type of immigration agreement that could satisfy security concerns and facilitate further economic integration in North America.

The first section recaps the story of NAFTA's success and reviews the achievements that Mexico has made in its original goal of economic integration. The second section highlights the limitations of NAFTA for the purpose of achieving prosperity in Mexico. Despite the significant contributions that NAFTA has made to the financial recovery of Mexico and in the achievement of economic stability and growth, it has not been enough nor could it be enough. While trade policy can be a powerful instrument to promote development, it cannot be the only one nor can it be a substitute for complementary domestic policies that address structural problems. The final section suggests ways to further develop economic and security integration in North America.

NAFTA: Commercial and Investment Success

The central purpose of NAFTA was to liberalize trade and investment between the three North American partners (Mayer 1998; Weintraub 1997). This goal has been achieved with results surpassing the predictions of major studies undertaken before the negotiations were completed.

Trade within NAFTA

Since NAFTA went into effect, trade flows between the partners have experienced substantial growth. Between 1993 and 2004, total trade among the NAFTA partners increased at an average annual growth rate of 6.4 percent from US $289 billion to US $698 billion. In the case of Mexico and the United States, two-way trade boomed at an average annual growth rate of 17 percent, tripling between 1993 and 2004, rising from US $85 billion to US $280 billion. Two-way trade grew from 34 percent of Mexico's gross domestic product (GDP) (measured at market exchange rates) to 63 percent. Mexican products increased their share in the US import market from less than 7 percent in 1993 to 16.6 percent in 2004. Since the implementation of NAFTA in 1994, Mexican exports and imports have increased 291 percent and 148 percent respectively, with a balance favourable to Mexico.

Other factors, besides NAFTA, explain part of this bilateral trade growth—notably the strong US economy in the 1990s, unilateral and multilateral trade liberalization, and the Mexican devaluation of the peso in 1994–5 (Krueger 1999; Flores and de la Peña Rodríguez 2005). Empirical studies, however, persuasively show that NAFTA was responsible for the *exceptionally* rapid expansion of Mexico-US trade. In an early study, Mexican economists Enrique Espinosa and Pedro Noyola (1997) demonstrated that the patterns of sector-by-sector trade growth could only be explained by the shape of NAFTA liberalization. More recent studies of NAFTA have reached similar conclusions. Ben Goodrich (2002), for example, uses panel techniques to assess the causal effect of NAFTA on North American trade. He reachs the conclusion that, in all six directions, North American merchandise trade substantially increased and often doubled compared to what trade would have been in the absence of NAFTA. Goodrich also shows that trade created by NAFTA far exceeds trade that is diverted.

An important implication of the dynamism of bilateral trade is that there has been a shift in the value-added composition of Mexican trade. In 1985, raw materials and mining products comprised 62.4 percent of total exports, of which the most important was crude oil. Starting in 1986, this proportion started to decrease until finally in 1993 it reached a level of 19.6 percent, of which oil represented 14.2 percent. At the same time, manufacturing exports grew every year from 1986 to 2004, each year surpassing the growth of the gross national product of manufacturing domestic output. This growth has meant that manufacturing exports have become the engine of growth for domestic output. The evolution of manufacturing exports has also shown a trend toward the production of more complex goods in terms of design, production, and commercialization. As two observers have remarked, Mexico has become a "reliable exporter of sophisticated products, from auto brake systems to laptop computers ... increasingly Mexican engineers are designing products and testing them in multimillion dollar research and development centers" (Smith and Malkin 1998).

Additionally, the impact of export activity on regional development has been particularly significant because it has become geographically dispersed. In the past, Mexico's export operations were concentrated in major cities such as Mexico City, Guadalajara, and Monterrey as well as in the northern border area. Today, almost all of the thirty-one Mexican states, including rural states such as Aguascalientes, Campeche, Durango, and Yucatan participate in international trade.

At the level of local government participation, state authorities have become aware of the potential benefits that exports can bring to their states and have acted to encourage exports and attract investment. For example, the state of Guanajuato, a major producer of apparel and footwear, has opened trade offices in cities such as Chicago, Dallas, Los Angeles, and New York as well as in London and Tokyo. In 1995, Guanajuato had 362 exporting firms. By the end of 1998, this number had reached 768. More than fifteen Mexican states have representation trade offices abroad, mostly in the United States. For example, the states of Campeche, Tabasco, and Yucatan have each opened trade offices in the state of Florida, and Jalisco has established close trade links with the states of Idaho, Oregon, and Washington. Trade has opened to sub-national authorities, providing new opportunities for bringing more national and foreign resources into these specific regions and encouraging the promotion of each state's development agenda.

Mexico-Canada trade has also increased under NAFTA, despite the geographic distance and limited historic ties. In 2004, eleven years after the implementation of NAFTA, Canada and Mexico's two-way trade reached US $8 billion, up from US $4 billion in 1993. Canada has become Mexico's fifth trading partner and its second most important market for exports. While bilateral trade numbers are small when compared to bilateral trade with the United States, the Canada-Mexico trade link has the potential for enormous expansion.

Foreign Direct Investment (FDI)

NAFTA is also an investment agreement, aimed at facilitating both foreign direct investment and portfolio investment. In this area as well, NAFTA has had a very dramatic impact, especially in attracting substantial amounts of FDI from Canada and the United States to Mexico, as compared to previous periods. From 1989 to 1994, the amount of FDI was on average US $4.6 billion per year, while from 1996 to 2000, it almost tripled to US $11.8 billion. FDI reached a peak of US $27.7 billion in 2001 and came down to an average of US $14.6 billion between 2002 and 2004. This growth in intra-regional FDI occurred in tandem with a tremendous expansion of intra-regional trade. The obvious and well-known conclusion is that NAFTA accelerated the rationalization of North American production facilities.

The connection between trade liberalization and investment growth is illustrated by three sectors in which commercial ties have been most extensive: the automotive industry, textiles and clothing, and the electronics industry. In these three sectors, deeper integration is clearly evident between the three economies. Canadian, Mexican, and US firms have relocated their production facilities and repositioned their supply patterns throughout the region, and they have used mergers and acquisitions across North America to strengthen their competitive stance. The reward has been higher productivity generally and a new role for Mexico particularly. Within Mexico, NAFTA has encouraged the development of more sophisticated automotive, textile and clothing, and electronic

TABLE 1 Mexican Sector Success under NAFTA

Sectors	Average annual growth of Mexican exports (%)	Percentage of US import market 1993–2003 (%)	New jobs
Electronic products	19.0	10.1–18.1	110,000
Automotive products (including auto parts)	14.8	7.1–14.0	200,000
Textile and clothing	19.1	4.4–10,6	260,000
Food, drinks, and tobacco	16.7	4.3–8.1	100,000

SOURCE: FLORES AND DE LA PEÑA RODRÍGUEZ 2005.

products—going beyond mere assembly—with significant research and development work now being conducted in Mexico. These sectors have also generated important well-paying jobs. Table 1 shows the strong rate of increase in Mexican exports in these sectors, their deep penetration of the US import market (which doubled in ten years), and the high proportion of jobs generated.

Commercial and Investment Success

While NAFTA has been a commercial and investment success, it did not, and could not, bring universal prosperity to Mexico. Mexico experienced in 1994–95 one of its worst economic crises since the Great Depression. This crisis cannot be blamed on NAFTA but, rather, on a combination of adverse political factors, unsound financial practices, and mismanaged monetary policy (Naim and Edwards 1997). For the purposes of this chapter, however, the important observation is that recovery from the peso crash of 1994–95 was remarkably fast compared to the recovery from the debt default and devaluation episode that began in 1982. In large part, the difference can be attributed to the existence of NAFTA.

In 1982, Mexico's immediate response to the debt crisis was to drastically slash imports, building a protective fortress through stringent import quotas and prohibitive tariffs. Mexican imports fell by more than 50 percent, from US $24 billion in 1981 to only US $9 billion in 1983. It took Mexico seven years to get back to pre-crisis import levels. After the 1994–95 peso crisis, by contrast, Mexico's membership in NAFTA did two things: it fostered a quick and ample financial rescue package, led by President Bill Clinton, and it guaranteed the continuity of Mexico's trade policy, led by President Ernesto Zedillo. Mexico actually accelerated its liberalization program, and pre-crisis import levels were restored in around eighteen months (World Trade Organization 1997).

Another revealing indicator is industrial production. After the 1982 debt crisis, it took Mexico about nine years to get back to its pre-crisis level of industrial output. In contrast, after the 1994–95 crash, it took Mexico less than two years to recover 1994 output levels (Heath 1998). Mexican employment declined by more than 4 percent in 1995, but between August 1995 and August 2001, the Mexican economy generated two million new jobs. Around a million of these jobs were related directly or indirectly to export activity. In 2001, the combination of the US recession and a strong peso exchange rate led some multinational firms in manufacturing to close down operations for the first time in many years, blaming high labour costs. This trend continued in 2002 and 2003 but stopped in 2004 since the economy had begun recovering and generating new jobs.

In terms of wages, however, while export growth has exerted a positive impact, the majority of Mexican workers have not seen an increase in real wages in over a decade. Fortunately, better times could be ahead on the Mexican wage front. Employment as a percentage of the labour force rose from 84 percent in 1993 to 95 percent in 2004. Meanwhile, the percentage of the workforce engaged in agriculture dropped from 28 percent to 17 percent (Organisation for Economic Co-operation and Development 2001). Tighter labour markets in urban areas could point to higher real wages in the next decade.

To conclude this overview, NAFTA has boosted North American trade and investment to a remarkable extent. Trade liberalization has played a major role in Mexico's rapid recovery after the financial crisis of 1995. When the peso crashed, the Mexican economy went through a recession that was deeper than that caused by the 1982 debt crisis. However, in the aftermath of the 1995 financial collapse, recovery was far more rapid than expected. Trade was central to this performance. Given the collapse of the domestic market, the external market became the main engine for economic dynamism. The GDP contracted 6.2 percent in 1995. However, if exports had remained stagnant, the free fall of the economy could have reached 11 percent, according to the Mexican Central Bank. Between 1994 and 1995, exports grew by 30 percent, most going to the United States and allowed Mexico to get back on track toward recovery.

Export activity currently accounts for half of Mexico's GDP growth and almost one-third of its overall GDP. In 2004, Mexico's GDP surpassed US $675 billion, while Mexico's total exports reached US $160 billion. Mexico has become the eighth largest trading nation in the world and the largest in Latin America. The bulk of these exports are manufactured products, which represent more than 85 percent of Mexico's total exports. Yet, Mexico faced economic difficulties in the 1990s and is experiencing slow growth at the present time as a result of the US recession of 2000–02 and, especially, as a result of a lack of significant structural reforms, for which consensus has not been forthcoming from the major political parties.

A North American Economic and Security Space

Mexico faces important challenges that must be addressed in the near future if it is to recover a sustained and robust economic growth. Mexico must grow at a level of 6–7 percent in order to prevent further unemployment. This rapid growth will have to be financed by increased exports and a higher rate of domestic savings. Given the role that North American markets, in particular, the United States, play in the Mexican economy and, especially, in Mexican industry, Mexican exports will have to maintain, increase, and solidify their presence in the Canadian and US markets.

Clearly, this goal represents a significant challenge, especially now that Mexican exports are being displaced from important sectors of the US and Canadian market by more competitive Chinese products and, more importantly, now that assured access to the US market is not certain given the security concerns that have become prevalent in the United States after the events of 11 September 2001. In effect, the attacks of 9/11 have added a new dimension to the NAFTA project. If economic borders have largely been dismantled under the banner of free trade, security borders have suddenly become more sensitive. After 9/11, the United States adopted a series of measures along its north and south borders, including the adoption of high-level alert, sustained, and intense inspections, which provoked a disruption of commercial traffic that lasted for several weeks with a concomitant crisis for just-in-time manufacturers, particularly auto companies, and an enormous decline in cross-border retail shopping and tourism. This level of security was reintroduced just before the United States started the invasion of Iraq, provoking a similar disruption of cross-border trade flows.

In order to prevent future disruptions to cross-border trade, the three countries have negotiated new agreements on "smart borders," which aim to secure the infrastructure and the flow of people and goods along North American borders (US Department of State 2002a). More recently, the three countries negotiated an agreement called the Security and Prosperity Partnership, which is aimed at getting rid of a set of policies and measures that stand in the way of more beneficial trade and investment flows, such as cumbersome rules of origin, complex anti-dumping procedures, burdensome regulatory requirements, and other restrictive measures.

All of these are sensible introductory measures to secure an open border for legitimate goods and services and to further the facilitation of trade. However, in order for the three countries to really achieve the deepening of North American integration and prevent a worst-case scenario on the security front, they will have to adopt an ambitious project that would serve to reorder the North American economic and security space. Such a project would address not only border and supply line inspections and trade facilitation but would also advance more ambitious cooperative polices on border management as well as focus on three other fronts, namely the elimination of external trade barriers, defence, and migration. The following sections suggest some ideas on what kind of new policies would be needed in the areas of border management, external trade barriers, and migration in order to achieve deeper integration in North America.

Border Management

The whole point of NAFTA is to eliminate economic barriers—tariffs and quotas—at the two borders. Apart from agricultural trade between Canada and its partners, and a handful of sensitive products traded between the United States and Mexico, economic barriers have largely disappeared. Until 11 September 2001, the purpose of border inspections was to ferret out contraband (especially drugs) and provide security against dangerous merchandise. The attacks of 9/11 have added a new concern, namely what we can call a "worst-case scenario," such as an attack by a trained terrorist entering the United States from Tijuana or Vancouver armed with biological or nuclear weapons or grain contaminated with natural or man-made biohazards shipped from the United States to Canada or Mexico.[3]

As noted earlier, in order to prevent this scenario, the three countries have negotiated the "smart border accords," and these agreements have made some progress to date. For instance, they have created the FAST programs in order to permit the rapid and secure passage of legitimate commerce through North American borders. However, so far only a minimum number of North American firms have registered in this program.

What is needed to prevent a worst-case scenario and really improve border management is to move security inspections away from the border to the plants where the shipments originate and to ensure continuous surveillance from the point of origin to the destination. The NAFTA partners have already taken the first step in addressing agricultural sanitary standards by relocating inspection and certification activities away from the border to the farms and plants where agricultural produce is grown or processed. US meat inspectors routinely visit Canadian packing plants, and US agricultural inspectors are posted at Mexican avocado orchards. The payoff is a faster trip across the border, plus better compliance with the standards. After all, it is more difficult to inspect a packed and re-frigerated container truck than it is to inspect an open field or processing plant.

What has already been accomplished in agriculture should be implemented in other segments of the merchandise trade. Such efforts will require a host of low-tech and high-tech innovations, including audited security built into production lines, akin to ISO 9000; sealed and tamper-proof containers; and the continuous tracking of containers (using a global positioning system) from origin to border to destination. The United States and Canada have made a start with a pilot program to inspect shipping containers destined for the United States at the Canadian port of entry. Those containers that arrive from Europe would be inspected in Halifax and those coming from Asia in Vancouver. It is only a start, since the pilot program does not address the far larger volume of traffic originating in US, Canadian, or Mexican plants. Yet the technology exists for inspection and surveillance from the point of origin to the point of destination. While it may be costly to implement, especially for small firms, the bigger obstacle is gaining political assent from each North American partner for the intrusive practices that entail the presence of foreign customs officials. Until this assent is forthcoming and new systems are put into place, NAFTA's future will be clouded by periodic episodes of border strangulation, as happened after 11 September.

External Trade Barriers

With respect to external trade barriers, normally when conversation turns to deeper economic integration—going beyond a free trade system—the approach that springs to mind is a customs union with a common external tariff (CET). This approach was pioneered by the 1957 Treaty of Rome for the European Economic Community and copied for numerous economic unions since that time.[4] While a CET has many attractions, and despite the fact that there has been increased talk of transforming NAFTA into a customs union, at the present time there is no agreement among the NAFTA partners on a formula for choosing tariff rates for a CET. Equally difficult would be the problem of coordinating NAFTA tariff offers in the context of the World Trade Organization (WTO), the Free Trade Area of the Americas (FTAA), or other bilateral trade negotiations. None of the NAFTA members would want to concede its own freedom to manoeuvre to the prior approval of its partners. Even less acceptable would be the delegation of negotiating authority to a supranational body, modelled after the first DG-1 (Directorate-General) in the European Commission.

It should be possible, nonetheless, to achieve many of the practical benefits of a common external tariff. The NAFTA partners could set a long-term goal of reducing their respective most-favoured nation (MFN) tariffs to the lowest MFN level applied by Mexico, Canada, or the United States, while each NAFTA partner would retain complete freedom to negotiate its rates in the WTO, the FTAA, and bilaterally. Rules of origin would be waived for tariff-free trade *within* NAFTA, provided that the exporting country did not import a significant quantity of the affected inputs at tariff rates more than (for instance) one percentage point lower than the MFN rates applied by the importing country. The waiver procedure could be invoked on an annual basis by each importing firm.

As a package, these reforms would not add up to a customs union. There would be no attempt to harmonize quotas. Individual NAFTA partners could still invoke anti-dumping and countervailing duties. External MFN tariff schedules would converge only gradually. Rules of origin would linger for many years. Nevertheless, from the vantage point of firms investing and trading within North America, these changes would go far toward eradicating the residual commercial borders that still separate Canada, the United States, and Mexico.

Migration

As already mentioned earlier, in order to prevent future disruption of cross-border trade, the three countries have already negotiated new agreements on "smart borders" that aim to secure the infrastructure and the flow of people and goods along the North American borders (US Department of State 2002a). All of these measures aim to "move the border away from the border" through fast-tracking pre-cleared travellers at border points; integrating border enforcement teams staffed by the two countries with common objectives and integrated actions; introducing Internet-based measures to simplify border transactions for small- and medium-sized enterprises; and providing infrastructure investment to improve access to border crossings through, for example, new highway bypasses that avoid congested downtown streets and the smart handling of goods and people at crossings. These are all sensible measures to secure an open border for goods and services.

However, there are a number of sensitive measures that relate to the movement of people that still are undefined. Many measures will speed the cross-border movement of business travellers. Even permanent resident cards are contemplated, including a biometric identifier. These measures also will undoubtedly increase confidence that people from Third World countries coming to North America do not have malign intentions. Yet what is not clear from the border plan is the treatment to be given to Mexican migrant workers. Within this category there are, as we know, two groups: those who already reside in the United States, a group whose number reaches between 3 and 4.5 million in the last decade (Pastor 2001; Camarota 2001); and those who will, in the future, come to the United States to work. All that was mentioned when the action plan was announced by presidents Fox and Bush in Monterrey, Mexico, was that the Cabinet-level migration group should continue negotiating this issue in the way that it was charged with in previous meetings between both presidents in Guanajuato and Washington. In these meetings, both presidents committed to a "grand bargain" in immigration flows from Mexico—that is, a search for alternatives to legalizing or regularizing the migrants who already reside in the United States and also adopting a more liberal approach for those who will, in the future, come to the United States to work.

The question, however, is whether the "grand bargain" approach is still a viable initiative after the 11 September events. For Mexico, no doubt, immigration is an issue that has to form part of the border partnership action plan. The Mexican government considers the legalization of immigrant workers to be a matter of human rights and social justice as well as a necessary step in the economic integration of North America. In terms of economic benefits, legalization will help ensure that the Mexican economy receives a growing flow of worker remittances, which now run to more than US $20 billion a year. Moreover, the legalization of millions of Mexicans working in the United States will improve their economic prospects and enable many to return to Mexico as successful entrepreneurs.

From the US perspective, feelings are equally strong. Some Americans flat out oppose any increase in immigration. More immediately, the attack on 11 September and the subsequent deterioration of the US economy have dampened discussions on the "grand bargain" that had started in the administration and Congress in the fall of 2001. The fact that many of the terrorists overstayed their visas cast a huge shadow over any legalization initiative.[5] The recession and rising unemployment gave fresh impetus to groups that oppose the opening of the border to migrant workers. According to recent polls, after 11 September, the American people grew more apprehensive about what they have perceived as weak border control and have voiced stronger support for enforcing immigration laws.[6] What does this imply for a grand bargain on undocumented immigration and the concept of a border partnership action plan? The shifting political landscape in the United States has superimposed security concerns on top of the already difficult economic issues wrapped up in immigration policy. Any deal on immigration will need to enhance the security climate by comparison with the current regime.

What kind of assurances could an immigration agreement provide that both satisfies security concerns and facilitates the creation of a secure border? The place to start is with the ongoing flow of migrant workers arriving in the United States. The United States should enlarge substantially the annual quota of Mexicans legally authorized to enter the United States on temporary (but renewable) work permits. In recent years, legal immigration from Mexico to the United States has numbered about 130,000 to 170,000 persons annually (US Department of Justice 2002). Illegal immigration numbers are of course speculative, but the US Immigration and Naturalization Service (INS) places the annual average at about 150,000 between 1988 and 1996 (US Immigration and Naturalization Service 2001).[7]

The way to tackle the flow problem is to start with an expanded number of legal visas, for example, 300,000 persons from Mexico annually. Additional visas should be issued on a work-skill basis (including unskilled workers), not on a family reunification basis (the dominant test for current visas). However— and this is where security is underlined—to obtain a temporary work permit, the Mexican applicant will have to undergo a background check designed to avert security threats. Once inside the United States, temporary permit holders would periodically need to inform the INS electronically of their address and place of employment. Permit holders could renew their permits as long as they were employed a certain number of months (for instance, eight months) in each rolling twelve-month period, had no felony convictions, and reported regularly to the INS. They could apply for US citizenship after a certain number of years (for instance, after a cumulative five years as temporary permit holders). In the meantime, they should accumulate public social security and Medicare rights as well as any private health or pension benefits.

Coupled with this substantial, but closely regulated, increase in temporary work permits, the United States and Mexico should embark on a joint border patrol program to reduce the flow of illegal crossings. The program should include features such as the enhanced use of electronic surveillance, the penalty of ineligibility for a temporary work permit for three years after an illegal crossing, and short-term misdemeanour detention in Mexico (thirty days, for instance) following an illegal crossing. No border patrol program will eliminate illegal crossings, but a joint program, coupled with a substantial temporary work permit initiative, could reduce the flow.

Finally, there is the very difficult question of perhaps four million undocumented Mexicans living and working in the United States. There is no magic solution. The foundation for my tentative suggestions is the proposition that nearly all of these people have made permanent homes in the United States, and they are not going to pick up their lives and return to Mexico. Under a set of appropriate circumstances, therefore, they should be granted residence permits with eligibility for citizenship. The appropriate circumstances that I envisage have two components—a threshold relating to illegal crossings and standards for individual applicants, including the following mandates:

- The resident permit program would be launched when the presidents of the United States and Mexico could jointly certify that the annual rate of illegal crossings does not exceed 50,000 persons. This would entail a reduction of more than two-thirds of the illegal crossings estimated in recent years. The resident permit program would be suspended in years when the presidents could not make this certification.
- Individual eligibility would require evidence that the person resided in the United States prior to the announcement of the program. Otherwise, eligibility standards would parallel those for temporary work permits discussed earlier.
- An applicant for a residence permit who could provide satisfactory evidence of residence in the United States prior to the announcement of the program would not be subject to deportation (whether or not he met other eligibility requirements) so long as he periodically reported a place of residence to the INS and committed no felony after the issuance of the residence permit.
- Holders of residence permits would be immediately eligible for public social security and Medicare benefits as well as private health and pension benefits. They could apply for citizenship after five years.

Conclusions

This chapter has argued that Mexico and the United States should broaden NAFTA with two chief goals: securing North American borders while keeping them open. In order to succeed, these new policies, which are tentatively coined a North American economic and security space, have to be sufficiently ambitious to evoke visionary leadership but sufficiently flexible to accommodate the political realities of North America. The closest analogue to a North

American economic and security space is the 1980s concept of a European economic space, which was designed to link the European Economic Community and the European free trade area. Until the European Union came into being with the Maastricht Treaty and absorbed most of European free trade area, the final destination of the European economic space remained a work in progress.[8] Similarly, the North American economic and security space should be a work in progress for at least a decade in order to foster the closer integration of North America while preserving the essential sovereignty of each partner.

NOTES

1 North American Free Trade Agreement between the Government of Canada, the Government of Mexico and the Government of the United States, 17 December 1992, Can. T.S. 1994 No. 2, 32 I.L.M. 289.

2 Security and Prosperity Partnership, 23 March 2005, http://www.spp.gov.

3 Under such a worse-case scenario, new security barriers could prove every bit as daunting to trade and investment flows as the tariffs and quotas that were negotiated away under NAFTA.

4 Treaty of Rome, 25 March 1957, http://europa.eu.int/index-en.htm.

5 According to some analysts, 11 September shifted the immigration discussion away from legalizing illegal migrants toward cracking down on them (Brownstein 2001).

6 In a national poll conducted after 11 September by John Zogby for the Center for Immigration Studies in Washington, DC, some three-quarters of Americans said that the government was not doing enough to control the border, and nearly as many said that it should greatly increase the resources devoted to enforcing immigration laws (Brownstein 2001).

7 Camarota (2001) estimates that total legal and illegal immigration from Mexico averaged about 400,000 annually between 1998 and 2000. By implication, his figures suggest that illegal immigration was running over 200,000 annually in recent years.

8 Treaty on European Union (Maastricht Treaty), 7 February 1992, http://europa .eu.int.

REFERENCES

Brownstein, Ronald. 2001. "Green Light, Red Light." American Prospect 12(20). http://www.prospect.org/cs/articles?article=green_light_red_light.

Camarota, Stephen, A. 2001. "Immigration from Mexico: Assessing the Impact on the United Status." Paper No. 19. Washington, DC: Center for Immigration Studies.

Espinosa, Enrique. J., and Pedro Loyola. 1997. "Emerging Patterns in Mexico-U.S.Trade." In Barry Bosworth et al., eds., *Coming Together? Mexico-United States Relations*. Washington, DC: Brookings Institution.

Flores, Quiroga Aldo, and Ricardo de la Peña Rodríguez. 2005. "Las relaciones economicas de Mexico con Norteamerica a 11 años del TLCAN." In *Revista Mexicana de Politica Exterior* 73 (February): 21–50.

Goodrich, Ben. 2002. *The Effects of Trade Liberalization on North American Trade*. Washington, DC: Institute for International Economics.

Heath, Jonathan. 1998. "The Impact of Mexico's Trade Liberalization: Jobs, Productivity, and Structural Change." In Carol Wise, ed., *The Post-NAFTA Political Economy: Mexico and the Western Hemisphere*. University Park, PA: Pennsylvania State University Press.

Krueger, Anne O. 1999. *Trade Creation and Trade Diversion under NAFTA*, Working Paper No. 7429. Cambridge, MA: National Bureau of Economic Research.

Mayer, Frederick W. 1998. *Interpreting NAFTA: The Science and Art of Political Analysis.* New York: Columbia University Press.

Naím, Moises, and Sebastian Edwards. 1997. *Mexico 1994: Anatomy of an Emerging-Market Crash*. Washington, DC: Carnegie Endowment for International Peace.

Organisation for Economic Co-operation and Development. 2001. OECD *Labour Statistics 2001*. Paris: Organisation for Economic Co-operation and Development.

Pastor, Robert. 2001. *Toward a North American Community: Lessons from the Old World for the New*. Washington, DC: Institute for International Economics.

Smith, Geri, and Elizabeth Malkin. 1998. "Remaking Mexico." *Business Week*, 21 December.

US Department of Justice. 2002. *Legal Immigration Fiscal Year 2000*. Annual Report Number 6. Washington, DC: Office of Policy and Planning, Statistics Division.

US Department of State. 2002a. "Smart Border: Twenty-Two Point Agreement-U.S.-Mexico Border Partnership Action Plan." http://www.state.gov/p/wha/rls/fs/8909.htm.

US Immigration and Naturalization Service. 2001. "Illegal Alien Resident Population." http://www.dhs.gov/xlibrary/assets/statistics/illegal.pdf.

Weintraub, Sidney. 1997. NAFTA *at Three*. Washington, DC: Center for Strategic and International Studies.

World Trade Organization. 1997. *Trade Policy Review: Mexico*. Geneva: World Trade Organization.

THE INESCAPABLE BORDER: IMMIGRATION FLOWS, HUMAN RIGHTS, AND POLITICAL REFUGEES

Rights at the Borders: Human Rights and Migration in the Canada-Mexico Relationship

Alex Neve

Global Rights Protection

This chapter considers the interplay of immigration flows, human rights, and political refugees in the Canada-Mexico relationship. At stake are crucial topics with major implications for significant numbers of people, the intensity of which has been dramatically underscored by the recent heated debate in the United States over proposed immigration law reforms in that country.[1] Behind these themes lies the notion of borders. Canada and Mexico, of course, do not share a border, far from it. In fact, the two nations are separated by the roughly 2,000 kilometres it takes to traverse the United States. Yet borders are, nonetheless, still significant in the Canada-Mexico relationship and are of considerable, even central, importance to each dimension of this article's theme—immigration, human rights, and refugees. And, of course, both Canada and Mexico do share a border with the United States, which is by far the most important border each of these nations faces. The distance to travel along these two borders is considerable, beginning with the Rio Grande, across the Prairies, and through the pine forests of eastern Canada, covering some 12,000 kilometres. This lengthy, convoluted ribbon weaves itself inescapably into numerous aspects of the Canada-Mexico relationship.

In human rights advocacy, we frequently repeat the refrain: human rights have no borders. And, of course, they do not. Yet this refrain is not just powerful rhetoric. It stands for the essential principle at the heart of global human rights protection—that human rights are universal. No one has more or fewer rights just because one is a woman or a man, because one is poor and not rich, of a particular religious faith, or because of one's political beliefs or the country in which one lives. There are no borders, only universality—a beautiful principle, full of great hope. This has been consistently affirmed since 1948, when the United Nations adopted the Universal Declaration of Human Rights, and through the adoption of other crucial human rights treaties at the level of the United Nations and within the Organization of American States.[2] The challenge, of course, arises in the practice because fundamentally rights are very much more and less enjoyed and found wanting for those precise reasons of economic status, religion, political views, and geography.

Cruelly, the promise of universality does know many borders—borders that can be excuses for human rights violations, as when nations assert their sovereignty and resort to using their borders as a means of fending off international concern and intervention in the face of mass human rights abuses and also when borders themselves become the locus of serious abuses such as when violence and perils are endured by the world's countless desperate border jumpers.

The Paradox of Borders and Canada's Refugee System

Paradoxically, borders are also a symbol of human rights protection, most obviously in the sense of escape. Thus, if the hard-line view of state sovereignty and borders keeps the world out when human rights violations occur, this same border offers a place of safety and potential rights protection, if and when it is possible to get out to the other side. This notion of the border as an avenue for escaping human rights violations plays out across borders around the world every minute of every day—and, certainly, it has been one notable aspect of the frontier relationship between Canada and Mexico. Refugees have fled from one country to the other for countless years. For many years now, significant numbers of Mexicans, consistently numbering over one thousand annually for the past five years, have sought asylum in Canada for a variety of different reasons, including claims of political persecution, cases in which police officers and other government officials have suffered repercussions for exposing corruption, claims of women facing domestic abuse, or claims of gay, lesbian, bisexual, and transgendered people experiencing violence and discrimination. Some have been credible, others not. Some have made well-founded claims, others more far-fetched. Many have been accepted, and most have been rejected.[3]

I myself spent some time as a member of Canada's Immigration and Refugee Board and heard many, many Mexican claims during a year with the board's Americas Team. The fact that so many claims have been made in Canada by citizens of a country perceived to have a democratic government—a country that is an important trading partner and close ally of Canada and a country well known to Canadians as an enticing holiday destination—has often sparked debates about Canada's refugee laws and policies. Some argue that there should be limits and restrictions on who can make a claim and who cannot.

However, the fundamental tenet of Canada's refugee system very importantly remains: that access to the system is universal and not tied to geography or nationality. No matter the nationality of a refugee claimant arriving in

Canada, he or she is entitled to a hearing to determine whether the claim is well founded. Claims that are not found to be ineligible come before the independent Immigration and Refugee Board for a hearing and determination.[4] Status is granted to those able to demonstrate a well-founded fear of persecution in their home country due to race, religion, nationality, political opinion, or membership in a particular social group as well as those facing a risk of torture or certain risks to life.[5]

It is also worth noting that, occasionally, there have been some "refugee" flows in the opposite direction. Most particularly, the thousands of Canadian Mennonites, largely from the province of Manitoba, who over a span of twenty years, beginning in the early 1920s, left what they felt was growing government encroachment on their freedom of religion in Canada. They chose new lives and new homes in the Mexican state of Chihuahua. Decades later, though, some of these Mennonites or their descendents have returned, some resuming life as Canadian citizens and others having to again make the journey as refugees.

Migration and Refugee Flows: Illegal Human Trafficking

Beyond traditional political refugees, there is another important migratory, border-related dimension to the Canada-Mexico relationship, with crucial human rights implications—namely, the flow of migrant labour from Mexico to Canada. Many individuals—thousands, in fact—come yearly under the official auspices of the agricultural worker program, which has been open to Mexican nationals since 1974. Currently, over 10,000 Mexicans are admitted temporarily to Canada every year under this program, almost all of them men.[6] Others, such as the nationals from countless other countries, reside in Canada as undocumented migrant workers, lacking official immigration status, perhaps having stayed on after the expiry of some other status or perhaps having been trafficked into the country and into Canada's sex trade through transnational criminal networks. And, of course, untold others never make it here, but might want to if the borders were not so high and the options for crossing were not so limited.

Migration and refugee flows, which are significant in this bilateral relationship, are one of the most pressing human rights challenges the world faces. Globally, massive numbers of people are on the move, certainly millions are within this hemisphere, and for many different reasons. Yet, almost always, this movement occurs under circumstances that give rise to serious human rights violations. Add the United States to our bilateral relationship and there is no doubt that migration is likely the most critical trilateral human rights concern that we face. The range of human rights violations associated with migration within North America is broad. Migrants are, by virtue of their temporary, uncertain, and sometimes unlawful status, vulnerable to exploitation and abuse. Both before and during border crossings, migrants face extortion, rape, threats, and other violence at the hands of *coyotes,* law enforcement agents, and private militia groups. The vulnerability continues after crossing the border, at the hands of exploitative employers, unscrupulous landlords, and violent spouses.

Given this North American context, it is notable that the UN special rapporteur on the human rights of migrants—an important post within the UN human rights system, which was established in 1999—chose Canada, Mexico, and the United States as among the first to which she carried out official visits in 2000 and 2002 (United Nations 2000; United Nations 2002a and 2002b). The first person to hold the special rapporteur's post was Gabriela Rodríguez Pizarro from Costa Rica. She held the post for six years and was followed by Jorge Bustamente from Mexico, who took up the post in August 2005.

Migration and human rights are undeniably and inextricably linked. Human rights violations of some description almost always are at the root of migratory movements—be it torture, rape, or mass killings that propel the so-called political refugees into flight or grinding poverty and a failure to protect basic economic and social rights that push migrant workers to seek out a brighter horizon. Violations far too frequently continue during migration, either at the hands of unscrupulous and ruthless *coyotes* and *passeurs,* harsh policing and border enforcement tactics, or now even the possibility of falling victim to private vigilante militias who have taken it upon themselves to help guard the border. And, sadly, violations may go on even at the end of the journey, particularly for the many, many migrants without lawful status, who find themselves easy prey and vulnerable to exploitation in many ways—forced into the sex trade, into unsafe and underpaid working conditions, or to endure domestic violence, all with the fear that to speak out and complain would be to risk exposure and eventual deportation. Such violations apply even when individuals do have lawful migrant status of some description, as is the case with Mexican agricultural workers or individuals who arrive under the live-in-caregiver program. The uncertainty of the status, which is of course not permanent, leads to some of the same trepidation and thus vulnerability to exploitation.

Internal Migration and Human Rights Abuses

It is worth noting that these concerns arise even when individuals never manage to cross an international border. Internal migration, within Mexico and also within Canada, gives rise to many of these same grave human rights problems. Think of the women from all over Mexico who have been drawn by the promise of jobs in the *maquiladora* world of Ciudad Juárez. Hundreds of these women have been killed over the past decade or have gone missing, and only recently have authorities begun to recognize it as a serious human rights crisis that demands a high-level, concerted, and very serious response.

The dramatic growth of the *maquiladora* industry in the area around Ciudad Juárez increased even more when the North American Free Trade Agreement (NAFTA) was established in 1994 between Mexico and its northern neighbours. After 1994, the industry spread into the country all the way to the city of Chihuahua.[7] However, the world recession that began in 2000 had a severe impact on the area. The *maquiladora* industry largely makes its profits by paying lower wages to its employees than those paid in the United States and other developed countries, a practice that is consistent with globalization in other parts of the world. However, within Mexico, the chance of earning a comparatively higher wage than elsewhere in the country has made the *maquiladora* industry a strong magnet for many people stricken by poverty as a result of economic crises or industrial restructuring and who go there to look for work, sometimes as a first step before trying to enter the United States.

For many years, women have made up the majority of the workforce in the *maquilas,* although at present the number of women is down to 50 percent. With regard to the role of the *maquiladoras* in Ciudad Juárez society, the Inter-American Commission of Human Rights special rapporteur on the rights of women reminds the Mexican government that it "bears responsibility for ensuring that the *maquilas* are meeting their duties under law to their workers, and has a special role in encouraging the *maquilas* to invest in measures to support the workers and communities that serve them and helping to channel such investment for the public good" (Amnesty International 2003; Amnesty International 2006a). I was in Ciudad Juárez in August 2005 and struck deeply by the many tragic dichotomies that pervade the area. Perhaps the most poignant image I found was symbolized by the numbers of dead women that have been found within an easy stroll of the bustling transnational assembly plants.

Moving north, one thinks also of the indigenous women from reserves across Canada, marginalized, dislocated, and drawn to the promise and hope of something else in Canada's urban centres—hope that is realized for some but cruelly betrayed for many others who fall further into despair and danger. Amnesty International issued a deeply disturbing report in 2004 entitled *Stolen Sisters,* documenting the alarmingly high levels of violence and discrimination experienced by indigenous women involved in the internal Canadian "migration" from reserve to city. The report notes:

> With the loss of traditional livelihoods within Indigenous communities, the opportunities for education and employment in Canadian towns and cities have become a powerful draw for a growing number of Indigenous people. Almost 60 percent of Indigenous people in Canada now live in urban settings. Critically, however, the majority of Indigenous peoples in Canadian towns and cities continue to live at a disadvantage compared to

non-Indigenous people, facing dramatically lower incomes and a shortage
of culturally appropriate support services in a government structure that
has still not fully adjusted to the growing urban Indigenous population.

In the 1996 census, Indigenous women with status living off-reserve
earned on average $13,870 a year. This is about $5,500 less than non-Indigenous women. Other groups of Indigenous women, such as Inuit and
Métis women, recorded slightly higher average annual incomes, but all
substantially less than what Statistics Canada estimated someone living in
a large Canadian city would require to meet their own needs. In fact, many
Indigenous women living in poverty not only have to look after themselves
but also must care for elderly parents, raise children or tend to loved ones in
ill-health, often with only a single income to live on. Homelessness and inadequate shelter are believed to be widespread problems facing Indigenous
families in all settings. (Amnesty International 2004, 12)

Laws, of course, are meant to provide protection and guard against abuse at
the regional, national, and international level. However, even though laws exist,
enforcement is invariably weak.

It is important to point out that Mexico has ratified the key international
treaty in this area, the International Convention on the Protection of the Rights
of All Migrant Workers and Members of Their Families (Convention on Migrant
Workers), but that Canada has not.[8] The convention has similarly not been ratified by the United States. This divergence in the three countries unfortunately
reflects a worldwide pattern. Countries that are the source of migrant workers
have signed on, while countries that are the destination have not.

North American Security Practices and Human Rights Violations

There has been more and more attention paid to North American borders over
the past decade. NAFTA, of course, has defined the commercial significance of
these borders, in its aim of opening them up as widely as possible for economic
traffic, but it is much more reticent in allowing people to move across them with
the same degree of freedom. More recently, national security has come to define
the borders as well. Security has, of course, long been a very visible and active
presence along the US-Mexico border, but it is now also becoming a major
aspect of the northern frontier as well. The case of Maher Arar is a high-profile
reminder that Arar, a Canadian citizen of Syrian origin, was arrested in the
United States in September 2002 while transiting on his way home to Canada
from a family vacation in Tunisia. Despite the fact that he was travelling on a
Canadian passport, he was taken from his prison cell after two weeks of detention in the United States in the middle of the night and summarily flown on a

private jet to Syria, where he remained imprisoned without charge or trial for
one year. He was held in abysmal prison conditions and was subjected to severe
torture before he was finally released and returned to Canada in October 2003.

There are worrying questions about the role of Canadian officials in Arar's
case, which are being examined in the course of a public inquiry expected to
conclude sometime late in the summer of 2006 (Commission of Inquiry into
the Actions of Canadian Officials in Relation to Maher Arar 2006). His case
has also come to symbolize, most certainly, a certain sense of US contempt for
the Canadian border and a callous willingness to figuratively close this border,
even to someone with a clear right to traverse it. It makes one wonder whether
there are any parallels to how officials of the US Drug Enforcement Agency
have viewed the Mexican border in the past with the notorious abductions of
Mexican citizens into the United States to stand trial.

There is more afoot in securing the borders of North America. The debate
about proposed new laws and practices with respect to passport requirements
when crossing from Canada into the United States is another reminder. So too
is the recent news that the minutemen militia, who are self-appointed vigilante
guardians of the US border with Mexico, have moved up the Pacific coast and
have begun patrolling along the border between British Columbia and the state
of Washington (CBC Newsworld 2006).

In March 2005, the three North American leaders gathered in Waco, Texas,
and announced the establishment of the Security and Prosperity Partnership
of North America, which calls for a "common approach to security to protect
North America from external threats, and prevent and respond to threats within
North America and further streamline the secure and efficient movement of
legitimate, low-risk traffic across our shared borders" (Security and Prosperity
Partnership 2005).[9] The Security and Prosperity Partnership was affirmed at
the March 2006 North American Summit in Cancun. However, nowhere does
the partnership turn any attention to the question of human rights and the
particular vulnerability of migrants in North America (Amnesty International
2006b; Amnesty International 2005).

There are 12,000 kilometres of border with serious implications for the
protection of fundamental human rights, but there is very little to show for
that in the deals and agreements negotiated among the North American governments. NAFTA is the most significant agreement to be developed, of course,
but it is about facilitating the cross-border movement of goods and services
and people directly associated with those goods and services and certainly not
about people more generally. When the Security and Prosperity Partnership
was adopted in March 2005 and strengthened in March 2006, North American
leaders updated to some degree their vision of the North American relationship. There are several references in that document to the flow of people within
North America, all prefaced with the qualifier "legitimate" and, in one place,

more precisely described as "facilitating further the movement of business persons within North America." Yet there is nothing in NAFTA and nothing in the Security and Prosperity Partnership about human rights and the movement of people or about human rights and migration, let alone an elaboration of a human rights-based approach to managing North America's borders. For that we are left looking elsewhere.

Refugees and Asylum: International Rights Conventions

As mentioned earlier, the one notable shortcoming of both Canada and the United States is their failure to ratify the key Convention on Migrant Workers. Canada, the United States, and Mexico have, however, all been actively participating for close to a decade now in an intergovernmental forum on international migration, which is often informally known as the Puebla Process and more officially known as the Regional Conference on Migration. Eight other Central American countries, with the addition of the Dominican Republic, take part in these ongoing meetings. Through this process, governments have set themselves a four-part human rights action plan, which includes: (1) full respect for existing legal provisions regarding the human rights of migrants; (2) strengthening those provisions; (3) ensuring the protection of refugees; and (4) addressing concerns about the health needs of migrants. It is all pretty soft at present—draft guidelines, ideas about pilot projects—and set against a backdrop where it seems clear that the real policies and practices are being hammered out elsewhere or simply being advanced unilaterally. Nonetheless, the Puebla Process is deserving of ongoing support, albeit cautiously.[10]

The plight of migrants within the context of intra-continental migration tends to dominate discussions of immigration and human rights in North America. There is, however, also a refugee flow between Mexico and Canada, as was highlighted earlier. Claims have risen significantly over recent years with just over 2,000 Mexicans seeking refugee status in Canada in 2004. There is some ease in doing so since there is no visa requirement for Mexicans wishing to travel to Canada, meaning that those with the means to fly are fairly readily able to get here and thus avoid having to cross the United States by land.

Refugees, including Mexican or other nationalities, seeking asylum in Canada or elsewhere have had a difficult time in this era of heightened global security. Worldwide, and certainly in both Canada and the United States, refugees are frequently held as being the source of insecurity in our midst. Refugee systems are porous, we are told, and Canada's system, in particular, is ripe for abuse—easy picking for would-be terrorists planning their next attack. As such, there are demands for restrictions, exclusions, more detention, and more deportations. In the rush to blame refugees, what is frequently overlooked is that, while there is inevitably room for abuse in any system that is about human beings and human lives, the vast majority of refugees themselves are fleeing insecurity and violence and need and deserve protection.

One very concrete outcome of this security-related focus on refugees has been the implementation between Canada and the United States of what is often termed the "safe third country" agreement, which was operational as of 29 December 2004.[11] Under this agreement, the bulk of refugee claimants who pass through one country on their way to the other will be bumped back to the first country and told to make their claims there. In practice, this means that a large percentage of the approximately ten thousand refugee claimants who pass through the United States each year on their way to Canada will no longer be able to access Canada's refugee determination system and will instead be required to make their claims for asylum in the United States.

The Challenges Ahead: Protecting the Safety of the Refugee

First, the simple, unchangeable reality of the refugee journey is that for many there is no other way to Canada other than through the United States. Certainly, for Latin Americans travelling overland this goes without saying. Mexicans, however, are likely the one exception to this pattern, since the bulk of Mexicans claiming refuge in Canada arrive by air, due to the fact that they do not require a visa to travel to Canada but do for the United States, a distinction that does not generally apply to other Latin Americans. And, of course, even for refugees from other parts of the world travelling by air, there are very few direct routes into Canada that do not involve a change of plane in the United States or perhaps in Europe.

Second, while this agreement is certainly described as a two-way street—a responsibility-sharing arrangement—the overwhelming impact will be on refugees travelling north to Canada. Very few refugees come through Canada on their way to make claims in the United States. For this reason, it is something that Canadian officials have long been interested in—a very crude way to reduce dramatically the numbers of refugees making claims in Canada every year. In any given year, between one-third and one-half of refugees claiming status in Canada arrive by way of the United States, many of them Latin American and many of them having passed also through Mexico.

So what is the concern? After all, is the real objective not to make sure that refugees are safe? Does it really matter whether the place of safety is in Canada or in the United States, even if the individual himself or herself may have particular reasons for preferring one to the other? The point is that safety is precisely what the fundamental test should be. Safety should be judged by one clear and essential standard—the international human rights obligations that are at stake. At the border, when decisions are being made and refugees are being told that they cannot cross and that they cannot make a refugee claim in Canada, human rights are very much in play. A number of fundamentally important human rights issues are being overlooked. Let me highlight two. First, to stop a refugee at the border and turn him or her back is to put that individual at risk of arbitrary detention. Second, if the refugee is a woman fleeing abuses such as domestic violence or so-called honour crimes, it is to put her at real risk of being denied the protection that is her right. .

This issue is raised as a bilateral Canada-US matter because it is a serious concern, and it is indirectly about Mexico as well because it can impact on Mexican refugees and certainly affects refugees who have passed through Mexico on their way to seeking safety in Canada. However, it is also mentioned because there has been much suspicion over the fact that there may be interest on the part of the US government in moving this model south and applying it to the US-Mexico border as well. The ultimate prospect—certainly not an immediate one, but not an entirely fanciful possibility—may be that refugees are bumped further and further south in the Americas and are ultimately unable to flee at all. It is one last telling reason why we need to commit to a North American human rights agenda with strong provisions about migration, including the protection of refugees, at its core.

Human Rights Co-operation: A Top Priority

These issues are pressing and are of a mounting, not diminishing, concern. The time for a new approach may be opportune. There is a new government in Ottawa, which is soon to be joined by a new administration in Mexico City. In Washington, President George W. Bush is moving into the end of his presidency and is weighed down by the Iraq War and low popularity. It may well be the moment for Canada and Mexico to seize and define a North American human rights agenda. One possible agenda for strengthening human rights protection for migrants in North America emerges very clearly from the reports coming out of the UN special rapporteur on the human rights of migrants in Mexico, the United States, and Canada. Five key themes run through all of those reports and, with an additional point regarding refugee protection, offer a six-point human rights agenda for the protection of migrants and refugees in North America.

First, better legal protection is needed, which certainly means that Canada and the United States should both move to ratify key international instruments such as the Convention on Migrant Workers and also the two recent protocols to the UN Convention against Transnational Organized Crimes, one dealing with human smuggling and the other with human trafficking.[12] It also means stronger laws at the national level. Throughout North America, there should be laws in place that ensure that the basic human rights of migrants are effectively protected and that a lack or uncertainty of immigrant status is not a barrier to individuals taking steps to lodge complaints and seek a remedy when their rights have been abused.

Second, better actual protection must stand behind stronger laws. A comprehensive action plan needs to emerge, including improved policing practices, enhanced training, better mechanisms to monitor abuses, effective and accessible complaints mechanisms, and the insurance that anyone who violates the rights of migrants is held accountable and brought to justice. A forum such as the now yearly North American summits that have led to the Security and Prosperity Partnership would be an ideal venue to see common best practices agreed to and implemented throughout all three countries.

Third, North American governments must provide increased support for civil society. In all three countries, it is apparent that civil society groups are often the ones most easily able to access, and thus provide protection and support to, vulnerable migrants. Their ability to continue with this work has to be expanded and must be well resourced and supported.

Fourth, governments should improve the status afforded to migrant workers to ensure that workers and their families are able to enjoy their rights, as laid out in the Convention on Migrant Workers. For instance, Article 30 of the convention guarantees the children of migrant workers the same access to elementary school level education as is the case for nationals of the state. It appears that President Fox's push for a migrant workers program of some description for Mexicans in the United States is not progressing. Yet these are precisely the ideas and proposals that have to advance—new approaches that will afford migrants their rights.

Fifth, all three governments must commit to adopting refugee laws and practices that conform to the requirements of international standards, which include the interpretation and application of the definition of refugee, the grounds for detention of refugee claimants, and the protection of fundamental economic and social rights such as the right to work, to health care, and to education. Until such a time as there is common standards, which are fully compliant with international law, "co-operative" undertakings such as the agreement between Canada and the United States should be abandoned.

Finally, governments of all three countries must do more to deal with racism and xenophobia. The special rapporteur noted this concern, for instance, following her 2002 visit to the US-Mexico border region—on both sides of the border:

> During her visit, the Special Rapporteur noted a certain tendency on the part of some segments of the US population to consider undocumented migrants as criminals and drug traffickers who pose a threat to national security ... The Special Rapporteur is concerned at reports about groups

of ranchers along the border who make xenophobic and racist comments about migrants on the internet ...

In Mexico, the Special Rapporteur was also concerned at the stigmatization of the migrant population (by some municipal authorities and public security officers). She noted that the abuses committed had undertones of xenophobia and discrimination. A mayor with whom the Special Rapporteur met asserted that, when they arrived at the border, migrants became beggars, prostitutes, criminals, or drug addicts and posed a threat to public safety. (United Nations 2002b)

A concerted, collaborative effort among the three North American governments to confront this bigotry and hatred is sorely needed.

NOTES

1 The "Sensenbrenner Bill," *Border Protection, Antiterrorism, and Illegal Immigration Control Act of 2005,* H.R. 4437, was passed by the United States House of Representatives on 16 December 2005. The bill proposes increased penalties for illegal immigration and would classify both illegal aliens and anyone assisting them as felons. It is presently under consideration by the United States Senate.

2 Significant human rights treaties include the Universal Declaration of Human Rights, 10 December 1948, G.A. Res. 217(III) UN GAOR, 3rd Sess., Supp. No. 13, at 71, UN Doc. A/810; the International Covenant on Economic, Social and Cultural Rights, 19 December 1966, 6 I.L.M. 360 (1967); the International Covenant on Civil and Political Rights, 19 December 1966, 6 I.L.M. 368 (1967); and the American Convention on Human Rights, 22 November 1969, 9 I.L.M. 673 (1970).

3 In 2004, Canada's Immigration and Refugee Board finalized the cases of 2,684 refugee claimants from Mexico. The acceptance rate was 25 percent, which was down slightly from 27 percent in 2003 and 24 percent in 2002. See Immigration and Refugee Board, Refugee Protection Division, *Statistics,* http://www.infosource .gc.ca/inst/irb/fedo7-e.asp.

4 Canada's *Immigration and Refugee Protection Act,* R.S.C. 2001, c. 27, does exclude some individuals from access to the refugee determination system, including those who have committed serious crimes, pose a threat to national security, or have previously made a refugee claim in Canada.

5 These rights are protected under Canada's *Immigration and Refugee Protection Act,* R.S.C. 2001, c. 27.

6 The Seasonal Agricultural Workers Program, Foreign Affairs Canada, http://www .dfait-maeci.gc.ca/mexico-city/immigration/agricultural-en.asp.

7 North American Free Trade Agreement between the Government of Canada, the Government of Mexico and the Government of the United States, 17 December 1992, Can. T.S. 1994 No. 2, 32 I.L.M. 289.

8 International Convention on the Protection of the Rights of All Migrant Workers and Members of Their Families, United Nations, 11 September 2007. http://www2 .ohchr.org/english/bodies/CMW/docs/CMW.C.AZE.1.pdf.

9 Security and Prosperity Partnership, 23 March 2005, http://www.spp.gov.

10 Regional Conference on Migration, http://www.rcmvs.org.

11 Agreement between the Government of Canada and the Government of the United States of America for Cooperation in the Examination of Refugee Status Claims from Nationals of Third Countries, signed 5 December 2002, operational 29 December 2004, http://www.cic.gc.ca/english/department/laws-policy/menu-safethird.asp.

12 UN Convention against Transnational Organized Crimes, 2000. http://www.uncjin .org/Documents/Conventions/dcatoc/final_documents_2/convention_eng.pdf.

REFERENCES

Amnesty International. 2003. "Mexico: Intolerable Killings—Ten Years of Abductions and Murders of Women in Ciudad Juárez and Chihuahua." Online index no. AMR 41/026/2003. 11 August.

————. 2004. "Stolen Sisters: A Human Rights Response to Discrimination and Violence against Indigenous Women in Canada." Online index no. AMR 20/003/2004. 3 October.

————. 2005. "Carta abierta de AI dirigida al Presidente Bush, al Presidente Fox y al Primer Ministro Martin con motivo de la reunión en Waco." 23 March. http://www.amnistia.org.mx/modules.php?

————. 2006a. "Mexico: Killings and Abductions of Women in Ciudad Juarez and the City of Chihuahua—the Struggle for Justice Goes On." Online index no. AMR 41/012/2006. 20 February.

————. 2006b. "Open Letter to Stephen Harper, George W. Bush and Vicente Fox," 28 March. http://www.amnesty.ca/archives/trilateral_summit_open_ letter_2006.php.

Borjas, G., and J. Crisp, eds. 2005. *Poverty, International Migration and Asylum.* Basingstoke, Hampshire: Palgrave Macmillan.

CBC Newsworld. 2006. *Minuteman Volunteers to Patrol Canada-U.S. Border for Illegal Migrant.* 28 March. http://www.cbc.ca/world.

Cholewinski, R. 1997. *Migrant Workers in International Human Rights Law: Their Protection in Countries of Employment.* Oxford: Clarendon Press.

Commission of Inquiry into the Actions of Canadian Officials in Relation to Maher Arar. 2006. *Arar Commission Reports Expected to Be Released by End of Summer.* 11 April. http://www.ararcommission.ca/eng/ release_0411e.pdf.

Hathaway, J. 2005. *The Rights of Refugees under International Law.* Cambridge: Cambridge University Press.

International Organization for Migration. 2005. *World Migration 2005: Costs and Benefits of International Migration.*

Kyle, D., and R. Koslowski, eds. 2001. *Global Human Smuggling: Comparative Perspectives.* Baltimore: Johns Hopkins University Press.

Martin, P., S. Forbes Martin, and P. Weil. 2006. *Managing Migration: The Promise of Cooperation.* Lanham, MD: Lexington Books.

Security and Prosperity Partnership. 2005. *Implementation Report—Security Agenda. Homeland Security Fact Sheet.* 27 June. http://www.spp.gov/ SECURITY_FACT_SHEET.pdf?dName=fact_sheets.

Simmons, A., ed. 1997. *Refugees, Human Rights and Free Trade in North America.* New York: Center for Migration Studies.

United Nations, Special Rapporteur on the Human Rights of Migrants. 2000. *Visit to Canada,* UN Doc. E/CN.4/2001/83/Add.1 (21 December).

———. 2002a. *Visit to Mexico.* UN Doc. E/CN.4/2003/85/Add.2 (30 October).

———. 2002b. *Visit to the Border between Mexico and the United States.* 2002b. UN Doc. E/CN.4/2003/85/Add.3 (30 October).

4

Human Rights and Mexican Foreign Policy

Ana Covarrubias

Human Rights: An Ambiguous Place in Mexican Foreign Policy

The subject of human rights is not new in Mexican foreign policy although there is no question that its importance has significantly increased in the last five to ten years. Since the end of the Second World War, Mexican foreign policy, like that of many other countries, has faced the dilemma of supporting the principle of non-intervention or promoting the protection of human rights. In dealing with this dilemma, Mexican governments have supported the human rights international regime by accusing states of violating human rights selectively, while they have endorsed the idea that human rights were a domestic matter most of the time.

Mexico's foreign policy did not evolve at the same pace as the human rights international regime in the post-Second World War era, nor did it solve the contradiction between the defence of non-intervention and the promotion of human rights. Belatedly, however, Mexican governments have recognized that human rights are a legitimate foreign policy issue, and the promotion of such rights has now become a foreign policy priority. Mexico's new attitude was both the result of the influence exerted by the international system to improve the state of human rights in the country and a deliberate choice for change. This chapter will focus on the international system (foreign actors) as a source of foreign policy change, although without totally ignoring domestic circumstances. It will argue that the Mexican governments have reacted to pressures and the influence of external actors, thus making human rights in foreign policy an instrument for most of the period under study. However, the most drastic change in favour of human rights in Mexican foreign policy was a deliberate choice taken by Mexican authorities to assure Mexico's democratic viability. After Vicente Fox took office in 2000, human rights were considered to be more a value than a strategy, but domestic circumstances suggest that there is a long way ahead before such new attitudes toward human rights are consolidated in Mexico's politics and society. The 2005 reports by Amnesty International and Human Rights Watch, for example, recognize the government's commitment to improve the state of human rights in the country, but they underline the rather poor results so far. The reports identify Mexico's major human rights violations, stressing the persistence of torture and impunity. As specific cases are concerned, both documents underline the unsolved cases of murdered women in Chihuahua (*las muertas de Juárez*) and the so-called "dirty war" in the 1960s and 1970s (Amnesty International 2005).[1] According to Human Rights Watch, it is unlikely that Fox's government will be able to advance its initiatives to solve the pending cases of human rights violations before the end of 2006.

Supporting the Human Rights International Regime: 'As Long as It Applies to Others'

Human rights were a subject of Mexican foreign policy long before the Cold War, the emergence of Zapatismo, or the election of Vicente Fox. At the Chapultepec Conference in 1945, the Mexican government insisted that human rights should be incorporated into international law and that states and individuals both should have rights and duties. A few months later, the Ministry of Foreign Affairs concluded a report on the Dumbarton Oaks proposals that criticized them for not including a human rights declaration (United Nations 1945). The ministry suggested that a declaration of the rights and duties of nations and a declaration of the rights and duties of men should be attached to the charter of what would become the United Nations to expose more faithfully the ideals of democratic nations. The Mexican government even suggested that international mechanisms should be established to guarantee the application of the general principles included in both declarations.

Mexico's position in 1945 stands in sharp contrast to the country's attitude regarding human rights thereafter. In 1945, the government expected a new international organization that would privilege law over politics. Yet once it was clear that the United Nations was more a political, than a juridical, organization, Mexican foreign policy tended to support non-intervention as a means to protect the domestic jurisdiction of states. Human rights would fall into the category of "domestic matters" (Castañeda 1995, 83–84).

During the Cold War, however, Mexican governments did not ignore the issue of human rights entirely, although their policy toward democracy and human rights was not consistent or constant. President Adolfo López Mateos (1958–64), for example, travelled only to those Latin American countries that had democratic regimes in 1960, but President Gustavo Díaz Ordaz (1964–70) rejected this criterion when he visited Central America a few years later. Díaz

Ordaz considered that such a distinction would imply a judgement of the Central American regimes and therefore intervention (Torres 1991, 156 and 197). President Luis Echeverría (1970–76) explicitly denounced human rights violations in Spain, Chile, South Africa, and Rhodesia. He ultimately broke diplomatic relations with Chile, suspended all communications with Spain,[2] and did not establish diplomatic relations with South Africa or Rhodesia (Rico 1991). The Mexican government even asked the Security Council to request that the General Assembly consider expelling Spain from the United Nations on the grounds of human rights violations. In 1979, President José López Portillo (1976–82) broke diplomatic relations with Nicaragua for the same reason—the massive human rights violations committed by Anastasio Somoza's government (UNAM, 1989, 33).

Defending Human Rights: A Matter of Conviction or Narrow Self-Interest?

The question at this point is whether foreign policy defended human rights out of conviction (as a liberal value) or whether it was just a justification that concealed other interests. Each example should be looked at in detail, but, in general, it could be argued that Mexico's policy was not a Liberal policy. This does not mean, however, that Mexican governments might have not defended human rights *per se*—human rights and other issues such as peace are difficult not to support since no state would deliberately choose to defend human rights violations. Supporting human rights was an easy thing to do, it was not costly, and it gave the Mexican government a prestigious standing. However, the examples mentioned earlier reflect more than anything the existence of other domestic and foreign policy objectives.

The rupture of diplomatic relations with Chile and the suspension of communications with Spain support the argument that one of Echeverría's main political objectives was to project the image of a progressive and democratic Mexico domestically and abroad after events in 1968.[3] Diplomatic rupture with Nicaragua, on the other hand, was the beginning of an active policy that was also defined as being progressive toward the Central American countries. The international system was obviously decisive for it provided the opportunities for Echeverría and López Portillo to act as they did, but it was more a choice than an imposition or a forced reaction. However, Echeverría's and López Portillo's policies were not necessarily "Liberal policies" as is demonstrated by the gap between domestic and foreign policy.

Human rights could have been defended elsewhere, but it was not clear that they would be defended in Mexico. Certainly, neither Echeverría nor López Portillo would have admitted external opinions about the situation of human rights in Mexico, let alone more direct foreign intervention. And regardless of whether the Mexican government was actually promoting and defending human rights in the country, it is also true that human rights in Mexico were not the subject of international discussion. The events of 2 October 1968, for example, when Echeverría was minister of the interior and Díaz Ordaz was president, had not attracted much international attention. Amnesty International only classified the participants in the movement as prisoners of conscience, and the Mexican government reacted by affirming that Mexico's domestic affairs were not the concern of other states and international actors (Sikkink 1993). In this way, foreign policy seemed to be an instrument to defend human rights without taking the risk of attracting international attention to Mexico.

The World Looks at Mexico

Mexican governments were therefore in a comfortable situation that allowed them to defend human rights abroad without having to account for the state of human rights domestically. This situation, however, started to change in the 1980s when the country began to "open up"—not deliberately, most of the time— and was seen and criticized by foreign actors. The debt crisis that began in 1982, the 1985 earthquake, the strengthening of drug trafficking and organized crime in Mexico, and electoral disputes throughout the decade were discussed beyond national borders. The earthquake revealed the extent to which Mexican police practised torture; the complaints presented by the National Action Party at the Inter-American Human Rights Commission (IAHRC) confirmed that Mexico's democracy was not working properly; and the assassination of Enrique Camarena, a Drug Enforcement Agency agent, in Guadalajara, Mexico, exposed not only the levels of corruption and impunity of Mexican authorities but also the extent to which drug trafficking cartels had increased their power.

The complaints presented by the National Action Party at the IAHRC and the government's reaction to this move illustrate nicely the links between the domestic and foreign levels. As the IAHRC endorsed the National Action Party's complaints, the Mexican government strongly reiterated its support for non-intervention, thus denying the validity of international human rights norms and, as a consequence, international action. In the first place, according to Mexican authorities, the IAHRC lacked any competence on "exclusively domestic matters."

If a "State agreed to subject itself to an international organization in matters relating to the election of its political organs, it would cease to be sovereign and to be a State."[4] In brief, the IAHRC was intervening in Mexico and violating its sovereignty.

Despite Mexico's defensive position and support for non-intervention, it continued to reiterate its commitment to the protection of human rights in other countries. International norms may have not been valid for Mexico, but they were valid for El Salvador, Guatemala, Chile, and South Africa.[5] Carlos Salinas de Gortari's (1988–94) presidential term illustrates the tension between the rejection of international norms and action and the need to concede. With respect to foreign policy, two examples of change or tactical concessions are worth mentioning: the World Conference on Human Rights in 1993 and the acceptance of foreign electoral observers in 1994. In both cases, there was resistance at the beginning and concessions at the end.

Post-1993: The Zapatista Uprising and Other Turning Points

In June 1993, during the UN World Conference on Human Rights, the Mexican government did not recognize that human rights were universal. Mexico supported international co-operation to "strengthen the efficacious and genuine protection of human rights taking into account the national perspective always" ("Derechos humanos" 1993, 40). In brief, according to the Mexican perspective, the defence of human rights should be impartial, objective, not selective, and not the instrument to "export" certain models of political and economic organization (ibid., 40–41). Apparently, Mexico realized that its position was shared by fairly useless partners and it may also have been receiving some pressure from the US government because by the end of the year its government endorsed the newly created office of the High Commissioner for Human Rights.

The decision to accept foreign electoral observers toward the end of Salinas' government has been explained by reason of the Zapatista uprising and the political assassinations of presidential candidate Luis Donaldo Colosio and José Francisco Ruiz Massieu, secretary-general of the Institutional Revolutionary Party in 1994, but it may be worth taking into account the general context of Mexico's foreign relations since international attention had already been attracted to Mexico. In 1990, for example, Americas Watch had published a report on the situation of human rights in Mexico and, for the first time, the US Congress had held hearings on the subject (Sikkink 1993, 432–33). Thus, Mexican authorities seem to have reasoned that the presence of electoral observers in 1994 might contribute to demonstrating the viability of a questioned regime and to legitimizing the Institutional Revolutionary Party, who was convinced it would win the elections. Additionally, some private foundations in the United States, such as the National Democratic Institute and the Carter Foundation, had insisted on the need for electoral observers (Benítez Manaut 1996).

What is interesting about Salinas' presidential term is that his government initiated a voluntary change in foreign policy that included an open rapprochement with the United States and, to a lesser extent, with other developed countries. Foreign policy change was not intended to include human rights issues, but Salinas' aggressive commercial diplomacy ultimately had significant repercussions in the area of democracy and human rights in Mexico. It was not possible to isolate human rights from other foreign policy objectives, and they became instrumental. The contradiction between the rejection of the validity of international norms applied to Mexico but not to other countries. The norm was valid for the Chilean and South African cases but not for Cuba. On the other hand, at the Organization of American States (OAS), the Mexican government considered that the Santiago's commitment to democracy and the renewal of the Inter-American system of the OAS which included Resolution 1080 (1991), the Washington Protocol (1992) and the Declaration of Managua for the Promotion of Democracy and Development (1993), which were all instruments adopted to actively promote democracy, gave the organization a non-desirable competence to judge and intervene in domestic processes of member states.

Human Rights and Mexican Politics

Salinas' foreign policy was designed to a large extent using the external world as a key point of reference as well as for domestic purposes—that is to say, NAFTA was the means of consolidating domestic economic reform. One might talk about a boomerang strategy for the economic sphere that had the unintended consequence of incorporating human rights issues into the agenda.[6] Obviously, domestic processes such as the political assassinations and the Zapatista uprising did not help to keep the issue of human rights out of the agenda, and the isolation of the subject became increasingly difficult. The government made some tactical concessions but reiterated its defensive position, and it denied the validity of the international norms applied by the OAS and those used in the Cuban case. The opportunities provided by the international system to strengthen a policy of defence of human rights (usually within the framework of defending democracy) were not easily taken by the Mexican government.

Thus, one might argue that change in foreign policy, but not in the area of human rights, originated from above and has to be understood largely in terms of the consolidation of a new economic model. Even though the subject of human rights was already part of the international agenda, there was no "imposition" on Mexico, despite increasing criticism about the poor state of human rights in the country. The Mexican government did seek to become a member of the modern-countries club in NAFTA and in the Organisation for Economic Co-operation and Development, but such association did not require a change in the area of human rights, only tactical and instrumental concessions.[7] The identity sought by the Mexican government in being "modern" did not necessarily include democracy and human rights. Mexico looked at the world in a selective manner. A straight look at the international agenda of democracy and human rights took place a little later.

Mexico Looks at the World and the World Takes a Hard Look at Mexico's Record

The government of Ernesto Zedillo (1994–2000) illustrates the transition from Mexico's resistance of international pressure in the area of human rights toward a more systematic policy of tactical concessions and, finally, to the recognition of the validity of international norms. Changes in Mexican foreign policy throughout Zedillo's presidential term were clear and numerous. The Mexican government invited the IAHRC's representatives and other UN rapporteurs to the country, accepted the jurisdiction of the Inter-American Court of Human Rights, and signed a treaty with the European Union that included a democratic clause as well as the statute of the International Criminal Court (ICC). According to Foreign Minister José Ángel Gurría, the invitation of the IAHRC's representatives demonstrated the government's new attitude concerning the subject of human rights: "This is our approach; a new approach since things were not handled like this in previous administrations. On many occasions, Mexico had adopted a cautious position, a position of great prudence in our contacts, because we considered that those institutions questioned our country" (Aponte 1997, 1). The Mexican government decided not only to join the game but also to benefit from it. In justifying the recognition of the jurisdiction of the Inter-American Court, Minister Rosario Green underlined that such a forum constituted "a place to argue if we disagree; to present our evidence so that we are not judged *in absentia*" (Medina 1998).

The acceptance of the validity of international norms, however, was limited to norms within a state system. The Zapatista uprising and subsequent events such as the killings in Acteal in 1997 not only attracted international attention but also literally opened the door to foreign actors who came into the country to observe the human rights situation *in situ*. In this way, even though the government accepted international norms, it did not recognize that any foreign actor was legitimate to demand compliance. International non-governmental organizations (NGOs) were not valid interlocutors for Zedillo's government, as the conflict with Amnesty International general director, Pierre Sané, demonstrated.

The Mexican president refused to meet with Sané, arguing that no appointment had been arranged. A few months later, Zedillo met a group of NGOs in Paris, and Amnesty International was excluded. The meeting became an occasion for accusing the Mexican government of not having complied in the area of defence and protection of human rights in the country. Facing such criticism, the Mexican government proposed to restrict the placement of complaints by NGOs at the IAHRC, but the project was not approved at the OAS. Moreover, the Mexican government issued a law to control the visits of human rights observers to Mexico. According to this law, potential visitors had to apply to the Ministry of Interior for a special visa, and they had to demonstrate the "seriousness" of the organization they represented as well as their previous experience as international observers. Visits would only be possible in small groups and for a short period of time. Amnesty International and Human Rights Watch Americas immediately criticized the new legislation (Elizalde 1998, 12; Cason and Brooks 1998, 5).

Zedillo's About-Face on Human Rights Organizations

The fact that Zedillo's government decided not to recognize NGOs as interlocutors and to control their activity in the country did not mean, however, that it completely ignored the position of such actors. The government created a Comisión intersecretarial para la atención de los compromisos internacionales de México en materia de derechos humanos, in which NGOs could express their views. The creation of the IAHRC is also interesting since it filtered "the outside" to "the inside"—through governmental agents, and with the opinion of civil society, the commission would see to it that Mexico complied with the international norms that the country had already agreed with. The agreement was justified on the basis that "[t]he international community has promoted the universality of human rights through the validity and application of various international instruments which promote and protect them ... Mexico fully agrees, on the basis of the beliefs of its people, with the fight in favor of human rights; hence its participation in the process of protecting individual rights and fundamental liberties." Moreover, according to the agreement, one of the national development plan objectives was the rule of law "which would be inconceivable without complete respect for human rights ("Decreto por el" 1997)."

Were tactical concessions a choice or a reaction? It was a choice but a restricted one. We might even talk about a choice that was close to a forced reaction. The point at which conditionality became clearer was when the country was considering the democratic clause in the agreement with the European Union. Despite the fact that there was some discussion about the drafting of the clause, which was at some point considered to be an intervention, the Mexican government finally accepted it, arguing that both Mexico and the European Union guided their domestic and foreign policies "by human rights and the democratic principles of each sovereignty" (Vázquez and Ortiz 1997, 10). It should be mentioned that the agreement was Zedillo's primary foreign policy objective, and it was signed in his last year of office. Throughout the period, however, choice seemed to be rather free or to have had another purpose that was closer to the idea of constructing a different identity—a democratic Mexico. And it is at this point, of course, when domestic factors, linked or not to human rights issues and international NGOs, acquired a key role. Human rights violations in Mexico were no longer easy to ignore, and the government's efforts to keep away NGOs, domestic and international, only strengthened the image of a country whose human rights record was far from satisfactory.

A Human Rights Foreign Policy?

One of Vicente Fox's priorities as he took office was to consolidate Mexico's presence in the club of democratic countries. In his first annual report, Fox enumerated five "axes" that would guide his government's foreign policy, including "Foreign Minister Jorge Castañeda's declarations that Mexico recognized human rights as being universal and indivisible (Tello Díaz 2001, 22–24; Castañeda 2001, 72–73).

The purpose of giving human rights a key place in foreign policy, and the strategy that would be pursued, accordingly, had been clear since the National Action Party took office. Mariclaire Acosta was named under-secretary of foreign affairs for human rights,[8] and the ministry initiated a number of international activities that were expected to perform the same function that NAFTA had performed before—to commit the country to changing abroad in order to lock in domestic reform. Jorge Castañeda argues that foreign policy was not only the result but also the cause of domestic change, and it would be an instrument to achieve the consolidation of a new political culture. He explains: "We cannot tighten and deepen our links with other nations expecting that this interaction will not have consequences on us: the support in international fora for certain universal principles, and the adoption of positions consistent with the values we profess, impose on us the obligation to act in a compatible manner in our domestic regime" (Castañeda 2002). The day after Fox took office, his government signed a technical assistance agreement with the office of the IAHRC, and the foreign policy agreements and actions that followed were numerous: the legislation for international observers was repealed; General José Francisco Gallardo was freed,[9] as were some environmental activists from Guerrero; and the Argentinean businessman Miguel Cavallo was extradited to Spain for crimes committed during the military rule in Argentina. Mexico fully supported the Declaration of Quebec City, therefore endorsing the view that a democratic regime was an essential condition of membership in the hemispheric free trade area (and reinforcing its commitment to strengthen representative democracy, promote good governance, and protect human rights and fundamental freedoms).

The Fox Government and International Human Rights Norms

Mexico accepted the Democratic Inter-American Charter, and an assessment of the situation of human rights in the country was elaborated in coordination with the United Nations.[10] For the first time in the history of the bilateral relationship, policy toward Cuba included the issue of human rights on the island. Between December 2000 and October 2003, fifteen human rights representatives visited the country: ten from the United Nations, four from the IAHRC, and one from Amnesty International. Between 2001 and 2003, the government ratified four human rights instruments and accepted one, but it refused to ratify three and maintained reservations and declarations to thirteen international human rights instruments.[11]

The Ministry of Foreign Affairs has confirmed that Fox's government has signed the Inter-American Convention on the Forced Disappearance of Persons, the Facultative Protocol Relating to the Participation of Children in Armed Conflict, the Facultative Protocol to the International Pact on Civil and Political Rights, the Facultative Protocol to the Convention against Torture, Other Cruel, Inhuman or Degrading Treatment or Punishment, the Convention on the Inapplicability of Prescription to Military Crimes and Crimes against Humanity, the Facultative Protocol Relating to the Sale of Children, Child Prostitution and the Utilization of Children in Pornography, and the Facultative Protocol to the Convention on the Elimination of All Forms of Discrimination against Women. Mexico has also recognized the competence of the Committee for the Elimination of Racial Discrimination and the Committee against Torture, and partially withdrew its reservations and interpretive declaration to the American Human Rights Convention regarding the active vote of religious ministers and the celebration of religious public acts, as well its reservation to Article 25(b)) of the International Convention on Civil and Political Rights, regarding the active vote of religious ministers. Mexico, according to the ministry, is now part of the most important international human rights instruments.[12] The Mexican government has issued an open and permanent invitation to any UN system mechanism wishing to observe Mexico's human rights situation *in situ*.

Foreign policy change in the area of human rights is now a certainty. Did foreign policy change because the regime changed? The answer to this question depends on the date one chooses as the beginning of regime change. If Fox's government is considered to be the "new regime," the answer would be in the negative since foreign policy began changing before this government came into office. On the other hand, it could be argued that Fox's policy was precisely the result of previous regime change. A more plausible argument suggests that *"la alternancia"* sped up and probably consolidated change in foreign policy, but its course had already been established. In any case, the importance of *"la alternancia"* is beyond doubt. There is a clear democratic legitimacy that makes it easier to aspire to become a member in the club of democratic countries in the world. The reasons and justifications for change, however, provide new elements. In this sense, the rupture with the previous regime—that of the PRI—for which foreign policy had also been useful, allowed for a policy design that was not necessarily reactive to international "pressures" but which also took the initiative—that is, a policy directed more clearly toward the construction of a new identity.

Foreign Policy and the State of Human Rights in Mexico

Foreign policy seems to have changed enough in favour of human rights, but a key question remains. Has such change been effective in improving the state of human rights in Mexico? Has the strategy of committing the country to international norms worked to change norms and practices domestically? These questions are obviously not easy to answer, but it may be safe to argue that the change in foreign policy was quicker and easier than the change in domestic politics. Changing attitudes in the political class and in society in general is not as straightforward as changing the outlook of a small elite deciding that Mexico should join one or another international treaty.

Without underestimating the work of many individuals and organizations, even at the official level, one can suggest that the change in foreign policy did have a positive influence, at least in contributing to the awareness of human rights violations in Mexico. By opening the country up to the outside world, by inviting foreign actors to monitor elections and to observe human rights, and by recognizing a plurality of actors within and outside the country, Mexican governments are recognizing the seriousness of the situation and exposing some willingness to improve it. The external circumstances under which Mexico has managed to design a human rights foreign policy, however, are no longer favourable.

The New Challenges Ahead for Mexico's New President

There is no question that the decline of the importance of human rights in the US agenda has negatively affected all efforts undertaken since the 1990s to promote them in Mexico. Moreover, the war against terror seems to be contradicting the idea of this culture. In this respect, the Mexican government has supported resolutions at the United Nations and at the OAS to emphasize the importance of protecting human rights in the fight against terrorism.[13] However, it does not look as if present international conditions will change in the near future so that the continuation of a foreign policy that privileges human rights will indeed be a challenge to Mexico's new government. Thus, the support of the incoming president to such policy will in itself be a good sign in terms of the consolidation and permanence of human rights in Mexican politics.

On the other hand, no matter how universal human rights are and how influential the international system may be, the effective protection of human rights is not possible without a state that is willing to do so. Fox's government has promoted the compatibility of domestic law with Mexico's international commitments by proposing a series of reforms, including modifications to Articles 1, 2, 4, 18, and 115 of the Mexican Constitution, in order to prohibit discrimination and to strengthen the principle of equality of indigenous peoples. These changes were approved by Congress (Camacho 2005, 14–16). On 23 June 2004, the Chamber of Deputies approved a reform to Articles 14 and 22, openly prohibiting the death penalty. On 21 June 2005, after modifying Article 21, the Senate ratified a decree thereby approving the Statute of the International Criminal Court. President Fox also sent Congress an initiative to modify Articles 3, 15, 33, 73, 89, 102, 103, and 105 in order to grant human rights constitutional recognition in general. In March 2004, the president sent another initiative to Congress to modify the judicial system regarding judicial guarantees, persecution, minors' justice, and the jail system (ibid.).[14]

Despite all of these efforts to "harmonize" Mexico's international commitments with domestic law, the state of human rights in Mexico is far from satisfactory. As the reports from Amnesty International and Human Rights Watch indicate at the beginning of this chapter, good intentions and initiatives have not translated into a radical improvement of human rights. The case of numerous women murdered in Ciudad Juárez is a constant reminder of the government's limitations not only to prevent violations of human rights but also to punish those guilty of them. The consolidation and enforcement of domestic law to prevent and punish human rights violations is indeed one of the major challenges that Mexico's new president will face. The creation of a culture that is protective of human rights is indeed a huge task. More specifically, the new government will have to take some assertive action on specific cases, such as the death of women in Ciudad Juárez, the so-called "dirty war," the attacks on journalists and defenders of human rights, and equality for indigenous peoples, among others, if it wants to be taken seriously in the area of human rights.

Illegal Immigrants in a Hostile, Security-Focused World

Another challenge that is linked to human rights protection concerns Mexican illegal immigrants in the United States. The problem of illegal immigration is, of course, much more complex than just the violation of human rights, but one of Mexico's traditional positions about it has been precisely to focus on the defence of the immigrants' human rights (Griego and Verea 1998). The Mexican government has recently promoted resolutions to protect the immigrant's human rights in international fora, especially the United Nations and the OAS.[15] As is well known, President Fox's original proposal for a migration program did not progress, especially after the terrorist attacks in 2001, but recent rallies in American cities suggest that the subject might well become an important one in the bilateral agenda. It is likely that, whatever the outcome, the next Mexican government will continue to insist, bilaterally and multilaterally, on the obligation of host governments to protect the migrants' human rights regardless of their legal condition. The three main presidential candidates, Roberto Madrazo from the Institutional Revolutionary Party, Andrés Manuel López Obrador from the Democratic Revolutionary Party, and Felipe Calderón from the National Action Party, have of course underlined the importance of the migrants issue in their foreign and domestic policies. López Obrador has gone so far as to declare that his government's main foreign policy objective would be to defend the legal rights of immigrants in the United States by turning Mexican consulates into "something like" attorney offices (López Obrador 2006). Calderón and Madrazo continue to endorse the idea of an immigration treaty with the United States (ibid.). The three candidates, however, recognize the importance of undertaking effective industrial policies in Mexico as a means to decreasing illegal immigration to the United States.

As this chapter has demonstrated, Mexico's foreign policy has already contributed significantly to the awareness and, to a certain extent, to the improvement of human rights in Mexico. There is no doubt that a human rights foreign policy will continue to face a hostile international context and an extremely hard and complex domestic reality. During the presidential election, the climate of violence and impunity is as visible as ever. Police abuses and organized crime-related violence have accompanied the candidates' campaigns: steelworkers were violently removed from their work premises in the Mexican state of Michoacán in April; police in the state of San Salvador Atenco violently repressed a group of street vendors in May, and some were accused of sexually abusing at least twenty-three women; teachers were violently repressed in the state of Oaxaca in June; and a series of executions have taken place in different states of the republic. The most recent one involved seven people in the state of Guerrero ("Deja 2 muertos" 2006; Amnesty International 2006a; Amnesty International 2006b; Enfrenta Guerrero 2006).[16] There is little doubt that the next president will face a complex domestic situation, and, except for drug traffic-related violence and public safety, there are no clear signs as to whether the next president will have a human rights policy as such. The improvement of the state of human rights is indeed a domestic battle, but the role of foreign policy should not be underestimated as it may constitute a constant reminder of the importance of human rights. The election of Mexican ambassador Luis Alfonso de Alba to head the recently created UN Human Rights Council may help to reassure the international community that foreign policy continues to collaborate in developing a human rights culture in Mexico ("Asume México" 2006). This is a step in the right direction.

NOTES

1   See México, resumen de país, http://www.hrw.org/spanish/ind_anual/2005/mexico .html#mexico. The dirty war is known as the period between the 1960s and 1970s when the Mexican government implemented a series of repressive policies which included the "disappearence" and killing of political dissidents.

2 The Mexican government recognized the Spanish Republic so that diplomatic relations could not be broken.

3 It is generally agreed that Echeverría's foreign policy was designed to underline the progressive and nationalistic nature of the Mexican regime and to co-opt groups from the Left that had been alienated by the regime after the 1968 killing of students by certain Mexican police groups (it is not clear whether it was the army who opened fire) (Shapira 1978, 56; Rico 1991, 19–67).

4 The National Action Party complained about legislative elections in Chihuahua (1985), municipal elections in Durango (1986), state elections in Chihuahua (1986), and legislative and municipal elections in the state of Mexico (1990). See the following commission reports: Organization of American States (OAS), Inter-American Human Rights Commission (IAHRC), Resolution no. 01/90, cases 9768, 9780 and 9828 (Mexico), 17 May 1990; and Organization of American States, Inter-American Human Rights Commission, Doc. OEA/Ser.L/V/11.85, Annual Report 1993, 1 February 1993, and Doc. OEA/Ser./v/ii.85, Annual Report 1993.

5 See the following resolutions on El Salvador: Resolutions A/Res/38/101 (1983); A/Res/39/119 (1984); A/Res/40/139 (1985); and A/Res/41/157 (1986). On Guatemala, see Resolutions A/Res/38/100 (1983); A/Res/39/120 (1984); A/Res/40/140 (1985); and A/Res/41/156 (1986). On Chile, see Resolutions A/Res/38/102 (1983); A/Res/39/121 (1984); A/Res/40/145 (1985); A/Res/41/161 (1986); and A/Res/42/147 (1987). On South Africa, see Resolutions A/Res/ 39/15 (1984) and A/Res/41/95 (1986).

6 The work of Margaret Keck and Kathryn Sikkink (1998) refers to the "boomerang effect," and Sikkink and Thomas Risse (1999) suggest a "spiral model." What they propose is that foreign policy has domestic repercussions, and, through a spiral consisting of five stages, a repressive government ends up internalizing international human rights norms.

7 A good example of how international pressure promotes domestic change (however superficial) is the creation of Mexico's National Human Rights Commission. According to Kathryn Sikkink (1993, 433–34), President Salinas was so concerned about Mexico's external image that he took some preventive measures, such as the creation of the commission only a few days before he met President George Bush. Another example is the appointment of Jorge Carpizo (former US Supreme Court judge and president of the National Human Rights Commission at the time of his appointment) as general attorney a few days before Salinas met president-elect Bill Clinton.

8 Mariclaire Acosta is a well-known human rights activist and had long worked with different Mexican and international non-governmental organizations before taking office. Her appointment to the post was a clear signal of the government's opening.

9 General Gallardo's case was well known domestically and internationally. Gallardo was charged with fourteen offences by the military, but he and many others alleged that the ultimate reason for his imprisonment had been his proposal of creating an ombudsman for the military. The IAHRC and Amnesty International had

recommended Gallardo's release since 1997. See the Amnesty annual reports since then. http://www.amnesty.org/es.

10 Democratic Inter-American Charter, www.oas.org. As a result of this *diagnóstico*, President Fox was presented with a National Human Rights Programme (Programa Nacional de Derechos Humanos) on 10 December 2004. This program established guidelines for federal public administration offices to design public policy from a human rights perspective. It also stated the tasks and commitments of the executive in its relations with local governments and the National Congress (Camacho 2005).

11 http://www.comovamos.presidencia.gob.mx/.

12 México, Secretaría de Relaciones Exteriores. http://www.sre.gob.mx/substg/dh/.

13 United Nations Resolution E/RES/2005/80 (2005), presented since 2003, and Resolution AG/RES.2143 (XXXV–0/05) (2005) at the OAS, presented in July 2005 (Camacho 2005, 9).

14 The text of the initiative containing all proposals can be obtained at "Oficio con el que remite iniciativa de decreto que reforma diversos artículos de la Constitución Política de los Estados Unidos mexicanos, en material de derechos humanos," http://www.sre.gob.mx/substg/dh/.

15 For example, Mexico has promoted a resolution in the United Nations since 1998 (Doc. E/RES/2005/47 2005) and presented another resolution at the OAS in July 2005 (Doc. AG/RES.2130 (XXXV–0/05) (2005) (Camacho 2005, 9).

16 For all organized-crime-related violence, see the Mexican press from at least April 2006.

REFERENCES

Amnesty International, Mexican Section. Annual Report 2005 http://web.amnistia.org.mx/prensa/articulo_print.php?id=300&PHPSESSID=fd8eadb7.

———. 2006a. "Seguridad/preocupación médica/juicio justo y nuevos motivos de preocupación: Detención arbitraria/tortura (actualización núm. 1)," 17 May. http://web.amnistia.org.mx/prensa/articulo_print.php?id=366&PHPSESSID=985fba74da.

———. 2006b. "Temor por la seguridad de maestros y miembros del SNTE en Oaxaca," 15 June. http://web.amnistia.org.mx/prensa/articulo_print.php?id=375.

Aponte, David, "Gurría: se aceptarán recomendaciones de Rodley". 1997. *La Jornada*, 19 August.

"Asume México presidencia de Derechos Humanos en la ONU." 2006. *El Universal*, 19 June. http://www.eluniversal.com.mx/notas/vi_356387.html.

Benítez Manaut, Raúl. 1996. "La ONU en México: elecciones presidenciales de 1994." *Foro Internacional* 36(3): 533–65.

Camacho, Juan José Gómez. 2005. "La política exterior de México en la nueva agenda internacional: protección de los derechos humanos." Mexico City: Secretaría de Relaciones Exteriores [unpublished document].

Cason, Jim, and David Brooks. 1998. "Human Rights Watch: expulsar a extranjeros, acto 'arbitrario'" *La Jornada*, 16 May.

Castañeda, Jorge. 1995. *México y el orden internacional. Obras completas. I Naciones Unidas.* Mexico City: Instituto Matías Romero de Estudios Diplomáticos-El Colegio de México.

————. 2001. "Los ejes de la política exterior de México." *Nexos* (December): 66–74.

————. 2002. "Política exterior y cambio democrático." *Reforma*, 12 July. http://www.reforma.com.

Declaration of Managua for the Promotion of Democracy and Development. AG/DEC.4 (XXIII–0/93). Twenty-Third Regular Session. Managua, Nicaragua, June 7–11, 1993. OEA/Ser.P/XXIII.0.2, September 30, 1993, vol. 1. http://scm.oas.org/pdfs/agres/ago3807E01.pdf

Declaration of Québec City. Third Summit of the Americas to strengthen representative democracy, promote good governance and protect human rights and fundamental freedoms. http://www.summit-americas.org/Documents%20for%20Quebec%20City%20Summit/Quebec/Declaration%20of%20Quebec%20City%20-%20Eng%20-%20final.html/.

"Decreto por el que se constituye la Comisión Intersecretarial para la atención de los compromisos internacionales de México en materia de derechos humanos." 1997. 17 October. http://info4.juridicas.unam.mx/ijure/nrm/1/71/1.htm?=iste.

Elizalde, Triunfo, 1998. "Restricciones 'sin prcedente' en las nuevas reglas para observadores: AI". *La Jornada*, 31 de mayo.

"Enfrenta Guerrero domingo de sangre." 2006. *Reforma*, 26 June. http://www.reforma.com/nacional/articulo/661162/default.asp?Param=7&PlazaConsulta=.

García y Griego, and Manuel y Mónica Verea. 1998. "Colaboración sin concordancia: la migración en la nueva agenda bilateral México-Estados Unidos." In Mónica Verea Campos, Rafael Fernández de Castro, and Sidney Weintraub, eds., *Nueva agenda bilateral en la relación México-Estados Unidos*, 107–34. Mexico City: ITAM-UNAM-CISAN-FCE.

Henríquez, Elio, 1998. "Desmantelan otro cabildo Zapatista mil soldados y policías". *La Jornada*, 2 May.

Keck, Margaret E., and Kathryn Sikkink. 1998. *Activists beyond Borders: Advocacy Networks in International Politics.* Ithaca, NY: Cornell University Press.

López Obrador, Andrés Manuel. 2006. "Debe modificarse la política económica porque fracasó el modelo neoliberal vigente, afirma López Obrador." Palabras del candidato ala Presidencia de la coalición "Por el bien de todos," durante el encuentro con miembros de la Asociación de Académicos "Daniel Cosío Villegas," de El Colegio de México, 24 April. http://www.amlo.org.mx/noticias/impdocumento.html?id=18938&ref=discursos.

Luna, Lucía, 1993. "Derechos humanos: incorporan a México al club de los 'renegados.'" 1993. *Proceso* 869: 40.

Medina, María Elena, 1998. "Presentará Ejecutivo iniciativa en septiembre", Reforma.com, 5 May. http://busquedas.gruporeforma.com/reforma/ Documentos/DocumentoImpresa.aspx?¡Docid=3746-1031&strr= rosariogreen.

Protocolo de Reformas a la Carta de la oea, "Protocolo de Washington", December 14, 1992. 1–E.Rev.oea. oea/Ser.A./2Add.3. http://www.oas.org/ juridico/ Spanish/firmas/a-56-html.

Rico, Carlos. 1991. *Hacia la globalización. México y el mundo. Historia de sus relaciones exteriores*, vol. 8. Mexico City: Senado de la República.

Risse, Thomas, and Kathryn Sikkink, eds. 1999. *The Power of Human Rights: International Norms and Domestic Change.* Cambridge: Cambridge University Press.

Santiago Commitment to Democracy and the Renewal of the Inter-American System, AG/RES.1080 (XXI–0/91). Twenty-First regular session, Santiago, Chile, June 3–8, 1991. oea/Ser.P/xxi/0.2. Vol. 1. http://scm.oas.org/pdfs/ agres/ago3805E01.pdf.

Shapira, Yoram. 1978. *Mexican Foreign Policy under Echeverría.* Washington Papers. London: Sage.

Sikkink, Kathryn. 1993. "Human Rights, Principled Issue-Networks, and Sovereignty in Latin America." *International Organization* 47(3): 428–29.

Tello Díaz, Carlos. 2001. "Entrevista a Jorge G. Castañeda." *Arcana* (December): 20–25.

Torres, Blanca. 1991. *De la guerra al mundo bipolar. México y el mundo. Historia de sus relaciones exteriores*, vol. 5. Mexico City: Senado de la República.

Torres Carlos, Daniela Morales, Antonio Aguilera and E. Martínez, "Deja 2 muertos y más de 40 heridos desalojo de mineros en Michoacán." 2006. *La Jornada*, 21 April. http://www.jornada.unam.mx/2006/04/21/index. php?section=sociedad&article=053n1soc.

United Nations. 1945. "Opinion of the Department of Foreign Relations of Mexico Concerning the Dumbarton Oaks Proposals for the Creation of a General International Organization." In *United Nations Conference on International Organization Documents*, Doc. 2G/7(c). London and New York: Library of Congress.

Universidad Nacional Autónoma de México (UNAM). 1989. Centro de Investigaciones Interdisciplinarias en Humanidades. *México en Centroamérica. Expediente de Documentos Fundamentales (1979–1986).* México, UNAM.

Vázquez, Antonio and Humberto Ortiz, "Lecomte: los resultados del 6 de Julio ayudaron al pacto comercial con la UE". 1997. *La Jornada*, 19 July.

The Inter-American Convention on Forced Disappearance of Persons and the American Human Rights Convention may be found at www.oas.org.

The Facultative Protocol Relating to the Participation of Children in Armed Conflict, the Facultative Protocol to the International Pact on Civil and Political Rights, the Facultative Protocol to the Convention against Torture, Other Cruel, Inhuman or Degrading Treatment or Punishment, the Convention on the Inapplicability of Prescription to Military Crimes and Crimes against Humanity, the Facultative Protocol Relating to the Sale of Children, Child Prostitution and the Utilization of Children in Pornography, and the Facultative Protocol to the Convention on the Elimination of All Forms of Discrimination against Women, the Committee for the Elimination of Racial Discrimination and the Committee against Torture may be found at www.un.org.

3

THE BUSH REVOLUTION IN FOREIGN POLICY: CANADA AND MEXICO AT THE CROSSROADS

5

The Inconsistent Neighbour: Canadian Resistance and Support for the US Foreign Policy Counter-Revolution

Stephen Clarkson

While all countries have to react to American foreign policy, the United States' two continental neighbours experience this dilemma with a particularly acute intensity. Given their near-total dependence on selling their exports to American customers and given the enormous power asymmetry between the global superpower and its geographical periphery, Canada and Mexico have encountered unusual difficulty during the opening years of the twenty-first century. They have been forced to reconcile the management of important policy differences with Washington on global matters with the maintenance of good relations with their economic locomotive. Before raising the diplomatic dimension of Canada's centre-periphery dynamic during the administration of George W. Bush, this chapter will examine to what extent the United States' forty-third president actually did precipitate a foreign policy revolution.

The Bush Counter-Revolution

The Tough New International Economic Order

Continuity was certainly the subtext as far as the United States' global economic policy was concerned. Indeed, George H.W. Bush, Sr., had presided over the opening years of the Uruguay Round (1986–94), which had climaxed with the Clinton administration's triumphant signing of the Marrakech Agreement Establishing the World Trade Organization in 1994.[1] The resulting World Trade Organization (WTO) signalled that American economic norms were being universalized in a muscular new hegemonic order in order to achieve the silent magic of the powerful new international legal order that President Theodore Roosevelt had begun ninety years earlier—an "open door" for US enterprise in every foreign state's market.

It was *muscular* because, as Sylvia Ostry observes, it had the strongest dispute settlement mechanism of any international regime (Ostry 2001). It was *hegemonic* because it was supported by all other capitalist states, in particular, the neo-conservative Canadian governments of Brian Mulroney and Jean Chrétien. This order was imposed on weak states in the global South, which were pressured to sign on with assurances that the liberated market would guarantee them perpetual growth.

While these norms had already been challenged through anti-globalization demonstrations in late 1999 in the streets of Seattle by non-governmental organizations from the North and behind closed doors at the same WTO ministerial meeting by many states from the South, Governor Bush remained as committed to global trade and investment liberalization as had Bill Clinton, the man he was campaigning to succeed in the White House. Fostering trade liberalization, which imposed US norms on its economic partners, remained part of Bush's vision for the world, whether multilaterally with the global defence of intellectual property rights for big pharmaceutical companies in the WTO's Doha round of trade talks; hemispherically in the push to have the North American Free Trade Agreement (NAFTA) model prevail over Brazil's preference for a more state-driven approach to a free trade area of the Americas;[2] continentally with its Central America Free Trade Agreement (2004); or bilaterally by signing trade deals with Chile and Singapore (United States 2002, 18).

The Soft Political Global Order

While a global regulatory regime favouring the further expansion of US transnational capital suited the Republicans just fine, Governor Bush clearly wanted to change the Democrats' internationalism. In light of the Clinton-mandated offensive to free Kosovo from Serbia, the Texan's admonition that the United States should be humble in its foreign policy suggested a less interventionist, more withdrawn global stance. Once ensconced in the White House, however, Bush gave conflicting signals, appointing the moderate Colin Powell to the Department of State while giving the aggressive Donald Rumsfeld control of the Pentagon. His own positions on matters international were telegraphed by Condoleezza Rice whom he installed as national security advisor. Pupil and professor interacted constantly, whether in the White House gym or the Camp David woods. *She* talked about proceeding "from the firm ground of the national interest and not from the interest of an illusory international community" (Hirsh 2002, 32). *He* described his foreign policy as a "new realism" in which America's efforts should steer clear of what he disparaged as "international social work." Instead, it should return to cultivating great power relations and rebuilding the military (Ikenberry 2002, 46).

In sharp distinction to Clinton's foreign policy, the Rice doctrine's implementation delivered a series of blows to the international order that had been recommended by hard-liners who worked out their program in such think tanks as the American Enterprise Institute. In rapid succession, the Bush administration announced its opposition to the Kyoto Protocol, the small arms convention, the Treaty between the United States and the USSR on the Limitation of Anti-Ballistic Missile Systems (Anti-Ballistic Missile Treaty), and the International Criminal Court.[3] This concerted counter-revolution, which moved American foreign policy toward a mix of behavioural unilateralism, ecological isolationism, and military triumphalism disconnected the Bush administration from the evolving multilateral order and placed it at odds with Canada's traditional penchant for multilateralism. In the short term, neither Canada nor the rest of the international community could do much beyond wringing their hands in collective dismay.

The Anti-Terrorist Security Order

The global security context following the end of the Cold War in 1990, which had been evolving confusedly for a decade in the more anarchic regions of the Balkans and Africa where concerns for human security had created new dilemmas of intervention for the international community in failed or failing states, was turned on its head in the course of two hours on the morning of 11 September 2001. The cataclysmic terrorist attacks on New York and Washington proved to be a political opportunity that allowed the fledgling Republican administration to save itself from the political doldrums in which it had been wallowing since its inauguration earlier that year. Exploiting the nation's trauma, it shifted its governing policy paradigm both internally and externally.

Domestically, the United States switched from a small-government neo-liberalism to a big-government security paradigm with its 2001 *Uniting and Strengthening America by Providing Appropriate Tools Required to Intercept and Obstruct Terrorism Act* (or USA PATRIOT *Act*).[4] Its homeland security response to the spectre of global terrorist networks flew in the face of the world order, which was based on trade and investment liberalization that had been constructed after the Second World War. This paradigm shift from economic border opening to military border closing was out of sync with the policy agendas of Uncle Sam's two territorial client-neighbours whose economic fortunes depended more than ever on maintaining an open frontier with the United States.

With the catastrophe dramatically proving how the same means that had generated America's growing wealth and prosperity—open economies and global communications systems—could be used to bring down the world's hegemon (Flynn, cited in Lachapelle 2001, 18), the president's handlers reinvented George W. Bush as a wartime president. Acting as the world's only remaining superpower and eschewing its traditional leadership role as the collaborative architect of a rules-based multilateral international system, the United States abruptly took on an unapologetically imperial role as unilateral enforcer of its new global-domination script (Nye 2002).

The Bush administration elevated the foreign war on terrorism to the top of its policy agenda in two stages to which Canada responded in two markedly differing ways. First, Bush's linking of his "war on terror" to the Taliban in Afghanistan caused Canada to revert to Cold War patterns in coordinating its military policies with the Americans to whom it offered practical support. When Washington engaged in a pre-emptive regime change in Iraq, dubiously rationalized by the Bush doctrine and misleadingly supported by questionable intelligence, the limits to Jean Chrétien's commitment to bilateral friendship became apparent.

Canada's Ambivalent Response

Whereas 11 September's attacks were understood abroad as *sabotage* requiring transnational cooperation among intelligence agencies, the US administration quickly constructed them as acts of *war*, requiring not just defence through improved counter-intelligence but also offence through military retribution and interdiction. Secretary of State Rumsfeld managed to restore the defence budget to Cold War levels in order both to pursue its war against Islamic *jihadists* and to fund his ballistic missile defence program (BMD), which was a repackaged version of the Reagan regime's ill-fated and satirically dubbed Star Wars project to shoot down missiles and so achieve US military control of space.[5]

In his speech to Congress on 20 September 2001, President Bush made it clear that he would not let any international institution stand in the way of his use of force when American security interests were perceived to be threatened. He also demanded full support from every other country by issuing a blunt ultimatum to world leaders: "Either you're with us or you're with the terrorists" (Hillmer, Carment, and Hampson 2003, 3). Within a month, he tested the fidelity of his allies by turning the "war on terrorism" into an actual war in the Himalayas.

Afghanistan and the Powell Doctrine

Buttressed by the worldwide outpouring of sympathy for Americans that followed the collapse of the World Trade Center's twin towers, Secretary of State Colin Powell assembled a supportive international coalition by promising a clear mission to topple the fundamentalist Taliban government in Afghanistan, which he credibly identified as harbouring Osama Bin Laden's terrorist operation, Al-Qaeda. Concurring with the international consensus that attacking the pariah Taliban and its associates in Al-Qaeda was justified, Ottawa signed on to the Powell doctrine. Somewhat belatedly in February 2002, Prime Minister Chrétien committed 750 Canadian soldiers from the Princess Patricia's Light Infantry Regiment to be deployed around Kandahar as part of a US army task force and under US command. This decision to go to war soon became embroiled in political controversy. Some Canadians were alarmed by the implications of their soldiers fighting *for*, rather than *with*, the Americans. More were shocked to learn that these troops were handing over captured Taliban fighters to their US military commanders who insisted that the Geneva Convention forbidding the use of torture in the treatment of prisoners of war did not apply to these enemy combatants.[6] The dismay generated by this violation of Canada's treaty obligations was compounded by the loss of four Canadian soldiers killed by American fighter pilots in a "friendly fire" incident, for which President Bush issued an offensively belated apology (Canadian Broadcasting Corporation 2005).

When Canada's support for the American war in Afghanistan was rewarded with increased duties imposed on British Columbia's lumber and the Prairie provinces' wheat shipments, Canadians learned that acting as an unconditional ally—even at the cost of breaking international law, violating its principles, and losing its soldiers—did not yield benefits in other areas of Canada-US relations, as had been anticipated in public by International Trade Minister Pierre Pettigrew.

Iraq and the Bush Doctrine

A year after the 11 September attacks, the Bush administration released its National Security Strategy (NSS), which proceeded from the proposition that the "United States possesses unprecedented—and unequalled—strength and influence in the world," economically, politically, and militarily (United States 2002, 1). Speaking the language of Wilsonian internationalism, much of the NSS's rhetoric gave the impression that continuity rather than change prevailed in the National Security Council. Other parts of the document demonstrated that the unilateralist group Straussean, a neo-conservative, anti-détente policy network from the old Reagan administration including Secretary of Defence Donald Rumsfeld, Deputy-Secretary Paul Wolfowitz, Vice-President Dick Cheney, and the arch-hawk Richard Perle, had won the struggle to redefine American foreign policy (Atlas 2003). The moderately multilateralist approach of Colin Powell, with its preference for deterrence and containment, had been shredded. In a blunt statement of faith in the value of hard power, the NSS legitimized America's right to strike pre-emptively in anticipation of any perceived threat to its interests.

Yet when the Bush administration constructed Iraq's weapons of mass destruction (WMD) as an immediate threat to US security, it became apparent that Canada would have difficulty keeping in step with the global leader. The notion of forced disarmament through pre-emptive regime change, which the Bush doctrine promulgated, was at odds with Canadian non-interventionist views on non-proliferation. Furthermore, Canadians did not feel threatened by Iraq. As the debate proceeded over whether the international community should attack Saddam Hussein, it became evident that there were limits to how far Jean Chrétien could be pushed by Washington. Owing to a lack of convincing evidence, the Bush administration had trouble developing rationales for war, based either on Iraq's possession of WMD or on its links with Al-Qaeda, and was no more persuasive when shifting the argument to the human rights purpose of liberating the Iraqi people.[7] When it announced it would enforce regime change *despite* Iraq's voluntary disarmament under the United Nations' scrutiny and regardless of the Security Council's position, the rift widened with Canada, whose foreign policy was still firmly rooted in respect for international organizations and the primacy of international law (Lyon 1989).

As the Pentagon moved its military machine to Iraq's borders, Jean Chrétien repeatedly stressed that war with Iraq was "not justified" (McCarthy and Koring 2003). His new minister of foreign affairs, Bill Graham, warned that regime change threatened to destroy "the world order as we presently know it," adding that "we do not believe we have a right to invade" (Trickey and Naumetz 2002). Defying Washington's desire for unquestioning support, Canada reverted to its traditional role of helpful fixer. Canadian diplomats made concerted efforts to bridge a bitter transatlantic divide with a compromise resolution at the United Nations that would have bought time by postponing the US attack.

Ottawa's position converged with that of its other NAFTA partner, whose seat on the Security Council placed it uncomfortably in the limelight, and the two peripheries coordinated their efforts to find a diplomatic alternative to war. During an official visit to Mexico in late February 2003, Prime Minister Chrétien discussed with President Fox his proposal for a more precisely detailed and extended ultimatum. Chrétien then followed up with a telephone call to President Ricardo Lagos in Santiago, since Chile was serving on the Security Council. Fox had also styled himself in the role of broker, trying to bridge the differences between the Anglo-American perspective and others: "We have to convince the United States that we have alternatives to attain the objective of disarming Iraq ... What we believe is that we still have time in formulas and proposals to do what we have to do without a war" (Laghi and Koring 2003). Mexican foreign minister Ernesto Derbez raised the Canadian proposal with Powell during a meeting in Washington the next week, but the Bush administration interpreted its northern neighbour's goodwill in trying to bridge the transatlantic divide as unhelpful meddling. US ambassador Paul Cellucci said Canada's proposal for a new UN resolution, which would give the Iraqi dictator a 28 March deadline, was "not particularly helpful" because it would allow Iraq to hold out longer: "We can't let this go on for ever" (Perkel 2003).

When Canadian attempts to avert war with Iraq failed, Jean Chrétien was forced to decide whether to join Bush's campaign. After much muddying of the waters—even Chrétien's own foreign minister exclaimed that Canada backed regime change—the Canadian prime minister made an uncharacteristically sharp and public response, warning that the United States' unilateral adventure in regime change would undermine the United Nations (Laghi and Koring 2003).

Chrétien's decision not to participate in a US-led invasion of Iraq infuriated critics at home and in the United States. Despite being consistent with Canada's role in building the post-war international order and its long-standing penchant for multilateralism, Chrétien's view that Saddam Hussein must be disarmed—but *only* with UN approval—was far from coherent and certainly not universally popular. Business leaders who feared US retaliation in the form of border blockages, clamoured for Canada's military participation in the conflict or, at the very least, for rhetorical support for the US war since it was the political symbolism of moral support that the White House was expecting from its "close friend and ally" (Sanders 2003). Pro-war leaders in Canada's western provinces feared US reprisals for not supporting the country's most important ally, while staunch opposition to the war in Quebec and an upcoming provincial election in that province pulled the Liberals' foreign policy in the opposite direction (Parkin 2003, 7).

US ambassador Paul Cellucci's rebuke that Washington was "disappointed" with Canada unsettled the Canadian domestic political order, strengthening right-wing critics in the House of Commons and emboldening the premiers of Ontario and Alberta to voice their support for Washington's war with Iraq. Following Cellucci's rebuke, approval of the prime minister's handling of the situation "declined a significant 10 points" since the previous week's polling (Ipsos News Center 2003).

Canada's policy priorities had been generally congruent with Washington's until its unilateral venture in Iraq broke the global consensus favouring multilaterally negotiated approaches for resolving serious threats to international stability. This leaders-level disagreement sent shock waves through the Canadian political system. Jean Chrétien's decision was initially contested, since 48 percent of Canadians supported Bush's war. Going into the third week of the war, Canadians were split evenly between those who supported (48 percent) and those who opposed (48 percent) the US-led military action. However, an Ipsos Reid/CTV/*Globe and Mail* poll revealed that "a division is clearly developing between the two solitudes." A slight majority (54 percent) of Canadians outside Quebec expressed approval of the war, compared to a minority (29 percent) in Quebec. This division between Quebec and the rest of Canada also emerged on the question of whether to help the US coalition after the military action had begun: 51 percent of Canadians supported such a move (58 percent in English

Canada and 28 percent in Quebec). The prime minister's approval rating on the handling of the Iraq situation remained steady at 55 percent—with a major difference between Quebec (75 percent) and the rest of Canada (48 percent). In fact, 50 percent of Canadians outside of Quebec then disapproved of his handling of the crisis (compared to the 50 percent of English Canada that had expressed approval one week earlier) (Ipsos News Center 2003). Beyond the poll data, Chrétien's decision resonated strongly with the left-of-centre public in Canada, many of whom thought this was "Jean Chrétien's finest hour" (Morris 2003).

Ultimately, Chrétien's decision proved popular, particularly when the United States' rapid military victory on the battlefield turned into a prolonged disaster afterwards. Yet Canadians' smugness about their government's boycott of the American war was ill founded. Ironically, the Canadians indirectly provided more military support for the United States in Iraq than all of the forty-six countries that were fully supporting it, with the exception of Britain and Australia, providing twenty-five war planners, naval protection in the Persian Gulf, and air space for two to three US airplanes per day to refuel in Newfoundland (Sanders 2003). Canadian naval units had been dispatched to the Persian Gulf where they constituted an inter-operating component of the American fleet patrolling Iraq's coastal waters. When the Department of National Defence decided in February 2003 to deploy 1,200 peace-building troops to Kabul, it was easing the Pentagon's military burden in Afghanistan, thus letting it concentrate on its challenges in Iraq. Ambiguity, not to say hypocrisy, also characterized the Canadian response to the United States' continental application of its renewed war doctrine.

North America and the Rumsfeld Doctrine

The US war on terrorism may have increased the distance between the political leadership of the United States and Canada, but it accelerated cooperation between Canadian and American military personnel. At the continental headquarters of the North American Aerospace Defence Command (NORAD) in Colorado Springs, the Canadian second-in-command had been in charge of North America's airspace on 11 September. This close intermeshing of the two armed services led to the establishment of a joint North American planning group to prepare contingency plans for maritime or land threats and for military assistance to civilian authorities in emergencies. The opaque nature of negotiating Canada-US military integration and cooperation meant that discussions took place with little public deliberation about the content and consequences of the Pentagon's new Northern Command. Similar opacity enveloped issues involving the technological feasibility and military rationale for Ballistic Missile Defence (BMD).

Offsetting the Canadian government's hesitation about accepting its armed forces' integration with the Northern Command and the weaponization of space that BMD would entail was the enthusiasm of Canada's military industry. Already integrated under such institutional arrangements as the defence production sharing arrangements, it stood to benefit from BMD as it had from building components of the Pentagon's weapons systems throughout the Cold War.

The internal feuding that divided Canada over Iraq was followed by a break from three norms that had characterized Ottawa's political relationship with Washington. The first deviation was seen when the provincial premiers, who were concerned that Chrétien was damaging Canada-US relations and that his policy on Iraq would spill over into commercial areas of crucial importance to them, took matters into their own hands (Foot 2003). Led by Ralph Klein and Gordon Campbell from Alberta and British Columbia, the premiers toyed with the idea of establishing parallel summit relationships of their own with the US government. Campbell and Klein actually did travel to Washington in June 2003 to discuss with Vice-President Dick Cheney such topics as US tariffs on BC lumber and the ban on importing Canadian beef following the discovery of "mad cow" disease in a Canadian bovine. Despite having been hit with trade sanctions following Canada's military contribution in Afghanistan and despite J.L. Granatstein (2003) insisting that "there will be no favours for Canada from the White House," the two premiers, the right-wing Alliance Party, and Canadian big business clung to the belief that unconditional Canadian support for the Bush administration's military operations would spill over as goodwill that would help resolve bilateral trade conflicts.

The second departure from earlier patterns was the abandonment of "quiet diplomacy," which was the practice of keeping Canada-US disputes over each other's policy out of the public eye. During the debate over Iraq, Jean Chrétien allowed minor incidents in Ottawa to become major irritants in Washington. After belatedly asking his communication director, Françoise Ducros, to resign for referring to President Bush as a "moron," Chrétien failed to discipline Member of Parliament Carolyn Parrish for her comment "damn Americans ... I hate the bastards." He let his minister of natural resources Herb Dhaliwal's questioning of Bush's leadership as a statesman go unrebuked while upbraiding Alberta premier Ralph Klein for publicly backing the US war in Iraq (Brean and Alberts 2003). These "brouhahas" made the front pages throughout Canada and the United States, and they registered in the White House.

Even Chrétien appeared to be practising public diplomacy when he questioned the US government's analysis of terrorism by linking the attacks to "root causes" of poverty and the "arrogance" of the West (Blatchford 2003). As if to emphasize that he was in no way George Bush's poodle, Chrétien went out of his way, before attending his final G-7/G-8 summit in Evian, France, to criticize the US government for its budgetary deficit (McCarthy and Laghi 2003). On the American side, US ambassador to Canada, Paul Cellucci, and Condolleeza Rice hinted strongly that there would be serious consequences for Canada's refusal to support the United States in Iraq (Brean and Alberts 2003; Appleby 2003).

In threatening reprisals, the Bush administration itself explicitly broke a third unwritten law in Canada-US relations—the practice of non-linkage. As a result of Bush's with-us-or-against-us position, many in Canada took Cellucci's "disappointment" with Canada as a thinly veiled threat to impose costs on Canadian exporters. Had they compared notes with their colleagues in such other capitals as Mexico City, where the US ambassador made oblique threats, doomsters on the Canadian Right might not have warned so portentously that "there will be no favours for Canada from Washington or anywhere its reach extends" (Granatstein 2003) and that there would be a "serious economic fallout," the only visible riposte was the cancellation of President Bush's first official visit to Canada scheduled in May 2003. Since the bilateral meeting's agenda was about securing US guarantees for Canadian energy supplies, some Canadians saw the snub as more *caritas* than curse (McQuaig 2003).

Other punishment was said to include the difficulty that the prime minister experienced in getting phone time with Bush to resolve the US embargo on Canadian beef exports, although Ottawa's ambassador to Washington later stated in public that he had encountered no difficulty in pressing the Canadian government's case (Kergin 2005). Jack Granatstein (2003) argued that, having upset the Bush administration over Iraq, Canada could no longer count on the White House to temper the excesses of Congress. Unremarked, the supraconstitutional norms enshrined in both NAFTA and the WTO trade rules (Clarkson 2002)—two pillars of Chrétien's economic legacy (Clarkson and Lachapelle 2004)—provided Canada with some protection against finger twisting by an unhappy hegemony wanting to crimp Canada's diplomatic autonomy through trade retaliation.

Despite doomsday forecasts from the Canadian Right that Canada would be punished for its opposition to the war with Iraq, no tangible punishment was ever experienced. Indeed, only a few weeks after his rebuke, the US ambassador to Canada confirmed that Canada-US relations were essentially "back to normal" (Cattaneo 2003), while his Canadian counterpart, Michael Kergin, publicly stated his view that the handling of Canada-US disputes concerning mad cow disease and softwood lumber were unrelated to Canada's refusal to sign on to the war in Iraq and missile defence (Kergin 2005). These views suggest that the temperature of Ottawa-Washington's diplomatic relations was not an accurate gauge of the actual Canada-US relationship. For his part, Chrétien toyed with the idea of using energy exports as leverage in the dispute over softwood lumber. Ultimately, he refrained from making any threat to link energy to lumber, presumably because, in the words of a former Canadian ambassador to Washington, the United States "could easily out-link Canada" (Gotlieb 2003, 25).

In the context of conflictual relations between the two capitals, the Canadian prime minister's efforts at rapprochement were negligible. The gulf between Canadian and American policy paradigms was given fiscal support in the 2003 federal budget, which confirmed that Chrétien's spending priorities leaned more toward socio-economic than military objectives (Canada 2003). He pushed ahead with plans to decriminalize the possession of small amounts of marijuana despite repeated warnings of reprisals at the border. He also signalled that the federal government would not try to overturn an Ontario court's ruling that sanctioned the marriage of same-sex couples, a development that was deeply offensive to such social conservatives in Washington as the chief justice of the US Supreme Court and the president himself.

Militarily, Chrétien deflected immediate US pressure for troops to help secure and rebuild Iraq following hostilities there. In its February 2003 decision to redeploy 1,200 troops as peace builders in Afghanistan, Ottawa sought a European partner to make sure that Canadian soldiers in the International Security Assistance Force would not be in Kabul under US command. On the medium-term issues involving integration in continental and space defence, the government tried to remain non-committal toward the American proposals and actions. Ottawa resisted the idea of folding NORAD into the Northern Command, which would integrate all Canadian forces under a single structure with the US army, navy, marines, and air force. This defence mega-structure would be responsible for the territory stretching from the North Pole to Guatemala and parts of the Caribbean including Cuba. In the longer term, Ottawa continued to show discomfort with the idea of responding by military means to an act of terrorism that it understood as an essentially a non-military threat.

Canada also resisted giving its full support for BMD based on its principled opposition to the weaponization of space. Yet while Ottawa officially opposed any measure that would render the Anti-Ballistic Missile Treaty obsolete and raise the spectre of a renewed arms race, the joint forces of economic integration and Canadian-American cooperation in the defence of the continent ultimately led Ottawa to move toward endorsing both proposals. While he shelved the decision on missile defence on 8 May 2003 within a matter of weeks (Leblanc and McCarthy 2003), Chrétien gave the signal to go ahead with talks to discuss Canada's "potential" participation (Sallot 2003).

Former finance minister Paul Martin took over the reins of government in December 2003. Although as the leader of the opposition, he had long criticized the Chrétien government's excessively anti-American stance, once in power, he now appointed as his defence minister David Pratt, a Liberal who was overtly committed to Canadian support for BMD. He regrouped the Canadian armed forces in a "Canada Command" that mirrored the Pentagon's Northern Command and restructured the government's security bureaucracy to mirror the US Department of Homeland Defence. He reorganized his cabinet structure to give priority to his personal management of Canadian-American relations. He strengthened the political capacity of Canada's US embassy and visited the

White House in order to express a new cordiality for the US president, who was receptive to this overture, relieved that Chrétien had departed.

Two years later, it was as if Martin had taken his contradiction-filled Canadian-American cues from his predecessor. Despite his major expansion of the Canadian defence budget and despite his continuing support for such US international economic objectives as the Free Trade Area of the Americas, he had managed to offend the White House. Although he had committed two thousand Canadian troops to waging active war in Afghanistan's southern region around Kandahar where the Taliban's forces were gaining strength, he had rebuffed President Bush's insistent request that Canada support the BMD program. He passed legislation to permit same-sex marriage and supported decriminalizing the possession of marijuana—two measures that were deeply offensive to the Republican Right. More provocatively, he had gone out of his way during the 2004 election campaign to criticize US social programs and even more provocatively criticized the US government's environmental policy in the 2005 election. With the US government refusing to comply with the NAFTA-based arbitral decisions on the two countries' long-standing dispute over US softwood lumber imports from Canada, Martin even became more confrontational than Chrétien, suggesting that Canada might divert its oil production to China.

Conclusion

Two years into his second term, George Bush's "transformational diplomacy" had come under considerable pressure. Its rhetoric is still a contradictory mix of missionary Wilsonianism and aggressive Manichaeism, and the US government remains committed to securing global military dominance. Nevertheless, George Bush has been trying to withdraw from an Iraq venture that is now widely seen, even in the United States, to have been a disaster in statesmanship. His emissary, John Bolton, has managed to hamstring some reform in the United Nations, but the US president had to acknowledge at the 2005 G-7/G-8 summit at Gleneagles that global warming is a reality, that humans are one of the chief causes, and that there is a need for multilateral action to contain it. Even the American war on terror was widely acknowledged to have aggravated, rather than mitigated, the threat of non-state actors in the United States. In short, the Bush administration's ideologically driven foreign policy has failed to deploy successfully its massive hard power while managing to undermine its precious soft power.

In this moment of need, the White House received an unexpected bonus. After five years of the Liberal Party's ambivalence, the government of Canada shifted to unambiguous support for Washington's agenda. Following his thin minority victory in the federal election of 23 January 2006, the new Conservative prime minister, Stephen Harper, moved quickly to establish his pro-American credentials. He flew to Kandahar where he endorsed the Canadian military engagement against the Taliban with Bush-like war-fighting words rather than failed-state, peace-building rhetoric. He advertised himself as the United States' ally with "boots on the ground" posters in the Washington metro that presented Canada as a military ally. He cut off Canada's financial support for the recently elected Hamas government of Palestine to show his solidarity with Israel, the United States' main ally against Muslim nationalism in the Middle East. He has expressed his scorn for the Kyoto Protocol on global warming. And he has demonstrated his full support for the fledgling Security and Prosperity Partnership of North America by participating enthusiastically in a trinational summit with Vicente Fox and George Bush in Cancún.[8]

In short, as Mexico prepared to follow Argentina, Brazil, Chile, and Venezuela in their political shift away from a US-led neo-conservative world order, Harper's Canada has lined up to buttress the Bush counter-revolution. The immediate payoff was a resolution to Canada's softwood lumber dispute with Washington based on Canada abandoning its previous insistence that the United States comply with NAFTA-mandated arbitration procedures. In the longer term, the benefits of such cozy relations among the continent's conservatives will have to be weighed against the costs of reinforcing the rogue Empire.

With the collapse of the Liberal Party's support in Quebec and the weakness in its leadership, it is possible that, by the time of the 2008 presidential elections, Stephen Harper will have been returned to office with his hoped-for majority. If the Republicans are unable to recover from the twin disasters of the war in Iraq and Hurricane Katrina, we may see a new disjunction between Washington and Ottawa, with conservative Canada once more resisting an American foreign policy revolution and, this time, returning to a liberal internationalist tradition.

NOTES

1 Marrakech Agreement Establishing the World Trade Organization, 15 April 1994, 33 I.L.M. 15 (1994).
2 North American Free Trade Agreement between the Government of Canada, the Government of Mexico and the Government of the United States, 17 December 1992, Can. T.S. 1994 No. 2, 32 I.L.M. 289.
3 Kyoto Protocol to the UN Convention on Climate Change, December 1997, 37 I.L.M. 32 (1998).
4 *Uniting and Strengthening America by Providing Appropriate Tools Required to Intercept and Obstruct Terrorism (USA Patriot Act) Act of 2001.* 26 October. http://www.selectagents.gov/resources/USApatriotAct.pdf. See also *The Anti-Ballistic Missile (ABM) Treaty* at a Glance. Daryl Kimball, January 2003. http://www.armscontrol.org/factsheets/abmtreaty.asp.

5   At US $390 billion in 2001, US defence spending exceeded the combined budgets of
    the next fourteen largest spenders (see Hirsh 2002). By 2004, this figure ballooned
    to US $455 billion, surpassing the combined total of the next thirty-two most pow-
    erful nations and accounting for 47 percent of the world total (see Starck 2005).
6   Geneva Conventions, 12 August 1949, 1125 U.N.T.S. 3.
7   Quite unlike the crisis in Kosovo, Iraq was not, at the time, engaged in a brutal civil
    war.
8   Security and Prosperity Partnership, 23 March 2005, http://www.spp.gov.

REFERENCES

Appleby, Timothy. 2003. "US Still Upset with Canada: Rice." *Globe and Mail*,
    31 May, A1.
Atlas, James. 2003. "The Nation: Leo-Cons; A Classicist's Legacy: New Empire
    Builders." *New York Times*, 4 May, A1.
Blatchford, Christie. 2003. "A Pious Sort of Speech, Root Causes and an Attitude
    of Moral Superiority: Chrétien Takes Shots at His US Host." *National Post*,
    14 February, A1, A16.
Brean, Joseph, and Sheldon Alberts. 2003. "US Loses Faith in Canada:
    Ambassador Cellucci Expresses Washington's Wrath." *National Post*,
    26 May, A1.
CAFTA (Central American Free Trade Agreement). 2004. http://www.ustr.gov/
    Trade_Agreements/Regional/CAFTA/Section_Index.html.
Canada. 2003. *The Budget Speech, 2003*. Ottawa: Department of Finance.
Canadian Broadcasting Corporation. 2005. "Friendly Fire Case: The Legal Saga."
    5 June. http://www.cbc.ca/news/background/friendlyfire/index.html.
Cattaneo, Claudia. 2003. "US Ties 'Back to Normal.'" *National Post*, 8 May, FP1.
Clarkson, Stephen. 2002. *Canada's Secret Constitution: NAFTA, WTO and the End
    of Sovereignty*. Ottawa: Canadian Centre for Policy Alternatives.
Clarkson, Stephen, and Erick Lachapelle. 2004. "Jean Chrétien's Continental
    Legacy: From Commitment to Confusion." *Review of Constitutional
    Studies/Revue d'études constitutionelles* 9(1–2): 93–113.
Foot, Richard. 2003. "Premiers Aim to Bypass PM on US." *National Post*, 8 July, A1.
Gotlieb, Allan. 2003. "Foremost Partner: The Conduct of Canada-US Relations."
    In Hillmer, Norman, David Carment, and Fen Osler Hampson. eds.,
    Canada among Nations 2003: Coping with the American Colossus, 19–31.
    Toronto: Oxford University Press.
Granatstein, Jack. L. 2003. "The Empire Strikes Back." *National Post*, 26 March,
    A15.
Hillmer, Norman, David Carment, and Fen Osler Hampson, eds. 2003. *Canada
    among Nations 2003: Coping with the American Colossus*. Toronto: Oxford
    University Press.

Hirsh, Michael. 2002. "Bush and the World." *Foreign Affairs* 81(5): 18–43.

Ikenberry, G. John. 2002. "America's Imperial Ambition." *Foreign Affairs* 81(5): 44–60.

Ipsos News Center. 2003. *Canada and the Iraq War: Two Solitudes Emerge.* Toronto: Ipsos Reid.

Kergin, Michael. 2005. "US-Canada Relations, 2000–2005: Five Seminal Decisions." Malim Harding Lecture, Munk Centre for International Studies, University of Toronto, 27 September 2003.

Lachapelle, Erick. 2001. *Canada's Policy Choices: Managing our Border with the United States.* Ottawa: Public Policy Forum.

Laghi, Brian, and Paul Koring. 2003. "Chrétien and Bush Clash over Regime Change." *Globe and Mail,* 1 March, online ed.

Leblanc, Daniel, and Shawn McCarthy. 2003. "PM Shelves Decision on US Missile Defence." *Globe and Mail,* 8 May, A4.

Lyon, Peyton. 1989. "The Evolution of Canadian Diplomacy since 1945." In Paul Painchaud, ed., *De Mackenzie King à Pierre Trudeau: quarante ans de diplomatie canadienne, 1945–1985,* 13–33. Montreal: Les Presses de l'Université Laval.

McCarthy, Shawn, and Brian Laghi. 2003. "Chrétien Jab Stirs Criticism in Ottawa and US." *Globe and Mail,* 28 May, A1.

———, and Paul Koring. 2003. "War Isn't Justified, PM Says." *Globe and Mail,* 19 March, A1.

McQuaig, Linda. 2003. "US Wants to Liberate Our Energy." *Toronto Star,* 20 April, A13.

Morris, Cy. 2003. "Kudos to Chrétien for Stance on War." *Straight Goods,* 22 March. http://www.straightgoods.com.

Naumetz, Tim, and Mike Trickey. 2002. "General Says Canadian Casualties 'a likelihood.'" *Ottawa Citizen,* 6 March.

Nye, Joseph S. 2002. *The Paradox of American Power: Why the World's Only Superpower Can't Go It Alone.* New York: Oxford University Press.

Ostry, Sylvia. 2001. "Global Integration: Currents and Counter-Currents." Walter Gordon Lecture, Massey College, University of Toronto, 23 May.

Parkin, Andrew. 2003. *Pro-Canadian, Anti-American or Anti-War? Canadian Public Opinion on the Eve of War.* Montreal: Institute for Research on Public Policy.

Perkel, Colin. 2003. "US–Canada Relationship Could Suffer, Cellucci Says." *Globe and Mail,* 1 March, A9.

Sallot, Jeff. 2003. "Ottawa to Move on Missile Defence." *Globe and Mail,* 29 May, A4.

Sanders, Richard. 2003. "Who Says We're Not at War?" *Globe and Mail,* 31 March, A15.

Starck, Peter. 2005. "World Military Spending Topped $1 Trillion in 2004." *Common Dreams News Center,* 7 June. http://www.commondreams.org/cgi-bin/print.cgi?file=/headlines05/0607-03.htm.

United States. 2002. *The National Security Strategy of the United States.* Washington, DC: White House, http://www.whitehouse.gov/nsc/nss.html.

6

The Bush Revolution in Foreign Policy and Mexico: The Limits to Unilateralism

Jorge Chabat

Introduction

The arrival of George W. Bush in the White House has produced radical changes in American foreign policy. These changes, which have been characterized by some authors as an irreversible revolution, represent a turning point for US international relations. However, this revolution is not about furthering America's goals but, rather, about policy instruments. Furthermore, the Bush revolution in foreign policy has redefined traditional US alliances and abandoned the multilateral approach favoured by the Clinton administration. The revolution has also redefined enemies and propelled the United States into Iraq for an occupation that has lasted more than three years and is predicted to carry over well into the next decade.

Domestically, the Iraq war has caused more than 2,000 casualties, has cost nearly US $200 billion, and has won President Bush the lowest approval rating of any president at this point in his second term, according to Gallup polls going back to the Second World War (Neil 2005). This shift in foreign policy has also affected the United States' neighbourly relations. Disagreements over the war in Iraq have strained US-Mexico relations and resulted in deep diplomatic crises for both countries. Bush's war on terror has resulted in a reshuffling of its priorities. In a matter of days, Mexico went from the top of the US agenda to an afterthought. Despite this reshuffling, US-Mexico relations have had their own momentum—the interdependence between the countries has substantially limited the Bush administration's margin for manoeuvre. This chapter will analyze the characteristics of the so-called Bush revolution in foreign policy, how it has affected its relationship with Mexico, and the possible trajectories for US-Mexico relations in the future.

The Bush Revolution in Foreign Policy: A One-Man Show

According to Ivo Daalder and James Lindsay (2003, 13), the Bush revolution in foreign policy has rested upon two beliefs: first, that the best way to ensure US security is by maximizing America's freedom to act, without depending on others for protection and, second, that the United States should use its super power status to democratize the world. Additionally, American foreign policy has been shaped by two characteristics: a decided preference for unilateral action and an inclination to use pre-emptive military action to attack potential enemies and produce regime change in rogue states (Daalder and Lindsay 2003; Fukuyama 2005).

The Bush foreign policy, conceived in response to the events on 11 September 2001, was further bolstered by beliefs associated with an important group known as the "neo-conservatives" (or neo-Reaganites), which was present in the president's inner circle from the very beginning. The word "neo-conservative," which initially had a large domestic policy component, now more specifically refers to advocates that believe US defence and national security interests should rest upon power and resolve, not upon diplomacy and treaties. Moreover, the group is known for its "deep scepticism of traditional Wilsonianism's commitment to the rule of law and its belief in the relevance of international institutions" (Daalder and Lindsay 2003, 15), a standpoint that has influenced the Bush administration's unilateral approach to foreign policy.

While the United States does not formally reject international institutions, the Bush administration has had no qualms about employing an "if it's good for Bush it's good for everybody else" doctrine of diplomacy. This attitude has not meant that current policy has embraced isolationism. Alliances with other nations—"coalitions of the willing"—have been sought in the war in Iraq but only with those nations willing to operate on US terms. The United States' unilateralism has provoked a "crisis of legitimacy," which has affected its relationships with other members of the North Atlantic Treaty Organization such as Germany and France (Kagan 2004; Tucker and Hendrickson 2004). This diplomatic conflict could, in theory, be counterbalanced by Bush's efforts to disarm and democratize the so-called "rogue" states.

Aside from the attacks, had US foreign policy simply reflected President Bush's conservatism, it would not be the muscular program that it is today. The best definition of US foreign policy under Bush, one of "democratic imperialism" (Daalder and Lindsay 2003, 15), is based upon the assumption that the "only route to lasting peace is through regime change, and once democratic regimes are established, they will live at peace and cooperate with one another" (Jervis 2005, 81). However, this alternative source of legitimacy—a very powerful one in the post-Cold War era—has been substantially eroded due to reports of human rights violations committed by members of the US army in Afghanistan and Iraq and of the appalling treatment of prisoners in Guantanamo Bay prison.

The Impact of 11 September on US Foreign Policy

As a consequence of the terrorist attacks in New York and Washington on 11 September 2001, the Bush administration redefined its priorities, putting the fight against terrorism and the defence of "the United States, the American people, and our interests at home and abroad by identifying and destroying the threat before it reaches our borders" at the top of its agenda. Furthermore, the support of democracy abroad was also emphasized among the goals of the 2002 "National Security Strategy of the United States." These goals involved expanding "the circle of development by opening societies and building the infrastructure of democracy" and supporting "moderate and modern government, especially in the Muslim world, to ensure that the conditions and ideologies that promote terrorism do not find fertile ground in any nation" (United States 2002, 2 and 6).

As mentioned earlier, Bush's iron-fist approach to protecting American interests has been a strategy embraced by members of his inner circle since the beginning. However, it was 9/11 that gave this approach political legitimacy: "Just as September 11 galvanized Bush to pursue his foreign policy revolution, it also swept away any inhibition he might have felt about speaking publicly about evil" (Daalder and Lindsay 2003, 87). As a direct consequence of 9/11, American foreign policy adopted strong moral language that resembled Ronald Reagan's 1982 "evil empire" lexicon, which worked well in galvanizing public support. Bush's popularity climbed, and Congress was unable to stop him. Three days after the 11 September attacks, Congress gave Bush authorization to retaliate against those responsible for the attacks. Seven weeks later, the *Uniting and Strengthening America by Providing Appropriate Tools Required to Intercept and Obstruct Terrorism Act* was approved, which broadly expanded the law enforcement's surveillance and investigative powers (Daalder and Lindsay 2003, 93).[1]

The Iraq Quagmire

Whatever the reasons for Bush's decision to invade Iraq—fighting evil, promoting democracy, or securing oil—its effects were disastrous for US relations with most European and Latin American countries. The conflict with Europe was particularly serious and significantly weakened post-Second World War alliances. For many nations in Europe and Latin America, the invasion of Iraq had nothing to do with the war on terror and more to do with an imperialist drive. Additionally, as mentioned earlier, human rights abuses by the US occupation forces in Afghanistan and Iraq and its treatment of prisoners in Guantanamo Bay, combined with the efforts of the US government to legalize torture practices ("Vice President for Torture" 2005), negatively impacted the legitimacy of Bush's only foreign policy—the democratization of "failed" regimes.

The main cost to the United States did not come from the lack of legitimacy of the war on terror but, rather, from the lack of results. After two and a half years of occupation, the instability in Iraq persists with the number of American deaths increasing every day. It has also been disastrous in economic terms, costing American taxpayers more than US $200 billion. Moreover, the energy expended in Iraq has considerably weakened the rest of Bush's foreign policy. Given the current domestic climate in the United States, another pre-emptive strike to depose governments in Iran, Libya, or Cuba is unimaginable. Additionally, Bush's decision to invade Afghanistan and Iraq did not work to prevent terrorist attacks in Madrid and London in 2005. In sum, the war in Iraq has substantially undermined the Bush doctrine. As Robert Jervis has pointed out, "Machiavelli famously asked whether it is better to be feared or to be loved. The problem for the United States is that it is likely to be neither." The failures of the Bush doctrine has left the United States looking neither strong nor benign, and we may find that the only thing worse than a successful leader is a failed one (Jervis 2005, 137–38).

The Second Bush Administration: In Search of the Lost Legitimacy

After two years of turbulent occupation in Iraq, Bush decided to make some adjustments in his foreign policy. He replaced Colin Powell, the overly liberal secretary of state, and appointed Condoleezza Rice, a member of the neo-conservative team, to the position. For many observers, this change would have meant a victory for hard liners and unilateralists over soft multilateralists. However, there are signs that this has not entirely been the case. Rice is a prag-matic politician, and, despite her background, the changes she has implemented in American foreign policy suggest a move in the direction of diplomacy and multilateralism rather than strengthening the Bush government's military ap-proach ("Condi's Challenge" 2005). There are some elements that support this assertion. On the one hand, the peace process in the Israeli-Palestinian con-flict made significant progress in 2005, which suggests a greater attempt by the United States to achieve a negotiated solution, even if Israel has to give up some of its demands.

In addition, there have been some clear signals of change in the use of di-plomacy. The Bush administration's call for UN support for democratic elections in Iraq demonstrates an acknowledgement of the importance of international organizations. As Robert Keohane points out,

> once they attacked Iraq they discovered that they needed international institutions, because you can't mobilize a longstanding coalition, which is legitimate, of democratic countries whose publics care about legitimacy, unless you are aligned in some way with an international institution—the UN or something else—which is seen as representing the views of not just ourselves. (Keohane, cited in Kreisler 2004)

There have also been changes in rhetoric employed by members of the Bush administration. In her statement before the Senate during her confirmation hearing to be secretary of state, Condoleezza Rice redefined US foreign policy goals, including: uniting the community of democracies "in building an international system that is based in our shared values and the rule of law," strengthening "the community of democracies to fight the threats to our freedom and democracy throughout the globe," and spreading "freedom and democracy throughout the globe" (Rice 2005). Rice also places an emphasis on the promotion of trade as a way to create jobs—a goal that has been reduced in importance since 11 September—and also made a surprising call for alliances and collaboration with "multilateral institutions" as a way to "multiply the strength of freedom-loving nations" (ibid.).

The United States also stressed job creation as the most urgent task to be undertaken in the region at the fourth Summit of the Americas, which took place in Mar del Plata, Argentina, on 4–5 November 2005. Even though the creation of a Free Trade Area of the Americas is still a long-term goal, the United States has recognized that the improvement of competition should be a priority in Latin America in the short term (United States State Department 2005).

Finally, another sign of change in US foreign policy is the appointment of Tom Shannon, a professional diplomat and expert on Venezuela, as assistant secretary of state for the western hemisphere. Shannon's appointment seems to indicate that the United States is taking a softer approach in the region, placing an emphasis on negotiation rather than military confrontation (LaFranchi 2005). In this regard, one question that remains unanswered is what the role will be for the Organization of American States in US strategy.

The United States' clear change in tone and its emphasis on non-military instruments to address the challenges that it is now facing can be attributed to complications associated with the Iraq war and the need for international legitimacy. Certainly, the political problems that President Bush faced domestically in 2005, such as the administration's delayed reaction to the victims of Hurricane Katrina, the scandal surrounding the revelation of the identity of an agent of the Central Intelligence Agency by trusted officials from Bush's inner circle, and the withdrawal of Bush's nominee to the US Supreme Court, Harriet Miers, contributed to this change in tone. Additionally, in the public mind, some of these problems are in some way related to the government's mistakes in foreign policy, particularly the invasion of Iraq.[2]

The weakness of the second Bush administration can be clearly seen in the president's sinking approval ratings, which, in May 2006, plummeted to an all-time low of 30 percent (Friedman 2006). The revelation of a massacre committed in November 2005 by the US marines against Iraqi civilians also contributed to the deterioration of Bush's image (Smith 2006). This situation and the prolongation of the Iraq occupation have substantially limited the United States' ability to engage in military operations in the rest of the world. As Mel Gurtov

(2006, 229) has pointed out, "now having undertaken a global war without front lines, the Pentagon finds itself with too many missions and too few soldiers."

Relations with Mexico: The Disagreement on Iraq

Over the last two decades, Mexico's gradual economic integration with the United States, as represented by the 1994 North American Free Trade Agreement (NAFTA), has not been accompanied by a similar process of political adjustment.[3] Traditional anti-US rhetoric shifted following the election of Mexican president Vicente Fox in 2000. Fox, a former chief executive officer of Coca-Cola, had a different view on what Mexico's relationship to the United States should be. Since the beginning of his administration, he made it evident that he would change traditional Mexican foreign policy. Fox considered that the foreign policy implemented by the Institutional Revolutionary Party was aimed to defend the regime and not national interests (Fox Quesada 2000b). Consequently, Fox proposed changes in many areas of Mexican foreign policy, including the relationship with the United States. One of the most significant changes that Fox proposed was to deepen and broaden NAFTA so that it would impact every region of the country (Fox Quesada 2000a).

"NAFTA plus" would further deepen US-Mexico economic integration, resulting in "convergences on the basis of fundamental variables of the economy: convergence of rates of interest, convergence of people's income, convergence of salaries." It would be a plan that, according to Fox, could take "10 to 20 years" to implement (Public Broadcasting System 2001). Following these ideas, Vicente Fox began to talk about an "open border" between Mexico and the United States before his electoral victory in July 2000 (Suarez 2000). Modelled on the European Union, an "open border" would allow for the free transit of American and Mexican citizens across their mutual border. Additionally, President Fox has insisted since the beginning of his administration that the signature of a migratory agreement between Mexico and the United States would imply the legalization of millions of illegal Mexican workers living in the United States. This proposal was the cornerstone of the relationship with the United States during the first years of the Fox administration. It was a permanent topic in all of the bilateral meetings and a strong demand in most of the Mexican media. However, this agreement was not achieved, in part because the US Congress is hostile to any amnesty for Mexicans living and working in the United States.

From the United States' point of view, Fox represented a healthy change in terms of a democratic transition, and the Bush administration warmly received the new Mexican government. In February 2001, President Bush visited Mexico on his first presidential trip outside the United States and met with President Fox at his ranch in Guanajuato. At their meeting, Bush expressed his support for a review of the so-called anti-drug certification process and congratulated Fox's efforts in fighting drug trafficking. Even though Bush was not enthusiastic about a migration agreement with Mexico, both Presidents did agree in their final joint statement to begin negotiating "short and long-term agreements" for migration and labour issues (United States 2001a).

A few months after President Bush's visit to Mexico, in the days leading up to 11 September, President Fox visited Washington on his first international trip as president. In light of the occasion, the most spectacular reception given to any Mexican president in the United States was prepared, and Bush expressed the importance that he placed upon the United States' relationship with Mexico: "The United States has no more important relationship in the world than the one we have with Mexico" (United States 2001b). Notwithstanding Fox's warm reception, it was quite evident at the meeting that Mexican enthusiasm about a migration agreement was not reciprocated by the Bush administration. Although it was in America's interest to maintain cordial ties and to advance the two nations' economic integration, President Bush did not seriously consider a migration pact that would imply the legalization of millions of undocumented Mexican workers. This refusal was due in part to the legal reforms that would be necessary, which would have to receive the approval of Congress. The final outcome of these migration reforms being discussed by Congress still remains unclear.

In 2001, bilateral collaboration progressed, especially in regard to the anti-drug campaign developed by the Fox administration, which led to the arrest of leaders of some of the most notorious drug cartels (Turbiville 2001; Chabat 2002). Collaboration on this front was so successful that both governments began to implement measures, such as the creation of a Federal Bureau of Investigation training school for the Mexican federal police, which would have been unimaginable a decade previously (Sandoval 2001). However, 9/11 changed the United States' priorities—drugs, economic integration, and migration sunk to the bottom of the new agenda.

US-Mexican relations deteriorated following the 11 September terrorist attacks due to the Mexican government's hesitation in giving full support to the United States after the terrorist attacks. What the Mexican government learned the hard way was that the logic of the new Bush doctrine was one of blind loyalties—you are either with me or against me. An impasse developed between the two countries as a result of President Fox's delay in travelling to Ground Zero in New York, which was seen by some sectors of the American public as "too little, too late" for a country that they had identified as being a "partner." US-Mexican relations continued to deteriorate following the United Nations Security Council's approval of Resolution 1441, which gave Iraq "a final opportunity to comply with its disarmament obligations under relevant resolutions of the Council" or risk facing "serious consequences as a result of its continued violations of its obligations" (United Nations Security Council 2002).[4]

Although Resolution 1441 was unanimously approved by the UN Security Council, Mexico's position was seen by some as being hesitant in supporting the United States. An editorial in the *Wall Street Journal* represented this hard-line position very well, criticizing Mexico for having joined the "soft-on-Saddam queue." The *Wall Street Journal* also made reference to Mexico's interests, linking the possibility of a migration accord with its support of the United States:

> Mr. Bush was already going to have to overcome opposition within his own party for a migration pact. The Mexican stiff-arm on Iraq will only convince more Republicans that our neighbors to the South are more useful as political piñatas than as partners. And Mr. Bush will be even less inclined to risk his own prestige to help out Mr. Fox. ("Our Friends at the U.N." 2002)

Although the discussion at the UN Security Council did not lead to an open confrontation between Mexico and the United States, it did foreshadow what was going to take place in the following months when the White House tried to pass a resolution that would authorize the use of force against Iraq.

Pressures for the Securitization of Mexican Borders

One of the direct consequences of the 11 September attacks was an increase in US concern about Mexican border security. In response to US pressures, Fox announced a revision of existing laws, mechanisms of surveillance, and safeguards in federal governmental facilities in order to prevent terrorists from entering Mexico from Guatemala. In October 2001, Ambassador Jeffrey Davidow complained that corruption in Mexico might have facilitated the entrance of terrorists into Mexico. Additionally, the Mexican government itself admitted that the possibility that terrorists could use Mexican territory to enter into the United States did exist (Novedades 2001). In this context, a "smart border" agreement was signed in March 2002 between Mexico and the United States to improve security along the US-Mexico border (Bumiller 2002). Still in 2004, journalist reports revealed that Al-Qaeda was purportedly connecting with local crime factions in Central America (Seper 2004).

Accordingly, plans were made to modify Mexican migration controls in order to include electronic mechanisms of surveillance. In July 2004, it was announced that a new integral system of migratory operation would be introduced, which would make it possible to track all legal visitors entering into Mexico (Mexico 2004). In addition, both countries have been contemplating the implementation of a program to pre-screen passengers from specific points of entry, such as Cancún, which would allow for the presence of US agents in Mexican territory.

As the Mexican experience has shown, despite diplomatic differences, collaboration in the area of security has been taking place since 9/11, fomented in part by the possibility of terrorists entering the United States through Mexico. The most effective way to prevent the threat of terrorism has been the development of intelligence capabilities. Consequently, collaboration between Mexico and the United States has been based upon intelligence sharing, which has provoked little response from the Mexican public.

The War in Iraq

During February and March 2003, US diplomacy pushed very hard to get authorization from the UN Security Council to invade Iraq despite reluctance from countries such as France and Russia. In this context, the Mexican vote became crucial, and President Fox was put in a very uncomfortable position. On the one hand, he realized that giving support to the United States could bring important benefits, such as the migration pact. On the other hand, there were important domestic costs associated with supporting the invasion, especially since 80 percent of the Mexican population opposed military intervention in Iraq and congressional elections in Mexico would be held that year ("Time to Be Counted" 2003).

Nevertheless, in the final phase of the American campaign to obtain the United Nation's approval for the war, President Bush made it very clear that he would not tolerate Mexico's opposition to the war. Although Bush discarded a "significant retaliation" against Fox's government, he pointed out that there would be disciplinary measures taken if Mexico persisted in opposing the war, comments that were echoed in similar statements made by the US ambassador to Mexico, Tony Garza (Carreño 2003a).

By mid-March 2003, it became evident that Mexico was not going to vote in favour of a US-led invasion to Iraq. In an interview on 12 March 2002, President Fox said that the decision on the vote at the UN Security Council would be a "state decision" involving the consensus of the country's main political forces and that it would not be difficult to say "no" to the United States (Noticieros Televisa 2003). This disagreement seriously affected US-Mexican relations, and the Bush administration openly objected to the lack of Mexican support for the war (Carreño 2003b).

Conservative sectors of the American public openly criticized Mexico's position. An editorial published in the *Wall Street Journal* on 12 March referred to Mexico and Chile's reluctant positions as a "fandango" and suggested that all trade benefits that both countries have enjoyed in their relationship with the United States should be cancelled: "Maybe we should transfer to Bulgaria—which is supporting us *sans* bribery—the trade benefits that these two nations have is apparently taken for granted" ("Bush in Liliput" 2003). The newspaper also warned about the long-lasting effects that this conflict with the United States could have: "These columns have long tried sympathetically to explain Mexican realities to our readers, but President Vicente Fox's UN war straddle will cost his country years of U.S. public goodwill" (ibid.).

Sweet Reconciliation or How Interdependence Makes for a Difficult Fight

Despite the serious conflict that has developed around Mexico's opposition to the invasion of Iraq at the UN Security Council, it could not last long. In March 2004, one year after the defeat of Saddam Hussein, President Bush and President Fox had a very cordial meeting in Crawford, Texas, in which Mexican border residents were exempted from the US-VISIT Program (Carreño 2004). After a few months of public confrontation, both governments had to return to the negotiating table since there were so many pending bilateral issues to be addressed. Even when there were no significant agreements at the meetings, the level of interdependence between the two countries was such that collaboration was crucial. The rapprochement with Mexico was not caused by weakness on the part of the US government or by a redefinition of the Bush doctrine but, clearly, was a result of interdependence.

From the Mexican perspective, the conflict with the United States confirmed that it was possible to disagree with the "Colossus to the North." However, the Iraq war incident showed that motives and arguments are important. Mexico shifted its position from arguing for the existence of weapons of mass destruction, sustained during the approval of Resolution 1441, to taking a pacifist stance by opposing the war. However, the insistence made by President Fox and the Mexican ambassador to the United Nations, Adolfo Aguilar Zinser, that if a vote had taken place Mexico would have opposed the war in Iraq was unnecessary and only succeeded in chilling relations with the US government. Although the chance of getting a migration agreement between the United Nations and Mexico was unlikely, it was evident that the conflict over the US invasion of Iraq complicated any discussion on this subject.

The Future of US-Mexico Relations

US-Mexican relations have been shaped by interdependence, and this interdependence has deepened over the last decade due the economic integration brought about by NAFTA. However, integration is not automatic. It needs constant support from both governments, and this support can be stunted as a result of conflicts, as has been shown during the war in Iraq. There are still certain sectors of the Mexican political elite who do not like Mexico's rapprochement to the United States. Even when this position is not supported in a clear way by the majority of the Mexican public, it represents a considerable obstacle for integration between Mexico and the United States (Centro de Investigación y Docencia Económicas 2004).

Still, it is reasonable to expect a change in the role traditionally played by Mexican nationalism. Over the last few decades, nationalism has been a constituent part of the Institutional Revolutionary Party's ideological appeal, particularly when democratic legitimacy was absent. However, since the Zedillo administration, nationalism has played a smaller role as a legitimizing factor because both Zedillo and Fox have claimed to be more democratic. From this point of view, it is feasible to expect that nationalist feelings will be less important in Mexican foreign policy in the future. Certainly, this process will not be quick and easy. It will continue to take time. This is not to say that there will not be disagreements between Mexico and the United States, but they will probably be based more on legal or technical issues than on questions of nationalism or anti-US feelings.

Conclusions

The Bush revolution in foreign policy, as can be seen in examining the case with Mexico, has affected the world significantly. The pressures placed on Mexico to support the war in Iraq were substantial. However, the war conflicted with Mexico's interests in many ways, affecting traditional Mexican support for international organizations and representing a very high domestic cost for the Fox administration. The final outcome of the disagreement with the United States proved that even though Mexico is highly vulnerable to the United States there is still some margin for manoeuvre due to the level interdependence between the two countries. In this sense, Mexico's opposition of the war in Iraq was successful. There were marginal costs for Mexico at the UN Security Council, and, in terms of the Mexico-US relationship, it did not alienate the Fox administration from the Mexican public. This public disagreement also complicated the negotiation of a migration agreement and delayed the possibility of a "NAFTA plus." Certainly, the conflict was inevitable, but it seems that public confrontation was avoided.

It is also worth mentioning that the third element of Bush's foreign policy revolution—the democratization of rogue states—could have been seen by Mexico in a more positive way, given the emphasis that President Fox has given to the promotion of democracy and human rights. However, this possible ground for support was overshadowed by the Bush administration's disdain for international organizations and the human rights abuses committed by the United States in Afghanistan and Iraq. If the United States decides in the future to channel its foreign policy objectives through international institutions, it is highly probable that it will be able to galvanize Mexican support. Notwithstanding this possibility, conflicts will continue to appear from time to time in the US-Mexican relationship. The challenge for both countries will be to accept the differences and support them with reasonable arguments.

NOTES

1 *Uniting and Strengthening America by Providing Appropriate Tools Required to Intercept and Obstruct Terrorism (USA Patriot Act) Act of 2001.* http://www .selectagents.gov/resources/USAPatriotAct.pdf.
2 When Hurricane Katrina hit New Orleans in September 2005, there were many who remembered that half of the Louisiana Guard were serving in Iraq.
3 North American Free Trade Agreement between the Government of Canada, the Government of Mexico and the Government of the United States, 17 December 1992, Can. T.S. 1994 No. 2, 32 I.L.M. 289.
4 This resolution reestablished the UN inspections of Iraqi facilities but was quite ambiguous about how and when these measures would take place if Iraq failed to comply.

REFERENCES

Bumiller, Elisabeth. 2002. "White House Announces Security Pact with Mexico." *New York Times,* 22 March, A18.
"Bush in Liliput." 2003. *Wall Street Journal,* 12 March.
Carreño, José. 2003a. "Amenaza Bush: Espero Disciplina de México." *El Universal,* 5 March.
———. 2003b. "Decepciona a EU la falta de apoyo de México." *El Universal,* 19 March, 4.
———. 2004. "Suspende EU 'fichaje' de mexicanos en la frontera." *El Universal,* 5 March, 1A.
Centro de Investigación y Docencia Económicas and Consejo Mexicano de Asuntos Internacionales. 2004. *Mexico y el Mundo: Global Views 2004. Mexican Public Opinion and Foreign Policy.* http://mexicoyelmundo.cide .edu/2004/%20Reporte%20Mexico.pdf.
Chabat, Jorge. 2002. "Mexico's War on Drugs: No Margin for Maneuver." *Annals of the American Academy of Political and Social Science* 582 (July): 134–38.
"Condi's Challenge." 2005. *The Economist,* 12 January.
Daalder, Ivo H., and James M. Lindsay. 2003. *America Unbound.* Washington, DC: Brookings Institution Press.
Fox Quesada, Vicente. 2000a. "Relación México-Estados Unidos, Chihuahua," 14 April. http://www.centrofox.org.mx.
———. 2000b. "Una Nueva Agenda en las relaciones entre México y Estados Unidos." Washington, DC. http://www.centrofox.org.mx/noticias.

Friedman. Thomas L. 2006. "Too Many 'Yes' Men Have Dragged Down Bush's Popularity." *Pittsburgh Post-Gazette,* 18 May, B-7.

Fukuyama, Francis. 2005. "The Bush Doctrine, Before and After." *Financial Times,* 11 October, 21.

Gurtov, Mel. 2006. *Superpower on Crusade: The Bush Doctrine in US Foreign Policy.* Boulder, CO: Lynne Rienner Publishers.

Jervis, Robert. 2005. *American Foreign Policy in a New Era.* New York: Routledge.

Kagan, Robert. 2004. "America's Crisis of Legitimacy." *Foreign Affairs* (March–April). http://www.foreignaffairs.org/2004/2.html.

Kreisler, Harry. 2004. "Theory and International Institutions: Conversation with Robert O. Keohane," *Conversations with History.* Institute of International Studies, University of California–Berkeley. 9 March. http://globetrotter .berkeley.edu/people4/Keohane/keohane-cono.html.

LaFranchi, Howard. 2005. "A Gentler Touch with Latin America." *Christian Science Monitor,* 6 October.

Mexico. 2004. "Presenta el INM nuevo sistema de control migratorio." 29 July. http://www.presidencia.gob.mx/buenasnoticias/index.php?contenido= 8740&pagina=27.

Neal, Terry M. 2005. "Bush's Poll Position Is Worst on Record." *Washington Post,* 11 April. http://www.washingtonpost.com/wp-dyn/articles/A43180-2005 April1.html.

Noticieros Televisa. 2003. "No es difícil decirle no a EU: Fox." El Noticiero con Joaquín López Dóriga. http://www.esmas.com/noticierostelevisa/ lopezdoriga/282572.html.

Novedades. 2001. "México puede ser trampolín para terroristas." 8 November.

"Our Friends at the U.N." 2002. *Wall Street Journal,* 29 October.

Public Broadcasting Service. 2001. "Interview with Vicente Fox." 4 April. http://www.pbs.org/wgbh/commandingheights/shared/minitextlo/int_ vicentefox.html.

Rice, Condoleezza. 2005. "Opening Statement by Dr. Condoleezza Rice. Senate Foreign Relations Committee." 18 January. http://foreign.senate.gov/ testimony/2005/RiceTestimony050118.pdf.

Sandoval, Ricardo. 2001. "Fox Pushes FBI School for Mexican Federal Police." *Dallas Morning News,* 20 May.

Seper, Jerry. 2004. "Al Qaeda Seeks Tie to Local Gangs." *Washington Times,* 28 September, 1.

Smith, Joan. 2006. "Haditha Was Horrifying, But It Was Not Surprising." *(London) Independent,* 2 June, 27.

Suarez, Ray. 2000. "A Conversation with Vicente Fox." Online News Tour, 21 March. http://www.pbs.org/newshour/bb/latin_america/jan-june00/ fox_3-21.html.

"Time to Be Counted: Mexico, the United States and Iraq." 2003. *The Economist,* 27 February.

Tucker, Robert W., and David C. Hendrickson. 2004. "The Sources of American Legitimacy." *Foreign Affairs,* November-December. http://www.foreignaffairs.org/2004/6.html.

Turbiville Jr., Graham H. 2001. "Mexico's Evolving Security Posture." *Military Review* (May-June): 39–46.

United Nations Security Council. 2002. "United Kingdom of Great Britain and Northern Ireland and the United States of America: Draft Resolution (Adopted as Resolution 1414 at Security Council Meeting 4644, 8 November 2002)." http://www.un.org.News/dh/iraq/res-iraq-07 maro3-en-rev.pdf.

United States. 2001a. "Joint Statement by President George Bush and President Vicente Fox towards a Partnership for Prosperity: The Guanajuato Proposal." *Weekly Compilation of Presidential Documents,* Washington, 26 February. http://frwebgate.access.gpo.gov/cgi-bin/getdoc.cgi? dbname= 2001_presidential_documents&docid=pd26fe01_txt-3.pdf.

————. 2001b. "Remarks at a Welcoming Ceremony for President Vicente Fox of Mexico." *Weekly Compilation of Presidential Documents,* 10 September. http://www.findarticles.com/p/articles/mi_m2889/is_36_37/ ai_79210653.

————. 2002. *The National Security Strategy of the United States of America,* September. http://www.whitehouse.gov/nsc/nss.pdf.

United States State Department. 2005. "U.S. Official Outlines Goals for Fourth Summit of the Americas," 29 September. http://usinfo.state.gov/wh/ Archive/2005/Sep/30-667427.html.

"Vice President for Torture." 2005. *Washington Post,* 26 October, A18.

4

NORTH AMERICAN SECURITY PERIMETER: THE MEGA AGENDA

7

Smart Trumps Security: Canada's Border Security Policy since 11 September

Wesley K. Wark

The Impact of 9/11

In the immediate aftermath of the 11 September terrorist attacks, the concept of border security took on a new and unfamiliar meaning for Canada. Canadians were long used to the idea of a demilitarized, "undefended border" with the United States. At the same time, the need for a protected and monitored border had long been apparent when it came to issues such as transnational crime, illegal immigration, gun trafficking, and even the mundanities of revenue generation through Canada Customs. Beyond its physical reality, the border had long been elevated to the status of cultural "trope," holding a meaning, however elusive, that was central to Canadian notions of distinctiveness from the United States (New 1998).

The comfortable duality of an undefended, but semi-secured, border was shattered by the 9/11 attacks. The border as cultural trope seemed suddenly quaint. Two urgent needs intruded, both of which shaped a new "securitization" of the forty-ninth parallel. The first need was to seal the border as a possible portal of terrorist activity. There was a very real fear in the immediate aftermath of 9/11 of further, imminent terrorist strikes on North American targets. An unprecedented effort had to be made against a wide range of activities, including the movement of terrorist individuals and cells, the transfer of money, the passage of weaponry, the concern about proliferation, especially involving dual-use technology, and the threat to cross-border critical infrastructure. The national security prerogative behind the effort to combat terrorism at the border was based on an appreciation of the need both to protect Canada from threats from within and to prevent Canada from being used as a doorway to the United States, or elsewhere, for terrorist activities. These prerogatives were ultimately written into Canada's national security strategy framework document, which was issued by the Paul Martin government in April 2004 (Canada 2004).

The second need was to align Canadian and American border security strategy. Of equal concern with the prospect of future terrorist strikes was the worry that a gap, real or perceived, could open up between Canadian and American doctrine. A post-9/11 dialogue had to be pursued between the two countries, each of which had potentially different conceptions of border security. The Canadian vision recognized the need for a tighter border but sought to emphasize the importance of sustaining an open conduit for trade and travel, which was essential to the Canadian economy. The pre-9/11 problems with the persistence of trade protectionism and border red tape, even in the context of the North American Free Trade Agreement (NAFTA), paled in comparison to the impact that a fortified border might have on the Canadian economy.[1] The American vision had a different perspective. Trade mattered as did the maintenance of friendly relations with a long-time ally and neighbour, but, as the phrase went, "security trumped."

The American security imperative had the upper hand in the days immediately following 11 September. North American airspace was closed to commercial flights, and planes were diverted to Canada. The land border was effectively locked down. The result on the Canadian side was congestion and long lines of transport trucks, the diminution of cross-border tourism, and a heavy, if short-lived, economic impact in lost business transactions. The restoration of a greater degree of normality to the border following 11 September was a relief, but it did not undercut the message of the early post-9/11 experience. Security could really trump trade.

Early on, the Canadian government found itself engaged in the task of selling an image of strengthened border security to the American public and of batting back false border threat stories. This campaign began immediately after 9/11 in the face of media concoctions on both sides of the border that some or all of the 11 September hijackers had come from Canada. And it has continued ever since.[2]

The Smart Border Declaration

Canadian border policy in the early crisis months after 11 September was based on the need to strengthen security controls at the border and to reach a renewed understanding with the United States about a secure and open border, which would be open, at the very least, to the right kind of trade and the right movement of people and goods. At the highest level, negotiations over a new framework for the border were handled by John Manley, the deputy prime minister, and his American counterpart in charge of homeland security policy, Tom Ridge. Responsibility for the American "file" in Ottawa was subtly shifted from the Department of Foreign Affairs and International Trade (DFAIT) to the Privy

Council Office, which was better able to serve the needs of Manley and his negotiations. These discussions ultimately led to the signing of the Canada-US Smart Border Declaration on 12 December 2001.[3]

The Smart Border Declaration talked about the inter-relationship between public security and economic security, a theme that would persist in all subsequent discussions of Canada-US border security. It used the phrase "zone of confidence against terrorist activities" to describe the plan for the strengthened border. The declaration came with a more detailed action plan for implementation, which originally had included thirty points but which had increased, by the time of writing, to thirty-two (Canada 2005b). With this action plan, the two governments made clear that future border security measures would be driven by a need for harmonization of policies and integrated efforts. The action plan was based on "four pillars": the secure flow of people; the secure flow of goods; a secure infrastructure; and coordination and information sharing. All of these initiatives built on previous efforts, even the one that was least in the public eye—intelligence sharing.

The Smart Border Declaration marked a victory for Canadian diplomacy, although like all diplomatic triumphs it had a temporal edge. The declaration had averted a potential crisis in Canadian-American relations in a way that satisfied Canadian needs. It served Canadian interests by demonstrating a commitment to beef up border security, while it retained a focus on facilitating the movement of people and goods. The American interest was served by this demonstration of a Canadian commitment to meet American security demands and to work in close partnership. American support for a reinforced, but traditional, border security strategy was enhanced by the fact that US security strategy was already looking well beyond the continental boundaries of the United States. By December 2001, when the Smart Border Declaration was signed, the United States was engaged in its campaign to destroy the Taliban regime and Al-Qaeda in Afghanistan and had begun to define an offensive, forward strategy in its global war on terror. The American "border" was being moved out into the world.

New National Security Institutions

Close cooperation on border security between Canada and the United States eventually fed into major institutional reforms in the Canadian government. In December 2003, a newly installed prime minister, Paul Martin, announced the creation of a major new ministry, the Department of Public Safety and Emergency Preparedness Canada (PSEPC). The stimuli behind the creation of the public safety ministry were in some respects similar to the forces that had earlier driven the establishment of the gargantuan Department of Homeland

Security in the United States. There was an equivalent Canadian need to create a department that would house and coordinate the major elements of the Canadian government's domestic security functions. There was, equally, the requirement for stronger leadership in what, after 11 September, had become a key government priority. The PSEPC, which was a large and senior Cabinet portfolio, replaced a second-tier ministry, the old Department of the Solicitor General. To give added clout to the new department, and to signal its political importance in Ottawa, the minister selected to head it, Anne McLellan, was also named as deputy prime minister. Enabling legislation for the new department, passed in the spring of 2005, spelled out the minister's role very broadly: "The Minister shall, at the national level, exercise leadership relating to public safety and emergency preparedness."[4]

While it might be easy to see the creation of the PSEPC (with its unintentionally Orwellian title) as imitating the homeland security initiative in the United States, there were significant differences in the design of the two agencies. The PSEPC's writ was not meant to extend quite so far as that of Department of Homeland Security, especially in the areas of immigration policy and maritime security. In the Canadian context, immigration policy functions remain vested in the Department of Citizenship and Immigration Canada. On the maritime security side, the PSEPC did not incorporate the Canadian coast guard or significantly encroach on the existing roles of departments such as Transport Canada and Fisheries and Oceans. Where the PSEPC did represent a greater concentration of power than even the Department of Homeland Security was in the realm of domestic security intelligence, where it assumed the old functions of the solicitor general for the Royal Canadian Mounted Police and the Canadian Security Intelligence Service, but added significant new elements of border security in the shape of the freshly minted Canada Border Services Agency (CBSA). The CBSA was to be the operational arm of the government when it came to monitoring and enforcing the border—it brought a significant and, it would prove, disputatious workforce into the ministry (the border guards and customs workers).[5]

The PSEPC was not a clone of the American Department of Homeland Security, but where the connecting tissue lay was in the need to have a powerful institutional structure north of the border that could interact with the American department. There had to be some kind of "Lego-fit" to smooth bilateral cooperation, and the PSEPC, which was similar enough in mandate and represented an equivalent power on the Canadian side of the border, was to be that fit with homeland security. With its control over key national law enforcement and security intelligence agencies as well as over border operations, the PSEPC was designed from the outset as the lead agency for border security. Yet it had to wait for its marching orders to be established.

A National Security Policy for Canada

Four months after the establishment of the new ministry, the Canadian government released a significant policy document entitled *Securing an Open Society: Canada's National Security Policy* (Canada 2004). Not only was this publication the first attempt made by the Canadian government to define its national security priorities after 11 September, it was also the first document ever to define Canadian national security strategy. The national security policy aimed at achieving three broad goals: (1) public safety in Canada; (2) the securing of Canada against its use by terrorists as a launch pad for attacks against allies (an implicit reference, of course, to the United States); and (3) making a contribution to international security. The focus of the document was on the first two goals. The policy also emphasized what can be called an "all hazards" approach to national security. It did not prioritize threats and steered clear of the suggestion that terrorism was of overriding concern, which might have made the document prone to the criticism of being too strongly influenced by American doctrine. Instead, it lumped together a wide range of threats from terrorism to natural disasters, organized crime, and health pandemics (ibid., in particular, chapter 1).

When it came to a discussion of border security, the national security policy emphasized the need to push ahead with work on the smart borders action plan and even to broaden it so as to bring it into line with the Canadian "all hazards" approach to national security by incorporating elements such as food safety and public health (ibid., 46). There was a suggestion of high satisfaction with the bilateral border security relationship, evinced by the idea that Canada should work to spread the message and "internationalize our Smart Border programs" (ibid.). The same note was struck in a progress report on the implementation of the national security policy, which was issued one year later in April 2005 (Canada 2005a).

The Security and Prosperity Partnership

Domestic national security reform and attention to the bilateral Canada-US border security framework were the dominant modes of activity for the Canadian government after 11 September 2001. Yet in March 2005, a new conceptual layer was officially added to the mix, although it had long been under discussion in public. The concept of a North American security perimeter was officially blessed at a trilateral leaders' summit, held at Baylor University in Waco, Texas. Presidents Bush and Vicente Fox and Prime Minister Paul Martin announced the Security and Prosperity Partnership of North America (*Security and Prosperity Partnership* 2005).[6]

Each of the North American partners came to the concept along different vectors, but the Canadian origins of the idea were significant. The notion of a

North American security perimeter was given an initial push by the private sector, especially the Canadian Council of Chief Executives (CCCE). Its president, Tom D'Aquino, had urged the business council to take up this cause in the aftermath of 11 September. D'Aquino presented an action plan at the CCCE's annual general meeting on 14 January 2003 and labelled the effort the Security and Prosperity Partnership (D'Aquino 2003). Some of D'Aquino's strategic plan was to find its way into the eventual announcement of the North American Security and Prosperity Partnership, especially the emphasis on deepening economic integration and the strong interrelationship between the economic and security foundations of any post-9/11 relationship between the North American states. D'Aquino saw 11 September as both a catalyst and an opportunity to move Canada and the United States into a tighter economic and security relationship. The focus was very much on bilateral relations but with some attention paid to Mexico, which was seen as a North American partner but with a historical relationship to the United States that was wholly different from that of the Canada-US relationship. The D'Aquino action plan was also marked by a note of pragmatism, arguing against radical changes to the political foundations of the relationship between the three sovereign states and in favour of a flexible model of bilateral and, on occasion, trilateral measures.

D'Aquino and the CCCE were convinced that Canada would have to take the lead in forging a new North American partnership. They saw themselves as fighting a post-9/11 version of the battle over free trade that had led to the Canada-US Free Trade Agreement and ultimately to NAFTA. There was some old business to be dealt with, particularly removing the frictions still occasioned by trade protectionist disputes, as well as a lot of new business, including one of D'Aquino's five priority areas: "reinventing the border" (ibid., 6). This initiative meant going beyond the model offered by the Smart Border Declaration of December 2001, which was seen as being too rooted in tradition. Going beyond this declaration meant embracing the concept of a North American security perimeter while transforming the Canada-US border into what was then called a "shared checkpoint within the Canada-U.S. economic space" (ibid., 7).

The next stage in the CCCE's crusade for a new understanding of the North American economic and security relationship came with the publication of a major paper in April 2004 entitled *New Frontiers: Building a Twenty-First Century Canada-United States Partnership* (Canadian Council of Chief Executives 2004). With this document, the CCCE continued to stress the need for a bold vision of border security, the requirement that Canada take a lead with its North American partners, and the value of a strategic approach rather than an ad hoc effort. However, the April 2004 study was also tempered by a greater realism and some fine-tuning to match Canadian public attitudes. The earlier call for a common North American biometric identity card was dropped, for example, as inopportune. In fact, what the 2004 study was doing was moving closer to a commendation of the principles of the Smart Border Declaration and, thus, backing up what the CCCE had previously decried as an overly traditional approach. The April 2004 paper also swung its attention much more firmly toward the economic integration agenda and away from the ambitious plans for security cooperation. The CCCE retained its call for a reinvigoration of Canadian military capabilities but, in the aftermath of the Iraq war, distanced itself a little from its earlier enthusiasm for a common global strategy with the United States, while stressing the need for strengthened Canadian-American continental defence cooperation. Interestingly, none of the fifteen key recommendations of the April paper specifically concerned border security.

The Canadian path to the announcement of the North American Security and Prosperity Partnership was laid, as we can now see, by a combination of factors: the success of the initial post-9/11 round of bilateral negotiations with the United States on border security; the reordering of government institutions and the creation of a new power base for national security decision making; the spelling out of a national security doctrine; and a powerful private sector push for greater levels of economic integration and security cooperation. The Canadian path to Waco, Texas, laid the greatest significance on bilateral Canada-US relations but was hopeful of some degree of trilateralism and open to the suggestion that there might be areas of mutual Canada-Mexico concern, whether it be in trade flows in the automotive sector, in the lessons to be learned from national approaches to border migration and anti-crime measures on our respective frontiers, or in the ways in which joint Canadian-Mexican *démarches* might have an impact on an otherwise asymmetric relationship with the United States. Yet it has to be said that the Canadian interest in a North American partnership remained firmly fixed on the North and on bilateral arrangements. The *Security and Prosperity Partnership* offered no challenges to the essential Canadian outlook. It, too, was rooted in bilateral arrangements rather than in anything more bold or innovative.

If the Waco, Texas, declaration seemed of little substance, there was always the question of what would come next? The leaders' statement was little more than an indication of intent. It balanced broad statements about promoting economic well-being with the promise of a "common approach to security" (Security and Prosperity Partnership 2005). Implicit in the document was a view that the three North American neighbours already possessed a shared vision of threats to security and that what was needed was the development of a shared response. In practice, little effort was made within the early framework of talks on the Security and Prosperity Partnership to establish a common approach to security threats. One can only speculate as to why this was, but it is plausible to argue that all three North American partners realized full well that there were significant differences in their approaches to national security priorities, especially between Mexico and Canada and Mexico and the United States. These differences were unlikely to be bridged by leaders' communiqués or solved without a lot of trilateral work. It was a case of sleeping dogs left to lie. Yet it would have consequences for the future of the Security and Prosperity Partnership idea. Common "architecture" would be difficult to construct without a common framework of thoughts about threats.

Beyond Words: Building the Security and Prosperity Partnership

The leaders' statement of March 2005 promised an ambitious agenda and set a direction but left it to the ministerial-led working groups to come up with more concrete plans, inside an initial deadline of ninety days. Two separate ministerial-led working groups operated to produce the required progress reports, one focusing on the security agenda and the other working on the prosperity agenda. Interestingly, the report issued in July 2005 makes a legible distinction (at least in the English version) between "economic integration" and "security cooperation." The reference to security cooperation is all the more important given the latitude conveyed in the partnership agreement for the promotion of bilateral activities, with a third partner coming on board as circumstances warranted.

The ministerial report deepened the impression that a trilateral security partnership meant less than it implied. References to initial results in the field of security focused on bilateral arrangements, almost exclusively involving Canada and the United States. None of the agreements involved direct Canada-Mexico cooperation. It is also noticeable that the discussions within the Security and Prosperity Partnership framework do not embrace the "all hazards" approach to national security that is fundamental to the Canadian doctrine. Health security, for example, is treated, for the most part, as falling within the broad economic domain.

Much of the detail about security cooperation in the ministerial report of July 2005 is cast in the form of good intentions and future plans, especially when it comes to any form of trilateral cooperation. The strategic emphasis in the security domain is less about integration of efforts and more about the establishment of compatible and comparable programs in all three North American states. The ministerial progress report clearly suggests that important distinctions remain in the minds of the three North American partners between plans for increased economic integration and proposals for security cooperation. The former are marked by considerable ambition, while the latter are marked by caution. This reflects, I believe, three realities as far as security arrangements are concerned. One is that approaches to security remain firmly within the traditional domain of national sovereignty in a North American context. States will continue to make security plans on the basis of perceived national needs, with the impetus for bilateral or trilateral cooperation flowing from that base calculation. The second reality is that North American security cooperation will proceed, as it has done in the past, on the basis of bilateral, as opposed to trilateral, arrangements. The centre of gravity of such bilateral arrangements will remain, for obvious reasons, the United States. Canada and Mexico will, for the foreseeable future, continue to manage separate security partnerships with the United States. The third, and most invisible, reality that underscores the approach taken to date in the Security and Prosperity Partnership is that each of the North American states has a unique doctrine of national security and a different set of appraisals of fundamental threats. Mexico remains the most disassociated of the three partner states, while historical alliance connections, shared war experience, and a long-established tradition of intelligence cooperation define the intimacy of the Canadian-American security relationship.

The true weakness of the prevailing concept of a North American security partnership lies not in the ways it bows to an ambition-shackling reality but in the manner in which its common-standards approach fails to take account of the diversity of national security doctrines between Canada, the United States, and Mexico as well as the absence of an agreed definition of threat. The solution would seem to be obvious, and yet it goes unmentioned in the official discussions of the Security and Prosperity Partnership. The obvious solution is to bring the three countries together in seeking to formulate a North American security doctrine and in generating a common assessment of shared threats. Such a solution is, in my view, not *directly* attainable in the foreseeable future.

A similar finding was reached by a C.D. Howe Institute seminar on Canadian-Mexican relations held in April 2005, which concluded that Canadian and Mexican priorities in North America differ significantly and that only limited areas of mutual cooperation exist, at present, in the security domain (Goldfarb 2005). The C.D. Howe Institute study put it this way: "An ambitious joint security and defence initiative between Canada and Mexico, or trilaterally, is unlikely to work or advance either country's interests effectively. If policymakers aim instead at what is achievable, there are a number of discrete areas in which Canada and Mexico working together—either bilaterally or within trilateral initiatives—could better advance their respective interests" (ibid., 7–8). Is there any room then for a big idea in the realm of border security?[7] Probably not. Yet there are little ideas that could have, in the long term, big idea consequences.

Shared Assessments of Threats

What is worth striving for within the slowly unfolding landscape of North American security is a greater degree to which we share threat assessments. There is ambition enough. Threat assessments are a coordinated product of a country's intelligence community. They are based on the flow of intelligence available to the state and the judgements applied by intelligence communities to that database, which is a unique cocktail of secret and open-source information.

They seek to define both short-term dangers to public safety and longer-term perils. Threat assessments typically look both inward to domestically generated concerns and outwards to dangers lurking in the international system. Generating accurate threat assessments poses significant challenges to an intelligence community, both in terms of quality and the methods of production. They are the informational building blocks for national security policy, not least because they suggest hierarchies of danger to the state.

The trilateral sharing of threat assessments would be fundamentally new and would require close cooperation between the security and intelligence communities of all three countries. In effect, it would require an extension of the historically deep-rooted Canada-US intelligence-sharing practices and traditions toward Mexico. The aim of such an endeavour would be to air both the similarities and differences in national security outlooks on the part of the three North American states, to find areas of convergence, to identify mutually agreed gaps and vulnerabilities, and to slowly lay the foundations for a common view on threats to national security. Without this common view, the trilateral partnership on border security has nowhere to go.

There has been some thinking done about the sharing of threat assessments, most notably in the work performed by an US Council on Foreign Relations (CFR) Independent Task Force on the Future of North America. The CFR task force, like the Security and Prosperity Partnership, traces it heritage back to the studies done by Tom D'Aquino's CCCE. In a report released on the eve of the Waco, Texas, summit, the chairs of the task force (John Manley for Canada, Pedro Aspe for Mexico, and William F. Weld for the United States) called for the creation of a "common security perimeter for North America" and argued that among the steps that could be taken was the establishment of a trinational threat-intelligence centre (Council on Foreign Relations 2005a). The task force released a more detailed study, entitled *Building a North American Community: Report of the Independent Task Force,* in May 2005, clearly hoping to influence the ministerial working group thought processes on the Security and Prosperity Partnership (Council on Foreign Relations 2005b). However, neither the language of a common security perimeter nor the specific proposal for establishing a trilateral threat assessment capability have made it into the Security and Prosperity Partnership recommendations to date.

Some hint as to why such an inclusion has not been done can be found in some brief dissenting opinions appended to the task force report. One, by Thomas Axworthy, casts into doubt the benefit of a common security perimeter concept, which would entail the harmonization of key immigration policies, including visa and asylum procedures. As far as Axworthy is concerned, the trade-offs involved in the loss of sovereignty are unappealing. Another suggestion, by Richard Falkenrath, notes that the United States is looking, in particular, for real gains on the security front from a trilateral partnership and argues that "the U.S. government in particular should insist on no less than parity between the economic and security agendas" (ibid., 33 and 35). Former Canadian ambassador to the United States, Allan Gotlieb, seconded Falkenrath's concern about the need to maintain focus on both the economic and security agendas.

Such dissenting views from prominent commentators indicate the difficulties involved in making progress on more deeply integrated North American security agendas. Falkenrath's views may be particularly uncomfortable for the Canadian government. At least in the Canadian government's case, the philosophy behind the Smart Borders Declaration was to see security as a necessary facilitator of free trade in goods and people. Security was not, in the Canadian perspective, an end in itself nor was it ever a trump.

Prospects for a genuine trilateral approach to border security in North America look set to falter at the fences of national security prerogatives and doctrine. Trilateralism, which is not far advanced to date, could easily dissolve back into its constituent bilateral parts. The Council on Foreign Relations was correct to see the value of joint threat assessments as an instrument within the framework of a common security perimeter, but it failed to see the Catch-22. The Catch-22 is that Canada, the United States, and Mexico will never get to a common security perimeter until they have a history of trilateralism in threat assessments and until this history, in turn, lays the foundations of congruent national security doctrines.

Assuming a start is ever made on the threat assessment front, there will remain a steep political hurdle. There will for the foreseeable future be a strong whiff of conspiracy surrounding the idea of trilateral border security. The threat assessment building block will never satisfy the political concern about secret sell-outs. Two illustrations will have to suffice. The first comes in the shape of the New Democratic Party's (NDP) response to the Security and Prosperity Partnership. The then NDP critic for international trade and globalization, Peter Julian, attacked the scheme as the product, pure and simple, of the CCCE and decried the assumption that "Canada and U.S. interests are the same in the long run as defined by a handful of multinationals that control most of North American trade" (Julian 2005).

A second illustration comes from a blog by a Ph.D. student at the University of Toronto, which probably captures the instinctual fears of many Canadians. Krista Boa writes: "The risks to privacy and civil liberties inherent in the Canada-U.S. Smart Borders program are more than the sum of its parts. It is an overall agenda to increase surveillance and information sharing between Canada and the United States. More attention needs to be given to the Smart Borders Action Plan as a systematic program that is rapidly eroding privacy while increasing surveillance" (Boa 2005). The hidden history of the Security and Prosperity Partnership and the vagueness, or lack of official definition, of the concept of a North American security perimeter give such views their plausibility. The Security and Prosperity Partnership has the potential to be a political bogeyman.

The Smart Identity Card, the Harper Government, and Common Sense

As governments change, new administrations will have to confront this bogey-man and find ways to allay fears about the downsides of closer economic and security ties between the North American states. In Canada, a newly elected Conservative government tentatively embraced the Security and Prosperity Partnership in its early months in office. At a trilateral leaders' summit held in Cancún, Mexico, in March 2006, the incoming Canadian prime minister, Stephen Harper, the second-term US president, George W. Bush, and out-going Mexican president, Vicente Fox, signed onto continued efforts to shape the Security and Prosperity Partnership. The leaders indicated five priority areas for the expansion of the partnership over the course of 2006–07. The five areas included the creation of a North American "Competitiveness Council;" the development of joint efforts to combat avian and pandemic influenza; the initiation of work on a plan for energy security; the continuation of cooperation on cross-border emergency management; and the development of enhanced initiatives for border security (*Security and Prosperity Partnership* 2006). The high-priority areas for border security were largely focused on the joint implementation of technological solutions to the management of cross-border flows of people and goods.

The 2006 Cancún summit effectively masked one growing irritant in Canada-US relations, namely the congressionally mandated requirement for secure identity cards for travellers across the Canada-US border. This issue was politely characterized in a single bullet point concerning the need to "develop standards and options for secure documents to facilitate cross-border travel" (ibid.). The bland statement hides the fact that US determination to insist on secure identity cards for travel (what form of card remains unclear) is likely to significantly hinder travel, especially by US citizens, and harm economies for a benefit in security terms that remains unclear. The smart identity card problem is an illustration of the ways that security imperatives, no matter what their merit, can still trump trade. It is also an important illustration of the fact that the Canadian approach to border security issues—in order to manage both economic and security matters as part of a whole rather than to disaggregate them into separate policy areas—can have real pitfalls.

For most economic integrationists, tacking on a North American security regime seems to be common sense. For those in Canada opposed to greater economic integration with the United States, tacking on a security regime makes no sense. Our problem is that we cannot talk sensibly about the need for a security regime on its own terms. We shy away from a definition of what a North American security perimeter might mean, preferring incremental steps without a larger map of the future. We lack even rudimentary consensus between the three North American neighbours on national security doctrine. There has been no effort made to build a common threat assessment to guide policy. In many respects, the Security and Prosperity Partnership, like the Smart Border Declaration before it, is built on conceptual sand. We should not be surprised that the historic cultural trope of the Canada-US border as a dividing line signifying difference has re-emerged. Increasingly after 11 September, it is not terrorists, but, rather, Big Brother (whether in capitalist or spy garb) who is trying to sneak across the border of our Canadian imagination.

NOTES

1   North American Free Trade Agreement between the Government of Canada, the Government of Mexico and the Government of the United States, 17 December 1992, Can. T.S. 1994 No. 2, 32 I.L.M. 289.
2   See, for example, the editorial by then Canadian ambassador to the United States, Michael Kergin, published in the *Washington Times* on 16 January 2003. Kergin's article was prompted by a false story about terrorists heading into the United States from Canada. He attempted to undercut the image of Canada as the Achilles heel of US homeland security by pointing to significant developments in Canadian national security since 11 September and the reality of close Canada-US border cooperation. See http://www.canadianembassy.org/ambassador/030116-en.asp.
3   Canada-US Smart Border Declaration, 12 December 2001, http://www.dfait-maeci .gc.ca/anti-terrorism/actionplan-en.asp.
4   Bill C-6, *An Act to Establish the Department of Public Safety and Emergency Preparedness*, S.C. 2005, c. 10.
5   The Department of Public Safety and Emergency Preparedness Canada (PSEPC) has a workforce of over 52,000 civil servants and an annual budget of CDN $5 billion. See PSEPC website at http://www.psepc-sppcc.gc.ca.
6   Security and Prosperity Partnership, 23 March 2005, http://www.spp.gov.
7   The attraction to big idea solutions to post-9/11 Canada-US relations was popularized by Wendy Dobson's (2002) article "Shaping the Future of the North American Economic Space" for the C.D. Howe Institute. Dobson's article received a lot of media attention and became the first in a regular series of commentaries on border issues published by the C.D. Howe Institute (*Border Papers*).

REFERENCES

Boa, Krista. 2005. "On the Identity Trail: Smart Borders: A Wholesale Information Sharing and Surveillance Regime." Personal blog. http://idtrail.org/content/view/185/42.

Canada. 2004. *Securing an Open Society: Canada's National Security Policy.* Ottawa: Office of the Privy Council.

———. 2005a. *Securing an Open Society: One Year Later. A Progress Response on the Implementation of Canada's National Security Policy.* Ottawa: Office of the Privy Council.

———. 2005b. Department of Foreign Affairs and International Trade. "Thirty-two-Point Action Plan," 13 January. http://www.dfait-maeci.gc.ca/can-am/main/border/32_point_action-en.asp.

Canadian Council of Chief Executives. 2004. *New Frontiers: Building a Twenty-First Century Canada-United States Partnership in North America. Discussion Paper.*

Council on Foreign Relations. 2005a. *Creating a North American Community.* Chairmen's Statement, Independent Task Force on the Future of North America, March.

———. 2005b. *Building A North American Community: Report of the Independent Task Force.* May.

D'Aquino, Thomas. 2003. "Security and Prosperity: The Dynamics of a New Canada-United States Partnership in North America." Presentation to the Annual General Meeting of the Canadian Council of Chief Executives, Toronto, 14 January. http://www.ceocouncil.ca.

Dobson, Wendy. 2002. "Shaping the Future of the North American Economic Space: A Framework for Action." C.D. Howe Institute Commentary 162, April.

Goldfarb, Danielle. 2005. "The Canada-Mexico Conundrum: Finding Common Ground." C.D. Howe Institute, *Border Papers,* no. 91, July.

Julian, Peter. 2005. "NDP Demands Transparency in Can/US/Mexico Talks." New Democratic Party, 27 June. http://www.ndp.ca/page/1444.

New, W.H. 1998. *Borderlands: How We Talk about Canada.* Vancouver: UBC Press.

Security and Prosperity Partnership of North America Established. 2005. Leaders' Statements and Agendas, 23 March. http://www.spp.gov.

Security and Prosperity Partnership of North America: Next Steps. 2006. Leaders' Statements and Agendas, 31 March. http://www.whitehouse.gov/news/releases/2006/03/20060331-1.html.

8

Mexico and North American Security

Jordi Díez

Introduction

The profound economic and political changes that Mexico underwent during the 1980s and 1990s did not appear to have a significant effect on its foreign policy. It continued to maintain, right until the end of the last administration of the Institutional Revolutionary Party, a relatively isolationist position in international affairs that was more interested in domestic security with a focus on organized crime.[1]

This pattern changed, however, when Vicente Fox assumed the presidency in 2000 and sought a more activist international role for Mexico through a foreign policy that followed two main tracks: a closer political relation with its northern neighbours and an active internationalism through a more prominent role within multilateral institutions, especially the United Nations. In regard to his relationship with his northern neighbours, Fox articulated his vision of a new North America early in his administration. At the Quebec City Summit of the Americas in April 2001, he declared his desire to establish a "North American Union," an arrangement that would be similar to the European Union and involve a common currency, a customs union, new political institutions, the harmonization of a wide range of policies, and the establishment of a North American regional development bank. Fox's proposals were received rather coolly by his northern counterparts at the time. Then Canadian prime minister Jean Chrétien rejected Fox's entreaty, stating that Canada's interests in North America were primarily economic, while President George W. Bush declared that closer co-operation could take place only on issues related to immigration.

However, the attacks on the United States on 11 September 2001 changed dramatically the nature of North American relations, igniting interest in closer co-operation among the three countries, especially on issues relating to security, border patrol, and immigration. Soon after the attacks, Fox declared: "We consider that the struggle against terrorism forms part of a commitment of Mexico to Canada and the United States, as a result of the need to construct the framework of the North American Free Trade Agreement within which we build a shared space for development, well-being and integral security."[2] The United States also expressed interest in further integration. Paul Celluci, then ambassador of the United States to Canada, urged for the need to update border policies and to harmonize immigration procedures. Canada, under former prime minister Jean Chrétien, called, in turn, for tougher screening measures at entry points so as to facilitate internal trade flows ("Don't Act Alone" 2002).[3]

This renewed interest in strengthening collaboration in North America crystallized in a call for the establishment of a North American security perimeter, an arrangement whereby the three countries would co-operate in a variety of areas creating a common security area within which trade would be protected (Fry 2003, 14–15). The three North American countries have taken several significant steps toward strengthening collaboration on security matters. In effect, security co-operation within the continent has never been as strong, and it has, in fact, been institutionalized between Mexico and the United States on some levels. Nonetheless, despite this new level of continental security co-operation, we are still far from the establishment of an international regime that would resemble anything close to a security perimeter. Indeed, what we are witnessing is the emergence of an informal North American security system unfolding along the two traditional axes that have historically characterized North American relations: the US-Canada relationship and the US-Mexico relationship. This chapter argues that, while security co-operation in North America has increased within the region, it has primarily unfolded through bilateral agreements and initiatives between the United States and both of its neighbours. We are therefore far from the construction of a formal trilateral "security perimeter."[4]

The chapter is divided into two sections. The first section reviews the various steps that have been taken in the area of security co-operation in North America since 2001 by looking closely at the Mexican case. As we shall see, co-operation has taken place mostly through bilateral agreements. In the case of Mexico, some of these agreements have essentially amounted to the institutionalization of security relations with the United States, which is a remarkable development, given Mexico's historic reluctance to establish formalized links with the US security establishment. The second section looks at the obstacles that are likely to impede the establishment of a continental security perimeter: the divergent priorities of the three countries and the changing political realities.

Security in Post-9/11 North America

The attacks of 9/11 on New York and Washington brought about a fundamental change in the dynamics of North American relations. Since the signing of the

North American Free Trade Agreement (NAFTA) in 1994—when the idea of North America as a regional entity crystallized—trilateral relations have primarily focused on economic integration.[5] However, with the events of 9/11, security rose to the top of the US national agenda, as the defence of the "homeland" became the most important priority for the Bush administration under the banner of the "war on terror." Within this new context, economic and political relations between the United States and its two neighbours became subordinated to the security concerns of the United States. The need for security collaboration among the three countries subsequently increased to levels never seen before, as Canada and Mexico have gradually increased their co-operation with the United States. Nonetheless, given the nature of North American relations, increased North American co-operation on security matters has mostly evolved through bilateral agreements and initiatives. Despite the adoption of NAFTA, North American relations have, for the most part, unfolded along its two traditional axes: the US-Canada relation and the US-Mexico relation. As a result, the United States has signed several bilateral agreements with both of its neighbours.

Canada and the United States

In the case of Canada and the United States, co-operation in the areas of security and defence has existed since the establishment of the US-Canada Military Cooperation Committee in 1946 and the creation of the North American AeroSpace Defense Command (NORAD) in 1957. Yet it increased and strengthened on a variety of other areas after 9/11.[6] Within weeks of the attacks, Canada established a borders task force with the intention of developing a new strategy to manage the forty-ninth parallel within the new security reality. This task force eventually led on 12 December 2001 to the signing of the Canada-US Smart Border Declaration between the two countries.[7]

The Smart Border Declaration, which institutes measures to facilitate the flow of goods between the two countries, set the stage for increased bilateral co-operation. Under the declaration, both countries created integrated border enforcement teams (IBETs).[8] The IBETs comprise multi-agency groups of several law enforcement officials from both countries and different levels of government that share information and intelligence, sometimes daily, on matters related to national security and organized crime.[9] Subsequently, on 3 December 2002, both countries signed the Joint Statement of Cooperation on Border Security and Regional Migration Issues. Pursuant to this statement, both countries agreed to include Canadian personnel in the US Anti-Terrorist Elite Group. It also allows members of the Royal Canadian Mounted Police to have access to US intelligence.[10] Moreover, on 4 December 2003, both countries joined the Free Trade Secure Trade Programme (FAST). The FAST program consists of the registration of business people who belong to the Customs-Trade Partnership against

Terrorism, allowing them to cross the border more quickly using special lanes.[11] In regard to defence, co-operation has intensified across several areas, and both countries have been negotiating a new agreement that would see the expansion of NORAD to include maritime surveillance ("NORAD" 2006).

Mexico and the United States

Security co-operation between the United States and Mexico has also increased since 9/11. Soon after the attacks, Mexico ordered measures to protect oil fields and platforms in the Gulf of Mexico, and a security belt was established around the whole country. The Mexican armed forces also immediately implemented Operation Sentinel (Operación Centinela), with 18,000 personnel from the armed forces committed (Benítez Manaut and Rodríguez Ulloa 2006, 26). Moreover, the Mexican government stepped up security efforts and assigned increased security and surveillance responsibilities to various ministries: the Ministry of Defence was tasked with airport security and special surveillance across the border; the Ministry of the Navy and the Attorney General's Office were directed to facilitate collaboration with the Federal Bureau of Investigation (FBI) and the Drug Enforcement Agency; the Ministry of Public Security and the National Institute for Migration were asked to redouble efforts of surveillance on borders and bus stations; and the Ministry of Tourism created the National Security Commission to guarantee the security of national and foreign tourists.

Mexico went beyond the immediate steps that it took right after 9/11 and has reached several agreements with the United States to coordinate efforts on several fronts. A version of the Smart Borders Declaration that was agreed upon by the United States and Canada was adopted and signed by the United States and Mexico on 22 March 2004.[12] The Mexican-US Smart Borders Accord is more limited in scope than its northern counterpart, but it does replicate some measures, such as the sharing of information on individuals who "pose a threat" and the establishment of an "advance passenger information" exchange system.

Both countries have also agreed to a more fluid exchange of intelligence and security information and have advanced toward greater coordination on migration matters. Moreover, during the visit of then secretary of homeland security, Tom Ridge, to Mexico in February 2004, the two countries signed a memorandum of understanding in which the United States guaranteed that the repatriation of Mexican nationals would be done in a humane and secure manner. A joint communiqué was also issued at the time, which established the Plan for Border Security (US Government Accountability Office 2005). This plan ratified and expanded a plan previously signed in 2001, and it agreed upon measures to facilitate the exchange of information to fight the organized trafficking of people as well as the establishment of exchange programs for the training of personnel in charge of carrying out the plan. Further, in late 2003, the Fox administration authorized the deployment of agents from the FBI to operate in Mexico City's international airport ("Agentes al servicio" 2004). Finally, since 2003, 237 Mexican military personnel have participated in the newly established Counter-Terrorism Fellowship Programme in the United States.[13]

This level of co-operation between the two countries is certainly unprecedented, fuelled by the perception of nationalist public opinion that no formal engagements should be undertaken with the United States as they might pose a threat to the country's sovereignty. It is worth noting that a majority of Mexicans generally approve of increased security co-operation with the United States. For example, while the Mexican media decried Fox's decision to allow FBI agents to operate in Mexico City's airport, citing a violation of the country's sovereignty, 63 percent of Mexicans supported the initiative (Chicago Council on Foreign Relations et al. 2004). What appears to be of particular relevance is the fact that security relations between the two countries have gone beyond mere co-operation on these issues and have assumed a certain level of institutionalization. Mexico's intelligence institution, the Centre for Research on National Security, and the US Information Analysis and Critical Infrastructure Protection Directorate, within the Department of Homeland Security (DHS), have established six interministerial working groups devoted to the protection of critical infrastructure along the US-Mexican border (Benítez Manaut and Rodríguez Ulloa 2006). These groups are presided over by a "bilateral steering committee" and are organized by sector: energy, health, agriculture, water, telecommunications, and transportation. Local agencies in Mexico have also increased co-operation with US federal agencies, such as the FBI, and the DHS is currently developing Operation Ice Storm. This operation consists of a plan of action to implement immigration and customs regulations in collaboration with Mexican authorities (ibid.).

Trilateral Co-operation

The North American Security and Prosperity Partnership, which was launched by the leaders of the three countries at their high-level meeting in Waco, Texas, in March 2005, seems to indicate progression toward the construction of a trilateral arrangement and quite possibly the institutionalization of a North American security perimeter.[14] However, upon the release of the Security and Prosperity Partnership's goals in June 2005, it became clear that the agreement calls for further co-operation on border controls, transportation, and emergency planning procedures and that it deals mostly with regulatory issues on migration and automobile integration. Although defence and security co-operation figure in this new partnership, it is limited to maritime and port surveillance, and, on the defence file, it is primarily a US-Canada affair.[15] At the meeting held on 31 March 2006 in Cancún, the three North American leaders declared their intention to "advance the agenda" of the Security and Prosperity Partnership. However, the next phase of the partnership deals mostly with issues of business competitiveness, avian influenza preparedness, energy, and border management. On the security front, steps are being taken to coordinate efforts on disaster management, both natural and man-made. However, there is nothing in the document that would point to the building of a security perimeter.

What we have witnessed, then, is a strengthening of co-operation among the three countries, which in certain areas has become institutionalized, rather than the emergence of an international security regime. Despite calls for the establishment of a security perimeter, the three countries appear to be continuing to operate along the two traditional axes, with stronger co-operation between Canada and the United States on the defence and security fronts. Increased co-operation has taken place primarily through bilateral agreements and initiatives. The United States has naturally remained at the centre of security relations in the continent, but it has carried out co-operation bilaterally with its two neighbours.

Mexico's Approach to Regional Security

Several factors appear to explain the fact that Mexico has not sought the same level of co-operation with the United States that Canada has, especially on the security file. Among many in Mexico's political elite, the link between security and trade was not rapidly or easily recognized. Despite the fact that over 92 percent of Mexico's exports go to the United States, Mexico was not quick to react to the new security reality to ensure that trade continued to flow without any disruption. Mexico did not act quickly to protect its trade with the United States after 9/11. In effect, Fox was not among the first heads of state to offer official condolences to the United States and to offer assistance. Such hesitation lies in stark contrast with Canada's swift reaction as it proceeded almost immediately in establishing a task force to look into ways to protect trade within the post-9/11 reality. In Canada, the economic consequences from a disruption to trade with the United States became all too obvious in the hours after 9/11, given how highly integrated the two economies have become.[16] The Smart Border Declaration was in fact a Canadian initiative (Welsh 2004, 58–59).

Part of the reason why Mexico has dragged its feet on the security front is because it has traditionally looked inward on matters of security and has a different conception of security. Mexico has traditionally held an inward-oriented view on security, and when it has included an international dimension it has primarily consisted of issues such as drug trafficking and organized crime. The Fox administration attempted to reframe the notion of national security upon coming into office. Its national development plan of 2001–06—the development plan that every Mexican president is constitutionally obliged to formulate for his administration—was rather vague, however, stating that the new government would adapt the country's national security to the "new times and the new phenomenon of vulnerability." However, the new approach to security still focuses on national domestic issues, such as corruption, environmental degradation, and organized crime. At the international level, Fox's administration, in fact, disengaged from security regimes by withdrawing from the Inter-American Treaty of Reciprocal Assistance in 2002.[17] Moreover, security issues in Mexico have continued to revolve around human security, and it has in effect become an area of priority for the Fox administration, given its deterioration over the last few years, trumping issues of national security.

Furthermore, political leaders in Mexico, regardless of their party, appear to be constrained in their ability to engage overtly with the United States on security and defence issues given the perceived nationalist sentiments harboured by the population. Even though polling figures show that a majority of Mexicans support co-operation with the United States on security matters,[18] there is a generalized perception that Mexican public opinion is overwhelmingly nationalistic, with some anti-US overtones—something to which the political leadership feels that it must listen. In part, this opinion is due to the role of the media, which does tend to be generally nationalistic, perpetuating the perception.

Finally, in regard to defence, there is immense opposition within Mexico's army to increased collaboration with the US armed forces in any significant way. Although Mexico's navy appears to be prepared to do so, the top brass of Mexico's army have continually expressed their lack of interest in expanding defence collaboration with the United States. They have reiterated that their priorities are domestic—natural disaster relief and combating drug trafficking have historically been their areas of operation (Díez and Nicholls 2006). The Mexican armed forces have therefore not pushed for further co-operation from within Mexico, something that could apply pressure on the government to increase cooperation with the United States.

The Prospects of Trilateral Security Co-operation in North America

As we have seen, security co-operation in North America has primarily unfolded on a bilateral level. A question naturally arises whether there are any prospects for the establishment of a trilateral security regime in the continent. It would appear that, at least discursively, the three countries are still interested in building on NAFTA and on furthering North American integration. This much was evident with the Security and Prosperity Partnership. Yet it is not clear that the desire to further continental integration necessarily equates to a call or a vision to establish a security system.

For instance, Canada has expressed an interest in further integration. In the international policy statement revealed by former Prime Minister Paul Martin in May 2005, his administration reasserted its commitment to North America and emphasized aspects of co-operation. It also stated that it considered Mexico to be a strategic partner. However, there has been no initiative to establish a continental security system. As for the current Conservative government of Prime Minister Stephen Harper, it is still unclear what his position on North American relations is, and, should he have a vision for the continent, he has yet to unveil it. His minority government was elected on "five priorities" that are entirely domestic in nature (tax policy, the introduction of an accountability act, a child care allowance, combating street crime, and health care waiting-time guarantees). In terms of security, Harper has begun to negotiate a new agreement to expand co-operation with the United States in defence matters through an extension of NORAD, but it does not include Mexico ("Tories Poised" 2006).

Four Factors Working against a Formal Security Regime

In the case of Mexico, greater co-operation with the United States on security issues has been forthcoming from the Fox administration, as we have seen, but several factors have complicated any push for further integration. The first one is Fox's inability to reach an agreement with the Bush administration on immigration. A central policy objective of his foreign policy was the establishment of a temporary workers program for Mexicans living in the United States. Reaching a migratory agreement with the United States seemed likely at the beginning of Fox's term, given that President Bush was receptive to the idea. At their first meeting in Crawford, Texas, in August 2001, Bush declared his willingness to work on this file and to push a workers program through Congress. Two weeks after the meeting, however, the attacks of 9/11 occurred, and migration was relegated to the bottom of the US national agenda.

Attempts to increase integration will be difficult unless a migration agreement is reached, since the protection of Mexican workers in the United States is cited as the country's number one foreign policy priority by 88 percent of Mexicans (Chicago Council on Foreign Relations et al. 2004). President Fox is by all accounts something of a "dead duck" president given that he has less than a year left in office and is constitutionally barred from re-running. It is therefore very unlikely that new momentum will emanate from Mexico over the next year. The prospects of establishing a new migratory system in the United States will most certainly depend on the manner in which the issue is resolved within the US Congress rather than on any agreement reached between the two countries. As we witnessed in the spring of 2006, despite the mass mobilizations that took place across the United States by illegal workers (mostly from Mexico), the new migratory bill unravelled in the US Senate due to partisan motives.

Second, the enthusiasm with which Mexicans supported NAFTA when it was first adopted has subsided substantially. For example, 70 percent of Mexicans say that NAFTA has had a positive effect on the US economy, while only 44 percent think it has had a positive effect on the Mexican economy. Moreover, 70 percent of Mexicans believe that the United States has benefited the most from NAFTA, while only 8 percent believe Mexico has benefited the most (ibid.). The economic benefits that President Carlos Salinas de Gortari promised with the advent of NAFTA have not materialized. Although Mexican exports to the United States and Canada have indeed trebled since its coming into effect, poverty has not been reduced in any significant way, and it appears that the wealth has failed to be distributed equitably. Income distribution has widened over the last decade, and the country has started to experience a stark regional differentiation where southern states have failed to reap the benefits of free trade and have lagged behind (Middlebrook and Zepeda 2003).

Third, in the same manner in which the US failure to abide by NAFTA rulings on the lumber dispute is eroding the legitimacy of NAFTA before Canadian public opinion, several disagreements between Mexico and the United States on some areas (that is, the US refusal to allow Mexican transportation trucks to enter the United States) have had a similar effect in Mexico.

Fourth, the US decision to act outside multilateral institutions in the invasion of Iraq has fuelled the distrust and suspicion of US intentions among a great number of Mexicans and augmented anti-American sentiments. This perception is in part due to the faith that Mexico has historically placed on multilateralism and non-intervention. For example, 55 percent of Mexicans believe that the US role in the world is negative, 43 percent express distrust of US foreign policy, 77 percent believe that the United States should not become the policeman of the world, and 60 percent believe that strengthening the United Nations is a very important foreign policy goal, compared with 38 percent of Americans (ibid.). It appears that any attempt to further integration would first have to address these negative feelings in public opinion at some level.

More fundamentally, however, the main obstacle for further integration beyond areas of trade regulation and border management is the disparate national priorities of the three governments. For the United States, homeland security has become the number one priority for the current administration, and all other issues have been placed much further down the list. For Canada and Mexico, trade with the United States continues to be of the utmost importance, but, for Mexico, issues of economic development, drug trafficking, and personal security are atop its citizens' priorities. Any attempt at further integration will not go far unless these issues are formally addressed. And although some within Mexico's administration are said to be trying to resume talks for further integration, given the recent improvement of relations between Mexico and the United States (Wood 2006), the time left in Fox's administration is, as mentioned, limited.

It is also unclear whether a new administration in Mexico City would bring about a significant change in Mexico's position on North American security. A week before the election, the two leading candidates, Andrés Manuel López

Obrador of the Democratic Revolutionary Party and Felipe Calderón Hinojosa of the ruling National Action Party, were in a statistical tie in opinion polls. If Calderón is the winner in a closely fought election, it is unlikely that he will change North American relations in any fundamental way. Calderón has declared that he will not change Mexico's foreign policy, and López Obrador's policy proposals on security, unveiled on 2 October 2005, deal mostly with personal security, corruption, and organized crime. There is no mention whatsoever on security collaboration with Mexico's northern neighbours. On the defence front, López Obrador has pledged to expand the role of the armed forces through a constitutional reform and to fight drug trafficking. Yet there are no proposals on defence co-operation with the United States or Canada.

According to some theories of regime formation, the establishment of formal regimes is to a great extent determined by the convergence of the interests of the stakeholders (Keohane 1983; Stein 1983; Axelrod and Keohane 1986). Neo-liberal institutionalists argue that formal regimes, which are based on collaboration as opposed to co-operation, are unlikely to emerge when stakeholders maintain widely disparate goals, since the decisions they make will produce sub-optimal results, given the differential in objectives (Stein 1983). If theories can be used to look into the future of a North America security perimeter, it appears that, given that the three countries have varied objectives, the likelihood of the emergence of a formal security framework is rather small.

The Need for Closer Co-operation

It can well be argued that continuing to pursue the formation of a formal security system is not in the interest of the three countries. Despite the fact that security does not have the same level of priority for the three countries, steps can be taken to institutionalize security relations in North America and to create a formal security perimeter. The debate should not be on whether closer co-operation on security should take place but, rather, on how. At a very pragmatic level, the economies of Mexico and Canada are extremely dependent on the free and stable flow of goods across borders: 92 percent of Mexico's exports and 86 percent of Canada's exports go to the United States. As a result, any disruption to trade caused by a security threat, whether it is terrorist or otherwise, would have an enormous effect on the economies of the two countries. Should an attack on the United States be carried out by an individual or group of people using either Canada or Mexico as an entry point, the consequences would be disastrous. Of course, a formal security arrangement would not provide any guarantee that this would be prevented. Yet it would at least share the responsibility more equally and diminish any attempt at closing down the borders.

Mexico lacks the resources necessary to step up security in any significant way and has other priorities. The establishment of a formal security regime would potentially result in the transfer of resources from its northern neighbours, which will, in turn, allow it to strengthen some of its notoriously weak and corrupt security institutions. The wave of violence that took place in some border cities during the summer of 2005, during which several police officers were killed by organized crime and dozens of others jailed for having collaborated with drug traffickers, is but an example of such institutional weakness. The federal government was forced to relieve the municipal police of its security responsibilities and send in the army under the "Secure Mexico" program.

How Far Are Canada and Mexico Willing to Go?

There exists the view in Canada and Mexico, among the political elites, observers, academic circles, and significant sectors of society, that any pursuit of further security integration would inevitably result in the loss of sovereignty and would represent the imposition of the priorities of the United States. Peter Andreas (2003, 11) captures that feeling exquisitely when he refers to the positions of Canada and Mexico within a post-9/11 world as one of "two scared mice next to a neurotic elephant." He argues that, given the structural imbalance and power asymmetries in North America, Washington "has significant policy leverage over its immediate neighbours, leaving them with limited space to manoeuvre. Here the United States largely sets the policy agenda and narrows the room for autonomous policy choices" (ibid., 12). US immigration policy is the most dramatic case in point of US unilateralism.

Yet, as Jennifer Welsh (2004, 58–60) shows, the proposal to reach the Smart Border Declarations in the region was a Canadian initiative and a policy triumph for Canada. She details how the United States had no clear vision of what the post-9/11 borders should look like and how Canadian officials elaborated a plan that was eventually adopted by the United States. As we have seen, a version of the plan was replicated along the Mexico-US border. This was not an imposition of the United States on Canada and attests to the extent to which Canada still enjoys policy-making autonomy.

However, more importantly, the establishment of formal institutions would make it easier to provide greater transparency and accountability in security co-operation. As mentioned earlier, security co-operation in North America has been strengthened in several areas. But there is some evidence that such cooperation has involved areas that are not known to the public, such as anti-terrorist and military training. In an interview with Loretta Bondì (2004, 86), a high-ranking US official, she states that "we do a lot of that [anti-terrorist training] because Mexicans badly need it. We try to keep it quiet since Mexicans are very sensitive to that."

The same official stated that her agency has been putting together a "counter-terrorism training package," which includes basic investigation, interview, and interrogation techniques as well as crisis management, hostage negotiations, evidence gathering, and surveillance (ibid.). The same informal arrangements are occurring in other areas, such as defence co-operation. Despite the Mexican army's official position that they do not wish to strengthen co-operation with the United States, a Mexican general declared that co-operation is taking place and will take place regardless of formal institutions.[19] Moreover, even when information is released on the training of personnel, there are, at times, discrepancies between the numbers of participants reported by the Ministries of Navy and Defence and those reported by US institutions. For example, according to the information provided by the two ministries to the daily *El Universal,* only thirteen Mexican military personnel had participated in the newly established Counter-Terrorism Fellowship Programme. According to the numbers provided by the US State Department, the number is 237 ("Militares toman" 2006; Center for International Policy 2006). On another occasion, the spokesperson for the US State Department's Southern Command stated that personnel from the Mexican navy had attended exercises in Texas in 2004, while a spokesperson from the Ministry of the Navy denied the event ("Refuta México" 2005). The point is that a great deal of unofficial co-operation has taken place, and it is likely to continue to do so. The formalization of these relationships through their institutionalization could potentially make it more transparent.

Admittedly, a complete openness of security relations would not be guaranteed through the establishment of formal institutions. Indeed, by definition, intelligence has to be secretive. Yet the institutionalization of co-operation that is already taking place in some areas, irrespective of the establishment of formal institutions, would make it easier to initiate increased transparency. And although it is difficult to oversee security agencies and bring them into account, it is not impossible. For example, Canada's National Security Strategy, unveiled in April 2004, allows for the inclusion of civil society groups in the formulation of national security policy as well as a mechanism of oversight. The roundtable on security was established to oversee security institutions and ensure that they do not overstep their responsibilities.

Given the distrust for supranational institutions that has long existed in the United States, the establishment of a supranational security institution is unlikely to transpire. But institutionalization can nevertheless take place at a lower level. The establishment of institutionalized intra-ministerial co-operation is a feasible and viable option. The close relationship that was established between Mexico's Centre for Research on National Security and the US Information Analysis and Critical Infrastructure Protection Directorate, through the creation of working groups, is an obvious starting point, and their expansion to trilateral institutionalization could be pursued. This is feasible because it is in the interest of Canada and Mexico to keep their borders open and for security relations to be rendered more transparent and accountable without formal institutionalization.

Conclusion

The coming into effect of NAFTA in 1994 crystallized the idea of North America as a regional entity. Whereas, prior to this point, North America referred to the United States and Canada, NAFTA appears to have expanded the definition of the continent to include Mexico. Since its enactment, NAFTA has increased relations among the three countries as trade and investment increased to record levels. However, these relationships remained primarily limited to economic terms. Notwithstanding the calls for the expansion of NAFTA made by President Fox upon coming into power, Canada and the United States have continued to see NAFTA purely as an economic agreement. The attacks of 9/11 fundamentally changed the nature of North American relations as security rose to the top of the US national agenda around the defence of the homeland. Relations between the United States and its two neighbours would therefore have to deal with security matters centrally. What we have seen, as a result, is an unprecedented level of co-operation on security matters since 9/11, since both Mexico and Canada have willingly chosen to participate.

In the case of Mexico, security co-operation has even been institutionalized in some areas, a remarkable development given the country's historical reluctance to establish formal links with US security institutions. Nonetheless, despite calls for the establishment of a North American security perimeter, security co-operation in post-9/11 North America has evolved mostly along the two traditional axes of North American relations: the US-Canada axis and the US-Mexico axis. As this chapter has attempted to show, we are far from the establishment of a formal, trilateral security structure since security co-operation has primarily been done through bilateral agreements. The prospects for the establishment of such a structure remain bleak as the three countries seem to have disparate national priorities.

NOTES

1 Mexico's foreign policy during Institutional Revolutionary Party's (PRI) rule was firmly grounded on the principle of non-intervention and characterized by an inward-looking position on security matters. For an overview of Mexico's traditional foreign policy during PRI rule, see the text by Mario Ojeda (1981), and for an overview of Mexico's security approach to its foreign policy see the text by Raúl Benítez Manaut (1996). Mexico's foreign policy underwent some modifications during the 1990s, but these changes were limited to economic matters as President Carlos Salinas de Gortari (1988–92) sought increased economic integration with the United States (Heredia 1997).

2 Speech made by President Vicente Fox at the Meeting for the Evaluation of Co-ordinated Action for Border and National Security, Tijuana, Mexico, 3 October 2001.

3 See also http://www.dfait-maeci.gc.ca/canada-magazine/issue14/14t3-en.asp.

4 Here I use Stephen Krasner's (1983, 142) classical definition of what an international regime is: "Implicit or explicit principles, norms, rules and decision-making procedures around which actors' expectations converge in a given area of international relations."

5 North American Free Trade Agreement between the Government of Canada, the Government of Mexico and the Government of the United States, 17 December 1992, Can. T.S. 1994 No. 2, 32 I.L.M. 289.

6 Co-operation between the two countries began almost immediately as Canada allowed the diversion of more than 220 commercial jetliners to its airports and placed its entry points in a state of emergency. Canada-US cooperation on border management predates the 9/11 attacks, however. In 1995, they signed the Accord on Our Shared Border—see http://dsp-psd.pwgsc.gc.ca/Collection/Ci51-95-2000E .pdf—and, in 1997, both countries' immigration departments (Citizenship and Immigration Canada and the US Immigration and Naturalization Services) began developing a regional approach to migration issues through the Border Vision program, which eventually resulted in the launch of the Canada-US Partnership Forum (Benítez Manaut and Rodríguez Ulloa 2006).

7 Canada-US Smart Border Declaration, 12 December 2001, http://www.dfait-maeci .gc.ca/anti-terrorism/actionplan-en.asp. The agreement involves twenty-two specific points on which both countries decided to collaborate. For further details, see http://www.whitehouse.gov/infocus/usmxborder/22points.html.

8 The integrated border enforcement teams have increasingly been used along the US and Canada border. They proved vital in the arrests of the seventeen alleged terrorists in the greater Toronto area in June 2006.

9 Further information on the Free Trade Secure Trade Programme can be found on the RCMP website at http://www.rcmp-grc.gc.ca/security/ibets_e.htm.

10 Joint Statement of Cooperation on Border Security and Regional Migration Issues, 3 December 2002, http://canada.usembassy.gov/content/textonly.asp?section=can_ usa&subsection1=borderissues&document=borderissues_statement_120301.

11 Canada Border Service Agency website, at http://www.cbsa-asfc.gc.ca.

12 White House website, 22 March 2004, http://www.whitehouse.gov/infocus/usmx-border/01.html.

13 For more information on the Counter-Terrorism Fellowship Programme, see Training Data: Mexico, http://www.ciponline.org/facts/fmtrmx.htm.

14 Security and Prosperity Partnership, 23 March 2005, http://www.spp.gov.

15 The details of the Security and Prosperity Partnership were released in June 2005 and can be found at Security and Prosperity Partnership, http://www.spp.gov.

16 As Stephen Flynn (2002, 60) reported, "within 36 hours after the September 11 attack, DaimlerChrysler announced that it would have to close one of its assembly plants because Canadian supplies were caught in an 18-hour traffic jam at the border. Ford announced that five of its plants would have to lie idle the following week. The cost of this loss in productivity?: each assembly plant produces on average $1 million worth of cars per hour." More trade occurs between the United States and

Canada at the Detroit-Windsor border than occurs between the United States and the European Union (Grunwald 2001).

17 Inter-American Treaty of Reciprocal Assistance, 2 September 1947, http://www.state .gov/r/pa/prs/ps/2001/4988.htm.

18 See the results on questions relating to security cooperation (Chicago Council on Foreign Relations et al. 2004).

19 This refers to statements made by General Alvaro Vallarta Cecena in declarations made on 17 April 2002 (18 April 2002).

REFERENCES

"Agentes al servicio de EU vigilan el aeropuerto del DF, Admite la PFP." 2004. *La Jornada*, 1 January. http://www.jornada.unam.mx.

Andreas, Peter. 2003. "A Tale of Two Borders: The U.S.-Canada and the U.S.-Mexico Lines after 911." In Peter Andreas and Thomas J. Biersteker, eds., *The Rebordering of North America: Integration and Exclusion in a New Security Environment*, 1–23. New York and London: Routledge.

Axelrod, Robert, and Robert O. Keohane. 1986. "Achieving Cooperation under Anarchy: Strategies and Institutions." In Kenneth A. Oye, ed., *Cooperation under Anarchy*, 225–54. Princeton: Princeton University Press.

Benítez Manaut, Raúl. 1996. "Sovereignty, Foreign Policy and National Security in Mexico, 1821–1989." In Hal Klepak, ed., *Natural Allies? Canadian and Mexican Perspectives on National Security*, 57–90. Ottawa: Carleton University Press and Canadian Foundation for the Americas.

———, and Carlos Rodríguez Ulloa. 2006. "Homeland Security in North America: From NAFTA to the Security and Prosperity Partnership of North America." In Jordi Díez, ed., *Canadian and Mexican Security in the New North America: Challenges and Prospects*, 25–38. Kingston and Montreal: McGill-Queen's University Press.

Bondì, Loretta. 2004. *Beyond the Border and across the Atlantic: Mexico's Foreign and Security Policy in Post–September 11th*. Washington, DC: Center for Transatlantic Relations.

Center for International Policy. 2006. *Training Data on Mexico*. http://www .ciponline.org/facts/fmtrmx.htm.

Chicago Council on Foreign Relations, Consejo Mexicano de Asuntos Internacionales, and Centro de Inverstigación y Docencia Económicas. 2004. "Global Views 2004: Comparing American and Mexican Opinion and Foreign Policy." http://www.ccfr.org/.

Díez, Jordi, and Ian Nicholls, eds. 2006. *The Mexican Armed Forces in Transition: Security Issues in the Western Hemisphere*. Strategic Studies Institute. Carlisle, PA: US Army War College.

"Don't Act Alone, PM Tells Bush." 2002. *Globe and Mail*, 10 September.

Flynn, Stephen. 2002. "America the Vulnerable," *Foreign Affairs* 81(2): 60–74.

Fry, Earl. H. 2003. "North American Integration." Center for Strategic and International Studies. *Policy Papers on the Americas* 9(8): 1–23.

Grunwald, Michael. 2001. "Economic Crossroads on the Line." *Washington Post,* 26 December, A1.

Heredia, Blanca. 2000. "El dilema entre crecimiento y autonomía: reforma económica y reestructuración de la política exterior en México." In CEI-COLMEX and IMRED, eds., *La política exterior de Mexico. Enfoques para su análisis México.* Colmex-IMRED, 1997, 81–99.

Keohane, Robert O. 1983. "The Demand for International Regimes." In Stephen D. Krasner, ed., *International Regimes,* 141–71. Ithaca, NY: Cornell University Press.

Krasner, Stephen, ed. 1983. *International Regimes.* Ithaca, NY: Cornell University Press.

Middlebrook, Kevin J., and Eduardo Zepeda. 2003. "On the Political Economy of Mexican Development Policy." In Kevin J. Middlebrook and Eduardo Zepeda, eds., *Confronting Development: Assessing Mexico's Economic and Social Policy Challenges,* 3–52. Stanford: Stanford University Press.

"Militares toman en EU curso contra terrorismo." 2006. *El Universal,* 8 January.

"NORAD to Include Maritime Surveillance." 2006. *Globe and Mail,* 20 February.

Ojeda, Mario. 1981. *Alcances y límites de la política exterior de México.* Mexico City: El Colégio de México.

"Refuta México a EU sobre colaboración militar." 2005. *El Universal,* 17 March.

Stein, Arthur A. 1983. "Coordination and Collaboration: Regimes in an Anarchic World." In Stephen Krasner, ed., *International Regimes,* 115–40. Ithaca, NY: Cornell University Press.

"Tories Poised to Sign a New Defence Pact with U.S." 2006. *Globe and Mail,* 20 February.

United States Government Accountability Office. 2005. "Border Security: Opportunities to Increase Coordination of Air and Marine Assets." Report to the Chairman, Subcommittee on National Security, Emerging Threats, and International Relations, Committee on Government Reform, House of Representatives. August. http://www.gao.gov/new.items/d05543.pdf.

Welsh, Jennifer. 2004. *At Home in the World: Canada's Global Vision for the Twenty-First Century.* Toronto: HarperCollins.

Wood, Duncan. 2006. "Sharing the Wealth? Economic Development, Competing Visions, and the Future of NAFTA." In Jordi Díez and Ian Nicholls, eds., *The Mexican Armed Forces in Transition: Security Issues in the Western Hemisphere,* Strategic Studies Institute, 39–50. Carlisle, PA: US Army War College.

5

OPEN REGIONALISM AND THE NATIONAL INTEREST: NEW DYNAMICS OF DIVERGENCE

9

North American Energy Security: A Common or Divergent Future?

Isidro Morales

Policy makers in the United States have long coveted Mexico's oil and gas reserves. They would like a single North American market for oil and gas, with as much of the industry as possible being privately owned. Although many concerns remain the same as in the past—dealing with risk management and various uncertainties—the current strategy is based upon the assumption that the price of oil will remain at US $60 a barrel or higher. With energy prices surging, Canada and Mexico have a strategic interest in developing their energy resources and consolidating their position as tier-one suppliers to the United States. Although there is no consensus on the shared energy risks and threats, the Security and Prosperity Partnership, a North American energy security initiative that was launched in 2005, requires the three countries to negotiate their respective energy interests.[1]

This chapter will focus on the Mexican side of the equation. Mexico and the United States have followed parallel energy paths in spite of the fact that Mexico's energy sector has remained effectively outside the North American Free Trade Agreement (NAFTA) and that the government has consistently maintained a state monopoly over its energy resources.[2] Contrary to what most people think, Mexico's domestic energy production, export markets, and global strategic commitments are not incompatible with US security concerns. At present, Mexico is increasing its stake in the North American market—a trend that analysts expect will make Mexico a major player in the most sensitive area of US foreign policy. The challenge is to balance private sector involvement with Mexico's state-run oil enterprise. The consensus is that the current balance is unsustainable and that, in the future, the Mexican state will have less direct control of its lucrative energy exports.

Towards a Continental Energy Partnership: Main Goals and Concerns

Energy co-operation in North America became a reality during the negotiations of the Canada-US Free Trade Agreement (CUSFTA) in 1989 and was further strengthened by the creation of NAFTA in 1994. Based on CUSFTA, Canada guaranteed energy supplies to the United States.[3] Through NAFTA, Mexico began liberalizing cross-border energy trade in gas and electricity while maintaining the state's monopoly on upstream and downstream activities. Private investment was also permitted in domestic gas distribution and transportation as well as in independent electricity producers, provided they sold their output through the national electricity network, which was still monopolized by the state.

In 2001, Presidents George W. Bush and Vicente Fox, and Prime Minister Jean Chrétien created the North American Energy Working Group, which was an interministerial task force with the goal of sharing information and data for improving and enhancing energy trade and interconnections within North America. The meetings and publications of this trilateral group have become more relevant since the terrorist attacks of 11 September 2001 and since Hurricane Katrina hit the Gulf Coast in the fall of 2005. Once energy became a major pillar of the Security and Prosperity Partnership, the future of Canadian and Mexican energy markets was reframed under a "continental" strategy.

The report published by the Security and Prosperity Partnership in June 2005 calls for the creation of a "policy environment" in which both sustainable production and the efficient use of energy supplies could be promoted.[4] It also recognizes that energy has become "critical to the prosperity and security" of the two nations. Such high-level initiatives and the growing pressures prevailing in energy markets due to a tight supply combined with the natural disasters striking the US Gulf Coast has made regional energy cooperation a priority. This type of "regional partnership" is fully consistent with what current secretary of state, Condoleezza Rice, has called "transformational diplomacy"—a new, post-deterrence diplomatic order that the second term of the Bush administration has been aggressively pursuing. Through these regional alliances, the major goals of the United States, including combating terrorism, defending against weapons of mass destruction, and democratizing "rogue states," could be better achieved (Rice 2006).

Since Canada and Mexico are the two single largest suppliers of oil to the United States, the major goal of this North American strategic partnership, in terms of energy security, is to keep both of these partners reliable and safe for the United States. In 2005, Canada supplied 16.3 percent of US gross oil imports, and Mexico supplied 15.4 percent. Canada is a major gas exporter to the United States, providing around 15 percent of its domestic consumption. The fact that the energy grids of these two countries are so highly interconnected with US markets (especially in the case of Canada) makes both of them an extension of the US homeland, at least in terms of their security concerns. The United States has been interested not only in the steady increase of both conventional and non-conventional sources of oil and gas from each of its North American partners but also in the safety and integrity of critical infrastructure for the conveyance of energy flows into the United States.

Due to its continued dependency on oil and gas, it may also be argued that the United States is highly interested in maintaining, and possibly increasing, its import share from these two countries in the future.[5] According to recent studies, in the year 2030, oil and gas will still amount to 61 percent of US overall energy consumption.[6] Thus, as a result of the new global strategy for enhancing energy security in the United States and regional priorities raised by the Security and Prosperity Partnership, it is anticipated that Washington will focus on the following issues in the years to come:

- The increase of non-conventional oil (and gas) in Canada. With the equiv-alent of 178 billion barrels of established reserves, the oil sands have made Canada, mainly Alberta, the second largest reserve in the world, second only to Saudi Arabia (National Energy Board 2004, 4). This amount pro-vides the equivalent of forty years of oil consumption in the United States at the current rate and makes Canada the closest and safest supplier for the United States. Since Canada has liberalized its oil and gas markets with the enforcement of the CUSFTA, there is no major "structural barrier" impeding the development of this major source of non-conventional oil. However, two major uncertainties loom on the horizon: the development of the oil sands is feasible only if oil prices remain above US $30 per barrel[7] and the additional costs that the energy industry will have to "internalize" if Ottawa is to attain the goals of the Kyoto Protocol.[8]
- The development and expansion of the appropriate infrastructure in both Canada and Mexico to enhance oil and gas exports to the United States. Due to the characteristics of Alberta's oil sands (heavy oil that can be processed with technically upgraded refineries), most Canadian non-conventional oil will be exported to the United States, at least in the short to mid-term. This means there will be a further "continentalization" of pipelines and the upgrading of refinery processing in the United States. With respect to gas, neither Canadian nor Mexican production will be able to supply growing US demand for gas imports in the short to long term, even if the Mackenzie Valley gas pipeline begins operating in 2011 (Energy Information Administration 2006). Thus, locating liquefied natural gas facilities is required by both countries.
- Increasing investment in Mexico's energy industry. As previously stated, NAFTA brought about a modest liberalization of Mexico's gas and electric-ity sectors. The big question currently is whether the Fox administration, or a new incoming one, will extend NAFTA's treatment to other areas of

the industry. From a US perspective, enhanced participation by private companies is desirable if Mexico's oil exports are to be sustained, and even increased, in the medium to long term.

- The security and reliability of the continental energy grid. So far, the US proposal is to transform the current North American Electricity Reliability Commission into an organization in which Mexico will join as an observer.

Mexico's Current Energy Quandaries

According to Mexico's Constitution and energy-related regulatory legislation, overall hydrocarbon resources belong to the state. The status of Mexican oil and gas reserves is similar, in some way, to Canada's except that Canadian provinces own the reserves and receive royalties from the companies that exploit them. In contrast, according to Mexican legislation, only the state is entitled to explore, develop, and produce hydrocarbon resources, including the production and distribution of electricity nationwide. Until 1994, when NAFTA came into effect, no private participant—either national or international companies—was allowed access to Mexico's energy sector, with the exception of turn-key-projects and subcontractors providing specific services to one of the two major state monopolies: Petróleos Mexicanos (PEMEX) and Comisión Federal de Electricidad (CFE).

Mexico's energy legislation reflects its own history. For most of the twentieth century, state energy monopolies played a major role in industrializing the country. During the latter part of the century, both PEMEX and the CFE became icons of nationalism and state-led policies that promoted growth and welfare by keeping domestic energy prices below international levels. Since this monopoly survived NAFTA, the Mexican government may still differentiate between national and international markets when fixing energy prices. From the early eighties until the present, PEMEX has been a major oil exporting company as well as a major source of fiscal income for the government.[9] Since the 1980s, all governments, including the current Fox administration, have used oil revenues to pursue ambitious social and macroeconomic policies.

The use (and misuse) of this fabulous oil revenue has made it possible to finance the so-called "oil boom" of the late seventies and early eighties, during which oil production almost tripled. When international prices collapsed and Mexico's foreign debt skyrocketed, the oil revenue guaranteed the repayment of the "fresh loans" that the government needed during the eighties and early nineties (Morales, Escalante, and Vargas 1988). In early 2005, after the peso crisis and the financial bailout provided by the Clinton administration (US $20 billion in loans), Mexico's oil revenue and reserves became the backbone of the government's entire financial structure.

Mexico's Public Energy Culture

Thus, keeping the oil monopoly in the hands of the state is a matter that goes beyond historic, nationalist, and policy considerations. For the Mexican government, the administration of an oil rent (for better or for worse) has become a strategic factor in funding government expenditures and for backing a growing foreign debt. For these reasons, none of Mexico's political elite or public opinion makers would dare advocate, at least openly, for the privatization of the oil sector, since doing so could jeopardize their own political careers. What is at stake, as will be discussed later, is whether or not to modify the investment climate in the energy sector in order to introduce opportunities for private sector participation.

Mexico's oil revenue has always been perceived, by the Mexican political elite, political stakeholders, and public opinion, as a cash cow to be used for financing social and/or industrial policies. However, from the 1980s to the present, political elites have also used the oil revenue for dealing with successive financial crises such as in 1986 when oil prices collapsed. Mexico's oil income was put on the table in order to restructure unpaid loans and to guarantee the repayment of new ones.

This may explain why, during the past decade, Mexico has put considerable effort into increasing oil exports in spite of the fact that less and less public money has been channelled into the energy sector. While Mexico was exporting 1.3 million barrels per day in 1994, by the year 2000 exports had increased to 1.6 million barrels per day. These exports were progressively concentrated in the United States as the country of destination, rising from 73 percent in 1994 to 85 percent of all Mexican exports by the end of 2004 (Shields 2005, 45). President Fox maintained this upward trend, trying to reap the benefits of a tightening international market. In 2004, oil exports reached the historic high of 1.87 million barrels per day. In terms of value, export income jumped from US $7.5 billion in 1994 to US $23.397 billion in 2004 (Petróleos Mexicanos 2005). Although revenues have fluctuated during the past decade, since 2002 they have gained upward momentum with the beginning of a new "expensive oil" era.

It is also important to highlight the fact that although Mexico's nationalist energy policies have provoked tensions with its northern neighbour on some occasions, they have never directly challenged US strategic interests. In the early 1980s, Mexico became a major oil exporter at a time when the United States and other Western countries were dealing with oil shortages and price instability. At that time, Mexico also agreed to sell oil to fill the United States' strategic petroleum reserve. In spite of the rhetoric of sovereignty underlying Mexico's nationalist approach to energy matters, Mexico never joined the Organization of Petroleum Exporting Countries and never threatened to use its oil exports as a "weapon" to gain strategic concessions from the United States (Meyer and Morales 1990).

All of these trends clearly indicate that Mexico's energy policies have been compatible with US interests and concerns in the oil market. However, what has become an issue in this new era of strategic "continental" partnership is whether Mexico will be able to maintain its own energy trends and provide solutions to its own energy bottlenecks, while continuing to be a reliable exporter to the United States and/or other international markets as well as a reliable partner with respect to NAFTA and its "partnership" commitments. From this perspective, the main "hot issues" for Mexico's energy agenda, which currently have an impact on the continental energy partnership, are twofold: the sustainability of current exports and the development of the investment climate in this industry.

The Sustainability and Potential Increase of Mexican Oil Exports

The dramatic drop in Mexico's proven reserves in recent years is the result of the reclassification of basic petrochemicals made by PEMEX in 2003, in order to comply with international standards,[10] and the inability of the company to compensate for the depletion of its stock with additional reserves.[11] Of greater concern is the fact that most of the current oil production is only sustained by one field, Cantarell, the offshore reservoir located south of the Gulf of Mexico. In 2004, 72 percent of oil production and 17 percent of natural gas came from this highly productive field (Petróleos Mexicanos 2005). Experts suggest that this rich field is about to enter a state of decline and estimate that production will be halved by the year 2010 (Baker 2005).

The current secretary of energy and the director of PEMEX agree that Mexico needs to maintain annual investments of US $10 billion if Mexico's oil production is to be sustained or even increased to four million barrels per day. According to them, investments should be as high as US $15 billion annually or US $25 billion over the next twelve years if Mexico wants to increase its production to five or six billion barrels per day, respectively (Shields 2005, 87).

During the Fox administration, in fact, investments have increased, reaching almost US $11 billion in 2004. However, since 1997, more and more of these investments are not being made by PEMEX but are being made by outsourcing services such as drilling and exploration to private companies. This formula for financing infrastructure projects by redirecting public expenses was first employed during the Zedillo years,[12] but President Fox has used it extensively in order to finance new investments in the oil and gas sector.

In 2004, private companies funded 90 percent of PEMEX's overall investments through this mechanism (Petróleos Mexicanos 2005, 8). The Fox administration has praised this investment design as the way to go if PEMEX wants to maintain and/or increase its production while maintaining the constitutional gridlocks pending in this industry. At the same time, this formula has relieved the government from the need to divert its oil revenues to fund the exploration of oil reserves and other energy-related projects. As in the past, the current administration continues to "confiscate" most of PEMEX's revenues.

Since 1998, when the Ministry of the Treasury levied more than 60 percent of the company's revenues, PEMEX has been operating under a financial deficit, despite the windfalls of recent years. At the end of the day, if private investments funded through the PIDIREGAS formula are not paid directly by PEMEX (because of this huge transfer of resources), they become a liability for the company and for the Mexican government. Opposition parties have been critical of this formula because it prevents major fiscal reforms within the state company and, at the same time, is obscuring the level of indebtedness. A major debate has begun in Mexico over the way new investments in the oil and energy sector have been funded in recent years. There was no agreement on this issue during the Fox administration. Although there seems to be a general consensus that the status quo is not sustainable, differences erupt when the debate turns to the nature of a new investment regime for the industry. This volatility is well reflected in the case of gas and power generation.

The Evolution of the Investment Climate in Electricity and Gas

NAFTA made it possible for private utilities to participate in the generation of electricity and to take part in cross-border transactions. It even allowed small producers to generate electricity for their own consumption or in combination with others. In all cases, power production was understood to be a surplus that a company possessed and that could be traded only through the national transmission network of the CFE, which is the Mexican power monopoly. Changes in Mexico's domestic regulations confirmed this situation. However, in early 1999, President Zedillo submitted a constitutional reform proposal to Congress, in which power generation ceased to be a monopoly of the state. Only the transmission network would remain in the exclusive operation of the state. If the reform had been approved by Congress, NAFTA treatment would have been extended to the power sector, allowing private utilities to increase their shares in a growing market (Beltrán Mata 2005, 152–53). However, the proposal was rejected, demonstrating for the first time that a divided Congress, with no party holding the majority, could become a major counterbalance to executive initiatives.

Two years later, President Fox submitted a timid regulatory reform proposal to an even more divided Congress, in which private utilities could increase their market share in the power sector (always selling through the CFE). Congressmen challenged the proposal at the Supreme Court of Justice, alleging that the executive branch did not have the authority to decide on this matter and that only the legislative branch did. This open confrontation between key legislators from the opposition and the president shaped the environment in which the Fox administration attempted to modify the energy sector's investment regime. Fox was never successful in passing major reforms in this regard. In contrast, due to a surge in gas and, consequently, in electricity prices, following the destruction of Hurricane Katrina, the Fox administration returned to price caps in order to ensure that Mexico's manufacturing sector would remain competitive.

What was distinctive about the Fox administration was that it fostered the increase in private sector participation in the development of the Burgos Basin. Located in northern Mexico near the Texas border, this gas reservoir, with attractive reserves of non-associated gas, became the target of Fox's energy policies in order to abate the growing imports of natural gas in this particular region. While Mexico exported marginal amounts of gas in the early eighties, by the early nineties it had started to import increasing volumes. Mexico still has large gas reserves, although most of them remain associated with oil production or are still prospective.

Furthermore, PEMEX continues to lack a sufficient number of transmission pipelines in order to supply growing consumption levels in the northern industrialized states, especially Nuevo León, whose capital, Monterrey, has become the country's major post-NAFTA industrial site. Imports from Texas have become a more attractive option than pumping gas from fields in the south of Mexico. When the country shifted to using gas for fuel and residual oil for the production of electricity in the nineties, demand for natural gas increased dramatically, raising imports to 27 percent of current domestic consumption. If consumption trends continue to rise at the same rate, imports could constitute 50 percent of overall consumption by the year 2012 (Shields 2005, 63). Growing imports are perceived in the country to be a failure of the state monopoly to ensure self-sufficiency and to protect the Mexican economy from the fluctuations of higher international prices. Nonetheless, the government is currently anticipating that growing imports could be supplied by incoming liquified natural gas shipments from Mexico's Atlantic coast via Altamira and from the Pacific Coast via Baja California.[13]

Outsourcing Operations in the Burgos Basin

Since the Burgos Basin reservoir contains non-associated gas and its production could easily supply additional gas to the Nuevo León region, the development of the Burgos Basin has become very important for the Fox administration. From 2003 to 2005, PEMEX tendered multiple service contracts (MSCs) for developing the Burgos Basin. MSCs continue PEMEX's tradition of outsourcing specific services that the company cannot develop on its own. However, the difference this time is that the MSCs are long-term clustered contracts. The MSCs encompass a pool of service contracts that have existed before but which, this time, will be tendered to a single company regardless of the output generated from the developed gas fields. As such, there is no risk-taking component and no performance-related compensation. As in the past, these contracts do not allow for any share of, or participation in, Mexico's gas reserves or production. A fixed amount is paid for the services provided by the companies on a yearly basis. According to estimates by PEMEX, private companies have invested US $5.9 billion through this scheme. This investment will let the government boost gas production from the Burgos Basin reserves by 605 million cubic feet daily by the year 2008.[14]

However, MSCs have been criticized for several reasons. They have not attracted any of the major oil and gas companies, perhaps because these companies would not be allowed a share of the gas reserves. Since a fixed amount is paid to service contractors, the development of some fields could be more expensive than anticipated if their productivity is not high. A major criticism of the opposition parties is that MSCs violate the Mexican Constitution, since they allow private companies to drill and perform maintenance services in exploration and production activities. Senator Manuel Bartlett of the Institutional Revolutionary Party has attempted to block MSCs but has not been successful in challenging the legality of these operations at the Supreme Court level nor in civil tribunals (Fuentes 2005).

The controversies over MSCs have further discouraged potential investors in the Burgos Basin and heated the debate on the need to change the status quo within the energy sector. During the Fox administration, this debate became polarized between the diverging interests of the president and the Congress. While President Fox pushed for constitutional change in order to let private investors legally participate in the exploration and production of non-associated gas, congressmen engaged in heated debates on the need for fiscal reforms in order to partially reduce PEMEX transfers to the treasury. In the end, President Fox was unsuccessful in pushing for constitutional change in Congress. Although, in December 2005, Congress voted on and passed a new fiscal regime for PEMEX, under which the company would be entitled to use approximately 2.5 to 3 billion barrels to fund its investments.

Managing US Security Concerns: The Future of Mexico's Energy Production

Mexico's oil wealth has traditionally increased the government's bargaining capacity with the United States, particularly at times when the possession of natural resources could be used for strategic purposes. Historians have argued that the exploitation of the oil industry in 1936 was politically acceptable to the United States because Washington was not interested in alienating its southern neighbour when the possibilities for war were escalating in Europe. Forty years later, when two oil shocks made energy security a major foreign policy goal of the United States, Mexico capped exports to the United States and became a major player in world oil markets. Even so, during the NAFTA negotiations, oil remained off the agenda in order to give the agreement domestic legitimacy.

At the turn of the twenty-first century, energy security is once again a buzz-word in US foreign policy. However, this time Mexico does not seem to have any leverage on the situation, and there are both international and domestic reasons for this state of affairs. At the international level, the major difference is Canada's emerging role as the energy powerhouse of North America. Growing exports of bitumen and synthetic oil from Canada, as well as Venezuelan ship-ments, will compensate for the eventual decline of Mexican exports. As long as prices remain competitively high, Alberta producers will have the incen-tive to boost their production. Americans have also become less vulnerable to high oil prices. With prices ranging from the low to high forties, the American economy is estimated to keep growing in the long term. In addition, US fed-eral policies are betting on an "expensive oil" scenario in order to diversify the energy mix, stimulate technological change, and develop sources of non-con-ventional oil, gas, and fuels (Energy Information Administration 2006). For Washington, high oil prices will also stimulate additional production from "out-of-risk" areas, all of which will contribute to satisfying the increasing world demand for oil.

In contrast, on the domestic front, Mexico's addiction to oil revenues has become a major flaw in the sound evolution of its energy industry. Mexico's historical inability to craft major fiscal reform has made PEMEX exports the main source of income for the government. This addiction to oil revenues has persistently used up the valuable financial resources provided by the state oil monopoly, preventing it from maintaining reserves in order to guarantee its current oil production rates continue in the future and causing it to increase gas production in order to abate growing imports. If there are any security concerns in Washington with regard to Mexican oil wealth, they are due precisely to the uncertainties of future production.

Major Policy Options for Mexico: Tough Love/Hard Choices

In many ways, Fox's final plea to open up natural gas exploration and produc-tion activities to the private sector and the fact that the fiscal reform finally passed through Congress have framed the current "energy reform" debate in Mexico. As a result, two major options loom on the horizon for Mexican energy politics. The first one has been clearly articulated by the Fox administration and by Mexico's new president Felipe Calderón Hinojosa. According to this strategy,

NAFTA treatment should be extended to include the energy sector, allowing private companies to participate in upstream oil, gas, and electricity activities. This proposal would in fact continue the pattern of institutional change that Mexico has pursued since the 1980s.

However, if Mexico decides to extend NAFTA treatment to upstream oil and gas, the government must be successful in pushing through a major constitutional reform—something the Fox administration failed to do. In order to pass a constitutional amendment, two-thirds of the votes of the federal Congress are required as well as two-thirds of each state legislature. Although an assessment of market reforms in the country goes beyond the parameters of this chapter, it must be highlighted that they make up the backbone of major state reforms witnessed in Mexico over the past twenty years. As a result of these reforms, government policies have become more predictable and more open to multiple stakeholders. In principle, if a National Action Party government sticks to its commitments and does not privatize PEMEX or the CFE, opening the sector further will have a positive impact on Mexico's energy sector. It would result in the two oil monopolies increasing their capital for investment and would force them to become more transparent, efficient, and open to stakeholders other than those currently running the company. Again, this scenario would require constitutional reform in order to clarify the scope and extent of private participation in the energy sector. Such a reform would require a great deal of political capital. If the current government intends to follow this route, it should be careful to earmark capital to implement the fiscal changes necessary to make PEMEX and the CFE more attractive to potential investors or competitors.

The second option was clearly articulated by the Democratic Revolutionary Party and its presidential candidate Andrés Manuel López Obrador. Under a Democratic Revolutionary Party government, Mexico's addiction to oil income would probably be maintained, if not increased. The government would capitalize on huge oil revenues in order to run public programs ranging from infrastructure to income subsidies for deprived populations. Although Mexico would keep exporting most of its petroleum to the United States, the eventual decline in production could become a bargaining chip on the bilateral front, although its political strength for advancing Mexican interests would be limited. The risk associated with this option is that it could potentially result in pressure and retaliation from Washington in other fields of the bilateral agenda.

No constitutional reforms or changes to the PEMEX fiscal regime would be associated with this option. The major consequences associated with this scenario would affect the mid- to long-term future—namely, would Mexico's energy sector survive if it was modernized, even gradually, in the years to come? Will social spending fuelled by oil income boost the Mexican economy's productivity and competitiveness? Will the government be ready to manage its dependence on oil revenues in the case that oil revenues shrink?

In spite of the differences between these options, it is obvious that the status quo is unsustainable. If Mexico's oil output is to be sustained, it is clear that investments will have to be increased since it is unlikely that sufficient funds will be found in state-owned enterprises in the oil and electricity sectors. Therefore, new private-public partnerships are likely to be forged. What form they will take needs to be worked out. One scenario is that PEMEX will be the lead partner; another finds that private investors will have a much more dominant role with the Mexican state being held at arm's length. As the new government looks to reform Mexico's energy sector, little radical change is likely to occur. The need for continuity and stability is well understood by both the National Action Party and Democratic Revolutionary Party. Mostly importantly, the idea of expanding the role of the market within a state system of regulation is fully compatible with current US perceptions and interests in terms of their continental energy security concerns.

NOTES

The author would like to thank the School of International Service and the Center for North American Studies (CNAS) at the American University for hosting him during the 2005–06 academic year. Thanks also to the financial sponsorship of the CNAS, without which this research would not be possible.

1   Security and Prosperity Partnership, 23 March 2005, http://www.spp.gov.
2   North American Free Trade Agreement between the Government of Canada, the Government of Mexico and the Government of the United States, 17 December 1992, Can. T.S. 1994 No. 2, 32 I.L.M. 289.
3   Canada and the United States agreed to limit export/import restrictions, keep the proportion of energy exports relative to total supply, and avoid dual pricing.
4   The details of the Security and Prosperity Partnership were released in June 2005 and can be found at http://www.spp.gov. Compare with *Security and Prosperity Partnership of North America: Report to Leaders,* trilingual version, June 2005, http://www.spp.gov/spp/report_to_leaders/Trilingual_Report_to_Leaders.pdf.
5   According to some authors, whether or not the United States reduces its oil imports from Gulf producers is irrelevant (21.7 percent of its imports in 2005). Oil markets are global and fully integrated (Cordesman and Al-Rodhan 2005). This is true in terms of the evolution of crude oil prices. A disruption in any part of the world immediately impacts all countries involved in energy importing. However, in terms of strategic options, the United States' growing reliance on "high risk" countries or areas could become a liability. Since the fall of the shah in Iran, the United States does not import oil from there. Washington has also imposed sanctions—through oil embargos—on Iraq and Libya. If the "war on terror" is going to last, as it has been repeatedly announced by the Bush administration, Washington will be keen to keep, and/or to increase, its oil imports from "out-of-risk" regions.

6 Oil and gas imports will amount to 64 percent of petroleum consumption, and gas imports will amount to 21 percent of overall gas consumption (Energy Information Administration 2006, 64).

7 Supply costs for bitumen range from CDN $10 to $16 per barrel, and synthetic oil ranges from CDN $22 to $28 (compare with National Energy Board 2004, 7).

8 Kyoto Protocol to UN Framework Convention on Climate Change, December 1997, 37 I.L.M. 32 (1998). Some authors have estimated this internalization cost of US $6 per barrel (Brownsey 2005, 16).

9 Currently, the revenue of Petróleos Mexicanos (PEMEX) constitutes 35 percent of the government's overall income.

10 Reclassification of basic petrochemicals began in 1986 with the reduction of state exclusivity from seventy products to thirty-four. This is important because basic petrochemicals are assigned exclusively to the state. A reduction in the number of basic petrochemical products implies an increase in the participation of the private sector in the petrochemical business.

11 Proven reserves fell from 24.7 billion barrels in 1999 to 12.882 billion barrels in 2005. These are reserves from which current production is being obtained. As such, they will be depleted in ten years if PEMEX fails to increase its reserves in stock in relation to oil output (Petróleos Mexicanos 2005).

12 In Spanish, this formula is called *proyectos de infraestructura diferidos en el registro del gasto,* the acronym of which is PIDIREGAS.

13 The development of infrastructure and the construction of regasification plants are currently being accomplished, and the government anticipates that part of the liquefied natural gas shipments could eventually be re-exported to the United States.

14 See the Pemex website, http://www.pemex.com.

REFERENCES

Alberro, Jose Luis. 2005. *A US-Mexico Partnership in Energy: A Policy of Convenience.* US-Mexico Policy Bulletin, Issue 4. Washington: Woodrow Wilson International Center for Scholars.

Baker, George. 2005. "Mexico's Presidential Elections Trigger Oil Policy Debate." *Oil and Gas Journal* 103(42): 20–24.

Beltrán Mata, José Antonio. 2005. *México: Crónica de los negros intereses del petróleo.* Mexico City: Grupo Editorial Diez.

Brownsey, Keith. 2005. "Alberta's Oil and Gas Industry in the Era of the Kyoto Protocol." In Bruce Doern, ed., *Canadian Energy Policy and the Struggle for Sustainable Development,* 200–22. Toronto: University of Toronto Press.

Calderón Hinojosa, Francisco. 2005. *El reto de México.* Mexico City, electronic version.

Cordesman, Anthony, and Khalid R. Al-Rodhan. 2005. "The Changing Risks in Global Oil Supply and Demand: Crisis or Evolving Solution?" First Working Draft, 3 October. Washington, DC: Center for Strategic and International Studies.

Energy Information Administration. 2006. *Annual Energy Outlook 2006: With Projection to 2030.* Washington, DC: US Department of Energy.

Fuentes, Víctor. 2005. "Libran litigio contratos de PEMEX." *Reforma,* 9 November.

López Obrador, Andrés Manuel, 2005, *50 compromisos para recuperar el orgullo nacional.* Mexico City, electronic version.

Madrazo Pintado, Roberto. 2005. *Bases para un gobierno firme y con rumbo.* Mexico City, electronic version.

Meyer, Lorenzo, and Isidro Morales. 1990. *Petróleo y Nación (1900–1987). La Política Petrolera en México.* Mexico City: Fondo de Cultura Económica and SEMIP.

Morales, Isidro, Cecilia Escalante, and Rosio Vargas. 1988. *La Formación de la Política Petrolera en México, 1970–1986.* Mexico City: El Colegio de México.

National Energy Board. 2004. *Canada's Oil Sands: Opportunities and Challenges to 2015.* Calgary, AB: National Energy Board.

Núñez-Rodríguez, Eduardo. 2004. "Mexico's Changing Energy Regulatory Framework: Liberalization under NAFTA Chapter 6?" In Kevin C. Kennedy, ed., *The First Decade of NAFTA: The Future of Free Trade in North America,* 253–69. Ardsley, NY: Transnational Publishers.

Petróleos Mexicanos. 2005. *Anuario Estadístico, 2005.* Mexico City: Petróleos Mexicanos. http://www.pemex.com/files/content/Anuario_Estadistico.pdf.

Rice, Condoleezza. 2006. "Remarks at School of Georgetown School of International Service." US Department of State, Washington, DC, 18 January.

Shields, David. 2005. PEMEX: *La reforma petrolera.* Mexico City: Editorial Planeta.

10

The End of Neo-Liberal Regionalism in Mexico?

Rosalba Icaza Garza

Introduction

This chapter explores the failure of neo-liberal regionalism as an experiment in the development of the last three *sexenios* in Mexico.[1] In particular, it examines why this policy option has failed to advance conditions for an equitable, participative, and inclusive development in Mexico and explains the extent to which the policy's discursive tenets have slowed down the substantive democratization of contemporary regional governance. After the 2006 elections, Mexico's political landscape seems to be pushing it away from confronting the high costs of this market-driven reliance on export-led growth. At the regional level, the political advances of the Mercado Común del Sur (Mercosur) and the Alternativa Bolivariana par alas Americas (ALBA), combined with the stalled negotiations of the Free Trade Area of the Americas (FTAA) and the seeming inability of different sectors of civil society to propose alternatives, further complicate the regional political landscape.

To address these issues, this chapter examines two examples of neo-liberal regionalism: the North American Free Trade Agreement (NAFTA) and the Economic Partnership, Political Coordination and Commercial Agreement between the European Community and Mexico (EC-Mexico Agreement).[2] Certainly, these cases need to be analyzed as two different kinds of trade regionalism. NAFTA is concerned with the free transit of goods, services, and capital and contains investment rules, intellectual property rights, dispute settlement procedures, and parallel agreements on labour and the environment. In contrast, the EC-Mexico Agreement goes beyond the bounds of a conventional free trade agreement and contains a democratic clause and discusses political co-operation and co-ordination. Nonetheless, the argument presented in this chapter emphasizes the *commonalities* between these agreements, particularly focusing on those provisions that shape economic partnerships and that represent, it is argued, the formal expressions of neo-liberal regionalism with long-term policy consequences.

The discussion is divided into four sections. The first section introduces some working concepts and presents a brief examination of key conditions at the national and regional level that have challenged neo-liberal regionalism as a dominant paradigm in regional governance. The second section analyzes the socio-economic implications associated with the discursive and institutional frameworks of neo-liberal regionalism. The third section looks into the democratic shortfalls of this policy option and its implications, at the national level, for deepening and enhancing democratic regional governance. The concluding section offers some final thoughts with respect to future challenges that the Mexican government will face as a result of thirteen years of neo-liberal regionalism.

Neo-Liberal Regionalism: Conceptual Issues and Emergent Challenges

In this section, "regionalization" refers to a process by which regions as territorial spaces are made and re-made. For example, the region of North America has been transformed through shifts in policies, patterns of production, and migratory and capital flows. "Regionalism" is understood here as a set of policies framed by particular ideational aspirations that have been undertaken by governments and other region-building agents to participate in the governance of regionalization. In short, regionalism describes how and by whom a region is built up and managed (Grugel and Hout 1999; Marchand, Boas, and Shaw 1999; Scholte 2004).

Traditionally, regionalization processes have been described as essentially "economic" and led by a production rationale. However, an alternative viewpoint sees regionalization as a political economic process, interrelated not only to material forces but also to patterns of ideas and institutional frameworks reproduced and modified through the interventions of different sorts of agents such as governments, private capital, and/or communities (Hettne and Söderbaum 2000, 457–59; Marchand, Boas, and Shaw 1999, 900).

Moreover, from a political economic perspective, regionalization processes denote *de facto* trends of economic, political, social, and/or cultural integration and complementarities or co-operation among different units, whether countries, sub-regions, or communities. These trends are not understood as given or fixed and may or may not lead to the formalization of regional governance arrangements (Hettne and Söderbaum 2000; Marchand, Boas, and Shaw 1999).

A further foundational point for our discussion is that contemporary processes of regionalization appear to encourage the proliferation of suprastate laws, institutions, and public practices of regionalism that, in some cases, have a notable degree of autonomy from the states and the general public. For example, certain trade dispute resolution mechanisms empower regional private arbitrators in panels that are not open to those sectors of society likely to be affected by the resolution, such as consumer or environmental groups, peasants, and labour unions (Scholte 2004, 27; Wise and Gallagher 2006). Relying upon the foregoing argument, the following sections discuss how Mexico's thirteen years of neo-liberal regionalism illuminate the impact of this kind of supranational autonomy and, in particular, how neo-liberal regionalism affects the realization of equitable and sustainable social development agendas at the local, national, and regional policy levels.

The Rise and Fall of Neo-Liberal Regionalism as an Alternative

In the early 1990s, the open regionalism promoted by the Economic Commission for Latin America (ECLAC) was marked by "economic reductionism," as this policy was linked to economic efficiency and competitiveness (Grugel and Hout 1999, 9–10; Gudynas 2005; Mittelman 2000, 126–27). In contrast to the "closed" regionalism of the 1960s and 1970s, "open" refers to "inclusion," which, in trade policy terms, means non-discriminatory measures and low-entry barriers. It was during those years that Carlos Salinas de Gortari's government in Mexico became a key promoter of open regionalism, believing that it was a non-discriminatory policy option. Later, under Ernesto Zedillo and Vicente Fox's administrations, open regionalism frameworks were endorsed due to their perceived compatibility with the multilateral goals of the World Trade Organization (WTO) (Belanger and Mace 1999, 18–35).

Overall, it was expected that this policy would be welfare maximizing for the entire international economy since trade and investment distortions and discriminatory policies would be avoided (Gudynas 2005). Open regionalism would enhance ECLAC's position in the world economy, reducing its vulnerability and external dependence on foreign capital, as this policy focused on selective integration and trade liberalization in accordance with national interests (European Commission for Latin America 1990; European Commission for Latin America 1991). Accordingly, several Latin American countries enacted unilateral trade liberalization laws and flexible foreign investment regulations.

In Mexico, open regionalism has been instrumental for neo-liberal policy reforms (Icaza Garza 2004). In particular, open regionalism discourses and policy frameworks have been employed by governing and economic elites only when these complemented and contributed to the advancement and consolidation of domestic neo-liberal reforms. For example, it has been argued that NAFTA—commonly cited by ECLAC in the 1990s as an example of open regionalism—worked to *lock in* neo-liberal reforms in Mexico (Lustig 1998; Wise 1998) Accordingly, it needs to be stressed that Mexican "open" regionalism is better understood as an expression of the worldwide ascendancy of neo-liberal regional strategies that characterized Latin American public policy in the early 1990s.

Open Regionalism or Neo-Liberal Regionalism in Mexico?

For some commentators, a neo-liberal regionalist framework contains elements of "open regionalism" in the sense that it is not about shrinking from external competition but, rather, about "catching up" with the processes of regionalization through trade and investment liberalization (Hettne 1993; Mittelman 2000). Nevertheless, in neo-liberal regionalism frameworks, it is free trade that turns national markets into economic units, and, as such, this policy option basically encourages the free operation of rule-based markets. The rationale behind neo-liberal regionalism is that a fully integrated global market renders more benefits than "middle-step" regional liberalization or integration. For example, a fully integrated market among North American nations would indicate a better insertion of the three countries' export sectors into other regions.

However, contrary to the objectives of open regionalism's frameworks—particularly those advocated in the 1990s by ECLAC—neo-liberal regionalism tends to subordinate certain economic sectors/activities and, sometimes, even national economies to the requirements of global markets. In many cases, it serves to undermine local or domestic productive chains (Mittelman 2000, 112). In Mexico's case, this can be seen by examining the *maquiladoras* (in-bond processing plants), which are one of the key economic activities in the NAFTA era. In 2001, almost 100 percent of the *maquiladoras* were handled by foreign private firms established in Mexico. However, the spillover effect of these operations on the broader economy was very limited because, among other reasons, only "a narrow range of processing or assembly operations benefited the labour market" (for instance, the local suppliers) (Polaski 2003, 16). For example, in 2002, almost the 97 percent of the components in this sector were imported and only 3 percent were produced locally (Dussel Peters 2003, 48–56).

In the late twentieth and early twenty-first centuries, Mexican *maquiladoras* operated as huge assembly lines and, to a large extent, disconnected from national productive chains. These operations were highly dependent on the requirements of the US market and competed aggressively to increase their market share relative to that of other low-income countries such as China (Buckman 2005). This sector had important socio-economic effects for Mexico, such as increasing inequality gaps between those regions and localities where *maquiladoras* had been established and those where other activities constituted the main source of income (for example, peasantry and migrant remittances) (Arroyo Picard 2000). In many cases, *maquiladoras* were also located in export processing zones, and these regions stand in sharp contrast to their more conventional counterparts with respect to foreign direct investment, employment, and wages.

Understanding the Rise and Fall

For some commentators, the lost opportunities of the 1980s, combined with the state's failure to develop further, challenged open regionalism's political legitimacy and "paved the way" for the ascendance of neo-liberal orthodoxy among decision makers in the region (Gwynne and Kay 2000). Two further factors that also contributed to the legitimization and subsequent implementation of neo-liberal regionalist agendas were the emergence of regional blocs in Western Europe and East Asia and the decrease in the United States' world competitive rate, which incited private capital flows to shift toward Latin American countries.

Additionally, important changes in values and perceptions among Latin American economic and governing elites—predominantly relating to their views on the United States and on liberal democracy in general—were also crucial for the ascendance of neo-liberal regionalism. In particular, the role played by a powerful and influential technocratic elite in Mexico (namely, US educated officials with degrees in economics) was crucial for the installation of a neo-liberal orthodoxy with a strong trade deregulation agenda. These events have been identified as a "convergence" between the economic and political elites in Latin America and market economy principles and liberal democracy. For some, this convergence clearly manifested itself in the so-called Washington Consensus and in the "There Is No Alternative" (TINA) manifesto, which was famously cited by Margaret Thatcher (Centeno and Silva 1998, 1–13; Gwynne and Kay 2000).

Nevertheless, the mid-1990s financial crises in the Latin American communities pushed forward not only a reformulation of the Washington Consensus but also a reassertion of alternative views on development in opposition to the TINA manifesto. One commentator accurately expressed the opinion that the Washington Consensus had become nothing more than another "agenda" (Gore 2000). For example, the so-called "Southern-Consensus" of the late 1990s was promoted by the UN Development Programme, the UN Conference on Trade and Development (UNCTAD), and some Southern governments as a post-Washington Consensus attempt to re-position an alternative view on development and to challenge narrow economic interpretations on regional integration (ibid.). Contemporaneously, the TINA manifesto started to be challenged by the Association for the Taxation of Financial Transactions for the Aid of Citizens (ATTAC) as well as by other members of the global justice movement, whose proposals were sloganized in the phrase "Another World Is Possible" (Birchfield and Freyberg-Inan 2004; Buckman 2005).

Meanwhile in Latin America, newly elected left-leaning governments in Argentina, Brazil, Ecuador, Nicaragua, and Venezuela have deepened the debate around the development of more and better organized opposition to the trade terms dictated by the United States in the FTAA (Newell and Tussie 2006). In addition, civil society groups and social movements that had been opposed to neo-liberal regionalism gathered around broad coalitions such as the Hemispheric Social Alliance to oppose the FTAA (Saguier 2004). Opposition groups rallied around efforts to contest and subvert the unquestioning logic of neo-liberal regionalism (Hemispheric Social Alliance 2002). For groups facing the democratic deficit of neo-liberal regionalism, embracing the principles of extended subsidiarity as applied to decision making was attractive. Such efforts involved making substantial decisions at the lowest level possible with the full participation of those affected by such decisions (Icaza Garza 2004).

In Mexico, a reformulation of the Washington Consensus agenda was endorsed by the governing and economic elites as well as by civil society and groups that had sought "a reform of the reforms." These second generation reforms included, among other things, an efficient, transparent, and accountable oversight role for the state respecting market operations and the involvement of private actors in allocating public goods for alleviating poverty. As for regionalization, the official discourse in Mexico shifted gradually from a narrow economic interpretation toward the inclusion of some redistributive notions. A good example of this was the Fox administration's early promotion of the North American community proposal—the sub-regional co-operation scheme known as "Plan Puebla Panama"—which integrated poverty alleviation issues and European Union–style cohesion funds for the development of depressed sub-regions and acknowledged the relevance of civil society, business, and government "partnerships."

As for those sectors of Mexican civil society that were critical of neo-liberal regionalism and the post-Washington Consensus reformist agenda, it has been argued elsewhere that through transborder civic activism these sectors became engaged in the political economy of regionalization and that their interventions affected, to some extent, the social dimension and the democratic qualities of NAFTA and the EC-Mexico Agreement (Icaza Garza 2004). Further, in relation to social development and trade economics, many groups advanced reformist agendas and alternatives to neo-liberal regionalism that were far less radical than many supposed. In particular, Mexican transborder civic activists that were opposed to neo-liberal regionalism have held an agenda on social development that is closer to the ECLAC and UNCTAD proposals on trade and development than to the more radical elements of the anti-globalization movement (for example, de-linking plans) (ibid.).

On the other hand, some of these groups have called for more radical changes to citizenship and for the elimination of social hierarchies. For example, some groups have advocated that trade liberalization should be tied to a democratic deliberation in which the economic sectors and actors concerned would participate. These proposals were deemed to be more likely to bring about equitable solutions that were clearly different from the dominant neo-liberal approaches to regionalization with their link to liberal (minimal) notions of democracy (ibid.). Paradoxically, governing authorities in Mexico have been more receptive, at least rhetorically, to developing the regionalization agenda as a more participative process and have consistently rejected proposals advocated by Mexican civil society groups that are against neo-liberal regionalism as a development paradigm (ibid.).

Who Has Gained from Neo-Liberal Regionalism?

Neo-liberal regionalism, as an official part of the Mexican development strategy, has had mixed results. In particular, as expressions of neo-liberal regional governance, both NAFTA and the EC-Mexico Agreement have had an impact by creating social policy with important implications for social redistribution and social provision at the national and sub-regional levels. These regional governance arrangements have maximized welfare but only for small sectors of society in Mexico, posing important challenges for an equitable, sustainable, and participative development strategy. These agreements have not resulted in better socio-economic conditions or more efficient institutions for dealing with income inequality or any other core social problem in the country. Instead, the distribution of benefits associated with the implementation of these regional governance frameworks has created few winners and many losers, challenging the model's utility for successful social development.

Although it should be acknowledged that income inequality in Mexico was a huge structural problem predating these two regional governance arrangements, the implementation of the agreements as part of the export-oriented model of development is associated with the worsening of income distribution in Mexico. In fact, income inequality has split along regional dimensions: those in the north and centre of the country that are connected to maquiladora production and with access to credits (for example, agribusiness) are better off than those in the south, which have remained disconnected (Dussel Peters 2003, 266–71; Morales 1999).

Assessments critical of NAFTA have noted that the agreement has not met its three primary objectives: more and better jobs, the reduction of the flow of Mexican migrants to the United States, and the development of a modern, export-oriented Mexican agricultural sector. Since the formal introduction of NAFTA in 1994, 550,000 new jobs have been created in the manufacturing sector (mainly in *maquiladoras*) and more or less the same number have been created in the service sector (although these jobs are typically unstable and underpaid) (Buckman 2005, 126). However, these gains have been offset by the loss of 100,000 jobs in the non-export manufacturing sector and by 1.3 million jobs lost in the agricultural sector. These latter losses have been tied to the flow of cheap subsidized US farm products flooding Mexican markets as a result of NAFTA (Audley et al. 2003, 3–6; Polaski 2003, 17–20).[3]

Furthermore, with respect to Mexico's overall trade performance under NAFTA, one source suggests that although the country converted a net trade deficit with the United States into a net surplus, three realities are not being considered. First, this positive result was probably not due to NAFTA but, rather, to the 1994–95 currency crisis. Second, there is a growing net deficit in agricultural trade with the United States, and, third, export manufacturing, as mentioned earlier, is focused on low-skill assembly line manufacturers (*maquiladoras*), which have inherently low levels of domestic-added value (Buckman 2005, 126).

On the whole, while the total volume of Mexican exports has increased since trade liberalization policies were implemented, it has not resulted in a better and more equitable distribution of wealth. At the beginning of the trade liberalization reforms, 15 percent of Mexicans lived in extreme poverty; by 2002, this figure had increased to 28 percent (Rozo Bernal 2002, 21–24). In sum, as one commentator noted, "far from reducing Mexican inequality, NAFTA contributed to increase it to high levels, thereby undoing many of the gains of previous decades" (Buckman 2005, 126).

NAFTA was the first free trade agreement signed between such unequal partners on the basis of national treatment status. In Mexico, the shift from most-favoured-nation status policies toward those associated with national treatment occurred in the absence of comprehensive adjustment programs that could have been promoted by the government to help deal with the associated negative consequences of this shift. Sector-specific industrial policies were simply abandoned in favour of sector-neutral policies, under the assumption that disparities in development levels would be overcome by giving into the less developed party's gradual tariff reduction schedules. This was also the case with regard to the EC-Mexico Agreement as will be seen in the next section.

According to the EC-Mexico Agreement, the free trade agreement signed with Mexico was negotiated by taking into account development asymmetries, meaning that Mexican producers enjoyed preferential timing in trade liberalization. Accordingly, Mexican fisheries' imports from the European Union, for example, would be totally free of quotas and tariffs by 2010. Industrial goods' quotas and tariffs were reduced by 47 percent in 2000, and, by 2007, these imports will be 100 percent free (Inter-American Development Bank 2004).

Beneath this "preferential timing" policy lies an important issue. These negotiations guaranteed NAFTA parity in real time to some European goods and service markets, such as the automobile industry. In other words, some European goods would have free access to the Mexican markets at the same time as US and Canadian products. This has occurred without due consideration for the needs of the affected sectors and producers. From the perspective of Mexico's negotiators of the EC-Mexico Agreement, trade has been too insignificant to cause huge distortions to non-competitive Mexican producers (Szymanski 2002).

Furthermore, despite UNCTAD's warnings with respect to the elimination of all existing capital controls as part of any free trade agreement, the Mexican government signed a reciprocal investment promotion and protection agreement (IPPA) with every EU member country. The IPPAs were aimed at increasing productive capital inflows to Mexico through financial deregulation. However, three years after the implementation of the agreement, flows of foreign direct investment coming from Europe seem to be contributing to increasing sub-regional disparity. For example, 78.7 percent of foreign direct investment was concentrated in urban centres such as Mexico City, Nuevo León and the state of Mexico (Rozo Bernal 2002, 77–79).

How Neo-Liberal Regionalism Undermines Democracy

The NAFTA and the EC-Mexico Agreement have undermined the full realization of a substantive democratization of regional governance. Their institutional arrangements have dubious democratic credentials, and the agreements have had the effect of undermining, not enhancing, popular control and equality in policy making. At the institutional level, NAFTA and the EC-Mexico Agreement undermine a full realization of democracy in various ways. For example, it has been extensively documented how the negotiations of NAFTA and the EC-Mexico Agreement were in the hands of governmental officials and conducted beyond public scrutiny. As proposals, they were not subject to robust examination in a broader pubic forum.

Moreover, the institutions created for the enforcement of NAFTA and the EC-Mexico Agreement have themselves largely remained outside of effective public scrutiny. For example, the key decision-making "body" in NAFTA is the Free Trade Commission. This entity does not have a fixed timetable for meetings, and, when meetings are held, it is on an irregular basis (Canadian Trade Ministry 2004). Moreover, the real "decision makers" of NAFTA are the ad hoc committees and working groups whose procedures are far from transparent— so much so that one of the avowed priorities for the Canadian government in 2004 was to enhance the transparency, accountability, and effectiveness of these bodies.

On the whole, NAFTA's dispute resolution mechanisms are also far from being democratic in nature. NAFTA investment provisions establish the *de facto* power of private actors in the development of administrative law in non-public (closed) tribunals. Under NAFTA's Chapter 11 dispute resolutions framework, private arbitrators are even empowered to sanction states in closed hearings (Barenberg and Evans 2003, 16). Moreover, NAFTA as "a WTO-plus" agreement calls for unrestricted rights of repatriation of investment capital, payments, profits, and royalties, along with a guarantee of "fair" compensation for expropriation (Shadlen 2003). Yet notwithstanding the extensive powers and rights provided to these private actors, NAFTA also mandates that none of the resolutions created to address environmental and labour concerns are binding upon these actors.

As for the EC-Mexico Agreement, important democratic shortfalls surrounding the creation of the Joint Council (as the body with authority to complete free trade negotiations) have been noted at procedural levels. The creation of this body was made possible by the enactment of an "interim agreement," which was signed in parallel with the EC-Mexico Agreement. The interim agreement was the mechanism that gave "fast-track" negotiation power to the European

Commission because it was focused on the trade of goods—a common policy—and, hence, was within the competence of the European Commission. While the EC-Mexico Agreement went through an extensive ratification process by the parliaments of each of the EU member states, the interim agreement was not subjected to similar analysis (Szymanski 2002, 16–23).

Moreover, it has been argued that the existence and activities of the Joint Council contravene the provisions of Mexico's Constitution, since the council remains under the purview of the executive branch of the two parties: in Mexico, the president, and in the European Union, the European Commission. Nevertheless, under Mexico's Constitution of 1917, the legislative branch (that is, the Senators Chamber) should ratify all executive decisions on foreign policy. As such, the decisions of the EC-Mexico Agreement's Joint Council should have had to pass through this legislative branch. This issue was raised in the report presented to the European Parliament by Member of European Parliament (MEP) Caroline Lucas, as speaker of the European Commission on industry, foreign trade, research, and energy, in January 2001, but, notwithstanding this discussion, none of the Joint Council's resolutions have been ratified by the Mexican Senate (Lucas 2001).

In addition, the EC-Mexico Agreement contravened the EU general mandate with regard to the negotiation of free trade agreements with third parties. Specifically, this agreement was signed and ratified without undertaking a sustainability assessment of the implications of a free trade agreement for the weaker party (Mexico). At the first forum to be held, "European Union-Mexico Civil Society Dialogue," held in Brussels in 2002, a representative of the European Commission agreed that sustainability impact assessments had to be carried out prior to the negotiation of an agreement, but this has not happened. The directive was not issued until after the negotiations had commenced with Mexico. The European Commission has paid for some of this work to be done by private think tanks, but the public has been effectively excluded from the process (Ciudadanos and Copenhagen Initiative for Central America and Mexico 2002).

Both the long-term process of democratization and the current struggle to consolidate a formal democracy have direct implications for the Mexican state and, hence, for the development and consolidation of NAFTA and the EC-Mexico Agreement. For example, some wonder if Mexico's authoritarian regime had the moral or political right to negotiate a free trade deal with two democracies when the NAFTA negotiations began in 1991 (Aguilar Zínser 1994, 205–7). After the defeat of the Institutional Revolutionary Party in the 2000 presidential election, the European Commission was one of the suprastate bodies that praised the democratic record of the Mexican state, despite worldwide criticism of its poor human rights practices.

In the case of NAFTA's ratification and its accompanying reforms, it has been emphasized that both were approved by a Congress dominated by the executive's power and amid a lack of public information. In 1991, representatives from the left-wing party Democratic Revolutionary Party requested information from the executive on the progress of the negotiations, but their efforts were in vain (see Interview 3 in Appendix 2).[4] In fact, the Democratic Revolutionary Party was unable to obtain the official text of the NAFTA negotiations until March 1992 when it was provided by allies within the civil society groups that were opposed to free trade (see Interview 5 in Appendix 2).

Mexico lacks reliable and effective accountability mechanisms through which to hold state authorities accountable for their actions. This is particularly true with regard to foreign affairs and foreign trade policy. In 2002, a Social Organizations Liaison Unit was created within the Ministry of Foreign Affairs to address the demands of civil society groups in relation to the WTO ministerial meeting held in Cancún and, later on, in relation to the Summit on Financing for Development in Monterrey. So far, this office—which until 2004 had only three people as permanent staff and no formal criteria to define what they meant by "civil society organization"—is the main body at the federal level responsible for dealing with issues of civil society and Mexico's foreign trade relations (see Interview 2 in Appendix 2).

The one-party-dominant system has meant that state authorities in Mexico at the federal, municipal, and local levels, together with the legislative branch and the judiciary system, largely remain out of public sight, not only with regard to free trade and the processes of regional integration but also in relation to many other public concerns. Notwithstanding this situation, the end of the Institutional Revolutionary Party's majority in the National Congress in 1997 opened up space for opposition parties to demand more transparency with regard to foreign policy. For example, during negotiations with the European Union, deputies and senators from the Democratic Revolutionary Party held information sessions to discuss the possible effects of the agreement (see Interview 3 in Appendix 2). Moreover, as part of the process of formal democratization in Mexico, local and federal courts, which were previously controlled by the federal executive and the Institutional Revolutionary Party, started to handle issues related to the enforcement of NAFTA and the EC-Mexico Agreement. In 2004, for instance, the Federal Court of Justice in Mexico handed down an unprecedented decision in favour of local authorities regarding NAFTA's international disputes regime. The court concluded that the federal government did not have the authority to compromise local resources for the payment of obligations relating to NAFTA's international panel resolutions ("Determina la SCJN" 2004).

To a large extent, the previously mentioned democratic deficits are grounded in how democracy is discursively addressed. As in other neo-liberal regional and global institutions, the official discourses in NAFTA and the EC-Mexico Agreement reduce democracy to a set of institutions and procedures in order to guarantee effective representation. When democracy is discursively linked to the process of building up citizenship through consultations and "ownership," mechanisms are created to promote this.

Due to the ongoing transition toward formal democracy in Mexico, a discourse on democracy as represented by the execution of fair and clean elections has prevailed for a long time within Mexican state institutions. More recently, democracy has been understood as the promotion of the rule of law, the effective separation of Republican powers, and the accountability of governing authorities. Meanwhile, its practice is understood much more narrowly by the governing elites. They have not supported a political culture linked to the building of citizenship and enhancing popular control. An example that clearly illustrates this prevailing notion of democracy lies in how civil society's involvement in the governance of regionalization has been addressed. In NAFTA and the EC-Mexico Agreement as well as in numerous institutions of the state in Mexico, "civil society" is most commonly understood as comprising non-governmental organizations (NGOs), business organizations, academics, and, sometimes, labour unions. From this perspective, the official documents of NAFTA and the EC-Mexico Agreement acknowledge the importance of "engaging" civil society stakeholders in processes of regional integration. In theory, the involvement of civil society is seen as being necessary to the drafting and operation of policies and projects. However, the involvement of some civil society actors has occurred to the detriment of others. In these regional governance arrangements, the participation of business associations, think tanks, NGOs, and private foundations is more common. For example, in NAFTA's Environmental Cooperation Commission, there is a Public Joint Consultative Committee integrated by non-governmental counsellors.[5]

Moreover, government promotion of the engagement of civil society groups has been focused on social and co-operation aspects and on procedural aspects rather than on substantive tasks. For example, technical and economic matters remain in the hands of closed governmental circles: the working groups in NAFTA and the Joint Council in the EC-Mexico Agreement. In *European Governance: A White Paper* and in the report *The Commission and NGOs: Building Stronger Partnerships*, the importance of consultation with civil society organizations at all stages of policy development is stressed (European Commission 1999; and European Commission 2001a). Accordingly, the European Commission's report *Country Strategy Paper: Mexico (2002–2006)* calls for the involvement of civil society organizations in the implementation of social and political co-operation aspects within the framework of the EC-Mexico Agreement (European Commission 2001b, 15).

It is noteworthy that the main objective of political co-operation is the consolidation of the rule of law and democracy in Mexico as well as the protection of human rights and the promotion of the public's trust in public authorities and so on. In practice, this aspect of co-operation has been implemented though a program of reforms for the judicial system and through actions in the human rights domain that include governmental organizations and NGOs officially participating in Mexico (Ciudadanos and Copenhagen Initiative for Central America and Mexico 2002, 70–75; European Commission 2001b, 15). Nevertheless, in the case of the economic aspect of co-operation, the main counterpart officially recognized by the European Commission in Mexico is the Ministry of Finance.

Furthermore, the bodies responsible for receiving and representing demands made by civil society in these regional governance arrangements have a narrow range of authority and a lack of enforcement capacity. They are under-resourced and understaffed, and their resolutions are not binding. One source documented in 2002 that "after seven years and twenty-three complaints" placed with NAFTA's National Administrative Offices there have been "very few tangible results in terms of influencing government policies or private employers" (Brooks and Fox 2002, 361). In the case of the EC-Mexico Agreement, there are no concrete provisions or mechanisms regarding human rights or environmental protection. In contrast, Titles III, IV, and V on Trade and Capital Movements and Payments establish specific standards that are subject to legal oversight (Ciudadanas de Mexico Frente a la Union Europea and Copenhagen Initiative for Central America and Mexico 2002, 13–15 and 77–79).

As for Mexican state institutions, in separate interviews, two officials in the Ministry of Foreign Affairs acknowledge the lack of resources among civil society groups in Mexico, hence, their underrepresentation in terms of participation and involvement in public policies. However, due to the fact that the ministry lacks formal criteria to clarify what constitutes a civil society organization, most of the programs are focused on formal groups (see Interviews 1 and 2 in Appendix 2). Overall, the assumption is that a level of formality and institutionalization is equal to legitimacy and representation.

Conclusion

This chapter has explored the key conditions at the national level that have challenged neo-liberal regionalism as a dominant paradigm in regional governance in Mexico. So far, it is possible to argue that Mexican regionalism of the last three *sexenios* has not only been a reaction to the increasing trends of globalization and the regionalization of production and consumption but has also served the practical implementation of the neo-liberal restructuring agendas. Some of the consequences of this "instrumentality" for future governments have been discussed in this chapter.

Furthermore, it has been observed that the demand-side underpinning of the neo-liberal regionalist projects implemented in Mexico has weakened the state's capacities to exert full control on trade and investment operations and that this could have direct and indirect social costs, such as on the provision of public goods. On the other hand, a caveat is important here, because this "weakening" has not been an "imposition" but, rather, an autonomous decision made by national governing and corporate elites. In fact, neo-liberal regionalism and its associated outcomes have been the result of policy decisions undertaken in numerous cases thanks to the prevailing features of Mexico's political regime. To be more precise, Mexican authoritarianism is characterized by an overwhelming concentration of power in the federal executive branch, which has enjoyed *de facto* control over state institutions and has helped in the implementation of neo-liberal regionalist agendas. At the same time, the adoption of neo-liberal regionalism as a dominant policy framework to accelerate the regionalization process as well as the establishment of a "formal" democracy in Mexico have also been crucial. As discussed earlier, despite the ongoing transition to a "formal" democracy in Mexico, international trade negotiations have remained out of public sight and in the hands of "experts" for efficiency and "technical superiority" reasons.

Therefore, it is not surprising that Mexico (and other Latin American countries) have witnessed the emergence of resistance to any renewed effort at developing trade, particularly from the sectors of civil society that are critical of neo-liberal regionalism and that are articulating regional scopes of activism (Icaza Garza 2004; Saguier 2004). Accordingly, Leftist party candidates in Mexico's 2006 presidential elections endorsed the renegotiation of certain aspects of NAFTA and an overall rejection of neo-liberalism. By contrast, the formally elected president, Felipe Calderón Hinojosa from the right-wing National Action Party, has supported regionalism as it was promoted by his predecessor Vicente Fox.[6] It advocates a broadening and deepening of market-driven regional strategy.

At the regional level, alternative solutions to the failed negotiations of the US-led FTAA and the proliferation of bilateral free trade agreements (many of them currently under negotiation) are urgently needed. The Alternativa Bolivariana par alas Americas and the Mercado Común del Sur have often been seen as alternatives to what has been identified as neo-liberal regionalism. What appears to be lacking, however, are more democratic venues for large-scale participation by civil society actors that oppose neo-liberal regionalism. So far, the process of a critical re-evaluation of thirteen years of neo-liberal regionalism in Mexico could serve as a starting point.

APPENDIX 1: EVENTS ATTENDED

First Forum, "*European Union-Mexico Civil Society Dialogue*," Brussels, Belgium, November 2002.

APPENDIX 2: INTERVIEWS CONDUCTED IN MEXICO

Interview 1   Ernesto Céspedes, director, Global Issues General Direction, Ministry of Foreign Affairs, 10 November 2003, Ministry of Foreign Affairs, Mexico City.

Interview 2   Melba Pría, director, Social Organizations Liaison Unit, Ministry of Foreign Affairs, 27 November 2003, World Trade Centre, Mexico City.

Interview 3   Jorge Calderón Salazar, general director, Institute for the Studies on the Democratic Revolution, active member of the Democratic Revolutionary Party, former senator and member of Red Mexicana de Accion Frente al Libre Comercio and Ciudadanas de Mexico Frente a la Union Europea, 1 and 8 December 2003, Institute for the Studies on the Democratic Revolution, Mexico City.

Interview 4   Manuel Pérez Rocha, Mexico advocacy officer, OXFAM, former co-ordinator of Ciudadanas de Mexico Frente a la Union Europea and member of Red Mexicana de Accion Frente al Libre Comercio, 10 December 2003, Mexico City.

Interview 5   Alberto Arroyo Pichard, NAFTA and FTAA campaign co-ordinator, Red Mexicana de Accion Frente al Libre Comercio, 18 December 2003, Mexico City.

NOTES

The author is particularly grateful to Daniel Drache and also to her colleagues at the Iberoamerican Institute in Sweden: Edmé Domínguez, Maj-Lis Foller, Maria Clara Medina, Vicente Oieni, and Åsa Stenman for their insightful comments. Any shortcomings are, of course, the responsibility of the author.

1   The *sexenio* limits the president to one six-year term.
2   North American Free Trade Agreement between the Government of Canada, the Government of Mexico and the Government of the United States, 17 December 1992, Can. T.S. 1994 No. 2, 32 I.L.M. 289 [NAFTA]. Economic Partnership, Political Coordination and Commercial Agreement between the European Union and Mexico, 1 October 2000. *EUR-Lex,* Official Journal of the European Union. http://eur-lex.europa.eu/LexUriServ/LexUriServ.do?url=OJ:L:2000:276:0045:0061:EN:PDF.
3   Since 1994, the Mexican agricultural trade deficit has constantly grown as the Mexican government allowed substantial above-quota tariff-free imports in sensible products such as corn coming from the United States. Since the early 1990s, 50 percent of the corn eaten by Mexicans in their tortillas came from large, transnational US firms, and, in 2002, 35 percent of the beef and 20 percent of the potatoes consumed in Mexico were produced out of the country (Peridico Reforma, Section "Negocios," 19 July 2002).

4 In November and December 2003, fieldwork was conducted in Mexico for research entitled "Civil Society and Regionalization: Exploring the Contours of Mexican Transborder Activism." This research sought to understand the societal implications of free trade agreements for local communities in Mexico with respect to issues of identity formation and organizing strategies. See Appendices 1 and 2 for a complete list of the events attended and interviews conducted for this article. All of the interviews were semi-structured, conducted in Spanish, and lasted an average of one and a half hours.

5 For a complete list of the Public Joint Consultative Committee of NAFTA's Environmental Cooperation Commission, see http://www.cec.org/files/pdf/ ECONOMY/builde_EN.pdf. For a complete list of the Advisory Committee of the Labour Cooperation Commission, see http://www.naalc.org/english/review_part2 .shtml.

6 Andrés Manuel López Obrador from the Democratic Revolutionary Party and Patricia Mercado from the Social Democratic Alternative Party.

REFERENCES

Aguilar Zínser, A. 1994. "Authoritarianism and North American Free Trade: The Debate in Mexico." In Ricardo Grinspun and Maxwell A. Cameron, eds., *The Political Economy of North American Free Trade*, 205–16. San Martin: Nueva York.

Arroyo Picard, Alberto. 2000. *Derechos humanos y Tratado de Libre Comercio México-Unión Europea*. Mexico City: Heinrich Böll Foundation.

Audley, J.J., D.G. Papademetriou, S.A. Polaski, and S. Vaughan. 2003. *NAFTA's Promise and Reality: Lessons from Mexico for the Hemisphere*. Washington, DC: Carnegie Endowment for International Peace.

Barenberg, M., and P. Evans. 2004. *The FTAA's Impact on Democratic Governance*. Annual Conference of the International Studies Association, Montreal. http://convention2.allacademic.com/one/isa/isa09/index.php?cmd= isa04.

Belanger, L., and G. Mace. 1999. *The Americas in Transition: The Contours of Regionalism*. London: Lynne Rienner.

Birchfield, V., and A. Freyberg-Inan. 2004. "Constructing Opposition in the Age of Globalization: The Potential of ATTAC." *Globalizations* 1: 278–304.

Brooks, D., and J. Fox. 2002. *Cross Border Dialogues: US-Mexico Social Movement Networking*. Centre for US-Mexican Studies. La Jolla, CA: University of California–San Diego.

Buckman, G. 2005. *Global Trade: Past Mistakes, Future Choices*. London: Zed Books.

Canadian Trade Ministry. 2004. "How NAFTA Works?" Documento examinado, 26 July 2004, http://www.international.gc.ca.

Centeno, M.A., and P. Silva. 1998. *The Politics of Expertise in Latin America*. London: Macmillan.

Ciudadanas de Mexico Frente a la Union Europea and Copenhagen Initiative for Central America and Mexico. 2002. *Encuentro de Organizaciones Sociales y Civiles de México y la Unión Europea en el Marco del Acuerdo Global UE-México.* Memoria del Primer Foro de Dialogo con la Sociedad Civil México-Unión Europea. Mexico: Ciudadanas de Mexico Frente a la Union Europea, Copenhagen Initiative for Central America and Mexico, and Heinrich Böll Foundation.

"Determina la SCJN que el gobierno no puede comprometer participaciones de los estados." 2004. *La Jornada.*

Dussel Peters, E. 2003. "La polarización de la economía mexicana: Aspectos Económicos y Regionales." In J. Bailey, ed., *Impactos del TLC en México y Estados Unidos. Efectos subregionales del comercio y la integración económica.* Mexico City: Miguel Ángel Porrúa.

European Commission. 1999. *The Commission and Non-Governmental Organisations: Building a Stronger Partnership.*

_____. 2001a. *European Governance: A White Paper.* Brussels: European Commission.

_____. 2001b. *Country Strategy Paper: Mexico (2002–2006).*

European Commission for Latin America, ed. 1990. *Production Transformation with Equity.* Santiago, Chile: European Commission for Latin America.

_____. 1991. "El desarrollo sustentable: transformación productiva, equidad y medio ambiente. CEPAL: Santiago.

Gore, C. 2000. "The Rise and Fall of the Washington Consensus as a Paradigm for Developing Countries." *World Development* 28: 789–804.

Grugel, J., and W. Hout. 1999. "Regions, Regionalism and the South." In J. Grugel and W. Hout, eds., *Regionalism across the North–South Divide: State Strategies and Globalization,* 3–13. London: Routledge.

Gudynas, E. 2005. "Open Regionalism or Alternative Regional Integration." In A. Program, ed., International Relations Center, 26 October. Silver City, NM: International Relations Center. http://americas.irc-online.org/pdf/columns/0510gudynas.pdf.

Gwynne, R., and C. Kay. 2000. "Views from the Periphery: Futures of Neo-liberalism in Latin America." *Third World Quarterly* 21: 141–56.

Hemispheric Social Alliance. 2002. *Alternative for the Americas,* http://www.asc-hsa.org.

Hettne, B. 1993. "Neo-Mercantilism: The Pursuit of Regionness." *Cooperation and Conflict* 28: 211–32.

Hettne, B., and F. Söderbaum. 2000. "Theorising the Rise of Regionness." *New Political Economy* 5: 457–72.

Inter-American Development Bank. 2004. *Integration and Trade in the Americas.* Special Issue on Latin American and Caribbean Economic Relations with the European Union. Washington, DC: Tercera Cumbre, UE-ALC, and Inter-American Development Bank.

Lucas, C. 2001. *Informe*. Brussels: Comisión de la Unión Europea.

Lustig, N. 1998. *Mexico: The Remaking of an Economy*. Washington, DC: Brookings Institution.

Marchand, M., Martin Boas, and Timothy M. Shaw. 1999. "The Political Economy of New Regionalisms." *Third World Quarterly* 20: 897–910.

Mittelman, J.H. 2000. *The Globalization Syndrome: Transformation and Resistance*. Princeton, NJ: Princeton University Press.

Morales, I. 1999. "NAFTA: The Institutionalisation of Economic Openness and the Configuration of Mexican Geo-Economic Spaces." *Third World Quarterly* 20: 971–93.

Newell, P., and D. Tussie. 2006. *Civil Society Participation in Trade Policy-Making in Latin America: Reflections and Lessons,* Institute of Development Studies Working Paper 276. Brighton: IDS.

Polaski, S. 2003. "Jobs, Wages, and Household Income." In John Audley et al., ed., *NAFTA's Promise and Reality: Lessons from Mexico for the Hemisphere*. Washington, DC: Carnegie Endowment for International Peace. http://www.carnegieendowment.org.

Rozo Bernal, C.A. 2002. "Los primeros resultados en flujos comerciales y de capital a dos años del TLCUE." In Copenhagen Initiative for Central America and Mexico, ed., *Memoria del Primer Foro de Diálogo con la Sociedad Civil México-Unión,* 78. Mexico City: Europea, Ciudadanos, Copenhagen Initiative for Central America and Mexico, and Heinrich Böll Foundation.

Saguier, M.I. 2004. *Convergence in the Making: Transnational Civil Society and the Free Trade of the Americas*. CSGR Working Paper No. 137/04. Coventry: Warwick University.

Scholte, J.A. 2004. *Globalization and Governance: From Statism to Polycentrism,* CSGR Working Paper. Coventry: Warwick University.

Shadlen, K. 2003. "Regional versus Multilateral Strategies for Economic Integration: NAFTA in the Context of the WTO." In *Mexico Changing Place in the World: Features of Contemporary World Politics Affecting Mexico*. Oxford: Centre for Mexican Studies, Oxford University.

Szymanski, M. 2002. "El Nuevo Acuerdo entre México y la Unión Europea: El Primer Vínculo de Libre Comercio entre Europa y el TLC." In A. Lebrija and S. Sberro, eds., *México-Unión Europea. El Acuerdo de Asociacion Economica, Concertación Politica y Cooperación. Sus aspectos fundamentales,* 11–45. México: Miguel Ángel Porrúa, ITAM, and IEIE.

Wise, C. 1998. "Introduction : NAFTA, Mexico and the Western Hemisphere." In C. Wise, ed., *The Post-NAFTA Political Economy: Mexico and the Western Hemisphere,* 1–40. University Park, PA: Pennsylvania State University.

Wise, T.A., and K.P. Gallagher. 2006. *Doha Rounds and Developing Countries: Will Doha Deal Do More Harm Than Good?* RIS Policy Briefs. Medford, MA: Global Development and Environment Institute, Tufts University.

6

ASIAN TURBO-CAPITALISM AND THE BRAZILIAN MIRACLE: WINNERS AND LOSERS?

11

The Dragon in Aztec Lands

Victor López Villafañe

The New Economic "Tug-of-War"

The massive Asian presence in the American market continues to surge. Double-digit growth in Asian exports has produced an unprecedented cycle of industrial growth in Chinese industries. The liberalization of the Chinese economy in 1978 and its corresponding competitive advantages, especially in the cost of the labour force, has propelled the Chinese economy into the US market (Villafañe 1994; Villafañe 1999). Though most of the early Chinese exports to the US market were actually made in Hong Kong and Taiwan rather than in China, nowadays, China itself is producing goods for export since foreign companies, mainly from Asia and North America, use China as the workshop of the global economy.[1] Chinese economic power is the result of disciplined state planning and success-ful industrial strategies. These strategies have their own problems and challenges, which, in general, are not appreciated in the West nor analyzed in terms of the risks they entail.

For Mexico and Canada, Chinese competition poses a number of problems. First, both countries are more dependent on the US market than they were twelve years ago when the North American Free Trade Agreement (NAFTA) was signed.[2] Second, China has close to an absolute advantage over the other coun-tries given its huge population of workers and low labour costs. Its competitive edge is driven by supply chain management networks and a focused state-di-rected industrial strategy that makes China a formidable and long-term compet-itor. Finally, many US companies are forming partnerships with Chinese firms. These partnerships have given China even greater market power, making it a very tough competitor for all three NAFTA countries. Today, China is the second most important commercial partner for the United States, Mexico, and Canada. Thus, the relations within the region as well as the economic conditions and priorities have been modified. What is the effect of the increasing participation of China in the NAFTA region? How have the United States, Canada, and Mexico responded to this new power?

Mexico's Response to the Dragon

Mexico has been profoundly affected by China's rise as a global economic power. Chinese products compete with Mexican products on the international market, and, as a result, China has replaced Mexico as the main trading partner to the United States. This outcome reflects an unprecedented shift in the commercial balance of power. The United States remains Mexico's chief trading partner, receiving 85 percent of all Mexican exports. However, in a way that no one could have predicted, China has become Mexico's second trading partner. The Chinese success story is well documented. The commercial deficit between Mexico and China reached US $12 billion in 2004 and US $15 billion in 2005. This imbalance is more than enough reason for Mexican elites to begin the process of rethinking the trading policy toward China. Mexico cannot maintain a deficit of this magnitude over the long term. If this imbalance is unsustainable for Mexico, does China have an incentive to revise its own commercial policy toward Mexico? In order to answer this question, it is important to examine the relationship between both nations as well as the situation of Canada and the United States in relation to China.

Today, China is an amazing economic power with record-breaking growth and incredible market power within its population of 1.3 billion citizens. Its gross domestic product (GDP) has been growing at an average of 9 percent annually since the beginning of the economic reforms in 1978 (see Figure 1). The surge of Chinese trading is affecting countless industries throughout the country due to its export power. China is becoming one of the top trade powers of the world. Within this framework, China has proposed to double its GDP from the year 2000 to the year 2010—a goal that is obtainable and realistic, according to the Chinese prime minister Wen Jiabao. This continued GDP growth is possible since China's annual growth is also growing at 7.5 percent, which is two percentage points less than the one attained in 2005. Between 1980 and 1997, China quadrupled its GDP, and, between 1978 and 1999, China increased its saving capacity by 280 percent. By achieving the goal that it has set for itself, China will increase its GDP per capita from US $1,600 to US $1,700 dollars, which is a significant improvement in living standards.

In 2005, the Chinese treasury collected around 3 trillion yuan, and China's international commerce exceeded US $1.38 trillion. China is the second recipient of foreign investment in the world (after the United States), with more than US $70 billion invested in 2004. Furthermore, China has outgrown its original reputation as a storehouse for cheap labour and is now a source of technological, industrial, and business innovation. Mexico, in sharp contrast, has been experiencing irregular growth since NAFTA. From 1994 to 2001, Mexican exports to the

FIGURE 1 NAFTA–China Commercial Balance

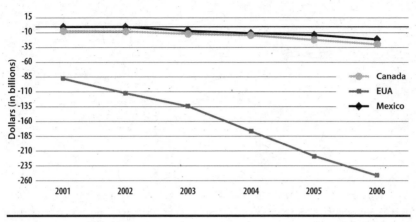

SOURCE: EUROMONITOR INTERNATIONAL.

United States almost tripled from US $50 billion to US $136 billion. After 2001, however, Mexico experienced a decrease in growth, as China began to increase its exports to the United States. For these reasons, China has displaced Mexico as the United States' second most important commercial partner in 2003.

The American Influence

The relationship that both China and Mexico have with the United States influences the effect that China has on other NAFTA member countries. Mexico is the third exporter to the United States, with a total of US $200 billion sold in the year 2006. It was the second exporter to the US market until 2002 when Mexican exports were surpassed by China. China's exports to the United States in 2006 totalled US $300 billion, representing almost the same amount as Canadian exports to the United States (Figure 2). These figures show us that even though imports from Mexico to the United States continue to increase, their growth is not enough to compete with China, which means that Mexico is losing out on new capital investment and the establishment of new enterprises.

This condition becomes more troubling when we notice that although Mexico's participation with the United States is declining, there is no corresponding increase in trade with other countries. In other words, Mexico is highly dependant on the United States, second only to Canada in the consumption of US goods and services. For example, in 2004, Mexico imported US goods to a total of US $111 billion, while China only imported US $35 billion during the same year (Figure 3). In fact, there has been a rise of nearly 13.7 percent in the number of US imports coming into Mexico during 2003–04, while US imports to China have only increased by 6.1 percent.

FIGURE 2 Real GDP Growth in NAFTA and China, 1990–2006

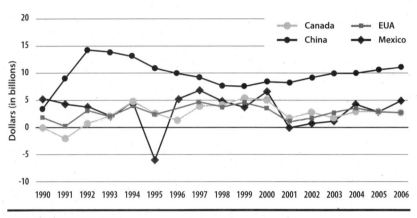

SOURCE: EUROMONITOR INTERNATIONAL.

FIGURE 3 US Imports

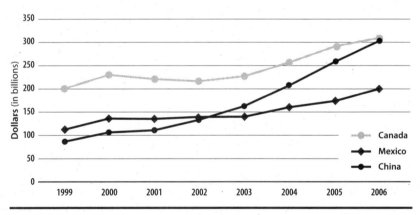

SOURCE: EUROMONITOR INTERNATIONAL.

The number of US goods imported to China is also growing, but China is still enjoying a huge trade surplus. The United States experienced a trade deficit of US $235 billion with China in 2006 (Figure 4). This amount is much greater than the deficit the United States holds with the other members of NAFTA. In 2003, the United States had a US $52 billion deficit with Canada and a US $41 billion deficit with Mexico. These numbers demonstrate the importance of the economic relationship between the United States and China and show how commercial activity is declining between the United States and other NAFTA member countries such as Canada and Mexico, despite the free trade agreement designed to promote North American integration.

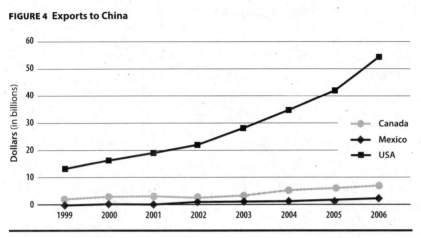

FIGURE 4 Exports to China

SOURCE: EUROMONITOR INTERNATIONAL.

China and the Productive and Commercial Networks in North America

The Chinese advantage over Mexico does not only lie in wage differences but also in the strategy behind every product. While Chinese goods are supported by the state, Mexican goods are produced in a private system. This difference explains the continuing success of China, even though Mexico offers better regulation, enhanced protection of intellectual property, greater productivity of qualified workers, a lower cost for the transportation of goods to the United States, and, above all, preferential access to US markets due to NAFTA (Oropeza 2005). Rather than being the solution to Mexico's trade woes, however, NAFTA may be part of the problem. For its part, Mexico believed that NAFTA would act as insurance against foreign competitors and provide secure access to the US market. This belief has resulted in a loss of an industrial and technological long-term strategy in the Mexican public and private sectors. China's economy, on the other hand, has benefited not only from its exclusion from NAFTA rules but also from a cheap labour force, skilled professional human resources, and institutional backup via state-created special economic zones for exporting projects.

For Mexico, free trade with its northern neighbors has had a positive effect in key industries, most of them controlled by multinationals, such as the automobile and electronic industries. These small gains come at a price, however, since NAFTA has brought Mexico a series of social and economic losses, such as agricultural unemployment. In contrast, China has not needed a free trade agreement to enter strongly into the US economy, which has meant that, for

FIGURE 5 Exports to the United States, 1999–2001

Winners	Gains		Losers	Losses	
China	134	46%	Japan	−112.6	38%
Mexico	48.9	17%	Taiwan	−36	12%
Ireland	17.1	6%	Canada	−27.5	9%
Russia	9.4	3%	UK	−20.9	7%
Others	83.4	28%	Others	95.8	33%
Total	292.9	100%	Total	292.9	100%

SOURCE: CHAMI BATISTA 2005.

China, the increase of business with the United States has been the result of its many competitive strengths.[3]

Further compounding this problem for Mexico is the direct competition between Chinese and Mexican products within the US market (see Figure 5). If we compare the main winners and losers in the United States between 1999 and 2004, we see that Mexico is in second place with a total of US $49 billion worth of products exported to the United States. Although Mexico outperformed Japan (28 percent), Canada (23 percent), and Taiwan (7 percent) in the amount of goods exported to the United States, all gains were dwarfed by China's US $134 billion worth of goods exported to the United States.[4]

The Export Game

In 2002, 61 percent of Mexican exports competed directly with Chinese exports in the US market (Hicks, Luis, and Humberto 2003). Fifty-five percent of the Mexican exports to the United States have been in the electronics, automobile, and auto parts sectors—sectors in which Mexico competes directly with China. The rest are in the telecommunication equipment, office and personal computer, professional and scientific equipment, and metallurgical and textile manufacturing industries (Cortés, Ignacio, and Castillo 2004). By 2003, Mexico outpaced China only in the telecommunications, electronics, professional equipment, and automotive sectors. During this time, China overtook Mexico as the main exporter of apparel for the United States when sales reached US $7.3 billion (in contrast to the US $6.9 billion sold by Mexico in the same year). China has also become the number one furniture-producing country in the world, while Mexico has dropped to the eleventh position since 2003.[5] For Mexico, it seems as though no industrial sector is unaffected by Chinese production. Even the automotive industry may be at risk if concrete actions are not taken soon. China

FIGURE 6 Growth of Manufacturing Industries, 1997–2007

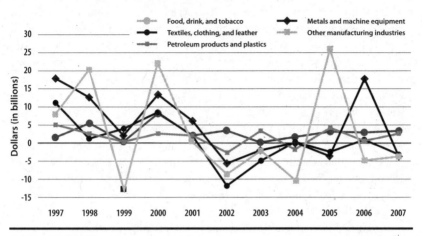

SOURCE: EUROMONITOR INTERNATIONAL.

has been consistently increasing its exports in the auto parts and automobile production industries. By 2010, China is expected to become the third largest automobile producer worldwide (Figure 6).[6]

In October 2005, the Bank of Mexico announced that the decline in business with the United States over the last five years has resulted in a loss of almost US $30 billion for Mexico. This loss implies a drop of almost one GDP percentage point annually and explains why the promised target of 5 percent GDP growth was not achieved in 2005. The increasing Chinese presence in the United States has also meant the loss of at least 730 assembly plants and almost 230,000 jobs in Mexico from 2000 to 2003. In fact, the Mexican Social Security Institute declared that from October 2000 to April 2005, the Mexican manufacturing industry had lost 824,000 jobs (Instituto Mexicano Del Seguro Social 2008).

Mexican/Chinese competition has also resulted in a slowing of growth in Mexico's manufacturing sector, especially in 2001, as Figure 5 shows. The drop in the Mexican manufacturing power is not only due to Chinese competition but also to the slow growth of the Mexican economy and its internal market. These indicators show that Mexico needs to redefine its objectives and policies toward China as soon as possible. If this situation with the United States continues unchecked, major industrial and employment losses will result.

Changing US Attitudes

The relationship that the United States maintains with China is hardly free of conflict. By August 2005, China was the United States' second biggest creditor,[7] holding a debt that translates to US $248 billion. In this same year, China's imports to the United States exceeded American exports to China by five times (Mekay 2005). Therefore, even though the United States recognizes that Chinese participation in its market is beneficial, there is an increasing perception of China as an economic and military threat. This perception is made evident in the statement made by Roger W. Robinson, Jr., vice-president of the United States-China Economic and Security Review Commission (uscc): "The impact of China in the economy of our nation ... affects ineluctably our national security" (ibid.). In fact, the relationship between China and the United States resembles the previous relationship between the United States and the former Soviet Union but includes economic dependency as well as a fear of China's military strength. The United States is also concerned about competition on world energy markets since China is now responsible for 40 percent of the world demand. Finally, the United States is worried about China's proximity to hostile countries such as Iran, Sudan, North Korea, and, in Latin America, countries such as Venezuela.[8]

The United States faces the dilemma of maintaining an effective and stable relationship with China as a growing partner and principal source of capital while, at the same time, protecting itself from China as a potential military threat and a strategic rival. In other words, both China and the United States are simultaneously each other's best partner and biggest political threat (Solomon 2005). However, according to Joseph S. Nye, there will not necessarily be a need for war between the two superpowers during the twenty-first century since military confrontation is not an inevitable outcome. If the Chinese transition remains peaceful, it will benefit China as well as China's regional neighbours, and the United States will be better off (Nye 2005). The US-China relationship is characterized by increasing interdependence in various areas of mutual interest. This makes a military confrontation between the two superpowers a very risky endeavour. In the future, changes to the world strategies of both countries are likely to occur as each one tries not to lose their international power.

To date, the United States is following a "congagement" strategy toward China—that is, a combination of containment and engagement. This strategy is characterized by rapprochement and economic exchange with China as well as the simultaneous establishment of new military alliances with China's closest neighbours. For example, the US government has recently established several alliances consisting of the following: agreements for the installation of aircraft carriers and anti-ballistic missiles in Japan; consent with India to share nuclear technology for space and civil purposes; an exchange of military training in Vietnam, with an emphasis on linguistic and medical programs; and troop training in Indonesia (Solomon 2005).

Economic relations between the United States and China are certainly not cut and dry and, in fact, may be nearing a breaking point. Recently, the US government has decided to economically act more aggressively toward China. For example, after the US Congress recommended to the uscc that the purchase could be dangerous, the Chinese National Oil Company was prevented from acquiring Unocal Corporation from its American owners. Similarly, the US Congress has made proposals to tax Chinese merchandise entering the US market. Another proposal is to freeze the assets of Chinese firms involved in the production of weapons and missiles. Finally, perceptions of American citizens toward China have been changing. These new perceptions derive from a fear about the discriminatory treatment of American merchandise in China compared to the treatment of Chinese products on American soil.

China's Response to the United States

The changing US attitudes toward its eastern partner suggest that China should start to re-evaluate its own policies and economy with respect to the North American region. This challenge is not a small one for China because access to, and participation in, the US market is fundamental to the Chinese economy. For this reason, if the advice of organizations such as the USCC is to reduce access and impose tariff barriers against Chinese imports, it would be very costly to the Chinese economy.

To address this real possibility, China has attempted a rapprochement with Mexico. In the 2003, Hu Jintao, the Chinese president, declared Mexico a strategic partner for the first time. As a strategic partner to China, Mexico is given preferential treatment in Chinese investment and trade. Furthermore, in the last two years, Mexico and China have made efforts to sign treaties in the fields of agricultural products; to co-operate in the mining sector; to draft agreements avoiding double taxation; to increase social development; and to regulate the illegal import of Chinese merchandise into Mexico. In addition, a major cultural exchange took place between the two countries. In 2006, China hosted a number of important events that focused on promoting Mexican art, culture, and history in China. This year, Mexico was invited to be the guest of honour at the Beijing Film Festival and was also recognized at the Shanghai International Film Festival, which dedicated a week to showcasing Mexican films.

Why has there been this sudden Chinese interest in Mexico? Mexico has preferential trade access to the US market and is geographically close to the United States. Moreover, the Mexican economy is suffering much more than any other country in the world due to Chinese economic competition and is highly dependent on the US economy. A Mexican economic crisis would affect the US economy and therefore could have impacts on the Chinese economy. This situation is reminiscent of the one that occurred during the 1970s and 1980s when Japanese participation in the US market started to cause alarm. The solution adopted by Japan was to conceal their exports by investing in emergent economies in Asia, Latin America, and Canada in order to reduce American concerns. If China wants to lessen political friction without losing ground in the US market, the strategy of investing to create exporting platforms could be a good one. Mexico, in turn, could become an interesting partner in this challenge for economic and strategic reasons.

China's interest in Mexico could turn out to be an enormous opportunity. If Mexico could redefine its relationship with China, it could generate a strategic alliance and a partnership that would permit development and growth for both sides. Mexico has not ignored this potential opportunity. It is ready to collaborate with the Asian giant, and Mexico's readiness is reflected in many new developments. These include the proposal for a consulate in Guangzhou; the decision to export auto parts to China; and the recent decision made by a group of Mexican corporations such as GRUMA, the Mexican giant multinational producer of corn products, to participate in the Chinese market. In 2007, this company opened a new plant in Shanghai to produce and supply corn products for the Chinese market. These demonstrations of economic goodwill are reciprocated by China, where approximately 160 companies are currently doing business in Mexico and additional plans for direct investment are already being made.[9]

The Great White Panda: A Strategic Alliance

In these new partnership developments, Mexico can take some lessons from Canada. Canada has already demonstrated a successful example of a similar partnering strategy in its development of a special and privileged relationship with the entire Asia-Pacific region and especially with China. While Canada-US relations have experienced a slight downturn because of the Canadian-Chinese partnership, and although the cost of Canadian raw materials and energy has increased with the growing Chinese demand, Canada seems to believe that the benefits of involvement in the Chinese market outweigh the drawbacks. Former Canadian prime minister Paul Martin and his government recognized that China would turn out to be the most important economy of the twenty-first century and that it is located in the heart of regional and global chains of supply and demand that affect Canada. As a result, Canada aimed toward doubling its commercial exchanges with the Asia-Pacific region in general and particularly with China by the year 2010 (Canada 2005).

The relationship between Canada and China has resulted in the purchase of PetroKazakhstan, a Canadian oil company in Kazakhstan, by the Chinese oil company China National Petroleum Corporation. Canada has taken advantage of having the biggest Chinese diaspora to create business, support academic exchanges, and promote itself as the link between the Asia-Pacific region and North America. One important and possible key Canadian difference with Mexico and the United States is the enormous population of Asian origin that now lives in Canada. Fifty-two percent of Canada's immigrants come from the Asia-Pacific region, and 10 percent of Canadians have family there (ibid.).

In summary, Chinese relations are different for each NAFTA partner and highly asymmetrical. At the present time, the foreign policy for the national security of President George W. Bush's administration, and the priority that the US market represents to China, allows both Mexico and Canada an opportunity to launch new strategies of economic and political engagement in which China will be a decisive factor. If this situation is handled carefully, it will allow Canada and Mexico to obtain beneficial trade agreements and position themselves in a vital partnership with China.

Conclusion

Even though Chinese economic participation is considered a new phenomenon and a recent threat for Mexican, Canadian, and US industries, its impact has been highly visible in recent times. Despite this, however, there have been few studies conducted on the relationship between NAFTA member countries and the growing Chinese-US economic relationship. One of the results of this relationship is that Mexico has been losing ground in the US market. To turn this trend around, Mexico needs to consider an economic alliance with China, which would enable continued participation in the US economy. In addition, Mexico should consider other options such as marketing products to economies outside the United States in order to make up some of the ground it has lost to China in the American market.

China's commercial friction with the United States is increasing because of the US trade deficit with China. This deficit is becoming a fuel that feeds the political reactions of the US Congress toward the Asian giant and, in turn, means that China will have to adopt new strategies if it wants to continue trading in the United States without becoming a political target of the US system. These strategies could translate into a major commitment with other NAFTA economies to establish productive networks for business. Following this logic, Mexico and Canada could become important locations for new Chinese investments. Since commercial friction with the United States will become a big concern to China during the next few years, China may open parts of their market to American enterprises in an ongoing effort to allay economic fears.[10] The North America region is very important for China. Total trade in the region as a whole is increasing, and China is becoming a major trade partner for the United States, Canada, and Mexico. Mexico, for example, is one of China's key trading partners in Latin America, together with Brazil. In addition, China is likely to establish alliances with Mexico and Canada in order to reduce the bulky commercial deficit of the United States and obtain major regional integration in the North American market. Moreover, its growing economic participation in these two countries will increase political dialogue and facilitate China's entrance into the North American economic region in the near future.

Back in North America, Mexico requires new strategies if it is going to compete with Chinese products. It should develop bigger and better technological capacities, and it should tailor exporting strategies for specific sectors (such as in regions inside the US southwest).[11] Mexico is confronting Chinese industries principally in the US market, but the real threat to Mexico arises in the decline of its manufacturing capacity and the slow growth of its internal market. Without industrial growth, technological innovation, and massive and continuous job creation to help Mexico deal with its structural unemployment, Mexico could suffer even bigger losses in the US market.

In conclusion, the relationship between Mexico and China is politically and economically important. Today more than ever, the possibilities of confrontation and co-operation appear at the same time. There is confrontation because Mexico has lost much from Chinese competition in the North American market, and there has to be co-operation because the economies of both countries could benefit from a strategic partnership that gives China greater exposure to a US market while simultaneously offering Mexico increased access to markets outside of North America. Whatever the outcome, we currently stand at a crossroads where the possibility for a new and more constructive economic relationship is imminent.

NOTES

The author would like to thank Ana Fernanda Hierro, research assistant of the Robarts Centre for Canadian Studies; and Jaigris Hodson, research associate at the Robarts Centre for Canadian Studies and graduate student at York University, for their help and collaboration.

1 In some branches such as electronics, computing, and telecommunications, the exports made by foreign companies goes from 60 percent up to 95 percent.
2 North American Free Trade Agreement between the Government of Canada, the Government of Mexico and the Government of the United States, 17 December 1992, Can. T.S. 1994 No. 2, 32 I.L.M. 289 [NAFTA].
3 According to John Audley (2004), the Mexican agricultural sector, where one fifth of the population still works, lost 1.3 million jobs since 1994. On the other hand, NAFTA imposed restrictions on technological transfers, which was an indirect benefit for Chinese development.
4 Jorge Chami Batista's (2005) study is based on the analysis method entitled constant-market share, which refers to the change that the exports could experience in a certain market—in this case, the United States. The factors to consider are: (1) the increase of the demand in the importer market, (2) the composition of the products, and (3) the changes in the competitiveness. This study reveals that between 1999 and 2004, Mexico's market participation declined by 6 percent.
5 Inside the national market, 40 percent of the furniture is imported, mainly from China.

6 In the year 2003, Chinese exports of auto parts reached US $6.5 billion, which was twice as much as the year before (Fishman 2005, 209).

7 Japan is the number one creditor of the United States.

8 Jay Solomon, "U:U: Increasingly Pursues Two Track China Policy, Economic, Security Goals Yield Approach Combining Engagement, Containment," *Wall Street Journal,* 17 November 2005; and Antoaneta Bezlova, "Politics: Bush Visit to Focus on China's Rising Economic Power," Global Information Network, New York, 16 November 2005. See also Mekay, "China Commission."

9 Like the Chinese enterprise investments in Cuatitlán, Estado de México, amounting to US $50 million in 2005 (*Milenio,* 19 October 2005).

10 In his visit to the United States, President Hu Jintao offered contracts to American companies to increase the Chinese purchases in the sectors of transportation, computers, and soybeans.

11 In this sense, one can be optimistic that the Silicon Border Development project is destined to strengthen the manufacture of semiconductors in Mexicali, Baja California, and thus supply the US market (*Biznews,* 7 April 2006).

REFERENCES

"Ambassador Rob Portman Delivers Remarks on China-U.S. Relations." 2005. Transcription. 14 November.

Audley, John J. 2004. NAFTA's *Promise and Reality: Lessons from Mexico for the Hemisphere.* Washington, DC: Carnegie Endowment for International Peace.

Bezlova, Antoaneta. 2005. "Politics: Bush Visit to Focus on China's Rising Economic Power." *Global Information Network,* 16 November.

"Buscan empresas mexicanas conquistar a chinos por el estómago." 2005. *El Financiero,* 18 November.

Canada. 2005. Department of Foreign Affairs. *Canada´s International Policy Statement.* Ottawa: Department of Foreign Affairs.

Chami Batista, Jorge. 2005. "Competing for the U.S. Import Market: NAFTA and Non-NAFTA Countries." Paper given at the Free Trade in the Americas Conference, Baylor University, Waco, Texas, 6 October.

"China Eyes Strong Growth to 2010." 2005. *Reuters,* 25 October, http://www.reuters.com.

"CNPC Completes Acquisition of PetroKazakhstan." 2005. *China View,* 27 October, http://www.chinaview.com.cn.

Cortés, Martínez, José Ignacio, and Omar N. Castillo. 2004. "La ventaja comparativa de China y México en el mercado estadounidense." *Comercio Exterior* 54(6): 516–28.

"Estiman baja de 3.0 por ciento en exportaciones de textiles y vestido. Las ventas en el mercado nacional crecerán 5.0 percent este año: CNIV." 2005. *El Financiero,* 18 November.

Fishman, Ted C. 2005. *China Inc.: How the Rise of the Next Superpower Challenges America and the World.* New York: Scribner.

Flores, Leonor. 2005. "Costó a México 30 mil mdd la pérdida de competitividad: Ortiz." *Milenio,* 5 October.

García, Myriam. 2006. "Da automotriz más inversión." *Reforma,* 12 January.

Hicks, Romero, José Luis, and Molina Medina Humberto. 2003. "La transformación económica de China y sus ampliaciones para Mexico." *Comercio Exterior* 53(12): 1155–65.

"Industry, Trade and Economy: Data and Análisis." 2005. *US Foreign Trade Highlights,* 25 July, http://www.ita.doc.gov/td/industry/otea.

"Instituto Mexicano Del Seguro Social." 2008. Retrieved 31 July 2008 from http://www.imss.gob.mx.

López Villafañe, Víctor. 2005. *The Dragon in Aztec Lands.* Toronto: Robarts Centre for Canadian Studies, http://www.robarts.yorku.ca.

Mekay, Emad. 2005. "China Comission Sounds Call for Punitive Action." *Global Information Network,* 11 November.

Nye, Jr., Joseph S. 2005. "The Future of US-China Relations." *PacNet,* 16 March.

Oropeza, Arturo. 2005. "México-China: La invasión del gigante amarillo." *Reforma,* 13 November.

Perrett, Bradley. 2006. "Update: China Economy Grew 9.8 pct in 2005—Vice Minister." *Reuters,* 1 January, http://www.reuters.com.

"Premier: GDP to Exceed US $1.85 trillion in 2005." 2005. *China Daily,* 20 October. http://chinadaily.com.cn.

Romero Hicks, José Luis, and Humberto Molina Medina. 2003. "La transformación económicade China y sus implicaciones para México." *Comercio Exterior* 53(12): 1155–65.

"Silicon Border Breaks Ground in Mexicali: Science Park Becomes a Reality." 2005. *TMCNet News,* 11 July. http://www.tmcnet.com.

Solomon, Jay. 2005. "U.S. Increasingly Pursues Two-Track China Policy; Economic, Security Goals Yield Approach Combining Engagement, Containment." *Wall Street Journal,* 17 November.

Villafañe, Víctor López, 1994. *The New Era of Capitalism: Japan and United States in the Pacific Basin, 1945–2002.* Mexico City: Siglo XXI.

———. 1999. *Asia in Transition: Boom, Crisis and Challenges.* Mexico City: Siglo XXI.

12

Brazil and Mexico: The Politics of Continental Drift

Edgar J. Dosman

Introduction: Brazil and Mexico in the Global System

Given their size and importance, Brazil and Mexico are not merely closely watched countries internationally but also key players in an inter-American system facing profound domestic and global challenges. By far the largest Latin American countries in population and economy, they are, at once, logical partners in strengthening regional growth and integration and historic rivals with divergent foreign policies and an underperforming bilateral relationship. This chapter will use the coincidence of 2006 national elections in both countries to assess the evolution of Mexican-Brazilian relations. More specifically, the discussion will focus on the implications of diverging globalization strategies since the 1980s, with particular attention to the redesign of Brazilian foreign policy and its regional strategy toward the Western Hemisphere. The final sections will examine the current status and outlook for Mexico and Brazil and their relationship with the North American Free Trade Agreement (NAFTA) after the July 2006 Mexican elections.[1]

Brazil and Mexico: Strategies of Globalization Compared

Mexico's political polarization in 2006, which was so clearly demonstrated in the July election results, could not have been anticipated six years earlier when Vicente Fox of the National Action Party won victory as president, breaking the monopoly of the Institutional Revolutionary Party and igniting a wave of optimism about future economic and political prospects. In 2001, he was the star of the third Summit of the Americas in Quebec, and Mexico was firmly established as one of the leading emerging global economies. NAFTA seemed to have delivered for Mexico, confirming the neo-liberal model chosen after 1982, with expanding employment and, now with Fox, a multi-party democracy as well. "With friends like Fox," American Robert Leiken enthused, the Americas were truly on the move (Leiken 2002). Even the sharp, but brief, peso crisis of December 1994 and the lingering Chiapas rebellion earlier that year could not dim the sense that Mexico faced a confident future. However, by 2006, the Mexican economy was trapped in a low-growth cycle, the country was polarized politically, and the benign Clinton years had been replaced by the geopolitics of George W. Bush. Mexico's foreign policy had atrophied under President Fox, and its position among the powers tracked the grim trajectory of declining national confidence. Brazil, in contrast, had recovered from severe challenges in 2000, including a currency crisis spreading from Asia and the proximity of financial turbulence in Argentina, to become a key global power by 2006 within a very select group of "emerging global actors."

Brazil and Mexico have pursued very different strategies of globalization since the 1980s. For Brazil, the end of the Cold War and the intensification of economic globalization coincided with the termination of military rule. Thus, its entire foreign policy required an overhaul. Most observers credit Brazilian leadership, particularly President Fernando Henrique Cardoso, for overseeing a coherent and successful transition. Brazil chose a regional approach, building from a South American base to a diversified international trade with roughly equal shares in Europe, North America, Asia, and Latin America, along with growing markets in the Middle East and Africa. As early as the mid-1980s, Brazil aggressively sought to enhance trade opportunities. The Mercado Común del Sur (Mercosur), a building block toward a potential South American community, was established in 1991 as a result of a rapprochement initiated by Brazil between it and Argentina. Since then, Brazil has pursued a vigorous multi-track international trade policy through Mercosur, the World Trade Organization (WTO), and the Free Trade Area of the Americas (FTAA), including free trade agreements between Mercosur and other countries or regions, with particular emphasis on a potential accord with the European Union. Brazil took a leadership role by bringing together the G-20 group of developing countries in global trade negotiations during the Cancún meeting of the WTO and has maintained its key role in the Doha Round (unlike Canada or Mexico) ever since (Schott 2004).

Over all, a robust Brazilian foreign policy has sought partners and strengthened ties in every region—China, India, South Africa, and other members of the G-20 (including being the host of a South America–Middle East summit in 2005). At the apex of this activism, it has underlined its commitment to UN-led multilateralism and rules-based governance by leading the UN Stabilization Mission in Haiti (MINUSTAH) and campaigning for a permanent seat on the UN Security Council. Beyond its acknowledged status as an essential player in the inter-American system, Brazil (the fifth most populous country in the world) is a credible claimant for a permanent seat on the UN Security Council, a major power in the south Atlantic, and the *de facto* leader of the ex-Portuguese colonial Lusophone world.

Mexico made a very different choice in the age of globalization, one that reflects the intractable reality of neighbourhood: geographic location, historic development ties, and the fact that NAFTA has produced a permanent and over-whelming US-dependent commerce. Mexico's entrance into NAFTA negotiations in 1990 implied fundamental changes in its foreign policy, including a new en-trance into the US and North American market and a strategic reorientation vis-à-vis Latin America (Hrsitoulas and Herz 2005). During the 1970s, Presidents Luis Echevarria and Lopez Portillo had played the role of an activist "Third World leader," seeing Mexico as an interlocutor between North and South and directly challenging US policy in Nicaragua and El Salvador. During the 1980s, this changed with the adoption of a neo-liberal economic model. Within the new NAFTA-based foreign policy vision, Mexico would be firmly anchored eco-nomically in North America but would try to diversify relations with free trade agreements around the world. Its success in negotiating a free trade agreement with the European Union in 2000, its application in 2004 for associate member status in Mercosur, and its initiation of a host of other free-trade agreements in Latin America and around the world exemplified Mexico's strategy.[2]

In practice, the international role of Mexico has diminished since the end of the Cold War, while the role of Brazil has expanded. Neither Mexico nor Canada has developed an effective doctrine or foreign policy adequate for the reality of NAFTA. Both form part of a reorganized North America under Washington's geopolitical leadership, including Central America and the Caribbean, in which transnational forces of migration, trade, drugs, and crime have created a complex and unattractive US-centred interdependence. Its location in South America, its far more autonomous economic structure, and its export diversi-fication have provided Brazil with greater scope to develop a more coherent foreign policy orientation.

Brazil as Partner: Strengths and Vulnerabilities

Given its size, clout, international visibility, and evident regional leadership role in South America, it is logical that Brazil should be included in the special category of "emerging global actors"—namely, large and dynamic developing countries that are also "regional leaders" anchoring important clusters in the international economy (Canada 2005). The popular term referring to Brazil, India, Russia, and China (BRIC) further identifies this grouping. Increasingly, they are being thought of as important players in the global economy, chal-lengers that are moving forward quickly in the global hierarchy and changing the international economic system. They are, in short, crucial future partners requiring priority attention (ibid., 22).[3] However, China, Brazil, and India are variously depicted as future superpowers, socially bifurcated, and therefore un-stable, giants prone to crisis, or simply large developing countries with cyclical ups and downs. Depending on the perspective, they are seen as possible threats, competitors, or potential partners. In assessing Brazilian foreign policy and the Mexico/NAFTA connection, it is therefore important to evaluate its strengths and vulnerabilities relative to other "emerging global actors." Where does Brazil really fit? Does it belong in the same category as China and India? (Coutinho 2005). For all of Brazil's international visibility, Mexico, with a much smaller population, can boast a comparable gross domestic product, and both have remained trapped for years in a comparable low-growth cycle while China and India have leapt ahead.

Brazil's economic strengths, however, appear impressive, beginning with a formidable and well-known physical and resource endowment that has marked its development since colonial days. Its deposits of coal and iron ore, for example, are legendary. Although Brazil emerged from military rule with one of the most closed economies in the world, the last decade has seen a rapid internationalization of the economy. Rivalling the United States as the world's largest agricultural power in grains and cereals (corn, soy, rice, sugar, and soybean meal), Brazil has benefited from the explosive growth of the international food market in recent years, fuelled in part by demand from China, which has prompted massive Brazilian exports (Watts 2006). In 2004, the country had a 31.21 percent increase in international trade on top of the 12.79 percent increase in 2003. Exports reached US $96.475 billion in 2004, yielding a trade surplus of US $33.67 billion. In 2005, this surplus rose again to a record US $44 billion, with a forecast for 2006 of US $132 billion (Gabeira 2005).

Brazil has also developed competitive industrial sectors that extend beyond its comparative advantages in agriculture-related or other commodity production, with leading global multinationals such as Vale do Rio Doce and Petroleo Brasiliera and including high-technology success stories such as Empresa Brasiliera de Aeronautica. Brazilian companies are increasingly visible abroad. Car production has expanded into the export market. High-profile Empresa Brasiliera de Aeronautica stands out as the standard-bearer of Brazilian product innovation. In intermediate technology areas such as steel, for example, the country's multinationals (such as Gerdau Steel) are world leaders and global investors. A population base of 185 million provides the advantage of a large domestic market to complement export opportunities. Combined with the continuation of macroeconomic stability as an official priority, such features make it a favoured country for foreign direct investment.

In the energy sector, Brazil has achieved self-sufficiency, unlike China or India, to compensate for its lack of petroleum reserves. It has done this under the leadership of Petroleo Brasiliera, the state energy company created in 1953 and through the development of alternative fuels such as ethanol. Few countries, the United States included, underestimate this accomplishment, which has required decades-long consistency in technology planning. Unlike China and India, which are petroleum dependent and currently scrounging the more unsavoury global locations for secure sources of oil and natural gas, Brazil can play a stabilizing role in South America's complex energy scene to the benefit of all parties—Hugo Chávez, Ivo Morales, Washington, and the Mercosur partners (Reguly 2006). Moreover, the evolution of Brazil's economy would not have been possible without strong human resources reflecting the high quality of its universities and research laboratories. Along with China, Brazil has the lowest "brain-drain" among developing countries (less than 5 percent). After decades of hyperinflation, Brazil has achieved and maintains a stable macroeconomic environment (Barbosa 2001). Economic growth of 5.2 percent in 2004, behind a booming and diversified international trade, promised a welcome return to expansion after years of relative stagnation.

Additional reasons for emphasizing Brazil's future possibilities include the return to stable democracy, including the election of its first labour government in 2002. Notwithstanding the scandals of 2005 in Brasilia, the stability of Brazil as a modern democracy is not in doubt. Indeed, by weathering this storm, the economy and the party system have been strengthened by confronting the crisis. In addition, and unlike China or India, Brazil enjoys a comparatively "benign neighbourhood" with uncontested borders and no actual or potential nuclear rivals (ibid.). As well as being its primary trade bloc, Mercosur comprises Brazil's core region geopolitically, a base for the gradual construction of a more integrated South America. While policing its vast borders remains a permanent challenge, not least with a civil war in neighbouring Colombia to the far north, Brazil does not face a military balance of power in South America and, therefore, has the luxury of relatively low military expenditures. Internally as well, Brazil faces no secessionist movements. Multicultural and open, despite enormous income distribution problems, the population is remarkably culturally cohesive.

However, Brazil's vulnerabilities offset its strengths and advantages and threaten the potential for a definitive breakthrough into the core economy status of China or India.[4] This concern is not merely based on the comparison of statistics, such as the vastly greater international bank reserves in these two countries, but it also concerns the underperforming growth rate since the end of military rule.[5] The relatively high growth rate of 5.2 percent in 2004 looks less impressive when considered against the growth rate of 2.5 percent in 2005 and in the context of eight previous years of intermittent stagnation. In 2001, for example, growth was 1 percent, while India and China's economies had literally taken off during these years. The enormous question hanging over Brasilia is whether strong economic growth will in fact continue should several years of an unusually favourable international environment end. Yet productivity fell in 2005, as did growth (4 percent), and the economy actually contracted during the third quarter, with a growth forecast for 2006 of only 3.6 percent. Such a figure in India (anything below 6 percent) or China (below 8 percent) would be considered a catastrophe. It is far too low for countries in transition to reduce poverty or inequality and still maintain industrial momentum. After years of witnessing anaemic growth, Brazilian planners appear resigned to low targets. Thirty years earlier, they would have assumed and expected nothing less than 6–8 percent, and annual growth actually exceeded 11 percent during the 1968–73 "miracle."

These lower expectations reflect a recognition of the impediments to growth in Brazil that China and India appear to have overcome or, at least, to have neutralized. Brazil's high debt servicing costs (US $267.89 billion between 1995 and 2004) equal the total of federal investment in education 3.5 times over. Reforms have been delayed in modernizing the state. Despite impressive trade growth and macroeconomic stability, Brazil still lacks an effective and supportive state bureaucracy; infrastructure investments to arrest the decline of cities and public security; fiscal reforms toward an effective tax system, currently hindered by red tape and chaotic tax administration; adequate public schools and health care, which require additional outlays for private insurance on top of taxes; and so forth. The costly outbreak of hoof and mouth disease in 2005 underlined the urgency of quality control and inspection. The main impact of recent political scandals in Brasilia has been the delay of addressing these problems and of creating a leaner and more efficient state to expand the internal market.

Other observers worry that Brazil may have caught a premature spell of "Dutch disease," a syndrome of booming commodities, over-valued currencies, and weak industrial productivity that squeezes profits and growth. Draconian measures (particularly high interest rates) used to maintain macroeconomic stability as a first priority raised the Brazilian real 13.7 percent relative to the US dollar in 2005 and contributed to the sapping of Brazil's overall economic energy. However, the official memories of hyperinflation remain vivid. Since President Luiz Inacio "Lula" da Silva adopted the macroeconomic approach inherited from Fernando Henrique Cardoso, on the argument that the growth cycle under way since 2004 would continue at an acceptable pace, and since the main opposition party is ex-president Fernando Henrique's Social Democratic Party of Brazil, policy consistency will likely continue. In short, Brazil has been applauded by the International Monetary Fund as a star pupil, paying out its US $15.5 billion debt in advance, but somehow missing key elements of China and India's "virtuous cycle," which is rapidly transforming these economies and their accelerated growth.

The problem of inadequate technological dynamism has also provoked a major debate about the future of Brazil. Empresa Brasiliera de Aeronautica and Petroleo Brasiliera are national symbols, but they are the exceptions to the rule. Isolated Brazilian successes in industries such as aerospace, electronics, steel, and industrial products have not generated a technological dynamism throughout the economy comparable with India (which has increased its information technology production twenty-fold since 1990). India's share of the global out-sourcing market was US $20 billion in 2005 compared with US $300 million for Brazil. In competitive areas, such as automobile production, Brazil has watched China's global market share grow from 3 to 7.9 percent since 1997, while the Brazil-Mercosur share has fallen from 4.7 to 3.9 percent in 2004 (2005). Brazil's comparative advantage remains in commodity production (70 percent of its exports) and particularly in food production and iron ore, and this image of the country as a "hewer of wood and a drawer of water" in the international hierarchy haunts its leadership. Moreover, having this comparative advantage is not without risks. The vast soybean farms reaching into the Amazon and Plate Basins may have long-term environmental impacts of unknown cost and severity.[6] Brazil's urgent challenge is productivity and international competi-tiveness in value-added goods across small and medium sectors as well as in transnational production.

Similarly, the undoubted defence advantages enjoyed by Brazil in South America are also offset by internal security problems such as civic and organized crime. Numerous adjoining states, including Colombia, Bolivia, Venezuela, and Paraguay, in particular, face active or insipient polarization, and these perme-able borders require increasing Brazilian attention. New factors such as impor-tant major natural gas reserves in conflict-prone Bolivia have created issues for Brazil and the other neighbours. Mercosur presents a similar dilemma of partial success, with severe structural problems impeding its consolidation even as its membership grows and international accords multiply. Mexico may have severe border difficulties with the United States and Central America, but at least it has secure long-term access to a core NAFTA market. In short, it is one thing to lead a region but quite another to deal with the long-term task of building a coherent South America. Like Mexico, Brazil's priority (regardless of the political party in government) is to accelerate growth and address the social deficit without a return to inflationary times.

Brazil's historical handicap of a socially segmented society is recognized as a major obstacle to its successful development and its most intractable challenge.[7] The social deficit inherited from the high levels of social exclusion and regional inequality, which has spawned poverty and marginalization, feeds alienation, urban violence, and organized crime. Under Fernando Henrique Cardoso, the Gini index of inequality finally moved slightly in the right direction. The elec-tion of the Brazilian Workers' Party in 2002 reflected a broad agreement on the centrality of social policy, but the last four years have demonstrated again that solutions are slow and difficult. Brazil finally faces favourable demographic trends: a low fertility rate will gradually lower pressure on education and other social policy budgets.

On balance, however, Brazil is increasingly important for Mexico and NAFTA because it is firmly established as the regional leader in South America and a powerful global interlocutor with an active and responsible multilateral foreign policy. The Washington-Brasilia axis is also the driving force behind inter-American relations, and Washington has *de facto* recognized Brazil's regional leadership aspirations. Severely overstretched, however, the United States currently needs Brazil to act as a bulwark of order in a turbulent region undergoing a tilt to the Left. Which other country could volunteer to lead MINUSTAH in Haiti, "manage" Hugo Chávez and the forthcoming Mercosur-Venezuela negotiations, normalize Evo Morales in the natural gas-rich neighbouring Bolivia, or deal with a host of similar issues that the United States has neither the credibility nor the resources to deal with (Schott 2004, 10; Hakim 2004)?[8] The Brazilian economy, which is seriously in need of a less restrictive macroeconomic framework, will not likely emulate China's "turbo-capitalism" or, indeed, its own period of equally torrid "savage-capitalism" of an earlier year, but it remains the largest and most autonomous economy next to the United States in the Americas.

Towards a Common Agenda:

Mexico and Brazil have different challenges—evident from their locations, cultures, and histories—the most notable being the management of the US relationship. But they also share obvious threats and broad interests across the agenda spectrum, including revitalizing growth and employment; tackling social exclusion, education, organized crime and violence; preventing conflict and managing borders with neighbouring states; and, above all, addressing increasingly pressing demands for equity and human sustainable development. Since solutions require international co-operation, both countries invoke the language of multilateralism, and both are members of the inter-American system and its regional governance instruments and opportunities. Indeed, the global threat to multilateralism in the George W. Bush era underscores the logic of intermediate power collaboration and, therefore, the importance to both Mexico and Brazil of deepening their relations to each other.

However, in practice, Mexico and Brazil have found themselves at odds on regional and international issues (although Mexico did join the G-20 at Cancún, and both Mexico and Brazil have rejected US unilateralism in attacking Iraq). The FTAA or MINUSTUH in Haiti offer highly visible examples of these countries' differing priorities. Six years of erratic Mexican foreign policy under President Fox may have contributed to the negative dialogue, but the bilateral differences between Mexico and Brazil are based on a more fundamental cleavage than personality or a particular issue such as the FTAA. From Brazil's perspective, Mexico's post-1990 choice of a NAFTA-based strategy implied that it had rejected the historic Latin American integration project initiated in 1960 with the Latin American Free Trade Agreement and had chosen instead to become part of North America, within the inner US geopolitical orbit. Mexico, in this optic, could no longer aspire credibly to play the intermediary role between North and South America. Indeed, from the perspective of the Brazilian Ministry of Foreign Relations, Mexico's decision to join the North fundamentally altered the political geography of the Western Hemisphere. "Latin America" no longer existed—in fact, the term disappeared in the official Brazilian category of regions. Instead, the Americas were "North America," including Mexico, and "South America" or an insipient "South American Community of Nations" with separate identities in the global system. Not surprisingly, Mexican diplomacy has resented this rebuff to its historic self-image as the bridging power in the Western Hemisphere. Recent Brazilian-Mexican disagreements, including Brazil's bid for a permanent seat on the UN Security Council, for example; its participation in MINUSTAH; its relations with Cuba and Hugo Chávez; its choice of candidate for secretary general of the Organization of African States; the future of the FTAA; the question of Mercosur associate membership; and so forth, are symptoms of a culturally embedded geopolitical discord between historic rivals.[9]

Nevertheless, Brazil's search for new trade partners has refocused interest on NAFTA as a key market.[10] After a premature enthusiasm for a special relationship with China, marked by a bilateral agreement to manufacture aircraft there with Empresa Brasiliera de Aeronautica as well as a unilateral designation of market economy status, Brazil has found fewer trade and investment returns than expected, at least in the short term. Disappointment in foreign direct investment has been matched by China's interest (and Asian countries in general) in importing Brazilian commodities rather than value-added goods and increasing its exports of manufactured goods to Brazil, which grew sharply in 2005. Although it is in third place in terms of market share, China as a "privileged partner" is likely to be viewed in Brasilia at least as much as a competitor. Its status as an international soybean and food basket and iron ore supplier for the Chinese economic powerhouse is not Brazil's image of a preferred future (Rohter 2005). In short, while Brazil's two-way trade with Asia increased from US $16,787 billion in 2002 to US $26,842 billion in 2004, it has not been the key to reducing dependence on the traditional markets (United States and European Union) or realizing the long-held dream of equitable and multisector strategic South-South partnerships (Hrsitoulas and Herz 2005, 237–39).

Brazilian-EU trade relations began at a high level with two-way trade amounting to US $40 billion in 2004, surpassing trade with the United States ($31,852 billion) by a significant margin, but it also remained stubbornly based in agricultural, mineral, and industrial commodities (Gabeira 2005, 49).[11] Moreover, the European Union's agricultural policies continually undermine progress toward an EU-Mercosur free trade agreement since the European sectors of greatest interest for Brazil remain heavily protected (Hrsitoulas and Herz 2005, 246–57).[12] The US market—for all its protectionism—is still more open to value-added goods than Europe, where the deafening volume of official invocations of solidarity with Brazil and Mercosur appears correlated with increasingly inventive trade restrictions (ibid., 240–43).[13]

In fact, Mexico and its NAFTA partners stand out as increasingly important economic partners for Brazil in the current international system. Both American and Canadian relations with Brazil have been carefully examined and cannot be addressed in this volume, but the rapid internationalization of the Brazilian and Mexican economies also offers mutual opportunities (ibid., 236–37).[14] In commercial relations, there are irritants, disputes, and industrial asymmetries (Mexico's petrochemical sector, for example, versus a greater Brazilian strength in steel), but, from Brazil's perspective, there is nothing comparable in its trade with Mexico to the aerospace rivalry between Empresa Brasiliera de Aeronautica and Canadian Bombardier. In fact, bilateral trade between Brazil and Mexico has grown solidly since the 1990s to sixth place, after the United States, Argentina, China, the Netherlands, and Germany, approaching US $2 billion from January to June 2005 and with the advantage of including a high ratio of value-added products.

While bilateral trade is one-sided in Brazil's favour, Mexico's foreign direct investment in Brazil of over US $3 billion in 2003 dwarfs Brazil's investment of only US $57 million in Mexico. Overall, the total is still small for such large traders (2.72 percent of Brazil's total foreign trade in 2002 and only 0.9 for Mexico) (ibid., 233–34). Moreover, Brazilian trade is concentrated in only eleven products, which is highly based in auto sector (50 percent of total trade). So far, the two governments have signed three economic complementarity accords, which have followed bilateral agreements on the automobile and auto parts sectors in 2000 and 2001: a limited Brazilian-Mexican preferential agreement; a commitment to proceed to a Mexican- Mercosur free trade agreement; and a Mexican-Mercosur accord to promote trade in automotive production (Hrsitoulas and Herz 2005, 234). Unlike China, Brazil does not threaten Mexico's export industries. With respect to certain products, the United States is Brazil's principal competitor. Moreover, respective private sectors in Brazil and Mexico are apparently comfortable with the existing narrow bilateral complementarity accords. On the other hand, there is enormous room for expansion in Brazilian-Mexican relations. The challenges, however, are enormous. The overwhelming continental focus of Mexican trade limits its interests and engagement at the WTO level. Yet, despite these obstacles, the goal of developing an effective multi-sector "emerging markets" dialogue with Brazil should not be underestimated. And, finally, the main achievement on both sides must be a recognition that Brazil and Mexico are important potential partners requiring priority attention.

Perspectives: The New Presidency of Felipe Calderón Hinojosa

The July 2006 presidential elections, with Felipe Calderón Hinojosa's extremely narrow and bitterly contested victory, obliged the new administration to reconsider foreign policy options toward Latin America, including Brazil. It was blindingly obvious that the coincidence of a divided electorate and a divided Congress as well as the accumulation of urgent public policy challenges, including illegal narcotics, civil insecurity, stagnant productivity, and fiscal reform, require priority attention to domestic reforms. Mexican foreign policy would have to support this overriding priority. During the election, the National Action Party had polarized the campaign against the Democratic Revolutionary Party, supporting President Fox's "North-American option" while using Hugo Chávez as whipping boy and public enemy no. 1 to defeat Andrés Manuel López Obrador. For its part, the platform of López Obrador promised a new approach not only to NAFTA but also to the entire conceptual framework underpinning Mexico's neo-liberal resurgence after 1981. His identification of social exclusion as the principal threat to Mexico's future captured the main theme of President Lula da Siva in his successful 2002 presidential campaign and also reflected the evident dissatisfaction throughout Latin America in recent years with the Washington Consensus. If López Obrador had indeed succeeded in winning the election—bearing in mind the uncertainties surrounding the actual implementation of his agenda, reflected in the variety of "Leftist" experiments that have occurred in Latin America when self-styled anti-neo-liberal parties have actually gained power—his administration would have undoubtedly redefined the North American connection while strengthening Mexico's political and economic relations with Brazil and Latin America.

Facing potential political deadlock after his victory was confirmed, Calderón Hinojosa lost no time in abandoning the foreign policy orientation of his campaign and reaching out to disaffected Mexicans. Distancing himself from his predecessor's unsuccessful foreign policy of antagonizing virtually everyone in Latin America while failing to strengthen US relations, he adopted instead a strategy of rebuilding relationships with all of the countries in Latin America regardless of political orientation in order to restore Mexico's regional and global prestige and underpin his credibility as a leader capable of representing national interests across the political spectrum. On 6 January 2007, he signalled the new approach by meeting with President Lula da Siva, re-launching the Brazil-Mexico Bilateral Commission and inviting Lula da Siva for a state visit in August. Later that month, Calderón Hinojosa pointedly replaced dialogue for confrontation with Hugo Chávez, quietly shelving his polarizing campaign rhetoric in a bid to normalize relations with Leftist governments in the region including Cuba and Nicaragua.

By the time he gave his first address to the nation on 2 September 2007, Calderón Hinojosa could claim considerable success in realigning Mexican foreign policy, with a new ambassador installed in Caracas, Nicaraguan president Daniel Ortega hailing Calderón Hinojosa for initiating "a new stage of friendship and cooperation," and Nestor Kirchner not only signing a "strategic partnership agreement" with Calderón Hinojosa but also vocally supporting Mexico's incorporation into Mercosur "as essential in the construction of Latin American countries and regional policies" (Mexico 2007a; Mexico 2007c).[15] In short, President Calderón Hinojosa had largely re-introduced pragmatism into Mexico's regional diplomacy. He had also demonstrated a more critical approach to a US relationship increasingly strained by the exhaustion of NAFTA, the failure of US immigration reform in May 2007, the escalation of casualties, and the construction of border fences, combined with a brutal crackdown on Mexican illegal migrants.

In this more promising environment, President Lula da Siva's state visit to Mexico on 6 August 2007 was successful, with Calderón Hinojosa hailing the bilateral relationship as the crucial political building block in the construction of Latin America. If Brazil and Mexico worked together, he noted, it would ensure that Latin America could occupy the place it deserved on the world stage. Both leaders underscored their joint, rather than diverging, initiatives in the G-5 (Mexico, Brazil, South Africa, India, and China) at the 2007 G-8 summit in Heiligendamm, at the G-20 in the Doha Round trade negotiations, and at the East Asian Latin American Co-operation Forum. With both Mexico and Brazil facing the economic slowdown in the United States and, possibly, the end of the spectacularly favourable international economic climate that had been in place since 2002, they also stressed the urgency of expanding bilateral trade beyond the 2006 level of US $6.7 billion, which remains "far below the full potential." Both countries were committed, they promised, to the development and integration of Latin America and the Caribbean (Mexico 2007b).

Nevertheless, given the geopolitical realities, the overlap of shared Brazilian-Mexican interests is (and will remain) limited. The Mexican economy remains tied to the United States, and notwithstanding Calderón Hinojosa's distancing himself politically from the hugely unpopular George W. Bush, his success in the anti-drug war, migration, and particularly in accelerating economic growth depend as much as ever on North America. Brazil's future lies in South America and its diversified global alliances in which Mexico plays only a secondary, if potentially important, role as partner. Nestor Kirchner's enthusiastic invitation to Mexico to join Mercosur is less a panacea for regional integration than a symptom of the southern bloc's declining cohesion. In other key areas, such as participation in international peace support operations such as Haiti or the G-4's UN reform project (Brazil, India, Japan, and Germany), Mexican-Brazilian interests continue to diverge. Neither bilateral opportunities nor the rebuilding of the inter-American system can be effective without the serious commitment of both countries.

With a Western Hemisphere mired in multiple challenges, including migration, security, borders, productivity, poverty reduction, and trade, the region desperately requires leadership and would benefit hugely from a more active collaboration between Mexico and Brazil. So far, given the omnipresent border crisis that Mexico confronts on its northern and southern borders, not to mention the China and Asian trade challenges, the Mexican media have not given Brazil and Latin America front-page attention. However, considering the first gloomy prospects, the evolution of Mexican foreign policy toward Brazil and Latin America since the exceptionally contested 2006 elections has been positive and welcomed. Although the initial fears of political polarization and stalemate have dissipated since the inauguration of President Calderón Hinojosa and his unexpected but welcome regional activism, policy sustainability depends on the success of his domestic reforms and his ability to relaunch productivity and growth. Brazil also faces urgent institutional challenges to accelerate economic growth, and improved relations with Mexico serve to offset irritating tensions with neighbours in South America. Overall, Brazil-Mexican relations have undoubtedly benefited from the advent of the government of Calderón Hinojosa in Mexico City, even if the underlying obstacles to deepening the bilateral relationship have not disappeared. A more serious political dialogue between the two Latin American giants is essential for progress in the Western Hemisphere and global multilateralism alike, but whether Mexico under the National Action Party can deliver remains to be seen.

NOTES

1 North American Free Trade Agreement between the Government of Canada, the Government of Mexico and the Government of the United States, 17 December 1992, Can. T.S. 1994 No. 2, 32 I.L.M. 289.

2 For a recent in-depth analysis of the relationship, see Antonio Ortiz Mena in Octavio Amorim Neto and Rafael Fernandez de Castro, eds., *Brasil y Mexico: Encuentras y Des encuentros* (Instituo Matias Romero, SRE Mexico, 2005).

3 It specifically includes China in East Asia, India in South Asia, and Brazil in South America (Canada 2005).

4 China's "turbo-capitalism" being the most evident current theme (Sandschneider 2006).

5 Of course, gloom about competitiveness and productivity is hardly limited to Brazil. Indian economists worry that their prospects cannot compare with China—everyone worries about China.

6 The comparative figures are China (US $769 billion), India (US $146 billion), and Brazil (US $50 billion).

7 Agricultural production actually fell in 2005.

8 *Social Watch* ranked Brazil ninety-fourth out of 191 countries surveyed in 2005. In 2006, after several years of stardom at Davos, Brazil was dropped from the featured triad of Brazil-India-China as the elite emerging powers. Scandals and slower growth had imperceptibly marked it down from these three Asian giants basking in international attention.

9 In this age of geopolitics, Brazil's focus on the United States as a commercial and diplomatic partner will continue to grow. Even in agriculture, the United States and Brazil share important objectives in the World Trade Organization and could work together in their common interest.

10 Mexico's sudden lifting and re-imposing of visa requirements for Brazilian visitors in 2004–05 did nothing to improve relations.

11 NAFTA has a limited international identity, but its underlying harmonizing dynamic is in steadily creating insipient trilateral regulatory regimes that affect external powers. Brazil discovered this fact during the "mad-cow" crisis (2000) when overzealous Canadian officials, acting on behalf of their NAFTA partners, temporarily banned beef imports for all three countries (Jubany 2001).

12 Brazil and India have been strong interlocutors in international trade circles since the formation of the UN Conference on Trade and Development, and it is not surprising that they lead the current G-20 group of developing countries. However, the two countries do not yet have strong trade or investment links—trade with India is about the same as that with Taiwan. Brazil has adopted a goal of emulating India's success in information technology outsourcing, hoping to enter the top five countries in five years (along with India, China, Russia, and Canada), but India is miles ahead. While both countries have agreed to strengthen high-technology collaboration, other countries (such as Canada) with powerful diaspora ties and established research linkages are claiming attention from India. Brazilian trade with Africa and the Middle East has also been advancing, and, under President Lula, Brasilia has conspicuously pursued these relationships, but, since overall trade volumes are beginning from a low base, the gains remain interesting and promising but not yet strong. Trade with Africa in 2004 rose to US $10.417 billion, which is one-quarter of the EU trade. Brazil–Middle East trade flows in the same year were US $6 billion.

13 It remains to be seen whether cultural and political dialogue, reinforced by a strengthened Ibero-American summit, can facilitate a new and more equitable relationship.

14 In certain key areas, such as information technology outsourcing, Brazilian success depends essentially on US access. In this case, India is Brazil's foremost competitor.

15 See Gabriel Luíz Gabeira (2005, 56) for a comparison of Brazil's trade with Mexico and other major importing countries.

REFERENCES

Barbosa, Rubens A. 2001. "A nova geografia economica do continente." *Political Externa* 10(2): 30.

Canada. 2005. *International Policy Statement: A Role of Pride and Influence in the World*. Ottawa: Department of Foreign Affairs and International Trade.

Coutinho, Luciano. 2005. "O Brasil na rabeira." *Folha de S. Paulo*, 30 October.

Gabeira, Gabriel Luíz. 2005. *Sintese da Economia Brasiliera 2005*. Rio de Janeiro: Confederacao Nacional do Comercio.

Hakim, Peter. 2004. "The Reluctant Partner." *Foreign Affairs* 83(1). http://www.foreignaffairs.org/2004/1.html.

Hrsitoulas, Athanasios, and Monica Herz. 2005. "Brasil y Mexico Enfrentan a la Seguridad Regional e International Despues de la Guerra Fria." In Antonio Ortiz Mena, Octavio Amorim Neto, and Rafael Fernandez de Castro, eds., *Brasil y Mexico, Encuentros y Desencuentros*, 229–70. Mexico City: Insituto Matias Romero.

Jubany, Florencia. 2001. *Getting over the Jet-Lag: Canada-Brazil Relations 2001*. Focal Policy Papers. Ottawa: Canadian Foundation for the Americas.

Leiken, Robert. 2001. "With a Friend like Fox." *Foreign Affairs* 80(5) (May/June). http://www.foreignaffairs.org/2001/5.htm.

Mexico. 2007a. Presidency of the Republic. Joint Press Conference by President Calderon and Argentinean President Nestor Kirchner, 30 July.

———. 2007b. Presidency of the Republic. Joint Press Conference by President Calderon and Brazilian President Luiz Inacio Lula da Silva, 6 August.

———. 2007c. Presidency of the Republic. Joint Press Conference by President Calderon and Nicaraguan President Daniel Ortega, 28 June.

Ming, Celso. 2005. "Algo novo das exportacoes." *O Estado do Sao Paulo*, 26 April.

Reguly, Eric. 2006. "China Treads Where Canada Won't." *Globe and Mail*, 2 May.

Rohter, Larry. 2005. "Brazil Weighs Costs and Benefits of Alliance with China." *New York Times*, 20 November.

Sandschneider, Eberhard. 2006. "A Guide to Dragon Care." *Internationale Politik: The Journal of the German Council on Foreign Relations* 7(1): 54–58.

Schott, Jeffrey J. 2004. *Reviving the Doha Round*. Washington: Institute for International Economics.

Watts, Jonathan. 2006. "A Hunger Eating Up the World." *Guardian Weekly*, 20 January.

7

BUILDING THE CANADA-MEXICO RELATIONSHIP:
THINKING OUTSIDE THE BOX

13

Thinking Outside the Box in Canada-Mexico Relations: The Long Road from Convenience to Commitment

Andrew F. Cooper

The Elusive Balance Point and the Super-Sized Neighbour

Canadian-Mexican relations can be described as being driven by a sense of convenience as opposed to commitment. Rather than operating as "like-minded" countries, these two countries have based their interconnection on an instinctive need to find ways of balance vis-à-vis the United States (Cooper 1999). This habit—although loosening somewhat under the weight of multiple contacts—is still strong enough to drive (and arguably distort) the relationship. Rather than building toward a strategic partnership based on their common geographical location and membership in the North American Free Trade Agreement (NAFTA),[1] Mexico and Canada have a tactical perspective that prevails with a deep overview of sensitivity and tension contradicted only with bursts of common purpose on an episodic basis directed at their super-sized neighbour.

Signs of this convenient behaviour obviously stood out prior to the NAFTA connection, as witnessed most famously by the shared resistance of the governments of Canadian prime minster Pierre Trudeau and Mexican president José López Portillo to Ronald Reagan's proposal (as part of his initial presidential campaign in November 1979) for a North American accord. However, it came to the fore during the launch of the NAFTA project when Canada, at least at the outset, was a "reluctant" participant. Having signed its own deal with its dominant trading partner, in the form of the Canada-US Free Trade Agreement, Canada was highly skeptical about the value of entering into a set of negotiations that would extend this type of arrangement to include Mexico. Symbolically, NAFTA raised the spectre that Canada would no longer be special. Instrumentally, it raised the danger of Canada joining Mexico as a spoke in the American hub. Also recognized by participant/observers was the fact that this ambivalent attitude toward NAFTA was only overcome by the Canadian instinct for being an insider as opposed to staying on the outside (Burney 2005).

Even in the post-integration era, the image of convenience—even opportunism—is compelling. The Jean Chrétien government did its best to put the brakes on President Vicente Fox's initiative for a NAFTA-plus agenda. And, despite the photo-ops of the three North American "amigos", at the April 2001 Quebec summit, the chemistry between Fox and Chrétien cooled considerably with Canada's reluctance to bite on the "big enchilada" (Cooper 2001). Whereas Fox called for an expanded NAFTA that would eventually become a hemispheric version of the European Union with borders open to immigration as well as trade, Chrétien rejected the idea after saying it was the structure of North America, with two smaller countries on either side of the powerful United States, that made the idea unworkable (De Palma 2001; Pastor 2001).

Yet, in early March 2003, at the most compelling moment of the Iraq crisis, Chrétien and Fox met and spoke to similar scripts about a compromise solution that would distance them from the Bush administration without putting them explicitly in the "un-willing" camp of France, Germany, and Russia. At a personal level, this meeting still exhibited some elements of tension (with Mexican newspapers commenting that Chrétien called Fox "indecisive"). On a structural level, however, the meeting was highly salient in showcasing a sense of solidarity against the US push to remove Saddam Hussein by force.

Paul Martin's main policy association with Mexico prior to becoming prime minister was his role with former president Ernesto Zedillo as joint chairs of the UN Commission on the Private Sector and Development. In conformity with this design, the Canadian-Mexican connection played out most robustly in the multilateral domain. Mexico was included on the list for a seat at the table of the proposed Leaders' G-20 Summit, based on the G-20 finance ministers that Martin had campaigned for during his time in office. Although set in a very different context of North/South relations, this initiative echoed, in procedural terms at least, some of the techniques used in the 1981 Cancún meeting of selective world leaders co-hosted by Trudeau and Portillo. More cautiously, Canada and Mexico took parallel defensive positions on UN reform at least in terms of an expansion of the permanent members of the UN Security Council. Yet, if they were at odds with the claims of the so-called G-4 (Germany, Japan, India, and Brazil), neither country was deemed a spoiler in the context of this drawn-out mode of negotiation.

Reframing the Disconnect in the Bilateral Relationship

Standing back from these snapshots, it seems contingent for any close analysis of the Canada-Mexico relationship to at least attempt to unravel this puzzle of convenience over commitment and to see if these constraints can be overcome. Thinking out of the box in this regard means focusing on two interconnected tasks. The first is to recognize, far more explicitly than is commonly presented, the diplomatic dimension of what the Canadian minister of industry, David

Emerson (before he moved over from the Liberals to the same cabinet post in the new Conservative government), termed the "tyranny of small differences"— differences that continue to beset the relationship (Emerson, quoted in Cheadle 2005). The second is to attempt to lay out some suggestions about how this distance can be narrowed, if not closed completely, at a time when there is new space as well as vulnerability in the North American architecture. The new Canadian government under Prime Minister Stephen Harper is North American in its sensibilities. However, how much room there is for Mexico in this framework is still open to question. Until Harper's participation at the second meeting of the Security and Prosperity Partnership of North America in Cancún, the slate was still bare.[2] President Fox, for his part, was concerned not only with his own legacy but also with a successful handover of power to Felipe Calderón Hinojosa from the National Action Party at the expense of Andrés Manuel López Obrador of the Democratic Revolutionary Party. Both leaders also must work under difficult conditions. Instead of being able to play a strong executive off against congressional pressures, they face a situation in which President George W. Bush is in free fall in the public opinion polls and has little in the way of leverage outside of resorting to the bully pulpit. They also must recognize that there is some long-standing baggage in the bilateral Canadian-Mexican relationship that cannot be dealt with easily.

The underlying struggle for diplomatic status between Canada and Mexico lies at the heart of this disconnect between a convenient and committed relationship. Mexico has reacted vigorously in the past to perceived slights, including, for instance, the episode surrounding Bombardier's bid for the contract on Mexico City's subway system. Canada suffers from a degree of anxiety over its reputation vis-à-vis with Mexico (Walker 2001). It sees its position as having a more diversified (if not as special as many would like it to be) position with the United States than Mexico does. After all, the relationship between Canada and the United States extends into many areas deemed to be off-limits by Mexico. To list just the basic ingredients of this complex interdependence, Canada belongs both to the North American Aerospace Defence Command and the North Atlantic Treaty Organization and has engaged in some areas of niche diplomacy (with Haiti, for example), which Mexico has refused to consider (Keohane and Nye 1977).

At least in the early stages of the Fox presidency, Mexico had the aura of an ascendant actor on the international stage that threatened this position. As reflected by their reciprocal visits, this up-and-coming position was highlighted by the (early) good relationship between Presidents Fox and Bush. The image of Mexico having the United States' attention was sensitive enough for Ottawa to handle. Yet the fact that Fox could take advantage of factors not available to Canada within the United States (the re-location of political power away from the north to the southwest and the growing abundance of Hispanic voters) lent a structural grounding to this dilemma.

This is not to deny that the "rise" of Mexico has been a complex phenomenon with different sorts of spillover effects for Canada. Organizationally, the bid by the Fox government for entry into the UN Security Council (even on a non-permanent basis) was a sharp departure from the historical Mexican position—and one that could be seen as curtailing some of Canada's activist diplomatic space. Yet, as illustrated by the Iraq dilemma, it also opened up some room for ad hoc coalitional opportunities.

A Value-Based Foreign Policy and Multilateralism

A similar measure of complexity is captured in the push for a strong values-based approach in the multilateral arena. The advent of democracy at home in Mexico brought with it some immediate signs that Mexican foreign policy would shift in some manner from its long-standing reluctance to be involved beyond it borders. Still, few commentators would have predicted such an initial rush. One motivation, of course, was the desire by the Fox government when Jorge Castañeda was still foreign minister to lock in the advances of Mexican democracy. Another rationale was to gain a greater role in international affairs more generally by playing the democratic card. As Castañeda rehearsed in one speech, Mexico's need was for a hybrid form of multilateralism that would blend the possibility of "constructing a counterweight—the only possible and viable one—to its vital but asymmetrical relationship with the United States" with one in which "State sovereignty [could] be reconciled with a new body of generally-observed norms" (Castañeda 2002).

This shift allowed Canada and Mexico to co-operate on some specific issues (most notably on the campaign to eradicate anti-personnel land mines). Nonetheless, the out-in-front style of the Mexico's new approach was not always in sync with Canada's own established position. Indeed, the Fox government can be criticized for overplaying its diplomatic hand not on border issues but, rather, on the issue of democracy promotion. These differences in style came out most notably in the contrast between Canada and Mexico's approach to Cuba. The hallmark of Canada's approach has remained constructive engagement. Mexico, by way of contrast, morphed from its strong association with the Castro regime to a more assertive and openly critical approach. The first hint of this changed approach came during President Zedillo's trip to Cuba in 1999, when he publicly stated that the Cuban people had a right to elect a government of their choice and gave leeway to his foreign minister to meet with Cuban dissidents (Oppenheimer 2002). These small derisions led to a surge of activity through 2002 with a number of highly publicized disagreements.

Variations on these themes can be found in an exploration of the fuller economic relationship between Canada and Mexico. To be sure, the mutual interests pertaining to the "NAFTA-ization" of the relationship have increased.

This attitude was demonstrated most obviously during the original summit held in March 2005 at Baylor University in Waco Texas, when, among other things such as the establishment of the Security and Prosperity Partnership of North America, both countries announced a commitment to pursue a North American steel industry strategy, to develop a continental compatibility in automobile standards, and to remove requirements for "rules of origin" on some US $30 billion of goods.

This pressure to act together has come not only because of the pressures of securitization within North America—as a consequence of 11 September and the inexorable move to privilege homeland security—but also because of the prospect of accelerated and ongoing pressures from emerging actors, most notably China, which are rewriting the rules of global commerce. One of Canada's chief organizations, the Canadian Council of Chief Executives (CCCE), for example, has expressed firm support for a new form of partnership in North America as a device for competing for investment and jobs with the new giants on the international stage (Independent Task Force on the Future of North America 2005).

The North American Dilemma: Too Many Constraints and Not Enough Opportunities

As played out on both the security and competitive scale, though, these pressures accent again the constraints on strategic co-operation due to countervailing holds. The CCCE—and, in its prior manifestation, the Business Council on National Issues—has only been a recent convert to an approach that goes beyond the main game of Canada-US relations. It did not play the same robust role on the NAFTA debate as it did on the Canada-United States Free Trade Agreement. Nor did the CCCE reveal any enthusiasm for President Fox's grand vision for North America prior to 9/11.

To its credit, the CCCE has engaged in a process of catch up, most notably via its participation in the Independent Task Force on the Future of North America, in which chief executive and president Thomas D'Aquino served as one of the vice-chairman. Yet, in doing so, it found itself up against a formidable set of political and institutional constraints. These constraints may be morphing with the demise of Liberal governments in Canada. Still, the prospect of a big bang or grand bargain on a new North American landscape is far off. A fine balance is still needed between the needs and interests of government and that of business—a search for equipoise that points to incremental solutions. As Harper declared during the Cancún summit: "It's not a case of leaders of countries seeking to impose [North American integration] upon society and upon the economy. What it is a case of is the business community, in particular, increasingly inviting us to co-operate more fully and to address a lot of structural inadequacies in NAFTA" (Harper, quoted in Wells 2006).

What must be recognized, however, is that the North American architecture—and especially the Canadian-Mexican relationship—is not simply about commercial design. Prior to 9/11, a key ongoing component of the Canadian approach to the architecture had been the maintenance of the differentiated status between the two countries generally and on border issues more specifically. On a crucial aspect of border management, Canada faced the threat of losing this status under section 110 of the US 1996 *Illegal Immigration Reform and Immigration Responsibility Act.*[3] Indeed, a full repertoire of lobbying techniques was used to try to delay, deflect, and/or temper the United States' push on cross-border controls. The focus of the Canadian effort was to point out the adverse effect of this legislation on the already congested traffic at entry points between the two countries (Cooper 2000; Zussman 2001; Drache 2004).

Post-9/11 Canada attempted to stick to this bilateral orientation. Unenthusiastic about explicit or implicit modes of trilateralism in this arena, Canada preferred to deal with the United States strictly on a one-to-one basis. By design, therefore, it chose to differentiate itself, both in terms of issues and solutions, from Mexico. While this stance could be justified on technical grounds (the two-speed approach), it also underscored important symbolic/political factors, which depicted Mexico not so much as a partner but more as a complicating factor in the neighbourhood. As in other areas of Canadian foreign policy, the incremental approach was judged to be the first best option. Any notion of a North American security perimeter was rejected in favour of a series of incremental and piecemeal measures with the focus on the more efficient management of the Canada-US border (Standing Committee on Foreign Affairs and International Trade 2002).

Despite the establishment of two "smart" borders, a coincidence of concern on issues such as a common fear about the further militarization of the border does not translate into a coincidence of interest about the modalities of policy. The Mexican government's focus, quite understandably, has been on the diffuse set of issues relating to migration across the southern US border. On the one hand, it is trying to offset the image of a "broken border" promulgated by commentators such as Lou Dobbs, the anchorman of the CNN business show, and, on the other hand, it is ensuring the well-being of the migrants themselves. Canada's official interests were far more discrete in nature, including the congressional requirement under the Western Hemisphere travel initiative that Canadians would require passports or passport-like documents to cross the northern border.

The impact of new competitors on the Canada-Mexico relationship is also highly complex, especially with regard to China. In declaratory terms, it allows the two countries to push toward co-operation. Prime Minister Paul Martin notably highlighted this fundamental change in "the nature of the world's economy" at Waco, Texas, as a catalyst for making "North America as competitive as possible (Martin, quoted in Delacourt 2005)." In practice, however, the "threat" from China is far more intense for Mexico than for Canada. Mexico sees itself, with some justification, as being under a massive threat from Chinese manufacturers (with the loss of nearly 200,000 clothing, textile, and other jobs between 2001 and 2003) and has (unlike the major South American countries) resisted efforts to recognize China as a market economy. Moreover, while there has been some Chinese investment in the Mexican mining industry, the constitutional restrictions on non-state firms exploring or producing oil puts Mexico in a very different situation than Canada (McKinley 2004). Despite the nod to a sense of historical solidarity as developing countries, therefore, Canada can more effectively put into place a measure of an extended relationship.

Formulating Some Proposals for Overcoming the Sense of Difference

As in any relationship, one of the best ways to become closer is for the two countries to do things together. In good part, this action still features the choice of working together to reduce the leverage of the United States either through bilateral or plurilateral means.

Yet, while highly salient on an issue-specific basis, these types of activities by themselves reinforce the convenient, but not always committed, tone of the relationship. To break down the sense of disconnect, there is a need to build trust and confidence in each other that goes beyond balancing "the powerful one." On some sensitive diplomatic issues, this means privileging each other over other choices. One sign of progress in this area from the Mexican side came with President Fox's support for Canada on the softwood lumber issue. A similar note of commitment from the Canadian side came through its recent support for the Mexican foreign minister, Luis Ernesto Derbez, in his bid to win the position of secretary-general to the Organization of African States. Not only did Canada follow the lead of the United States, which had made Derbez its backup option, but it also made him its first choice over José Miguel Insulza, Chile's interior minister.

Hemispheric Populism and the New Diplomacy: A Study in Contrasts

Yet while this type of support is necessary for a more committed relationship, it is still not enough. As the Derbez candidacy reveals, there is also a need for more detailed appreciation about not only the opportunities but also the risks of taking such a supportive stance. The image of Derbez as the candidate from NAFTA and the soon-to-be Central American Free Trade Agreement countries has isolated him from the South American "core" countries (with the exception of Peru and Bolivia, which had their distinct historical reasons for mobilizing against any candidate from Chile, and Colombia, the United States' close ally). It also helped create a backlash against Derbez in Mexico itself.

Splits in the context of the larger canvas of the Americas could force Canada to make choices that it has long avoided—a variant on the "with us or against us" scenarios between its economic partners in North America and an extended group of countries in South America. President Fox has little to lose by his energetic bid to distance himself from the populist stances of Venezuela and Bolivia. This stance has helped differentiate Mexico's comparative openness by way of trade and investment. By implication, it has placed López Obrador in the Hugo Chávez/Evo Morales camp. And it has the added bonus of signalling to the United States and Europe that there are safe bets in the Americas as opposed to uncertain options: "not everything is gold in China, in Asia or India" (Dombey 2006).

Canada, by way of contrast, has maintained a low-key approach to the populist regimes of South America. With some considerable investment in the resource sector, Canadian state officials and business interests have kept a low public profile on sensitive issues such as the announcement by the Morales government that it would nationalize the foreign-controlled gas sector. Certainly, there was no echo of the Fox critique of "demagoguery" and "deception" (ibid.). In traditional Canadian fashion, business representatives and state officials simply said that they would keep an eye on the situation.

With this contrast in mind then, far more detailed attention needs to be paid to a regular and multifaceted pattern of diplomatic engagement directed at elevating the knowledge base of the political/social systems of the two countries (Wilson-Forsberg 2002; Goldfarb 2005). One suggestion that is particularly pertinent is for the two countries to return to the idea of some form of a Canada-Mexico commission that would bring both state and non-state actors together on a regular basis. Such a forum must go beyond the notion of a small select wise men/women committee. Not only has this more limited option been tried through the independent task force sponsored by the Council on Foreign Relations, the Consejo Mexicano de Asuntos Internacionales, and the cCCE (co-chaired by John Manley, Pedro Aspe, and William Weld), but it also inevitably tilts the balance toward discussion of formal top-down integration options (customs union, common market, economic union) as opposed to informal bottom-up mechanisms that have been "signposted" already by the Security and Prosperity Partnership (Schwanen 2001, 47).

The first moves of Harper government's appear to be leading toward a business-centric model. At the Cancún meeting of May 2006, an announcement was made that a North American Competitiveness Council would be established, with representation from the Bank of Nova Scotia, Suncor, and Power Corporation, among others. Yet there is still time to stretch this type of contact to other areas of society. The danger of a business-centric approach will be that it will tap into sensitivities about a "silent" loss of sovereignty. As it is, Maude Barlow of the Council of Canadians, a nationalist group, has complained that "Stephen Harper brought Canadian CEOs with him to Cancun [proving] that he is standing up for the corporate sector without regard for what the public really wants or needs" (Council of Canadians 2006).

Another suggestion along the same lines would be to set up a version of the advocacy Secretariat that is established at the Canadian Embassy in Washington, DC, in Mexico City. Paralleling the US version, this institutional innovation would supplement the congressional liaison function of the embassy, with special attention as well to the facilitation of visits by provincial representatives, business people, and non-governmental organizations (NGOs). The office would also ratchet up the level of public diplomacy techniques available to Canadian officials via connections with media, cultural and academic personnel, and focus groups.

The Need for a Strategic Vision: Some Concrete Suggestions

All of these efforts would reduce the impression that the Canadian-Mexican relationship has been driven simply by day events and an ad hoc reaction to specific problems—the real box in which this relationship has become entrapped. Not only could a strategic vision be refined, but a system of networks could also be tapped into. Indeed, the timing appears to be good to run with this agenda from the perspective of both business and NGOs. As noted earlier, business groups, symbolized by the CCCE, appear to be far more engaged with Mexico than they were even at the negotiation of NAFTA (as witnessed by the enthusiasm for the Security and Prosperity Partnership and their active participation at the Cancún summit). It would seem that the continuing fears around an agenda about deep integration, the fixation of NGOs with NAFTA's Chapter 11, and the "race to the bottom" have arguably eased somewhat, allowing for some momentum to build on other initiatives designed both to build "like-mindedness" and to address key problems. One illustration that would be valuable on both counts would be a common initiative on the cross-border movement of small arms (and the implications for multi-level governance). An initiative of this sort would play well in Canadian cities such as Toronto, which has seen a rise in gun-related crime. It would also signal that co-operation at the borders can be accomplished, as opposed to just one NAFTA partner vis-à-vis another.

A number of other proposals would do much to build a sense of commitment. Through a bottom-up lens, an ambitious move toward a societal project— for instance, the option of investing in President Fox's "Vision 20/20" proposal for a social fund—seems unlikely at the moment. However, specific policies could be implemented that would at least provide markers along the route. Enabling small-scale, but highly symbolic, programs such as the one concerning the approximately 11,000 seasonal Mexican agricultural workers comes to mind. So, in a different manner, does the introduction of an equivalent program to the Fulbright scholarships in order to allow selective students and academics to forge connections in Canada and Mexico.

The Cancún summit telescoped activity on both of these fronts. On the educational front, the summit included a discussion about joint research and teaching initiatives between Canada and Mexico. On the seasonal worker issue, Harper agreed that an expansion of the temporary foreign worker program could possibly fill some labour shortages in Canada, above all in the booming resource economy of Alberta. This type of program has obvious political as well as economic benefits for Mexico, allowing its workers access to better paid jobs. The barrier remains immigration policies and the Canadian cultural problem with guest workers, which moves away from the traditional system of points-based immigration and replaces it with an emphasis on language skills, education, and family ties.

Through a top-down lens, one crucial ingredient is building momentum past former Prime Minister Martin's Leaders' G-20 proposal. The beauty of this plan is that it adds Mexico to the group including Brazil, India, Russia, and China in an expanded G-7/8. Both Canada and Mexico could lend momentum, for example, to the notion that a group of additional leaders meet in St. Petersburg to help break the deadlock on the World Trade Organization's Doha Round. With this possible breakthrough, the way would be open as well for an Leaders' 20-type meeting (with leaders from the emergent powers from the South in addition to the established members of the G-8) on issues such as energy security that weigh heavily on the minds of both Canada and Mexico. Indeed, another one of the other major features of the Cancún summit was the creation of an energy security initiative through the North American working group.

Diplomatic Networking: A Vital Component

Another sign of commitment might be for both Canada and Mexico to support each other's candidates for a top-level institutional position. One sign that a valuable process of learning is taking place is in connection with the Organisation for Economic Co-operation and Development, where the successor for Donald Johnson, the current secretary-general, has come from Mexico, in the figure of Angel Gurria. The fact that Canada supported Gurria's bid is an excellent sign of the evolving maturity in the relationship between the two countries.

Again, as in any relationship, these signs of commitment must be ongoing. If Canada is to be taken seriously as a partner, it must make sure that amid all of its other diplomatic connections Mexico does not get short shrift. Mexico, likewise, must scale up its delivery on a wide number of fronts. It must not only forego any hint of backsliding on democracy, but it also needs to keep trying to build a rules-based system. However, beyond that it needs to craft a more nuanced, multifaceted approach that allows some further glimpses of commonality in how the two countries see and deal with international issues. The assistance given by the Mexican military in the wake of Hurricane Katrina (via an army convoy, marines, and a navy vessel) may be a harbinger of this sort of parallelism, in that this work replicates in some ways the focus that Canada has placed on a rapid reaction force in disaster situations. It is significant from this perspective that among the recommendations of the Cancún summit was the advancement of co-operation on avian and influenza management as well as on co-ordinated training exercises in emergency response.

For both Canada and Mexico, furthermore, the relationship needs to span material as well as institutional/procedural matters. The original Security and Prosperity Partnership of North America, which was signed by Prime Minister Martin and Presidents Bush and Fox, lent some weight to the claim that things would be done differently (Canada 2005).

On closer examination, however, the Security and Prosperity Partnership was far less a big bang than an incremental shift in design. What was novel was the level of ministerial/bureaucratic engagement that the work plan entailed. The degree of trade-offs that were made possible between issues areas was also different. Yet in terms of the detailed plan, the statement lacked any ingredient to establish new or improved institutions. Most tellingly, the overall process lacked any compelling timeframe or responsibility to deliver results (Gotlieb 2005). Although the Cancún summit has done a good deal to reduce the air of convenience, it is too soon to tell whether the relationship between Canada and Mexico has actually reached a new stage of maturity or whether we are still in a position of having two bilateral relationships in North America with Canada and Mexico caught between their own main games with the United States. Given this context, moving to a committed relationship will not be a sudden or seamless movement.

Conclusion: Fine Tuning or a Course Correction?

Only an unmitigated optimist would predict that Canada and Mexico would be able to move away from their entrenched habits in dealing with each other. Indeed, there might be a temptation to backslide if the two countries go in divergent political directions with a Conservative government in Ottawa and López Obrador in Mexico City. Only by thinking outside the box—with a very different mental map and policy trajectory—can these obstacles be confronted. Moreover, this re-formulation of ideas and polices must be done in a context where both Canada and Mexico will face increasing challenges from the global

South, both in the Americas and beyond, and where the landscape of US politics is increasingly difficult to gauge. Amid these complexities, however, there is a growing awareness in both Canada and Mexico that there could be more to North America than convenient arrangements (debates encompassing the future of a limited and stalled NAFTA). The glimmer of opportunity—moving toward authentic discussion about potential options—should be seized, and new points of reference and cohesion located.

NOTES

1 North American Free Trade Agreement between the Government of Canada, the Government of Mexico and the Government of the United States, 17 December 1992, Can. T.S. 1994 No. 2, 32 I.L.M. 289.
2 Security and Prosperity Partnership, 23 March 2005, http://www.spp.gov.
3 *Illegal Immigration Reform and Immigration Responsibility Act,* U.S. Public Law 104–208. 30 September 1997. http://www.lib.umich.edu/govdocs/text/104208.

REFERENCES

Burney, Derek. 2005. *Getting It Done.* Montreal and Kingston: McGill-Queen's University Press.

Canada. 2005. Office of the Prime Minister. "Security and Prosperity Partnership of North America Established." Ottawa, 23 March. http://pm.gc.ca.

Castañeda, Jorge. 2002. Speech given by President Vicente Fox for the diplomatic corps in Mexico, National Palace, 27 June.

Cheadle, Bruce. 2005. "Three Nations Move to End 'Tyranny of Differences': Canada, United States and Mexico Commit to Broader Economic and Security Integration." *Canadian Press,* 28 June.

Cooper, Andrew F. 1999. "Coalitions of the Willing: The Search for Like-Minded Partners in Canadian Diplomacy." In Leslie A. Pal, ed., *How Ottawa Spends 1999–2000: Shape Shifting: Canadian Governance toward the Twenty-First Century,* 221–50. Don Mills, ON: Oxford University Press.

———. 2000. "Waiting at the Perimeter: Making US Policy in Canada." In Fen Osler Hampson and Maureen Appel Molot, eds., *Canada among Nations 2000,* 27–46. Don Mills, ON: Oxford University Press.

———. 2001. "Quebec as Democracy Summit." *Washington Quarterly* 24(2): 159–71.

Council of Canadians. 2006. "Three Amigos Summit Dramatically Advances Deep Integration," 31 March, http://www.vivelecanada.ca/article.php/20060403120600842.

Delacourt, Susan. 2005. "The Ties That Bind: Three leaders Sign Complex, Itemized Deal with Bush Pushing Security, Martin Trade Issues." *Toronto Star,* 24 March.

De Palma, Anthony. 2001. *Here: A Biography of the New American Continent.* New York: Department of Public Affairs.

Dombey, Daniel. 2006. "Fox Warns Leftist Policies Will Harm Latin America." *Financial Times,* 12 May. http://www.macleans.ca/.

Drache, Daniel. 2004. *Borders Matter: Homeland Security and the Search for North America.* Halifax: Fernwood.

Goldfarb, Danielle. 2005. "The Canada-Mexico Conundrum: Finding Common Ground." C.D. Howe Institute, *Border Papers,* no. 91, July.

Gotlieb, Allan. 2005. "Baby Steps towards a Partnership." *Globe and Mail,* 13 April.

Independent Task Force on the Future of North America. 2005. *Building on a North American Community: Report of the Independent Task Force on the Future of North America.* Ottawa and Mexico City: Council on Foreign Relations in association with the Canadian Council of Chief Executives and the Consejo Mexicano de Asuntos Internacionales.

Keohane, Robert O., and Joseph S. Nye. 1977. *Power and Interdependence: World Politics in Transition.* Boston: Little, Brown.

McKinley, James C. 2004. "Hu Signs Trade Deals during Trip to Mexico: Visit Gives Chance to Defuse Tense Relationship." *New York Times,* 14 September.

Oppenheimer, Andrés. 2002. "Cuba Trip to Test Fox's Democratic Credentials, and Word." *Miami Herald,* 24 January.

Pastor, Robert A. 2001. *Toward a North American Community: Lessons from the Old World for the New.* Washington: Institute for International Economics.

Schwanen, Daniel. 2001. "Interoperability, Not Convergence." *Policy Options,* November.

Standing Committee on Foreign Affairs and International Trade. 2002. *Partners in North America: Advancing Canada's Relations with the United States and Mexico.* Ottawa: Government of Canada.

Walker, William. 2001. "Bush Woos "Most Important" Mexico." *Toronto Star,* 6 September.

Wells, Paul. 2006. "Spring Break Summit." *Maclean's,* 24 April. http://www.macleans.ca.

Wilson-Forsberg, Stacey. 2002. "Canada and Mexico: Searching for Common Ground on the North American Continent." *Focal Policy Paper,* Doc. FFP-02-3, February.

Zussman, David. 2001. "What's after NAFTA?" Speech given to an Industry Canada Conference on North American Economic Integration, 21 June, Calgary, AB.

14

The Future of Mexico-Canada Relations: Bilateral and Trilateral Solutions in North America

Duncan Wood

Introduction

The past four years have been a difficult period for the North American partnership. The stresses and tensions brought on by the new security concerns of the United States and the war on terrorism have made it nearly impossible for a common agenda to emerge that is of mutual benefit to all three partners. The enormous differences that have emerged in the worldviews of the countries of the North American Free Trade Agreement (NAFTA) and the priorities they pursue have meant that significant progress on North American integration has been unattainable.[1] This is not to say that no new agreements have been negotiated. On the contrary, there have been advances, most notably in the area of borders and business integration. Yet it would be fair to say that the prospect of a new era of integration that satisfies all three countries is as distant today as it has ever been.

The purpose of this chapter is to set forward an optimistic, yet at the same time realistic, future for North America—a future to be found in bilateral rather than trilateral approaches. Despite the solid bases of NAFTA and the considerable advances made by the Security and Prosperity Partnership,[2] the divergence in the political agendas, interests, and even public opinion in the three NAFTA countries will make trilateral co-operation difficult, whereas more progress will be possible in coming years in the three bilateral relationships. What is more, in the specific context of the Canada-Mexico relationship, there is ample room for innovation and new initiatives. This chapter explores the possibility of enhancing sub-federal co-operation between the two countries in a number of distinct areas.

The three governments face an array of challenges before they can realistically talk of a "NAFTA-plus" arrangement. First, they must await "normalization" in US relations with the world in general and with its allies in particular as well as a subsequent change in the US foreign policy agenda. Second, public opinion in both Canada and Mexico must come to terms with a changed United States and be ready to get closer. Third, significant economic disparities among the three countries and among regions within the three countries must be addressed. Finally, and most importantly, a perception of mutual gain must emerge that would create the powerful lobby groups within the three states necessary to drive the process forward. Such an alignment of the "integration stars" would appear to be highly improbable in the near future. Divergence, as much as convergence, will mark the near future.

However, at the same time as trilateralism in North America has been facing these challenges, the bilateral relationship between Canada and Mexico has been going from strength to strength. The signing of a Canada-Mexico partnership in 2005, the increasingly close co-operation between the two countries in the United Nations, and the Canadian "courting" of Mexico in its 2005 International Policy Statement are discernable signs of the closeness in bilateral affairs. The warmth and enthusiasm of the reception given to President Vicente Fox in Alberta in September 2005 was also indicative of this closer relationship and stood in marked contrast to the disillusionment and disappointment felt toward him in his own country.

Yet this newfound intimacy in the relationship is not to be taken for granted. A range of challenges must be overcome in the near future if the progress of the past couple of years is not to be lost. Elections in both countries in 2006, combined with the problems of structural reform in Mexico's economy and the ever-present domination of the region by the United States, require that the advances made by the two countries be institutionalized and a new framework for deeper and more long-lasting co-operation be created.

This chapter argues that the way to succeed is to bring together stakeholders in areas of mutual interest for the two countries. Despite the divergence on trilateral affairs, there remains a wide array of actors and issues that permit co-operation on a bilateral basis. On a large number of diverse issues, the two countries have mutual interests, although these are not necessarily obvious at the federal level. Instead, sub-federal co-operation must be fostered by empowering and encouraging actors at the provincial/state, municipal, and community levels from both countries to come together to design collaborative projects for the long term. Subsidiarity is therefore a key concept in this chapter, as is the idea of the existence of specialized communities whose interests and worldviews would be served by closer co-operation.

The Problems Facing North American Integration

After eleven years, it would be accurate to say that NAFTA has been a partial success. For although trade levels among the three countries have increased dramatically, and foreign direct investment has become a driving force for integration, a number of challenges still remain. First, integration is far from complete.

While the Canada-US and US-Mexico economic axes of the region are flourish-ing, the Canada-Mexico economic relationship remains relatively underdevel-oped. At the same time as this national breach exists, regional differences are of crucial importance in evaluating the agreement. Whereas some regions of North America have become highly integrated (Ontario, California, and Nuevo León, for example), others (such as Labrador, Arkansas, and Chiapas) remain isolated by weak infrastructure, education, or communications from the opportuni-ties offered by NAFTA. Perhaps most significant from the point of view of the legitimacy of the integration process is the fact that large sectors of society in all three countries have yet to benefit from NAFTA. The owners of the resources in demand in the region (capital, skilled labour, technology, management, and so on) have all had the opportunity to benefit from higher levels of economic co-operation. However, the disadvantaged, uneducated, unskilled, poor, and marginalized have been excluded from the "NAFTA bonanza."

At the same time, we must note that the visions of the three countries with regard to North American integration are still highly divergent. Canada's main priority in NAFTA has always been to protect and expand its privileged economic relationship with the United States. The United States, on the other hand, has come since 9/11 to see NAFTA through the lens of security and borders, intel-ligence co-operation, and the control of the flow of people. Mexico's priorities remain the advancement of the migration agenda with the United States and, simultaneously, the protection of Mexico from too much interference by its northern neighbour.

The Security and Prosperity Partnership of North America, negotiated in March 2005, highlighted these divergent interests and the relative importance of the three NAFTA partners (Council for Foreign Relations 2005). This agreement reflected the interests and vision of the United States and, to a lesser extent, of Canada while neglecting the North American agenda of President Fox. Weakened at home through disillusionment with his *gobierno del cambio* (government of change) and his inability to deal with a hostile and unco-operative Congress, Fox was unable to secure any significant mention of migration in the March meeting. The Security and Prosperity Partnership's focus on borders and facilitating the business climate represented the agenda of powerful interests in the United States, interests with which Canada was able to come to an understanding. Thus, despite the signing of a three-party agreement, Fox's sorry figure at the Waco meeting suggested a further weakening of trilateralism in the region.

Another major obstacle to significant trilateral progress lies in the dispari-ties in levels of economic development and competitiveness among the three countries. Whereas the United States and Canada are highly developed, com-petitive economies with a healthy mix of agricultural, raw material, industrial, and services production, Mexico faces enormous challenges in terms of struc-tural economic reforms. Thus far, unable to make the full transition from a *maquiladora*, resource, and cheap labour-based economy, Mexico's international

competitiveness is under threat not only from China but also from other developing regional economies such as Brazil and Chile. The failure to move
Mexico's economy forward to a new stage of development and competitiveness
has made it a much less attractive and important focus for international investors. Although Mexico still receives significant foreign direct investment, there
is a feeling in Mexico and internationally that the country is losing ground
against other potential destinations. The interest in American and Canadian
business communities to promote deeper integration with Mexico, therefore,
is somewhat limited by the perception that other countries may in fact offer a
bigger bang for the buck. We now turn to an examination of specific elements
that challenge future trilateral co-operation in North America.

Agendas

By examining the respective agendas of the three NAFTA governments with regard
to the future of the area, we can detect a significant divergence. The problems
posed by competing visions of the future for North America have been discussed elsewhere (Wood 2006). The issues presented for discussion and negotiation in the North American area suggest to us that, while Canada and the
United States have been able to come to an understanding on the issues that they
want to move forward in their bilateral and trilateral agendas, Mexico stands as
an outsider in this game. Despite the fact that Mexico signed the Security and
Prosperity Partnership and that Fox's government officials have claimed that it
reflects the issues that are important to Mexico, it was clear that President Fox
was unable to move his agenda forward at the Waco, Texas, meetings.

What then are the issues that top the Canadian agenda in North America?
First and foremost, Canada has pressured the United States to keep the border
more, rather than less, open and to guarantee continuing Canadian prosperity
and economic growth. This is an agenda that was close to the heart of the previous Liberal government and remains a priority for the Conservative minority
government of Stephen Harper. Furthermore, the Canadians have been quick to
accept (as has happened frequently throughout history) that the issue of space in
North America has changed and, instead of merely waiting for the United States
to impose new arrangements, have anticipated US concerns over security and
pre-empted the United States by proposing new security and border agreements
in the region. What has changed, albeit to a minor degree, is the commitment on
the part of the Harper government to improve relations with the United States.
The limits to such a bilateral agenda, especially in light of current Canadian
public opinion make much closer co-operation between the Canadian and US
governments unlikely (see discussion later in this chapter).

With reference to Mexico on the North American front, the issue of migration has dominated the agenda under the Fox government. Admittedly, the early
halcyon days of the administration saw an overly enthusiastic call for a single
currency, which was rapidly rejected by the Canadians, and political probing

into the idea of a social fund and transfer payments for North America. The failure of these ambitious initiatives pushed the Fox government to focus more and more on migration. The subsequent failure of the Fox agenda on migration, especially after the events of 11 September 2001, left Mexico on the receiving end of North American initiatives.[3] Unlike the governments of Jean Chrétien and Paul Martin, Fox's team has been unable to anticipate US concerns and respond with a proactive approach to policy in the area of security and borders.

As for the United States, it is easy to sum up the North American agenda in three words: security, security, security. Of course, this is an exaggeration, as issues of prosperity, although taking a backseat to security, have always been, and will likely always be, present. But for now and for the foreseeable future, the US North American agenda, as well as its domestic and international agendas, is dominated by concerns of controlling borders and threat prevention. This is what has made the Canadian approach so effective—recognizing US concerns and dealing with them in a proactive manner that best protects Canadian interests. It is not to say that the Canadian government has been able to predict the future. Rather, it has learned to react quickly to changing circumstances and to recognize US concerns, albeit in a somewhat ad hoc fashion at times.

Interests

Although we might expect the three countries' agendas for North American co-operation to provide a direct reflection of their interests, this is only partially the case. Each of the NAFTA states has a broader set of regional interests than their trilateral agendas allow, given current political constraints. What is interesting is that, by focusing on interests, more room emerges for both convergence and divergence in North America.

Canada's primary national interest continues to be guaranteeing access to the US market in order to maintain Canadian prosperity. Unable to diversify its economic relations, despite repeated attempts to do so, Canada has accepted its fate as a North American nation that is overwhelmingly dependent on the United States. Readers of this text do not need to be reminded of the intensity of this dependence. However, it is worthwhile emphasizing once again the fact that, whereas Mexico sees its dependence on the United States as a handicap and limit, Canada has come to embrace the reality and use the assumption as a basis for foreign and domestic policy making. The Canadian government has, over the course of the last century, learned to incorporate the bilateral relationship as a basic assumption and factor it into its decision making in a diverse range of issue areas. The levels of interdependence brought by integration of industry and intra-firm trade have made this an unavoidable reality. Canada, however, has more at stake in North America than merely exports to the United States, even if only at a marginal level. Concerns of regional development, stability, health, education, and the environment, while not occupying the top of the agenda, are of clear interest to Canadian policy makers. As will be shown later in this chapter, although there is no room on the trilateral agenda for these items, Canada has sought other mechanisms to satisfy its concerns.

Mexico's primary interests in North America remain less fulfilled by the regional agenda than either of the other two NAFTA states. Migration stands out, of course, with Mexico unable to contemplate its own economic and political stability without the escape valve provided by half a million Mexicans migrating to the United States every year. Yet, despite the high profile of migration, it is far from being the only issue of crucial national interest for Mexico in the North American context. With desperate need for investment in roads and railways, agricultural development, urban infrastructure, and education, the current trilateral agenda simply ignores Mexican priorities. This is easily understandable when we consider that both Canada and the United States are unwilling to contemplate a development fund for Mexico when the country has such large trade surpluses with both in the context of NAFTA and has not taken the difficult decisions necessary to help itself over the last decade and a half.

Unsurprisingly, the current trilateral agenda most closely reflects US interests, with its heavy emphasis on security. But we must recognize that US interests are much broader in the region than just security. Immigration, as exemplified by the current politicized debate in the United States, is of central importance to the American economy, and the interests of US agriculture, industry, and services depend, to varying degrees, on receiving ongoing high levels of migrant workers. This, however, is unlikely to be treated as a trilateral issue, given Canadian resistance to the theme. A third issue that does show promise for regional treatment, however, is energy. Of crucial importance to the economy, energy dependence on the part of the United States is seen by the current Bush administration to be closely linked to broader discussions on national security and foreign policy as well as on economic growth and will continue to be seen in this way by future presidents. Guaranteeing access to oil imports from Canada and Mexico will be an increasingly prevalent theme in North America in the coming years. For the time being, however, given Mexican concerns over oil sovereignty and the perceived threat posed by US oil companies to this element of the *patrimonio nacional,* any meaningful agreement on oil seems distant.

Public Opinion

In both Canada and Mexico, anti-Americanism poses the biggest challenge to far-reaching progress on trilateral co-operation. There are, however, significant differences in the kind of anti-Americanism exhibited both north and south of the United States. In Canada, anti-US feelings usually run relatively shallow, with the current situation made much worse by anti-Bush sentiments. The normal state of affairs is one of affinity, tolerance, and partnership, even though Canadians generally feel superior, in moral and social terms at least, to their American cousins (Doran 2006). The experience of 9/11 is highly demonstrative of this idea. Canada responded to that traumatic event with an outpouring of popular support for the United States, most tellingly in the public gathering on Parliament Hill and the housing of stranded American travellers in Canadian homes.

In Mexico, on the other hand, anti-Americanism is deeply engrained, promoted by a public education system that for years promulgated an image of the United States as an imperialist threat, focusing on the Mexican-American war of the mid-nineteenth century. Such anitpathy was never truer than under the old Institutional Revolutionary Party regime in Mexico, when anti-yanquismo helped to legitimate the regime and divert attention away from failings in democracy and economic equity. As Rafael Fernandez de Castro and Jorge Dominguez (2001) point out, public opinion has been an important factor in determining the speed, if not the direction, of US-Mexico cooperation. What is more, it has generally been the Mexicans who have an unfavourable perception of their northern neighbours, rather than vice versa. While it is true that things are slowly changing in the country, particularly given the fact that so many Mexican families have relatives living in the United States, anti-Bush feelings have made matters worse. The enmity that has developed among ordinary Mexicans toward the US government in recent years is reflected in anti-Fox demonstrations, where he is, perhaps surprisingly to the informed observer, portrayed as a puppet of George Bush. Bush and the United States are increasingly seen as the representatives of global capitalism and globalization, neither of which has benefited the majority within Mexican society. Such attitudes are, of course, seen more generally throughout the American continent, particularly in the southern regions. Yet the intensity of current anti-yanquismo in Mexico stands in sharp contrast to the rosy hues of the early years of Fox and Bush.

And we must not forget that recent history has not made it any easier for Americans to have friendly feelings toward their neighbours. Despite the closeness felt after the 9/11 attacks between Canada and the United States, the UN debate leading up to the Iraq invasion severely strained bilateral relations and created an unfriendly feeling on the part of Americans toward their northern cousins. A common perception that Canadians are too liberal, too passive, and, ultimately, free riding on American security has come to pervade the American public. In the case of Mexico, Americans were extremely unhappy about the country's reaction, or rather non-reaction, to 9/11, and the intensifying migration debate has served to deepen anti-immigrant and, in turn, anti-Mexican feelings in key states. Anti-Mexicanism, although not a generalized social phenomenon in the United States, is exhibited by such movements as the Minutemen and the recent anti-immigration marches in California. As mentioned earlier, Americans have tended to have a favourable perception of Mexico and Mexicans, although periodic outbursts of anti-Mexican xenophobia seem to be a recurring problem in the bilateral relationship (ibid.).

A Bilateral Alternative: Canada-Mexico

There is ample room for a bilateral agenda for co-operation to emerge between the extreme north and south of NAFTA, independent of the giant that divides them. Canada and Mexico have made tremendous progress in recent years, in part because of the problematical nature of relations with the United States. The idea of the two countries working together more closely is not a new one. In the late 1990s, Isabel Studer (1997) argued that a strategic partnership was possible between the two countries. Later, Duncan Wood and George MacLean (1999) wrote of the possibilities of a new partnership between Canada and Mexico, focusing on the potential for co-operation in multilateral forums and in the region.

Before the 1990s, it was far from clear that the two countries were, as H.P. Klepak (1996) has put it, "natural allies," and, in recent times, the relationship has had its difficulties, such as in the period immediately following 9/11 when Canada preferred to negotiate bilaterally with the United States over new border arrangements rather than risk "Mexicanizing" the US-Canada border (Hristoulas 2003). Other tensions arose between Mexico and Canada in early post-9/11 discussions over the future of NAFTA, with the Fox government pushing for a NAFTA-plus solution which would involve a migration accord, a social fund, and heavy investment in infrastructure—the "whole enchilada." The standard Canadian response to appeals from the Fox government for support was simply "what's in it for us?" At the time, the Canadian government, as well as the business community, seemed to define North America in strictly Canada-US terms, including Mexico only "when possible" (Dobson 2002).

These tensions, however, began to dissipate as problems grew between the two countries on the one hand and with the United States on the other. The US war on terror and, in particular, the invasion of Iraq pushed Canada and Mexico toward a rapprochement. As their foreign policy agendas began to coincide, especially in the United Nations, a greater mutual understanding also began to emerge. The prevailing factor of pragmatism, which had been long visible in the Canadian approach to its relations with Mexico (Wood and Hristoulas 2002) and, more broadly, with Latin America, surfaced (Hristoulas 2006).

The creation of the Canada-Mexico Partnership (CMP) in October 2004 marked a significant step forward in bilateral affairs and was intended to develop the strategic relationship between the two countries.[4] It brought together leading figures from business and government in both countries to discuss bilateral co-operation in a broad range of areas. Initially, three working groups were created in the areas of urban development and housing (looking at both sustainable cities and housing), human capital, and competitiveness (Canada 2005).

Shortly afterwards, the Canadian government issued its 2005 International Policy Statement, which pleased its Mexican counterpart enormously. First, the statement emphasized the importance of North America as a priority for Canada, with the region defined in trilateral terms. Unlike in earlier formulations of North America, Ottawa had apparently now come to see Mexico as a full partner in the region for some policy initiatives. Second, the International Policy Statement was replete with references to Mexico as an important country for Canada not only in the region but also internationally as a partner in international institutions.

In September 2005 in another bilateral meeting between President Fox and Prime Minister Martin, the two mandataries celebrated the high level of cooperation between the two countries, giving particular emphasis to the temporary workers agreement that has seen around 13,000 Mexican agricultural workers come north to Canada for seasonal employment. Although it is only a small program, discussions have begun to consider expanding the program to include workers from other sectors.

Given this impressive progress in the past couple of years, it would be tempting for advocates of the bilateral relationship to sit back and rest on their laurels. However, it is clear that the current state of affairs is an unstable one, vulnerable to changes in the national governments of the two countries concerned and to changes in the United States. It must be remembered that 2006 produced federal elections in both countries. The victory of the Conservative Party in Canada could easily mean a swing back toward the United States to the detriment of Mexico, and the victory of Felipe Calderón Hinojosa in Mexico could mean a resurgent interest in North America in general. Unlike the US-Canada and US-Mexico axes of North America, the Canada-Mexico economic relationship lacks the same intense interdependence and is far from expendable in considerations of the national interest. Whereas the first priority of Canadian foreign policy may be to "keep the US border open" and to maintain the flow of goods south, it is difficult to imagine Canadians attaching the same importance to the flow of tourists to Cancún or Acapulco! Mexico is therefore not yet an "assumption" in Canadian politics in the same way that the United States is for both Canadians and Mexicans.

Nor have Mexico and Canada reached a level of cultural and societal understanding that facilitates stable long-term co-operation. Whereas Canada and the United States have reached an, at times, uneasy cultural accommodation over the last two centuries, and the United States and Mexico are experiencing a new level of cultural and social integration through the presence of tens of millions of Mexican and Latino migrants in the United States, Canada and Mexico remain distant neighbours. One idea that has been floated to bridge this cultural divide is to encourage more Mexican migration to Canada. This idea seems rather like putting the cart before the horse, however. Surely we need to decide if and why Mexicans are needed in Canada for economic purposes rather than just importing Mexican populations to encourage greater understanding! Nonetheless, the trend is for more and more Mexicans to look toward the Canadian option. Provinces such as Alberta that are experiencing prolonged and high rates of economic growth are consequently facing labour shortages—Mexicans are beginning to fulfil some of that shortfall, if only on a temporary basis.

Plotting a Sub-Federal Future for Bilateral Relations

Given these uncertainties and the current healthy nature of the relationship, the time is right to take steps to institutionalize the progress of the past couple of years and to lay the foundations for continued co-operation in the future. The best way to do this is not through the traditional means of federal government-federal government co-operation but, rather, through sub-federal and societal networks that are not subject to the same shifts in political winds that can jeopardize close co-operation.

Who will lead the process forward in such a way? Interestingly enough, from the Canadian perspective, the key political actor will probably not be the federal government. Instead, the process should be driven from the bottom up. In particular, provincial governments will explore the opportunities in the region to see what they can best take advantage of in a wide range of areas, from business to culture to education to sports. The growing interaction between provincial premiers and the governors of states in Mexico is testament to the will of this level of government to engage in non-traditional forms of diplomacy. Municipalities may also play a growing role, although this approach is not as well advanced at the time of writing.

Of course, this is not a novel approach to international co-operation. There is a long tradition in international relations of looking for sub-national drivers of bilateral and multilateral co-operation. In the 1950s and 60s, the neo-functionalist approach suggested that interested communities within society would push governments toward the creation of supranational arrangements. Robert Putnam's two-level games approach put forward the idea not only that domestic politics mattered in international co-operation and vice versa but also, more appropriately in the present study, that transnational alliances of domestic-level actors could be formed to secure international agreements.

What is more, the idea of sub-national governments moving forward with piecemeal co-operation suggests a notion reminiscent of the European model of integration. Subsidiarity, the idea that policy and government functions should be transferred to the lowest level of government capable of effectively carrying them out, has yet to be explored in North America but holds enormous potential for opening up relations between different areas within the region. The economic concept of growth nodes and the potential for synergy between the factors of raw materials, labour, and technology, which are so abundant throughout the region but widely dispersed, are areas that provincial and state levels of government are likely best able to explore. Complementarity in education, health care, and even employment needs are other areas that would benefit from a less macro, and more area-specific, approach. This is not to suggest that subsidiarity in North America acquire the *de jure* status it holds in the European Union but, rather, that a de facto approach to the concept holds great potential.

However, public authorities at the sub-federal level are not the only actors considered in this case. In addition, key communities holding specialized knowledge and sharing similar worldviews present a useful counterpart in, and also provide support to, the integration process. The epistemic community approach, which is focused on learning the issues of international politics with knowledge-based networks of professionals, achieved a respectable following in the early 1990s and may hold some wisdom for the future of bilateral relations. It is possible to identify groups in the two countries that approximate the established definition of an epistemic community—that is, a network of individuals with

- shared normative and principled beliefs,
- shared causal beliefs,
- shared notions of validity, and
- a common policy enterprise (Haas 1992).

For many years, North American integration has depended on the three national business communities for its impetus. Future co-operative efforts between Canada and Mexico, however, will benefit enormously from the participation and leadership of interested groups or stakeholders. In the areas outlined later in this chapter, there exist communities in both countries, as well as an interest on the part of their members, to move forward with bilateral co-operation.

The Example of the Canada-Mexico Partnership

A precedent exists for the kind of bilateral co-operation that brings in key stakeholders. The Canada-Mexico Partnership has produced a workable bilateral agenda marked by issues that are not necessarily of interest (or workable) at the trilateral level. Clear progress is being made in the Canada-Mexico Partnership, and, while the progress may not be earthshaking, it is nonetheless an example of what can be achieved outside of the trilateral environment.

Further Issues for Exploration at the Sub-Federal Level

Education

The Canada-Mexico Partnership has already identified human capital as a key component in the drive for international competitiveness and as an area in which Canada and Mexico can work together. The collaboration of the Association of University and Colleges of Canada and the Asociación Nacional de Instituciones de Eseñanza en Relaciones Internacionales, along with government agencies, has shown that space exists for the operation of a transnational epistemic community. Yet the steps taken thus far are but a small portion of what could be achieved, given the right circumstances.

Given the provincial domain over education, it would make sense for Canadian provinces to join these parties and directly engage the Mexican authorities to identify key areas of collaboration. Reducing the differences in the levels of public education from pre-primary through to university would clearly be in the interest of Mexico, but labour markets in Canada (and North America in general) would benefit from improved standards and the possibility of harmonized vocational standards.

A harmonization of educational standards may seem like an awfully ambitious goal given the enormous disparities between the two countries. Yet initial steps could be taken that focus on the university level. Canadian expertise in a state-run university system can be matched with the experience of Mexican experiments in private tertiary education—an experiment that has had mixed results to date, with certain examples of excellence. The highly entrepreneurial nature of Mexican university education, however, offers much to its Canadian counterpart, as do its links to Latin America and the challenging experience of working in a developing country.

Health and Social Security

Although Canadians are by now used to the idea of an imminent crisis in their systems of public health care and social security, they recognize that they are among the best-protected citizens in the world in this regard. Mexicans, on the other hand, have come to accept that the state cannot provide the necessary protection at a satisfactory level and have embraced a mixed system. Although the public health care system in Mexico cannot satisfy the needs of its clients and desperately needs new investment, there is no shortage of well-trained professionals. These professionals need money and the opportunity to practice.

One simple and seemingly straightforward mode of co-operation would involve the creation of training programs in Canada for Mexican health care providers (both doctors and nurses) with the necessary knowledge to allow them to practice in the Canadian context. Northern populations in Canada already suffer from a lack of health care providers. If we can bring in seasonal workers for agriculture, why not consider expanding the program in the area of health sciences? Given the fact that health comes under their mandate, the provinces would be key actors in this regard as well as the universities, doctors, and professional associations in both countries. The exchange of medical knowledge and expertise would presumably benefit both scientific communities as well as health care recipients.

A more radical idea would be a co-operative agreement to build health care facilities in Mexico (for example, in the vicinity of large "ex-pat" communities, such as Lake Chapala), where Canadians could go to receive medical attention.

If snowbirds already receive medical attention in Florida, why not promote the idea of lower-cost alternatives in Mexico? Private insurance companies are already experimenting with the idea of encouraging American and British clients to seek health care in India, at a fraction of the cost. Senior citizen care could easily be included in such an agreement, with the creation of long-term care facilities. Such healthcare could easily be covered by the state at a cost that is much lower than what it would cost for similar services in Canada. Alternatively, public-private collaboration between the public health service in Canada and private insurance companies could provide another option.

Infrastructure and Transportation

Mexico is in desperate need of heavy investment in its economic and transportation infrastructure. One outcome of the 2006 presidential election in Mexico is that there will likely be an increase in infrastructure spending. It would surely be in the interest of Canadian companies such as Bombardier to encourage a healthy dialogue with the Mexican government at such a time. However, an earlier, pre-election approach by groups of experts in infrastructure planning from Canada would ease the way for such a business opportunity to arise.

Canadian provinces and municipalities would be important partners if a dialogue on urban infrastructure was to emerge, and the discussions would fit in neatly with the sustainable cities program. The success of urban transportation systems in cities such as Toronto, Ottawa, and Montreal provide examples that Mexican cities may wish to imitate or at least to learn valuable lessons from. Investment in long distance transportation systems has been a crucial element of the Canadian national story, from railways to the trans-Canada highway. The engineering, planning, and financing expertise that is held by the Canadian government, as well as by private firms, would be of enormous benefit to Mexican planners.

Energy

Mexico is currently facing an imminent energy crisis. High prices for electricity and gas are compromising the competitiveness of Mexican business. Consumers are facing blackouts and an uncertain future in energy supply, and, most shockingly for the Mexican psyche, at current levels of exploitation and investment in exploration, Mexico will become a net oil importer at some point in the next ten years. What is more, there is a lack of well-trained engineers and geologists in the country (particularly in the area of oil exploration), which further compromises the possibility of a homegrown solution to the problem. Unfortunately, the debate over energy reform in Mexico remains dominated by oil and mired in outdated conceptions of sovereignty and the protection of the national treasure.

Already a number of Canadian firms are working with the Mexican government to deal with some of the myriad of problems facing the electricity and natural gas sectors. This co-operation is by necessity limited due to the strict public control over electricity generation. In the oil and gas sector, Petróleos Mexicanos's (PEMEX) experimentation with multiple service contracts has allowed limited collaboration with Canadian firms, but a full-scale entry into the Mexican energy sector is a long way off. Precision Drilling, for example, an Alberta-based firm, has been active in Mexico for several years now, often working in co-operation with American firms in multiple service contracts with PEMEX (Case 2003).

Canadian provinces (in particular, Alberta, Ontario, and Quebec) would be important partners in any discussion on energy reforms in Mexico. Alberta's hugely successful natural gas exploitation holds important lessons for Mexico, and Ontario and Quebec's experience with hydroelectric generation could help certain areas of Mexico to come up with alternative energy sources. While Canada does not hold any significant expertise in offshore deepwater oil drilling (where significant new oil reserves may be found in the Gulf of Mexico), the key benefit from the creation of an energy dialogue between the two countries would be the transfer of knowledge and expertise to help Mexico fully exploit its energy potential. In this sense, provinces, universities (offering training facilities), and industry associations would be important collaborators. In fact, the University of Alberta has already begun working with Mexican institutions on joint programs to train petroleum engineers.

Indigenous Affairs

While Canada has had a far from perfect record in its dealings with its indigenous populations (or First Nations), it would be fair to say that the current standard of living of the majority of Canadian First Nations citizens is far better than that of their Mexican counterparts. Of course, the histories of the two countries in their dealings with indigenous populations could hardly be more different. In Canada, it is a history of land treaties, separation, confrontation, and eventual cohabitation with the prospect of political and economic development, while, in Mexico, it is a culture of *mestizaje*, marginalization, and, ultimately, rebellion in 1994.

Significant sections of Canada's First Nations today have achieved greater political and economic autonomy and have begun to look outside of Canada for contact with other indigenous peoples. Recent years have seen a flurry of activity in this regard, with high-ranking indigenous individuals visiting Mexico. Cultural exchanges, discussions over economic co-operation, and, importantly, the visit of Paul Okalik, premier of Nunavut, in November 2004, have heralded this new era of "indigenous diplomacy."

Indigenous affairs will be of great importance to the next president of Mexico as levels of protest among the *pueblos indigenas* of southern Mexico are again rising. With the chaotic southern border already facing the challenge of rising levels of violence and disorder due to the *maras* (or gangs originating in Central

America), a constructive dialogue that leads to significant improvements in the standard of living of the indigenous population is desperately needed. It is in this respect that the Canadian federal and provincial governments, but, more importantly, the First Nations, may be able to play an "honest broker" role. The indigenous communities in both Canada and Mexico hold many of the qualities normally attributed to epistemic communities, particularly in the areas of shared normative and principled beliefs, shared causal beliefs, and shared notions of validity.

What do Canadian indigenous groups stand to gain from this co-operation? Key achievements would be a sense of prestige, international recognition, and, perhaps most importantly, a heightened sense of community and brotherhood in the hemisphere. The Mexican government stands to benefit as a process of dialogue replaces confrontation, as well as the potential for economic transfers from wealthier Canadian First Nations to marginalized populations in the southern states.

Federal Government Co-operation

This chapter has focused its attention on sub-federal co-operation. However, it would be foolish and short-sighted to ignore the numerous areas of interest and potential co-operation to both federal governments. Of course, the two federal governments need to lay the foundations and prepare a framework within which such sub-federal co-operation can take place. But we must also consider the interest that exists in federal collaboration in areas such as foreign policy, in particular, international institutions, fiscal reforms, and regional development (the abortive experience of the Plan Puebla-Panama contains many valuable lessons for both governments). A final area that may hold potential is that of peacekeeping and peace building. Although constitutional constraints limit the potential at the present time for military collaboration, the federal electoral institute has already been active internationally in Afghanistan and Iraq in promoting free and fair elections. What is more, the space exists for the transfer of peacekeeping expertise from the Pearson Centre, for example, to those agencies of the Mexican military (such as the navy) that are ready to listen.

Conclusion

Significant potential exists for future co-operation and collaboration between Canada and Mexico at the sub-federal level if an adequate framework can be created to promote a vibrant dialogue that includes relevant communities from both countries. Although such far-reaching collaboration may seem improbable at the time of writing, the example of the Canada-Mexico Partnership holds the potential for broader and deeper co-operation that can be continued by political authorities in the future at multiple levels.

NOTES

1 North American Free Trade Agreement between the Government of Canada, the Government of Mexico and the Government of the United States, 17 December 1992, Can. T.S. 1994 No. 2, 32 I.L.M. 289.
2 Security and Prosperity Partnership, 23 March 2005, http://www.spp.gov.
3 At the time of writing, the probability of significant immigration reform in the US Congress was, at best, uncertain. The passage of two bills through the legislature was imminent, but their outcome unknown.
4 Canada-Mexico Partnership, 24 October 2004, http://www.infoexport.gc.ca/science/mexico_home-en.htm.

REFERENCES

Canada. 2005. Office of the Prime Minister. "Canada-Mexico Partnership: Backgrounder," http://www.pm.gc.ca/eng/news.asp?id=598.

Case, Brendan. 2003. "Pemex to Enlist Oil Giants to Develop Gas Reserves in Northern Mexico." *Alexander's Oil and Gas Connections* 8(20). http://www.gasandoil.com/goc/company/cnl34246.htm.

Council for Foreign Relations. 2005. *Building a North American Community.* Independent Task Force Report No. 53. New York: Council on Foreign Relations Press.

Dobson, Wendy K. 2002. "Shaping the Future of the North American Economic Space: A Framework for Action." C.D. Howe Institute, *Border Papers*, no. 162, April.

Doran, Charles. 2006 "Canada-US Relations: Personality, Patterns and Domestic Politics." In Patrick James, Nelson Michaud, and Marc O'Reilly, eds., *Handbook of Canadian Foreign Policy*, 389–408. Lanham: Lexington Books.

Fernández de Castro, Rafael, and Jorge I. Domínguez. 2001. *Socios o Adversarios? México-Estados Unidos Hoy.* Mexico City: Océano.

Haas, Peter M. 1992. "Introduction: Epistemic Communities and International Policy Coordination." *International Organization* 45(1): 1–35.

Hristoulas, Athanasios. 2003. "Trading Places: Canada, Mexico and Continental Security." In Peter Andreas and Thomas Biersteker, eds., *The Rebordering of North America.* New York: Routledge.

———. 2006. "Canada in Latin America: A Foreign Policy of Ambivalence, Pragmatism, or Inconsistency?" In Patrick James, Nelson Michaud, and Marc O'Reilly, eds., *Handbook of Canadian Foreign Policy*, 317–36. Lanham: Lexington Books.

Klepak, H.P., ed. 1996. *Natural Allies? Canadian and Mexican Perspectives on International Security.* Ottawa: Carleton University Press.

Studer, Isabel. 1997. "Fundamentos y condicionantes de una sociedad estrategica: Mexico-Canada." *Revista Mexicana de Politica Exterior* 51: 45–83.

Wood, Duncan. 2006. "Sharing the Wealth? Economic Distribution and Competing Visions of the Future of NAFTA." In Jordi Diez, ed., *Canadian and Mexican Security in the New North America: Challenges and Prospects*, 11–24. Kingston and Montreal: McGill-Queen's University Press.

————, and Athanasios Hristoulas. 2002. "Idealismo Pragmático en la Política Exterior Canadiense: América Latina y la seguridad humana." *Comercio Exterior* 52(5): 426–30.

————, and George MacLean. 1999. "A New Partnership for the Millennium? The Evolution of Canadian-Mexican Relations." *Canadian Foreign Policy* 7(2): 35–55.

Civil Society and the Bifurcated State: Mexico in the Latin American Mirror

Carlos H. Waisman

This chapter conceptualizes the relationship between civil society and the state in Latin America. Mexico embodies the ideal type of the patterns discussed later in this chapter, and this focus will help us understand the dynamics of the relationship between state and society in Mexico and the quality of the country's democracy. Briefly stated, there is a long line of argument in social theory, according to which a strong civil society is a necessary condition for a high-quality democracy. This position is especially associated with the work of Alexis de Tocqueville, whose work has experienced an unusual revival, as scholars and social actors have tried to explain the processes of democratization in the past two decades as well as the variable outcomes of these processes (Tocqueville 1969).

The activation of civil society groups in different parts of society and different areas of the country, their organization and mobilization, have been a feature of the process of political transition in Mexico since the final years of the Institutional Revolutionary Party regime up to the present. The evaluation of the effects of these new social forces on Mexican democracy requires an understanding of the nature of civil society, of the different kinds of democracy that exist in Latin America, and of the mechanisms that link civil society and political institutions.

Civil society is a diffuse concept in the social sciences, and the fact that it has entered political discourse has further limited its applicability in academic research. For this reason, a theoretical excursus will be necessary. The first part of this chapter proposes a conceptualization of civil society based on Tocqueville's (1969, vol. 1, parts 1 and 2) analysis and a contemporary operationalization by Ernest Gellner (1994). The focus will be on the complicated issue of what constitutes a strong civil society. In the second part of the chapter, once civil society is defined with some precision, we find that the concept helps us understand central aspects of the relationship between state and society in contemporary Latin America in general and in Mexico in particular. The conclusion suggests that the feature of social dualization, which is present in most countries of the region and intensified in the recent period by economic liberalization, has produced what I call regime bifurcation.

Conceptualizing Civil Society

Civil Society and Democracy

The spectre of civil society is haunting the enemies of democracy and the market economy. Yet they should feel relieved. This spectre's insubstantiality has rendered it quite harmless. Since the meaning of the term "civil society" is so fluid, the propositions derived from it, loosely inspired in superficial readings of Tocqueville, are hard to test empirically. Civil society is supposed to be the magic bullet against the old and new enemies of democracy (communism and authoritarianism in the past, jihadism in the present) and market society, the midwife of democracy. However, these are little more than rhetorical images, due to the extreme fuzziness of the concept.

In the world of practical politics, the opponents of communism in central Europe in the 1980s, initially a small segment of the intelligentsia, seized on this term as a label. Since then, opponents of authoritarian and even populist regimes (for example, the government of Hugo Chávez in Venezuela) have done the same, whatever their level of civility. Governments and international organizations, both inter-governmental and non-governmental organizations (NGOs), have also appropriated "civil society" and used it vaguely to refer to non-governmental groups or institutions. Thus, a collection of speeches by an American secretary of state, dealing with variegated subjects such as freedom of the press, human rights, the recovery of Holocaust-era assets, democracy, refugees, and freedom of religion bears the title *Strengthening Civil Society and the Rule of Law* (Bureau of Public Affairs 2000).

The Inter-American Development Bank (IADB) points at more specific entities and defines civil society as the "set of citizens' activities, either individual or associative, in the economic, social and political fields" (Inter-American Development Bank, n.d., 7). This definition includes both private and public activities as well as, within the latter, both informal and associational ones. This document classifies "civil society organizations" (CSO) as follows: civic participation and social interest promotion CSOs, CSOs that render social services, CSOs that promote enterprises "established under a social criterion of integration and solidarity," and CSOs engaged in developmental philanthropy (Inter-American Development Bank, n.d., 18).

The International Monetary Fund, in a discussion paper about its relations with civil society, applies the term to international, development-oriented organizations based in the North and community and advocacy groups representing or favouring the poor and the underprivileged in the South (for example, Oxfam, Friends of the Earth, Forum of African Voluntary Development Organizations, and so on) (Dawson and Bhatt 2001, 6). An Oxfam publication on civil society defines its subject by arguing that civil society groups coalesce not on the basis of primordial attachments, such as ethnicity, language, or religion, but, rather, on "small issues" that cut across boundaries and bring people together in new coalitions, such as credit schemes or health clubs (Oxfam 2000, 128). The Johns Hopkins comparative non-profit sector project is a good example of this approach. It claims that civil society is a "major social force ... throughout the world ... that is comprised of] thousands of private community groups, health clinics, schools, day care centers, environmental organizations, social clubs, development organizations, cultural institutions, professional associations, consumer groups, and similar entities" (Salamon et al. 1999, xviii).

The term is used with greater specificity in academic discourse, generally meaning the realm of society that lies outside the state, but it still lacks conceptual rigor, and its operationalization is usually not very definite. Adam Seligman (1992, 3 and 5) defines civil society as all that lies within the public sphere and outside the state. Victor Perez Diaz (1993, 3 and 57) includes markets, voluntary associations, and the public sphere, as long as they are outside the control of the state. Jean Cohen and Andrew Arato (1992, ix) subsume the private realm within civil society. They define the term as "a sphere of social interaction between economy and state, composed above all of the intimate sphere (especially the family), the sphere of associations (especially voluntary associations), social movements, and forms of public communication."

Robert D. Putnam (1993, 90 and 86–91) focuses on civil and political associations. He argues that a civic community, the basis of democracy, is characterized by the values of participation, political equality, solidarity, trust, and tolerance, which are embodied, following Tocqueville, in civic and political organizations. As he explains, "a dense network of secondary associations both embodies and contributes to effective social collaboration." Finally, Larry Diamond (1999, 221) gives the term a definition closer to its Tocquevillean meaning: "The realm of social life that is open, voluntary, self-generating, at least partially self-supporting, autonomous from the state, and bound by a legal order or set of shared rules," excluding individual and family life, economic society (business firms), and political society (parties).

Beyond definitional differences (Seligman and Diamond focus on the public sphere and autonomy from the state, Perez Diaz, Cohen, and Arato include markets or family life, and Putnam does not distinguish between civil and political associations), it is imperative to specify systematically what constitutes a strong civil society or what makes a society civil. This is essential for the testing of propositions linking civil society with democracy. The reason is clear. The proposition that the mere presence of a civil society, or even of a vibrant one, is a necessary or even sufficient cause of the generation or the maintenance of democracy makes little sense. Highly mobilized and organized societies could be very highly polarized and, thus, inhospitable to democratic institutions. Weimar Germany, the Spanish II Republic, or Argentina and Chile in the 1970s are cases in point. Larry Diamond (1999, 401–29) and Michael W. Foley and Bob Edwards (1996, 38–52) have argued that a flourishing civil society could mobilize citizens to either strengthen or undermine democracy. Sheri Berman (1997, 401–29) has documented the nefarious role of Weimar Germany's vigorous civil society.

What these arguments miss is that the independent variable, in the Tocquevillean and Gellnerian tradition is not just a civil society but also a strong one, and "strong" does not just mean that major and highly mobilized social organizations exist. Moreover, the proposition would be that a strong civil society is a necessary but not sufficient condition of democracy. How could a major institutional complex have a single cause that is valid everywhere? Affirming the civil society hypothesis does not preclude the causal efficacy of the economic, political, and cultural determinants discussed since classical times, even though the hypothesis implies that these other determinants, from Seymour Martin Lipset's (1981, 27–30) level of economic development to Putnam's (1993) civic political culture, are mediated by civil society.

The Tocquevillean-Gellnerian Position

As is well known, Tocqueville argued that the central political process of the contemporary world is the spread of equality of condition, or the democratization of society, by which he basically meant the abolition of ascriptive privilege. When arguing that the process of democratization is irresistible and necessary, he referred to this sense of the term. He did not expect a democratic polity to be the necessary or even likely correlate of democratic society. In fact, his central point was that a democratic society would generate a strong tendency toward despotism. For Tocqueville, the state as an organization is inherently driven toward centralization. Unless societal forces check this tendency, a despotic regime would be the natural outcome.

He contended that equality of condition had two consequences: the disappearance of powers that had, in aristocratic societies, mediated between the state and the citizenry and the growth of political apathy (Tocqueville 1955). His argument in this regard represents an early use of an explanation based on mechanisms. Equalization of condition would lead to apathy because of the operation of two micro-mechanisms, which facilitate the centralization of power.

First, modern society produced growing individualism and, second, people are more interested in equality than in liberty (Tocqueville 1969, 507–9). Therefore, citizens are prone to surrender to the state.

The task of preserving political democracy, then, consists in creating countervailing forces not controlled by the state, which would involve citizens in the public sphere and block the centralization of power. Tocqueville was interested in studying the American polity because, from the standpoint of his theory, it appeared as a deviant case, a democratic society whose polity had remained democratic. As is well known, he concluded that this was due to a combination of peculiar factors: mores, institutions, and physical circumstances in descending order of causal efficacy (ibid., 305). However, in the end, his general argument (that is, what is generalizable from the American case) turned out to be more institutional than cultural. He focused on variables such as the existence of a strong web of independent voluntary associations, the separation of church and state, the existence of administrative decentralization and strong local government, the jury system, an independent press, and so on.

His well-known conclusion was, of course, "Tocqueville's law": "Among laws controlling human societies, there is one more precise and clearer ... than all others. If men are to remain civilized or become civilized, the art of association must develop and improve among them at the same speed as equality of condition spreads" (ibid., 517). In other words, the key for establishing and maintaining a healthy democracy is not the prevalence of virtue or civic values among rulers and citizens but, rather, the erection of societal barriers to state expansion and rulers' despotic inclinations. The centrality of this conclusion for the design of contemporary democracies is obvious.

Gellner's (1994) analysis represents the most encompassing and systematic application of the Tocquevillean concept to contemporary societies. As John Hall (1995, 15) has pointed out, his focus was on understanding civil society as the self-organization of strong and autonomous voluntary groups that balance the state. Civil society is autonomous in the sense that its constituent units are self-governed, but it is still linked to the state and it operates within its institutional channels. Gellner (1994, 5) defined civil society as "that set of diverse non-governmental institutions which is strong enough to counterbalance the state and, while not preventing the state from fulfilling its role of keeper of the peace and arbitrator between major interests, can nevertheless prevent it from dominating and atomizing the rest of society."

As Tocqueville before him, Gellner has argued that a strong civil society is inherently connected with democracy, to the extent that the two are different labels for the same type of society (and part of a broader institutional package involving the decentralization of economics and culture). "Without these institutional pre-conditions," he writes "'democracy' has little clear meaning or feasibility" (ibid., 189). However, separating analytically the system of voluntary associations from political and governmental institutions allows us to return to Tocqueville's original question and look into the relationship between civil society and democracy. If we make the distinction, Gellner's response in this regard would be consistent with Tocqueville's: a strong civil society is a necessary foundation for democracy.

Operationalizing a Strong Civil Society

It is now important to operationalize the term, in the sense that is most consistent with Tocqueville and Gellner's arguments, for the purpose of examining the relationship between the characteristics of civil society and the existence and quality of democracy. Civil society is a slice of society, whose core is the web of voluntary associations that articulate interests and values, and their system of interaction, as long as these units are not under the control of the state. It may contain *Gemeinschaften,* and eventually civil society as a whole may generate a strong *Gemeinschaft,* but it consists of (relatively independent) *Gesselschaften.* This slice of society, for Tocqueville, is different from what he called political society and, thus, from the party system. Of course, this conception of civil society also excludes economic society as well as the family and other institutions in the private sphere.

This definition has an important implication. In the tradition inherited from classical theory, and pace international agencies and NGOs, civil society includes associations representing both the underprivileged and the privileged, the excluded and the included (and also the excluders), the poor and the rich—in sum, the "good" and some of the "bad" people as well.

The next step is to address the operationalization of civil society's strength. For this purpose, it is useful to consider that three analytically distinguishable dimensions—density, autonomy, and self-regulation—constitute civil society. Density refers to the extent to which all of the major interest and value communities existing in a society are organized and mobilized. Elites usually are, so the issue is the extent to which non-elite social forces are also organized and mobilized. Autonomy implies self-rule rather than absolute independence from the state. Of course, there is no reason to assume that civil society organizations will always have an anti-governmental orientation or will refuse to participate in governmental activities. Self-regulation means that the units of the associational web, in representing the interests and values of their constituencies, function within the institutional channels of the democratic state. They may form coalitions and engage in conflict, but they act within the boundaries of the constitution and the laws.

These dimensions are relative, of course. In the most democratic of societies, some significant interest or value groups are not organized, associational autonomy is formally constrained by the laws and formally and informally limited by the government, and self-regulation is always bound by the legal, administrative, and political framework of the society. Based on the dichotomization of these dimensions, we can formulate four ideal types of society:

1. Density is low. In this kind of situation, few or no autonomous groups exist because of either non-mobilization or exclusion/repression. The latter is the simplest mechanism available to the state for reducing or blocking the autonomy of society. Russia in the Tsarist period is an example.
2. Autonomy is low. A situation in which there is a dense web of associations representing interests and values, but the web is heteronymous. State corporatism is a second, and more sophisticated, mechanism for the control of society by the state. If density is high, this is the pattern of relationship between the state and associations characteristic of totalitarian and some populist regimes. The Soviet Union is an extreme case, Mexico under the Institutional Revolutionary Party is a more partial one.
3. Self-regulation is low. Whenever this happens in societies in which the web is dense and its constituent units are highly autonomous, but there are intense cleavages, high polarization ensues. Weimar Germany, Lebanon today, Argentina or Chile in the 1970s are instances of this situation.
4. All of the variables are high. Only when the associational web is dense, autonomous, and has a high capacity for self-regulation—that is, for conflict resolution within the institutional channels of democracy—is civil society strong. For this to happen, Tocqueville's "art of association" should be supplemented by the "art of negotiation."

Therefore, what the Tocquevillean-Gellnerian proposition asserts is that this fourth type of society is a necessary, albeit not sufficient, condition for the generation and maintenance of a high-quality democracy. This latter criterion implies that the dependent variable itself also requires conceptualization. Indeed, it is possible to have a democracy, and a stable one, without a strong civil society. However, it is likely to be what Juan Linz and Alfred Stepan (1996) have called a low-quality democracy, varieties of which are Guillermo O'Donnell's (1994, 55–69) delegative democracy (a democracy with deficient accountability), Fareed Zakaria's (1997, 22–43) more extreme illiberal democracy (that is, a democracy in which the rule of law and civil rights have a low level of institutionalization), and Diamond's (1999, chapters 1–3) pseudo-democracy (an authoritarian regime with electoral façade). In fact, there are at least three different types of democracy with ascending levels of quality. These types include the basic electoral or Schumpeterian kind; the Dahlian or liberal one, characterized by high levels of inclusiveness and contestation and strong institutionalization of civil and political rights; and the republican type, which includes, in addition to the institutions of liberal democracy, a highly active and organized citizenry (Schumpeter 1987, 250–83; Dahl 1971). Based on this conceptualization, the chapter will now examine the emerging relationship between state and society in contemporary Latin America.

State and Society in Contemporary Latin America: The Template of Mexican Democracy

The Articulation between Society and the State

There is a rich tradition of associational life in Mexico and the other countries in Latin America. For a long time (and in societies under military rule since the reestablishment of democracy), old organizations such as trade unions, professional associations, entrepreneurial groups, churches, community organizations of all kinds, sports clubs, and so on have sustained a vigorous internal life and a very visible public presence. New organizations representing the poor and the excluded, many of them the victims of recent processes of economic liberalization, have come into being in the recent period (for example, the Zapatistas, the landless movement in Brazil, the organizations of the unemployed, or *piqueteros,* in Argentina, and so on), and some of them have displayed a high capacity for mobilization. Finally, organizations based on ascriptive identities (gender, sexuality, race, and ethnicity), which are akin to their counterparts in advanced industrial societies, have mushroomed. However, this intense associational landscape is not indicative of a strong civil society, at least in the sense discussed earlier. Large segments of society are not organized, some of those that are organized are not very autonomous, and some are not very civic.

Social and economic dualism has been a central, and enduring, characteristic of many Latin American societies (World Bank 2004). For most of the twentieth century, only Argentina and Uruguay, the region's most developed countries, which had eliminated their peasantries in earlier periods and whose population consisted largely of European immigrants, had avoided this trait. Dualism has intensified in the past two decades, this time in all countries, because of intense economic liberalization and most states' limited capacity to implement effective compensatory policies. Throughout the region, social polarization (and, in some cases, such as Venezuela and Bolivia, political polarization as well) has increased. Dualism has major implications for civil society, state-society relations in general, and the quality of the new democracies.

The institutions that are being consolidated in some of these polities differ substantially from those advocated by the classical liberal model and from the norms and practices that prevail in the established democracies of Western Europe and North America. These differences appear in three layers: the preservation of authoritarian residuals, the weakness of the rule of law, and the articulation between state and society. The focus in this chapter will be on the third. The first layer consists of the preservation of authoritarian residuals (for example, in Chile, where the Senate has been packed with "institutional representatives," mostly from state agencies that were the core of the previous military regime; or in Argentina, where presidents routinely circumvent Congress by abusing decree powers). The second layer concerns the fact that the rule of law has a low level of institutionalization in most of these polities. Governments make an instrumental use of constitutions and laws, the judiciary is ineffective, dependent or even venal, and substantial corruption exists.

Finally, there is the third layer. Clientelism has been pervasive in Latin America, state corporatism was an important feature of the institutional structure of some of its larger societies (Mexico, Brazil, and Argentina) during the period of intense urbanization and industrialization that followed the Second World War, and almost all of the countries in the region have experienced protracted authoritarian regimes, some of them quite coercive. These three institutional frameworks represent varieties of a state-society relationship in which government is the principal and the citizens are the agent—the exact reverse of the relationship presupposed by the ideal model of liberal democracy. An interesting peculiarity of Latin American states is that, while being in most cases weak vis-à-vis their elites and major powers, they have nevertheless developed these relationships of vertical control with their societies.

State corporatism, whose most durable manifestation in the region was the regime of the Institutional Revolutionary Party in Mexico, became unviable once the newly urbanized and industrialized societies outgrew their straightjackets. Authoritarian regimes succumbed to legitimacy vacuums, the mobilization of their societies, the effects of international demonstration, and the withdrawal of support from the major powers. However, clientelistic tendencies persist and mark the new democracies as fundamentally different phenomena from their counterparts in advanced industrial societies. As we will see, dualism and clientelism are inherently related and persistent, to the extent that they could be considered the "deep structure" of Latin American societies. The overall effect is partial democracy or the bifurcated state. Mexico is a case in point. It must be noted that "old" or established democracies have also been characterized by considerable dualism and some clientelism in the past (and some residues are still around), but the difference between them and the new Latin American democracies is substantial enough to produce a different relationship between state and society as a whole.

Dualism, Economic Liberalization, and the Bifurcated State

The argument for a bifurcated state can be summarized in three propositions. First, economic liberalization intensifies traditional dualism, and it has a contradictory effect on civil society. Second, a dualized society generates affinity with a bi-facial state. Third, the dynamics of democracy tend to reinforce dualism, as can be seen from the following discussion.

Economic Liberalization Intensifies Traditional Dualism and Has a Contradictory Effect on Civil Society

The liberalization of previously semi-closed economies (privatization, de-regulation, and the opening-up of the economy) is governed by the logic of differentiation (Waisman 1998; Lijphart and Waisman 1997, 235–37). The first effect of economic liberalization is the increase in both vertical and horizontal differentiation. Polarization between the affluent and the deprived widens, but there are "winners" and "losers" within most social classes, sectors of the economy, and regions, be they rich or poor. As some industries expand, either because they are internationally competitive or because they serve an expanding local demand, the fortunes of the social classes connected with them and the regions where they are located improve. Conversely, as industries contract because of their inability to withstand foreign competition or because they serve markets hurt by economic liberalization, their owners and workers suffer and so do the areas in which they operate.

The experience of advanced countries indicates that the very dynamics of capitalism, together with the effect of social policy, reduces the overall level of differentiation in a second stage (even though the development of capitalism keeps producing differentiation, both at the micro and the macro levels). However, this happens when effective market institutions and states are in place, something that does not happen in most Latin American countries. Thus, one can break the eggs but, in the end, fail to make the omelette. This may be the outcome of economic liberalization in some parts of the region. In medium and large Latin American countries in the 1990s, the period of large-scale liberalization, income inequality, measured by Gini indices, was substantially reduced only in Chile and stabilized in Mexico. It grew in most other countries, spectacularly in Argentina (World Bank 2004, 8). Whether and when this second stage will occur in Latin America is still an open question.

The consequences of this economic transformation on civil society have been contradictory. On the one hand, the strengthening of market mechanisms has produced the social dislocation discussed earlier. On the other hand, it has reduced the control of society by the state and solidified autonomous associations in some areas of society within the class segments and regions that can be considered the "winners" in the process of economic differentiation. As noted earlier, these "winners" are located in all social classes. If the Mexican automobile industry is internationally competitive, the companies producing cars benefit and so do the unions, the firms related to this industry via forward and backward linkages, and the regions in which the plants are located. The ensuing social environment has been conducive to the generation and strengthening of associations within these groups and the establishment of "civic" relations among different interest constituencies and between them and the government. An open market economy contributes to the emergence and consolidation of a bargaining culture among interest groups. This facilitates the spread of mechanisms for the management of social conflict that do not involve the state as a decision maker (a situation compatible, of course, with a governmental role as a regulator or last-instance adjudicator). This is the institutional environment in which societal self-regulation is likely to grow. Also among the "winners" are relations with the government that have tended to be the ones characteristic of democracy: demand making, offering of contingent support, and so on. Overall, these are the traits of what we have earlier called a strong civil society.

The other side of the picture is the weakening of civil society among the "losers." If the Mexican textile industry is not competitive, its firms disappear, their workers become unemployed, and the areas housing the mills turn into rust belts. The logic of differentiation has intensified pre-existing economic and regional cleavages, and the outcome is the segmentation of society into a "civic" pole, characterized by strong associations and the capacity for self-regulation and a "disorganized" or marginalized sector, with a low level of autonomous group organization, and a low capacity for sustained, organized, and independent mobilization.

A gulf in this regard exists in all democracies, to the extent that Ralf Dahrendorf (1988) has argued that the cleavage between the "organized" and the "disorganized" sectors is becoming the central one in advanced capitalist countries. However, the level of deprivation and inequality in the United States or Western Europe is incomparable with that of Latin America. World Bank income distribution tables contain empty cells for the former countries in the column entitled "Population under $2 a day," but the proportions were 43 percent in Brazil and 40 percent in Mexico at the turn of this century (World Bank 1999, 196–97). The ratio of income received by the tenth to the first deciles of the population was, at that time, seventeen in the United States and fourteen in Italy, compared to fifty-four in Brazil and forty-five in Mexico (World Bank 2004, 2).

The extent to which cleavages are cumulative is especially important for political institutions. Where the spatial organization of the economy into cores and peripheries produces a territorial concentration of civic and disorganized fragments, more or less like in the Italy as described by Putnam (1993), and real or imagined cultural differences between the areas in question exist, there is a potential for serious state crises. Such a situation could lead to the development of centrifugal forces in "rich" regions or the breakdown of state control in the poorer ones. The Zapatista movement in Mexico and the emerging conflict in Bolivia between the Santa Cruz and the Andean regions may represent a first indication of processes of this sort, the potential for which exists in most Latin American countries (especially in those where ethnic cleavages are correlated with socio-economic ones).

Thus, the effect of this fragmented society on democratic institutions is complex. There is no automatic link between a rich associational life and a high-quality democracy. The civic pole generates an involved citizenry that, in the process of advancing or protecting its interests and values, co-operates with or opposes the government while also limiting or balancing it. At the same time, the mere existence of a large disorganized pole invites governments and parties to relate to it through one of the several non-democratic linkages institutionalized in Latin America's recent historical trajectory.

A Dualized Society Generates Affinity with a Bi-Facial State

A setting of this type generates a propensity for what is being called a bifurcated state. This is due to two facts: the forms of political action to which the two poles of society are prone and the politicians' incentives. First, it should be obvious that two poles generate very different kinds of social input into politics. The civic pole produces citizens and citizen groups—that is, forms of political action characterized by the making of demands and the offer of supports, in which individuals and the associations they form view themselves as principals and the politicians as agents. The disorganized pole, on the other hand, is more likely to generate apathy, perhaps punctuated by short-lived mobilization, or the dependent participation characteristic of clientelistic or corporatist arrangements. People living below the poverty line, who are either unemployed or employed informally or intermittently and who, in some cases, live in environments characterized by social disorganization, lack the resources or the inclination for the sustained exercise of citizenship. Moreover, their deprivation renders them the ideal candidates for clientelistic or corporatist co-optation. Instances of independent mobilization are likely to be short-lived, often non-institutional, and, in some cases, violent. Since re-democratization, urban or rural *jacqueries* have occurred in several Latin American countries (Argentina, Bolivia, and Ecuador).

Politicians' incentives, especially in a democratic setting, are the other factor. Politicians and governments respond to demands, and marginal sectors and regions are unlikely to sustain high rates of social and political participation and to manage resources that are convertible into political influence. Political parties and government agencies will be more likely to interact with, and engage in, the civic segment and to deal with it based on the rules of citizenship. Therefore, democracy may become the game the winners play or at least a game whose most permanent players are the organizations and groups within the civic pole.

Parties and governments may build constituencies within marginalized groups and regions, of course, and these constituencies may jump to the centre of the political stage in some situations (especially when they display non-institutionalized forms of behaviour). However, the relationship between them and government and parties is likely to be clientelistic or state-corporatist and, thus, not conducive to the strengthening of civil society. Finally, if sectors of the marginal pole resort to violent forms of collective action, coercion may become the standard state response. Hence, the bi-facial state: liberal democratic vis-à-vis the civic pole and clientelistic, corporatist, or coercive vis-à-vis the disorganized one.

The Dynamics of Democracy Tend to Reinforce Dualism

It could be expected that democratic institutions, whose dynamics depend on citizens' preferences, will generate, unlike the authoritarian regimes that preceded them, incentives among politicians to focus their agendas on the reduction of the gulf between the two poles of society. The fact that, in many of these societies, almost half of the electorate lives under the poverty line should concentrate democratic politicians' minds. However, it is not so obvious that this will be the case. In societies whose economic performance is not impressive and whose governments' ability to extract revenue is limited, shifting resources to the poor and the excluded would imply withdrawing them from other groups, elite or non-elite, but still part of the civic pole. This does not mean, of course, that re-distributive policies are impossible in the absence of sustained economic growth, but they are unlikely. Governments undertaking this road in the periods of fiscal stringency that is so common in Latin America would collide with the segments most able to deploy political resources in all but the lowest social strata.

In fact, the norm seems to be that for democratic governments, even those on the Left, law and order and macroeconomic stability—that is, the "winner's" agenda, loom larger than re-distributive policies, which are consigned to the realm of political rhetoric, token social programs, or some effective but narrowly targeted ones. Even in the face of massive poverty and dislocation, attempts to reduce subsidies and dysfunctional entitlements to the non-poor have been sparse and limited. This situation in societies where, in many cases, the affluent profit from credits, specifically targeted tax benefits, and toleration for large-scale tax evasion and where the middle classes also enjoy the latter as well as generous pensions for high government officials and free higher education. Likewise, the privileged segment of the working class, the participants in the formal economy, is assisted with public-sector featherbedding and rigid labour markets.

These tendencies are evident in Mexico. Social polarization has increased since the beginning of the North American Free Trade Agreement, and the dynamics of democratization, especially since the demise of the Institutional Revolutionary Party regime at the turn of the century, has intensified the bifurcation of the state.[1] As the civic pole strengthens and negotiates political support based on the principles of citizenship, politicians' corporatist and clientelistic reflexes acquire more centrality as determinants of their behaviour toward the marginal pole (and, consequently, as criteria for the allocation of revenue).

As we can see, the relationship between civil society and democracy is very complex in Latin America. What are the prospects for these partial democracies? The desirable outcome, the emphasis on policies designed to reduce inequality and its consequence, the strengthening of civil society, and the expansion of citizenship presupposes a strong state. This road is easier for countries with effective economic institutions or that are locked into expanding trade areas, such as Mexico or Chile. However, the very establishment and maintenance of these institutions implies a high level of state capacity. In order to have a sustained high-level performance, an open market economy requires a state that is able to deliver a rule of law, manageable levels of corruption, the effective regulation of markets, adequate levels of revenue, and so on. This presupposes a government that is relatively insulated from distributional coalitions, and a (albeit modestly) Weberian state apparatus. These are in short supply in Latin America.

The alternative is not the scenario of centralization predicted by Tocqueville for situations in which societal barriers fail to prevent state expansion, since *both* civil society and the state are weak in most of Latin America. Rather, the alternative is the further decay of democracy and its transformation into a mere façade. Such a conclusion would happen if this Janus-like state, articulated with the large civic and marginal political cultures that exist in the two poles of the society, is institutionalized. It would amount to a return to the past—the renaissance, under a new guise, of the "liberal," limited democracy regimes that existed in much of the region before industrialization.

The implications of the foregoing analysis for Mexico are quite clear. The country is at a crossroads, and it faces two paths. The first implies radical change—the forging of a basic consensus among the major parties and social forces about using the country's relatively strong state (in relation to most other Latin American nations) to extract larger amounts of revenue and channel it toward effective, targeted social programs and education, in order to reduce inequality and expand the material basis of citizenship to the marginal pole. The second path, which politicians in Mexico and other countries in Latin America have justified many times with populist and sometimes even revolutionary rhetoric, is the inertial one—the preservation or deepening of dualism. This path implies the pragmatic exchange of revenue for support between government and the more civic pole of society and either the clientelistic engagement or benign neglect of the needs or interests of the disorganized or marginal pole. The choice is not structurally determined. In the next few years, and consciously or not, the major social and political forces will make this decision about the future of Mexican democracy.

NOTE

1   North American Free Trade Agreement between the Government of Canada, the Government of Mexico and the Government of the United States, 17 December 1992, Can. T.S. 1994 No. 2, 32 I.L.M. 289.

REFERENCES

Albright, M.K. 2000. *Excerpts of Testimony, Speeches, and Remarks on Strengthening Civil Society and the Rule of Law.* Bureau of Public Affairs Public Information Series. Document no. S1.2:F68. Washington, DC: United States Department of State.

Berman, S. 1997. "Civil Society and the Collapse of the Weimar Republic." *World Politics* 49(3): 401–29.

Bureau of Public Affairs. 2000. *Focus on Issues: Strengthening Civil Society and the Rule of Law.* Washington, DC: United States Department of State.

Cohen, J.L., and A. Arato. 1992. *Civil Society and Political Theory.* Cambridge, MA: MIT Press.

Dahl, R.A. 1971. *Polyarchy.* New Haven, CT: Yale University Press.

Dahrendorf, R. 1988. *The Modern Social Conflict: An Essay on the Politics of Liberty.* Berkeley: University of California Press.

Dawson, T.C., and G. Bhatt. 2001. *The IMF and Civil Society Organizations: Striking a Balance.* Washington, DC: International Monetary Fund.

Diamond, L. 1999. *Developing Democracy: Toward Consolidation.* Baltimore: Johns Hopkins University Press.

Foley, M.W., and B. Edwards. 1996. "The Paradox of Civil Society." *Journal of Democracy* 7(3): 38–52.

Gellner, E. 1994. *Conditions of Liberty.* London: Hamish Hamilton.

Hall, J.A., ed. 1995. *Civil Society: Theory, History, Comparison.* Cambridge: Polity Press.

Inter-American Development Bank. n.d. *Modernización del estado y fortalecimiento de la sociedad civil.* Washington, DC: Inter-American Development Bank.

Lijphart, A., and C.H. Waisman, eds. 1997. *Institutional Design in New Democracies. Boulder,* CO: Westview Press.

Linz, J., and A. Stepan. 1996. *Problems of Democratic Transition and Consolidation.* Baltimore: Johns Hopkins University Press.

Lipset, S.M. 1981. *Political Man.* Baltimore: Johns Hopkins University Press.

O'Donnell, G. 1994. "Delegative Democracy." *Journal of Democracy* 5: 55–69.

Oxfam. 2000. *Development, NGOs and Civil Society: Selected Essays from Development in Practice.* Oxford: Oxfam.

Perez Diaz, V. 1993. *The Return of Civil Society.* Cambridge, MA: Harvard University Press.

Putnam, R.D. 1993. *Making Democracy Work.* Princeton, NJ: Princeton University Press.

Salamon, L., et al. 1999. *Global Civil Society: Dimensions of the Non-Profit Sector.* Baltimore: Johns Hopkins Center for Civil Society Studies.

Schumpeter, J.A. 1987. *Capitalism, Socialism, and Democracy.* London: Allen and Unwin.

Seligman, A. 1992. *The Idea of Civil Society.* New York: Free Press.

Tocqueville, A. 1955. *The Old Regime and the French Revolution.* New York: Doubleday.

_____. 1969. *Democracy in America.* New York: Anchor Books.

Waisman, C.H. 1998. "Civil Society, State Capacity, and the Conflicting Logics of Economic and Political Change." In Philip Oxhorn and Pamela Starr, eds., *Market or Democracy?* 43–68. Boulder, CO: Lynne Rienner.

World Bank. 1999. *World Development Report 1998/99.* New York: Oxford University Press.

_____. 2004. *Inequality in Latin America: Breaking with History?* Washington, DC: World Bank.

Zakaria, F. 1997. "The Rise of Illiberal Democracy." *Foreign Affairs* 76(6): 22–43.

Contributors

Jorge Chabat is a professor of political science at the Centro de Investigación y Docencia Económicas in Mexico and is one of Mexico's experts on security and the border. He appears frequently on television and writes a weekly column on current affairs.

Stephen Clarkson is professor emeritus in the Department of Political Science at the University of Toronto and one of Canada's best-known experts on Canadian-American relations. His book *Uncle Sam and Us: Globalization, Neoconservatism, and the Canadian State* (University of Toronto Press, 2002) is a major examination of North American integration. He is presently writing a study of transborder governance in North America.

Andrew F. Cooper is an associate director and distinguished fellow at the Centre for International Governance Innovation and a professor of political science at the University of Waterloo. He is a leading authority in Canadian foreign policy and his latest book is on celebrity politics, *Celebrity Diplomacy* (Paradigm Publishers, 2007).

Ana Covarrubias is a senior scholar currently working at the Centre for International Studies at El Colegio de México, and her main interests are Mexican foreign policy (especially Cuba and Central America) and the links between human rights and foreign policy.

Jordi Díez is an assistant professor of political science at the University of Guelph and a specialist in North American security and civil-military relations. He is author of *Political Change and Environmental Policymaking in Mexico* (Routledge, 2006) and editor of *Canadian and Mexican Security in the New North America: Challenges and Prospects* (McGill-Queen's University Press).

Edgar J. Dosman is professor emeritus in the Department of Political Science at York University and is one of Canada's leading analysts of hemispheric relations with a particular focus on Brazil and Mexico. He has recently completed a biography of Raoul Prebisch, the first secretary-general of the UN Conference on Trade and Development and one of the century's most innovative developmental economists, which is to be published by McGill-Queen's University Press in 2008.

Daniel Drache is a professor of political science at York University and associate director of the Robarts Centre for Canadian Studies. He has written extensively on North American integration and the asymmetry of power. His latest book on North American governance is *La Ilusión Continental: Seguridad Fronteriza y Búsqueda de una Identidad Norteamericana* (Siglo XXI, 2007).

Rosalba Icaza Garza is a lecturer in governance and international political economy at the Institute of Social Studies in The Netherlands. She is interested in transborder activism and democracy and gender with a particular emphasis on Latin America and Mexico. Her latest publication, with Jackie Smith, Marina Karides, et al., is *Global Democracy and the World Social Forums* (Paradigm Publishers, 2007).

Isidro Morales is a professor of political science in the Graduate School of Public Administration and Public Policy at the Instituto Tecnológico y de Estudios Superiores de Monterrey. He has published extensively on the effects of NAFTA on regional development and the future of Mexico's energy sector. In 2006, he was visiting professor at the American University in Washington, DC.

Alex Neve is a lawyer who has practised, taught, researched, and adjudicated in the areas of refugee law and international human rights law. Since January 2000, he has been the secretary-general of Amnesty International Canada.

Gustavo Vega-Cànovas is a senior professor, researcher, and director of the Center for International Studies at El Colegio de Mexico. He specializes in international political economy, North American integration, and international trade regulation and is one of Mexico's leading scholars in the field.

Victor López Villafañe is a professor of political science and the director of the Centre for North American Studies at the Instituto Tecnológico y de Estudios Superiores de Monterrey. He is one of Mexico's best-known scholars on Mexico-Japan-China relations, and in 2008 he will be a guest of the Beijing Academy of Social Sciences.

Carlos H. Waisman is a professor of political science at the University of California–San Diego and the University of Buenos Aires. He has lectured and taught in many countries in Latin America on democracy, civil society, and political theory.

Wesley K. Wark is a professor of international relations at the Munk Centre for International Studies at the University of Toronto. A historian by training, he is one of Canada's leading experts on terrorism and homeland security. Currently he is engaged in completing a major book on homeland security and Canadian foreign policy.

Duncan Wood is a professor of political science and director of the program in international relations at the Instituto Tecnológico Autónomo de México. He is one of Mexico's experts on security and trade issues.

Index